LINCOLN'S PATHFINDER

LINCOLN'S PATHFINDER

JOHN C. FRÉMONT *and the*
VIOLENT ELECTION *of* 1856

JOHN BICKNELL

CHICAGO
REVIEW
PRESS

Published by Chicago Review Press Incorporated
814 North Franklin Street
Chicago, Illinois 60610
ISBN 978-1-61373-797-2

Library of Congress Cataloging-in-Publication Data
Names: Bicknell, John, author.
Title: Lincoln's pathfinder : John C. Frémont and the violent election of
    1856 / John Bicknell.
Description: Chicago, Illinois : Chicago Review Press, 2017. | Includes
    bibliographical references and index.
Identifiers: LCCN 2017006150 (print) | LCCN 2017008234 (ebook) | ISBN
    9781613737972 (hardback) | ISBN 9781613737989 (PDF edition) | ISBN
    9781613738009 (EPUB edition) | ISBN 9781613737996 (Kindle edition)
Subjects: LCSH: Frémont, John Charles, 1813–1890. | Presidents—United
    States—Election—1856. | Presidential candidates—United
    States—Biography. | United States—Politics and government—1853–1857. |
    BISAC: HISTORY / United States / 19th Century. | HISTORY / United States /
    Civil War Period (1850–1877).
Classification: LCC E415.9.F8 B49 2017 (print) | LCC E415.9.F8 (ebook) | DDC
    324.973/09034—dc23
LC record available at https://lccn.loc.gov/2017006150

Typesetting: Nord Compo

Printed in the United States of America
5 4 3 2 1

For Gary

Beneath thy skies, November
Thy skies of cloud and rain,
Around our blazing camp-fires
We close our ranks again.
Then sound again the bugles,
Call the muster-roll anew;
If months have well-nigh won the field,
What may not four years do?
                    —John Greenleaf Whittier,
        "A Song Inscribed to the Frémont Club,"
                National Era, November 20, 1856

CONTENTS

INTRODUCTION

THE PATHFINDER

John C. Frémont's reputation as the "Pathfinder" rested on the accomplishments of his five expeditions to the West, in which he explored the Rocky Mountains, the Oregon Trail, the Sierra Nevada, and other territory that was admittedly inhospitable—but nevertheless previously explored.

Frémont was not so much a pathfinder as he was a path populizer. Beginning with the reports on his 1842 and 1843–44 journeys to Oregon and—against orders—Utah and California that were lovingly edited by his wife, Jessie Anne Benton Frémont, the army officer gained a level of fame rare for a soldier who was not a hero in arms.

The Frémonts' *Report of the Exploring Expedition to the Rocky Mountains in the Year 1842, and to Oregon and North California in the Years 1843–44*, published in 1845, became an instant bestseller and all but holy scripture for immigrants heading west. John's detailed observations and Jessie's romantic notions and talents as an editor combined to cast the West in an entirely new light for many Americans. Previously derided as the Great American Desert, easterners began to see the possibilities in the new land, thanks in large part to the sweeping grandeur of the Frémonts' prose.

John C. Frémont, though a naturally reticent man, reveled in the glory. For the next decade and more, he was one of the most admired men in the country. Seventeen towns and counties were named or renamed in his honor, stretching from New Hampshire to Nebraska, which was not yet even a state. Far from a mere fifteen minutes of fame, Frémont's moment would endure twelve years, and he would make the most of that moment while it lasted, through multiple expeditions, triumphs and travails in the Mexican War, disputes with his powerful father-in-law, Missouri senator Thomas Hart Benton, legal wrangling over a gold mining claim in California, election as that state's first senator, and finally, nomination as the first presidential candidate of the new Republican Party.

And Jessie Benton Frémont would be right there every step of the way. Much more politically savvy than her husband, she was an aide-de-camp to her father, that most boisterous proponent of westward expansion, who was her husband's great political patron and protector and a volatile man whose relationship with his favorite daughter was unusually close and periodically tempestuous.

Her husband knew what he had in Jessie, and he was not reluctant to make use of the asset. She would play a role in the 1856 presidential campaign unimagined by any wife before her. Her own participation was unique enough, but it also marked the first time a cause and campaign of a major political party resonated with women—and with free people of color. The Republican Party was no bastion of equal rights, to be sure. While some abolitionists attached themselves to the party, its senior leadership and party platform claimed no more than an opposition to the extension of slavery into new territory. Some of these men—though not Frémont—were as racist as the slavery-supporting Democrats they opposed, although the foremost historian of the early days of the Republican Party wrote that "what is striking about Republican rhetoric during these years is not how often one encounters racist declarations, but how infrequently." The party of "Free Soil, Free Men, and Frémont" inspired a hope that things might be better, a hope that had never really existed until 1856. For many African Americans in antebellum America, that was astonishing enough.

Frémont would lose the election of 1856 to James Buchanan, who would go on to lead what many consider to be the most disastrous presidential administration in American history. Frémont would serve—not terribly successfully—in the war that followed. Both he and his wife would cause the commander in chief no small measure of grief.

But in 1856, the Pathfinder who had made his fame by following in the footsteps of others would, after all, blaze a trail. His campaign, unique in the annals of politics to that time, showed the way to victory for another candidate, a man less reticent personally and more prepared temperamentally for the rigorous challenge of national crisis. Where John C. Frémont led, Abraham Lincoln would follow.

PROLOGUE

"WE CAN'T CONCEIVE OF A GREATER PIECE OF MISCHIEF"

Congressman Abraham Lincoln had worked hard to elect Zachary Taylor president in 1848, and now, as Taylor took office and Lincoln left Congress after just one term, the congressman wanted his just reward.

The Illinois Whig's two years in the House were marked by his opposition to the Mexican War—the successful war of conquest that made Taylor a hero and got him elected president. But Lincoln had set aside Taylor's participation in the war he opposed as he campaigned tirelessly for the candidate, a career military officer, a slave owner, and a political blank slate. Lincoln had traveled extensively on Taylor's behalf, making speeches in Delaware, Maryland, and Massachusetts, as well as around his home state, and helped to disseminate mailings of pro-Taylor speeches and broadsides.

In return for his efforts, Lincoln wanted to be named commissioner of the General Land Office, a plum job for a westerner, in charge of managing and selling public lands. "This is about the only crumb of patronage which Illinois expects," Lincoln wrote, and whether it went to him or some other loyal Taylor supporter, he was insistent that it come to his state.

It did, but not to Lincoln's satisfaction. Despite his pleas that the appointment of Chicagoan Justin Butterfield "will be an egregious political blunder" that "will give offence to the whole Whig party here," Butterfield got the job.

Butterfield, like Lincoln, was an Illinois lawyer born elsewhere—New Hampshire, in Butterfield's case. One of his claims to fame was that he had once represented Mormon prophet Joseph Smith in federal court. Like Lincoln, he was a devotee of Whig icon Henry Clay. Unlike Lincoln, Butterfield had stuck with Clay in the brief contest for the Whig nomination the previous year, having "fought for Mr. Clay against Gen. Taylor to the bitter end."

After failing to secure the land office, Lincoln was offered the governorship of the newly organized Oregon Territory as a consolation prize. But he declined the post and decided instead to return to Illinois and practice law. He rode the circuit, traveling around central Illinois wherever court was in session to take on cases, and worked on retainer for the Illinois Central Railroad. It was not so much a retirement from politics as a simple recognition that, for the time being, his moment had passed.

It would take Lincoln's old Illinois friend and foe, Senator Stephen A. Douglas, to draw him back into the arena five years later. Douglas had been trying to organize the territory between the Missouri River and the Rocky Mountains since 1844. His motivations were partly patriotic. "It is utterly impossible to preserve that connection between the Atlantic and the Pacific, if you keep a wilderness of two thousand miles in extent between you," he reasoned. It was a "national necessity" that the "Indian barrier must be removed. The tide of emigration and civilization must be permitted to roll onward until it rushes through the passes of the mountains, and spreads over the plains, and mingles with the waters of the Pacific."

But, of course, creating that connection would serve Douglas personally as well. "Douglas had his eye fixed on the Presidency," Illinois lieutenant governor Gustave Koerner wrote. "He expected to get the nomination in 1856, but of course he must get the South, and they gave him to understand that if, in organizing the Territories, he should exclude slavery under the Missouri Compromise, he would not get any Southern support."

These personal and patriotic interests were not mutually exclusive—Douglas could boost his presidential aspirations not only by using the legislation to prove his southern bona fides but also by making his western backers happy with the northern route for a transcontinental railroad and opening new territory to white farmers. It was a win-win-win for Douglas.

In previous Congresses, southern opposition had blocked Douglas's efforts. They feared the creation of new free states north of the 36 degrees, 30 minutes latitude line established by the Missouri Compromise in 1820. And they wanted a transcontinental railroad built through the South, not the North.

The bill Douglas reported from his Senate Committee on Territories on January 4, 1854, attempted to assuage southern concerns. It proposed splitting the territory into two areas: Kansas, stretching from latitude 37 degrees on the south to 40 degrees on the north, and a much larger Nebraska, which included today's South and North Dakota, from 40 degrees north to 49 degrees north. Immediately, that created the suspicion that Douglas's motive was to create one free state and one slave state. Such a result might have been in Douglas's mind, but there were also practical reasons for dividing the territory, not the least of which was its enormous size. Railroad interests preferred separate jurisdictions, predicated on the building of separate central and northern routes to the Pacific. Iowa agriculture interests, allied with Douglas, also wanted a second, northern territory. On the question of slavery, Douglas's bill would leave that decision to the voters in each territory. Using language from the Compromise of 1850 that organized New Mexico and Utah—which Douglas had played an instrumental role in enacting—the new bill provided that "when admitted as a State or States, the said territory or any portion of the same, shall be received into the Union, with or without slavery, as their constitution may prescribe at the time of their admission." Of course, that ran directly counter to the geographic limitation imposed by the Missouri Compromise—that slavery would not be allowed north of the 36-30 line. And it was disingenuous at best. The territorial provisions of the Compromise of 1850 applied only to the lands annexed following the Mexican War, whereas the Missouri Compromise applied to the lands obtained in the Louisiana Purchase, which included the territory now in question.

Douglas's principle was no principle at all, and a well-earned reputation as a skilled legislative tactician—and for political skullduggery—ensured that his motives would be questioned. His none-too-subtle attempt to disguise repeal of the Missouri Compromise added to the suspicion. "We can't conceive of a greater piece of mischief than is here set on foot by our Senator," the *Illinois State Journal* editorialized. Commercial interests were wary, too. New York Whig merchants condemned Douglas for his "wholly gratuitous and entirely political" reopening of the controversy they had hoped was settled.

Douglas was playing a double game, which must have seemed even to him like walking on thin ice. He denied that his intent was to repeal the Missouri Compromise, but any fair reading of the legislation would lead to that conclusion. Instead of a win-win, Douglas was facing a lose-lose. Northern free soilers rejected the idea of repealing the outright ban on slavery north of the 1820 line. Southerners, who never liked the restriction to begin with, wanted the Kansas-Nebraska bill to explicitly repeal the restriction, which they believed had already been overtaken by the 1850 language in any case. And they saw inherent in Douglas's solution the death knell of slavery's expansion. If the Missouri Compromise rules remained in place until after statehood, few slave-owning southerners were likely to immigrate to the territory, making it highly unlikely that slavery would be approved later on.

"There cannot be a doubt as to the propriety and policy of repealing the Missouri compromise," reasoned Georgia senator Robert Toombs, a onetime southern unionist moving rapidly toward southern nationalism. "The North never did agree to it and never would sanction it since its adoption. They have adhered to its prohibitory provisions, but uniformly and nearly unanimously trampled its principles under foot so far as the South was to be benefited by it."

Douglas decided to placate the South further, dumping his New Mexico–Utah language in favor of outright popular sovereignty. He would give the people in the territory at the time of organization the right to vote on whether to allow slavery. But this still wasn't enough for southern hardliners, and Kentucky Whig Archibald Dixon offered an amendment on January 16 that would explicitly repeal the Missouri Compromise. "The citizens of the several States and Territories shall be at liberty to take and hold their slaves within any Territory of the United States, or of the States to be formed therefrom," the amendment read. Douglas didn't want to have that fight on the floor of the Senate, in part because Massachusetts abolitionist senator Charles Sumner had answered Dixon's amendment with one of his own explicitly endorsing the Missouri Compromise line. Douglas knew a debate on the hallowed compromise would be explosive and risked sinking the legislation. So he told Dixon, Toombs, and his other southern allies that he would do as they demanded.

But not quite. Douglas altered the language to say that the Missouri Compromise was "inconsistent with the principles of the legislation of 1850, commonly called the compromise measures, and is hereby declared inoperative." And still that was not enough. The South wanted one more word, and Douglas added it, from yet another amendment, this one by Alabama congressman Philip Phillips. The Missouri Compromise, the bill now read, was "inoperative and void." "It will triumph and impart peace to the country and stability to the Union," Douglas predicted. "I am not deterred or affected by the violence and insults of the Northern Whigs and Abolitionists. The storm will soon spend its fury."

With his southern ducks in a row, Douglas now had to line up the president.

Franklin Pierce, elected in 1852, had never believed the Missouri Compromise was constitutional to begin with, but he was still reluctant to repeal it. Pierce at first had favored Douglas's original approach: ignore the compromise and just do what the bill's supporters wanted with Kansas and Nebraska. Eventually, they reasoned, the Supreme Court would side with them and declare the territorial provisions of the compromise unconstitutional. But Secretary of War Jefferson Davis and the other southerners in Pierce's administration wanted a more affirmative statement, and Douglas wanted clarification before launching a Senate debate, which was scheduled to begin on Monday, January 23, 1854. Two days prior, Pierce met with his cabinet, which produced its own language and beckoned a congressional ally, Kentucky representative John C. Breckinridge, to deliver it to Douglas. In an administration increasingly bereft of reliable allies in Congress, the sturdy Breckinridge—six foot two, 175 pounds, with piercing blue-black eyes and black hair—stood as firmly as anyone in Pierce's corner.

After receiving the news from the White House, Douglas went to fetch Davis at his home, accompanied by several fellow senators—Finance

Chairman Robert M. T. Hunter and Foreign Relations Chairman James M. Mason, both of Virginia, Judiciary Chairman Andrew P. Butler of South Carolina, and Senate president pro tem David Rice Atchison of Missouri—and Congressman Phillips of Alabama. It was an all-star lineup, the leading lights of Congress. To abolitionists, it was a roll call of scoundrels. Atchison was "that lawless ruffian, the leader of the Missouri-Kansas bandits." Douglas was "that desperate demagogue and Iscariot traitor to liberty." Mason was "the infamous framer of the Fugitive Slave Law." Butler was among those "whose souls are steeped in pollution, whose hands and garments are dripping with the blood of enslaved millions."

The day before debate was to begin, this group went to the White House—Davis, Douglas, and Atchison in a carriage, the others on foot—where Davis went in alone to see President Pierce while Douglas and the southern contingent cooled their heels in a reception room. Pierce, who didn't like to conduct business on Sunday, agreed to meet with the group at the urging of Davis, who always liked to get the last word. Davis told the president that Douglas's Committee on Territories wanted to move ahead the next day on the legislation, so he needed to know beforehand whether the administration would support it. Next Douglas and Atchison spoke with the president alone, and then the others joined them in the quiet of the White House library. Phillips reported that a cold formality prevailed. The meeting lasted two hours, and Pierce warned the men that they were walking on a precipice. "Gentlemen, you are entering a serious undertaking, and the ground should be well surveyed before the first step is taken." But Pierce knew he was trapped. If he opposed the measure, its supporters would go ahead without him, leaving him without party backing for the final two years of his administration. He would be in the same position as John Tyler a decade earlier—a president without a party, with no hope for reelection. So Pierce listened to their arguments, and finally agreed to support the changes, even writing the final language out himself: that the Missouri Compromise had been "superseded by the principles of the legislation of 1850 . . . and is hereby declared inoperative and void."

Pierce had declared in his first annual message as president in December 1853 that the "repose" in sectional tension provided by the Compromise of 1850 "is to suffer no shock during my official term, if I have the power to avert it." Now he had taken a step that would shock the system to such a degree that civil war would become all but inevitable.

Pierce believed the Compromise of 1850 had settled the slavery question forever, and with the smashing Democratic victory in 1852 he was eager to move on to other things—obtaining more territory from Mexico for use as a southern route for a transcontinental railroad; expanding the American empire by acquiring Cuba and possibly Central America (where he turned a blind eye to the private adventures of American filibuster William Walker in attacking Nicaragua); spreading US influence around the world by increasing trade; and opening Japan to the West. Pierce's was an ambitious, expansionist vision, and he didn't want to be bothered by what he saw as piddling domestic concerns that should be considered settled in any case.

But the president's "repose" was, to a great extent, illusory. The Compromise of 1850 had calmed some waters while roiling others. Pierce simply chose to ignore the "shock" that had already occurred in the form of organized northern resistance to the Fugitive Slave Act, which had become personified in the publication of *Uncle Tom's Cabin* by Harriet Beecher Stowe. "What a sermon!" exclaimed Ohio free soil Democrat Salmon P. Chase of the most important novel ever written by an American. "I cannot read it without tears."

Neither could thousands of others, who now saw the Kansas-Nebraska Act as merely the latest and most egregious example of Congress caving in to the slave power, a straight line that began with the 1845 annexation of Texas and the Mexican War, led to the Fugitive Slave Act, ran through the Gadsden Purchase (which provided the territory for a southern transcontinental railroad), and included machinations to force US acquisition of slaveholding Cuba, as Pierce had outlined in his first annual message.

Rev. Theodore Parker, a prominent abolitionist, saw Kansas-Nebraska and the other tendencies toward support of slavery as something akin to murder, which would "make stillborn the infant liberty." Parker and three thousand other northern ministers signed a petition against the bill, declaring it "a great moral wrong," and sent the 250-foot-long paper to the Senate. Harriet Beecher Stowe used some of her royalties from *Uncle Tom's Cabin* to finance the effort. Pro-Nebraska New York Democratic

congressman William M. Tweed—the future Boss Tweed—called the petition "a profanation of the American pulpit."

Anti-Nebraska rallies were called for around the country, and many
prepared resolutions demanding not just that Congress defeat the Kansas-
Nebraska Act but that citizens organize a new political party that would
stand steadfastly against the expansion of slavery into the territories. Pro-
testers meeting in Amesbury, Massachusetts, approved a resolution opposing Kansas-Nebraska and appealing to a broader constituency by pointing
out that free labor would be barred from the "Great Central Garden" of
America if the territory became a slave state. It was a savvy political pitch,
and would be repeated in venue after venue as the debate continued.

A Fire Which May Consume
Those Who Kindle It

Ohio's Salmon P. Chase led the opposition in the Senate, with help from
Sumner, who came late into the battle, believing that strategically it would
be better to have more moderate members go first and because he wanted
to spend considerable time in preparing his remarks. New Yorker Gerrit
Smith and Ohio's Joshua R. Giddings led in the House.

On January 24, Chase asked for and got a week's delay in the debate,
claiming he needed more time to familiarize himself with the bill. In reality, he wanted time for public opinion to react to his magnum opus, "The
Appeal of the Independent Democrats in Congress to the People of the
United States." He had finished writing it on the nineteenth and sent it
off to the *National Era* on the twenty-second, the same day Pierce hosted
Douglas and the others in the White House.

In the appeal, Chase derided the Kansas-Nebraska Act as "a gross
violation of a sacred pledge; as a criminal betrayal of precious rights; as
part and parcel of an atrocious plot to exclude from a vast unoccupied
region immigrants from the Old World and free laborers from our own
States, and convert it into a dreary region of despotism, inhabited by masters and slaves." He called the Missouri Compromise "a solemn compact"
and expressed "indignation and abhorrence" at the idea that it might be
repealed. Below Chase's name were the other signatories: Senator Charles

Sumner and Representative Alexander De Wit of Massachusetts, Ohio representatives Joshua Giddings and Benjamin Wade, and Representative Gerrit Smith of New York.

Douglas began the floor debate on January 30, delivering a hostile, abusive diatribe against the bill's opponents. One journalist reported that he "lost his temper before he began." When Chase tried to respond directly to an insult, Douglas refused to yield, though it was a common senatorial courtesy. "I will yield the floor to no abolitionist," he bellowed.

When it was Chase's turn, his February 3 speech drew the biggest audience, including an unusually large number of women, who "crowded into and took possession of one-half the lobby seats on the floor of the Senate." Chase called the Missouri Compromise a "time honored and sacred compact," and derided the proposal that would scrap it. "You may pass it here, you may send it to the House. It may become law. But its effect will be to satisfy all thinking men that no compromises with slavery will endure, except so long as they serve the interests of slavery." And Chase made a pair of predictions. "This discussion will hasten the inevitable reorganization of parties upon new issues," he said, and "it will light up a fire in the country which may, perhaps, consume those who kindle it."

Sumner went a step further. "They celebrate a present victory," he said to the Ohioan, "but the echoes they awake will never rest till slavery itself shall die." On the floor, Sumner lambasted the South for reneging on the Missouri Compromise, by which the South had gained much, an "infraction of solemn obligations originally proposed and assumed by the South." Now, "with the consideration in pocket, it repudiates the bargain which it forced upon the country." He obliquely tarred Douglas with the "northern man with southern principles" brush, a line that drew applause from the gallery, and asserted that, contrary to Douglas and Pierce's contention that Kansas-Nebraska would settle the slavery question, "nothing can be settled which is not right."

Douglas challenged Sumner directly on the "northern man with southern principles" remark, but Sumner remained seated and quiet, refusing to rise to the bait. "He says nothing," Douglas sneered. "He has not the candor to admit it nor the courage to deny it." And he gleefully reminded

his colleagues that Sumner had condemned Martin Van Buren with the
same curse—before supporting Van Buren for president in 1848.

The debate ran through all of February and into the first days of March.
Southerners warned, as they had before and would again, that failure to do
their bidding would mean disunion. "If we let this opportunity of finally
settling it escape I see no hope in the future," Georgia's Robert Toombs
wrote to a friendly newspaper editor. "Dissolution will surely come, and
that speedily."

But there was more to it than that.

Georgia representative Alexander Stephens, a leading southern voice
who was also respected by many northerners, saw the measure not just as
central to settling the sectional question but as part of a grander strategy
to bring the country around generally to the proslavery way of thinking
about things. "The moral effect of the victory on our side will have a
permanent effect upon the public mind, whether any positive advantages
accrue by way of the actual extension of slavery or not. The effect of such a
victory at this time is important. We are on the eve of much greater issues
in my opinion." He meant the attempt to annex Cuba and add another
slaveholding territory to the Union. A victory on Nebraska, he believed,
would open up a world of possibilities.

They didn't let the opportunity escape, and it wasn't even close. The
Senate passed the bill 37–14 in the early hours of March 4. Eight southern
Whigs joined with all but five Democrats in approving the measure. Only
two southerners—John Bell of Tennessee and Sam Houston of Texas—
voted no.

The House debate was slightly shorter if no less shrill. Chase expressed
his hope that the House speeches on the bill would be "classified as obituary notices." Violence was threatened on more than one occasion, although
none actually came. Douglas hovered around the periphery of the House
floor to keep an eye on things. Opponents did what they could, attempting to get the measure referred to the committee of the whole—all of
Congress debating under committee rules rather than the more formal
House rules—which they believed would bury it beneath a pile of other
legislation. But they were out-maneuvered by Douglas lackey William A.
Richardson, who won a 109–88 vote to go into the committee of the

whole, then proceeded to win postponement of the eighteen bills lined up in front of the Kansas-Nebraska Act via eighteen separate roll call votes. On May 22, the House voted to remove from the measure an amendment added by the Senate that would have barred foreigners from holding office, then passed the revised bill 113–100. As in the Senate, only two southern Democrats voted no: John Millson of Virginia and Missouri's Thomas Hart Benton. But in what should have been recognized as an ominous sign for Democrats, forty-two members of their northern wing opposed the bill; forty-four supported it. The Senate, which had barely adopted the nativist amendment to begin with, did not object to its removal, and cleared the final version for the president's signature on May 26. Pierce signed it into law four days later.

Ignoring the regional split, proponents of the law expressed confidence that the storm would pass. "Nobody says anything now against it but the abolitionists," Alexander Stephens declared, with a touch of Falstaff. "Let them howl on—'Tis their vocation."

But Stephens and his allies proved poor prognosticators. Douglas encountered hostile crowds and virulent newspaper coverage on his extended trip home from the capital. "I could travel from Boston to Chicago by the light of my own effigy," he said.

The antislavery fire was growing hotter, and it was heating the presidential pot. Soon-to-be senator Henry Wilson told future colleague William H. Seward that "the time has come to dissolve the infamous union of Whigs of the North and South." The Massachusetts man told the New Yorker that he would support him for president in 1856—not as part of the Whig Party but in a new organization that would "combine in one great party all the friends of freedom."

Horace Greeley used his *New-York Tribune* editorial platform to predict that "passage of this Nebraska bill will arouse and consolidate the most gigantic, determined and overwhelming party for freedom that the world ever saw."

Passage of the measure coincided with the notorious arrest of a fugitive slave named Anthony Burns in Boston, further arousing an already primed populace. "That man must not be sent out of Boston as a slave," poet John Greenleaf Whittier wrote of Burns. "Anything but that. The whole people must be called out, the country must precipitate itself upon the city—an avalanche of freemen! . . . In the name of God, let the people be summoned. Send out the fiery cross without further delay!" Burns had lived free in the city for nearly a year, but the president wanted to make an example of him, so Pierce threw the full force of the law into action. US marshals and federal troops were employed to move Burns to court and, finally, to a ship in which he was "triumphantly carried back to bondage" in Virginia. A deputy marshal was killed in one of several melees involving law enforcement officials and enraged abolitionists.

The lethal combination of Burns's return to slavery and the Kansas-Nebraska Act moved even nonabolitionists to wonder what might come next. Massachusetts mill owner Amos A. Lawrence, one of those "infamous" cotton Whigs doing business with the South that Wilson had referred to—and a cousin by marriage of Franklin Pierce—confided to his diary that "we went to bed one night, old-fashioned, conservative, compromise, Union Whigs, and waked up stark mad Abolitionists."

"STAND WITH ANYBODY THAT STANDS RIGHT"

For slavery's supporters, the thin edge of the wedge to attack the South had been the Wilmot Proviso—a proposal to bar the extension of slavery into territories gained in the Mexican War. For slavery's opponents, the Kansas-Nebraska Act was the full force of the axe, and the blow splintered the Whig Party.

Radical abolitionist William Lloyd Garrison, publisher of the *Liberator*, had long ago sworn off politics as collaboration with evil; he'd recently burned a copy of the Fugitive Slave Act and the Constitution in protest of Anthony Burns's reenslavement. Garrison considered the idea of a political party dedicated to antislavery principles as "simply absurd." "No party can be national without being pro-slavery," Garrison concluded.

But while the new law struck Garrison simply as confirmation that the political process was a sham to be avoided, for others—including Abraham Lincoln—it was a clarion call to action.

Lincoln had effectively withdrawn from politics after leaving the House in 1849, failing to secure the position of commissioner of the Land Office,

ABRAHAM LINCOLN, CIRCA 1850.
Courtesy of Library of Congress

and rejecting the offer to become governor of Oregon. He practiced law, made some money, and spent considerable time doing what the twenty-first century calls networking. The connections he made would matter a great deal when he turned his attention back to the political arena.

The hastily organized meetings of spring 1854 had not stopped the Kansas-Nebraska Act, but they were bearing another kind of fruit. An organizational turning point came in June in Kalamazoo, Michigan, when a convention of nearly two hundred free soil Democrats agreed to abandon their own party line on the ballot and unite with anti-Nebraska "fusionists," a step that led directly to a July 6 meeting about sixty miles east in Jackson, one of several around the country that would later lay claim to being the birthplace of the Republican Party.

Lincoln was not yet quite ready to jump into the new pool. But he had begun to get his feet wet, and by autumn he was committed to the idea, in spirit if not in body. In August, in Winchester, Illinois, a small town about ninety miles north of Saint Louis, he presented "a clear, forcible, and convincing" argument against the extension of slavery . . . replete with unanswerable arguments, which must and will effectually *tell* at the coming election."

Three weeks ahead of the midterm elections, in a three hour and ten minute speech in Peoria on October 16, Lincoln wrestled in public with his, and others', hesitation. "Some men, mostly Whigs, who condemn the repeal of the Missouri Compromise, nevertheless hesitate to go for its restoration, lest they be thrown in company with the abolitionist. Will they allow me as an old Whig to tell them good humoredly, that I think this is very silly? Stand with anybody that stands RIGHT. Stand with him while he is right and PART with him when he goes wrong. Stand WITH the abolitionist in restoring the Missouri Compromise; and stand AGAINST him when he attempts to repeal the fugitive slave law. In the latter case you stand with the southern disunionist. What of that? You are still right. In both cases you are right."

The Kansas-Nebraska Act, Lincoln declared, ran counter to the founding principles of the nation. Slavery, according to the act's supporters, was now "a sacred right. Nebraska brings it forth, places it on the high road to extension and perpetuity; and, with a pat on its back, says to it, 'Go, and God speed you.' . . . Let no one be deceived. The spirit of '76 and the spirit of Nebraska are utter antagonisms, and the former is being rapidly displaced by the latter."

The midterms of 1854 would prove that was not entirely the case. The results of the election were shattering for pro-Nebraska Democrats, but far from an unalloyed victory for the nascent Republicans. Across the country, the unifying force of free soil served to defeat incumbent Democrats. But just as often the beneficiary was an antiforeign nativist party that dubbed itself the American Party but was more popularly known as the Know Nothings (for their secretiveness, not their lack of knowledge).

New Yorker George Templeton Strong wrote that his state's "antipathy to the Pope and to Paddy is a pretty deep-seated feeling." Strong didn't dismiss the possibility of "a religious war within the next decade, if this awful vague, mysterious, new element of Know-Nothingism is as potent as its friends and political wooers seem to think it is."

Lincoln hoped it wouldn't be, and he saw the danger in any necessity to break free. "I have hoped their organization would die out without the painful necessity of my taking an open stand against them," he wrote. He understood that a strong stand against nativism or temperance (another of the Know Nothings' signature causes) would wreck any hope of uniting the factions. But he couldn't wrap his head around the theory. "Of their principles I think little better than I do of those of the slavery extensionists. Indeed I do not perceive how any one professing to be sensitive to the wrongs of the negroes, can join in a league to degrade a class of white men."

That was a worry for another day. For now, the numbers were inspiring. New York Democrats fell from twenty-two seats in 1852 to six in 1854. Pierce administration allies won only four seats in Pennsylvania. In Ohio, anti-Nebraska candidates swept the twenty-one House seats. Eighty-four percent of northern Democrats—thirty-seven of forty-four—who voted for the Kansas-Nebraska Act lost. All told, Democrats lost two-thirds of the seats they had won two years earlier—and more states would be voting in 1855. The results were much the same at the state legislative level. Most starkly, the Massachusetts assembly elections yielded a legislature that included one Whig, one Democrat, one Republican, and 377 Know Nothings.

The gains at the state level and in the US House were a direct reflection of northern dissatisfaction with Kansas-Nebraska. But senators were still elected by state legislatures, and Lincoln had declared his intention to seek the seat held by Democrat James Shields, who had fought alongside President Pierce in Mexico. Anti-Nebraska fusionists had won a majority in the Illinois legislature, but Democrats retained a sizable minority, and possibly a plurality if the scattered anti-Nebraska forces could not unite behind a single candidate.

Two of the candidates had just been elected to other offices. Anti-Nebraska Democrat Lyman Trumbull had been elected to the US House, while Lincoln had served four previous terms in the statehouse, from 1834 to 1842, and had just been elected again in 1854, as a Whig. But state legislators were barred by the Illinois constitution from being elected by their own body to the US Senate. So having just won, Lincoln declined his seat on November 25 and announced his bid for the Senate. It's unclear if this was an oversight or a late decision, but the anti-Nebraska takeover of the general assembly certainly played a role in Lincoln raising his sights.

The legislature gathered on February 8, 1855. On the first ballot Lincoln led with 45 votes (out of 99), the incumbent Shields got 42, and Trumbull trailed with 5. The rest were scattered among other candidates. But after that, Lincoln's support began to stall. He was still a Whig, and while he shared the free soil position of the anti-Nebraska Democrats, they refused to support a Whig. After eight ballots, it was clear that while Shields was not going to be acceptable to the anti-Nebraska majority, the Whigs and anti-Nebraska Democrats could not settle between themselves.

The pro-Douglas Democrats decided to dispense with Shields and put forth the governor, Joel A. Matteson, who received 49 votes on the ninth ballot. He appeared poised to win on the next. Lincoln, accepting that this was not going to be his moment despite consistently receiving the most votes, released his supporters to Trumbull, who was elected on the tenth ballot.

Trumbull's victory was a signal event, even if it kept the eloquent Lincoln out of the Senate. The home state of Stephen A. Douglas, the leading proponent of popular sovereignty and the Kansas-Nebraska Act, had sent an anti-Nebraska man to the Senate. More would follow, even as free soil Democrats, newfangled Republicans, and Know Nothings struggled to refine their coalitions, which varied widely from state to state.

Throughout 1855, as emigrants from New England, Missouri, and elsewhere poured into Kansas, the debate raged on about how that territory should be governed. Missourians worried that to have free territory on a third side, joining Illinois to the east and Iowa to the north, would make slavery untenable by making escape too easy. But victory in Kansas would change the equation. "If we win," declared Missouri's David Atchison, "we carry slavery to the Pacific." And that goal should be reached by any means: "peaceably if we can, forcibly if we must." But Atchison was not returned to the Senate to make his case. The Missouri legislature, split among Atchison, proslavery Whig Alexander Doniphan, and Thomas Hart Benton, couldn't find a majority and left his old seat empty, although the lawmakers displayed a clear preference for Atchison and Doniphan, the two proslavery candidates.

While settlers were already rushing to Kansas, some thought Nebraska was not quite ready. Commissioner of Indian Affairs George W. Manypenny reported that there was no land there "in such a condition that the white man [could] lawfully occupy it for settlement." Extensive negotiations with the local Native American tribes would be necessary, and fighting was still going on in some places. Fighting of a different sort seemed to be on the near horizon in Kansas. Both proslavery and antislavery settlers were arming themselves, with assistance from interested outsiders. As the competing parties edged their way toward violence, elections in Kansas and across the country continued to show that the nation was sorely divided on the question.

The culminating moment came in October 1855, when Salmon Chase, author of "The Appeal of the Independent Democrats in Congress to the People of the United States," was elected governor of Ohio. Chase was a taciturn, stubborn man with few obvious political skills. But he had labored in the abolitionist vineyard for many years, and his fervor for the cause had at last met just the right moment. He courted the Know Nothings by enlisting their men as allies for lower offices, without overtly endorsing any nativist proposals. He made common cause with a less strident group who dubbed themselves the Know Somethings; they were anti-Catholic but happy to accept Protestant Irish and Germans into their ranks. At one point, Chase claimed to oppose the creation of any formal party, suggesting rather that the anti-Nebraska forces "catch the spirit of the people, to feel that transfused into us, to organize a peoples movement & overthrow the Slave Power. Party organization will come well enough afterwards if we succeed." He caught the spirit of the people enough to post a 15,000-vote margin of victory, although he ran behind other statewide fusionists, indicating perhaps the need for a more concrete party organization. But Chase had demonstrated that this disparate new group could build a winning coalition in a major state. He was certain it could do the same on a national scale in 1856.

{ 1 }

"A New Man"

The two would-be presidents stood face to face, but this was no debate. One was there simply to invite the other to dinner.

Ohio governor Salmon P. Chase had come to a modest redbrick home on F Street near the Capitol Building in Washington to ask New York senator William H. Seward to join him the next night—Saturday, December 29, 1855—at the home of longtime DC power broker Francis Preston Blair, "to meet some friends at his country seat," just outside the city limits.

It was the kind of get-together Seward preferred to avoid. He liked to leave the backroom dealing to his Albany amanuensis, Thurlow Weed, who relished the task. Seward, with a broad sense of humor and impeccable people skills, preferred the one on one, which he supposed was probably why Blair sent his opposite number—the humorless, all-business Chase—with a note rather than a delegation. But Seward knew better than to decline outright. Who else, he asked Chase, was going to attend? Chase had to confess that he didn't know, beyond the two of them, Blair, and Gamaliel Bailey, editor of the abolitionist journal the *National Era*, with whom Chase was staying while in town.

That was a giveaway. Bailey's attendance meant this would be a meeting about organizing the new Republican Party, in which Seward and Chase were the leading figures among elected officials. It was the editor's latest project, one that he and the staff of the Washington newspaper—the largest

abolitionist journal published in a slaveholding territory—had thrown themselves into with gusto, in the hope of keeping the party free of nativist
influence. That Blair was hosting meant there would be considerable talk
not just about organizational matters, such as the proposed national preconvention planned for some time in February or March, but also about
potential presidential candidates. If Blair was inviting both Chase and
Seward, other potential candidates were probably on the docket as well.
Seward knew that might include others like Chase who favored making
common cause with the nativist elements of the coalition. Seward told
Chase he would let him know, and Chase departed.

Not long afterward, another knock came at Seward's door. This time
it was Bailey, bearing a guest list. The editor said that in addition to those
Seward already knew about, other attendees would include a fellow New
Yorker and friend, Representative Preston King, as well as fellow senator
Charles Sumner and the leading anti-Nebraska candidate for Speaker of
the House, Nathaniel P. Banks, a Massachusetts man like Sumner but of
considerably more pliable convictions than his immutable colleague.

That sealed it for Seward. No one was sounder than Sumner on antislavery and immigration. But Chase, after some initial hesitation, favored uniting
with the so-called North Americans, the northern wing of the nativist Know
Nothing movement that opposed more Catholic immigration and full citizenship rights for many Catholics already in the country. Banks, on the other
hand, had originally been elected as a Know Nothing in the anti-Nebraska
sweep of 1854 and had demonstrated his ideological flexibility by moving
back and forth as electoral circumstances dictated. He seemed to be a solid
anti-Nebraska man and true opponent of the extension of slavery, but Seward
did not care to be seen in the company of such men. He had made rare
inroads for a Whig among the Irish Catholic leaders and voters concentrated
in New York City and along the route of the Erie Canal (which they had
helped build), by advocating bilingual education for newcomers (many of
whom spoke Gaelic) and backing proposals to let Irish children be educated
by teachers who shared their faith. He did not dare risk those relationships.

After Bailey left, Seward composed his reply to Blair, "approving of his
activity" but declining the invitation. He always tried to avoid "plans or schemes
for political action," Seward explained disingenuously—a ridiculous excuse

for a lifetime New York pol to offer, and one that didn't mesh with Seward's blunt confession to Weed that he didn't go to Blair's meeting because he didn't want to be seen associating with anybody who had ties to the Know Nothings. Seward was the public man, and he had to maintain appearances. Weed, the backroom conniver, told Seward after the fact that he should have gone.

At the least, he likely missed a good meal.

Blair's home, Silver Spring, sat just north of the line that separated Maryland from the District of Columbia. He had named his 250-acre estate and its twenty-room, three-story home, built in 1842, after the mica-flaked pool of water he and daughter Elizabeth found during a ride in the area two years earlier. Streams and orchards dotted the land, and the political visitors on December 29 passed through an ornate entry gate, traversed a stand of pine and poplar, and continued onto a carriage road lined with chestnut trees before crossing a quaint bridge to a circular driveway that deposited them in front of the grand home.

Chase was the last to arrive, but he got there in time to enjoy the delightful spread prepared by the family's slaves under the direction of Blair's wife, Eliza, a renowned hostess. After their meal, the men gathered in Blair's study to decide the fate of the Union.

SILVER SPRING.
Courtesy of Library of Congress

Francis Preston Blair was accustomed to power. He had come to Washington from Kentucky in 1830 at the request of President Andrew Jackson to run the administration's newspaper, the *Washington Globe*. He quickly became a favorite of the Democratic president, both professionally and personally. Serving as editor of the house organ, Blair wielded the kind of power that modern newspaper editors only dream of. As an informal adviser to the president, he sat in councils of state at which policy was determined, then went back to the *Globe* office to assign reporters to cover the news he had just helped make.

But he was more than a member of Jackson's "kitchen cabinet." The Blairs adopted the recently widowed Jackson into their family. They bought a mansion—Blair House—across the street from the White House. Eliza Blair knitted socks for the president. Daughter Elizabeth lived in the White House for part of her youth and served as part-time secretary. On his deathbed in 1845, the childless Jackson gave his wife Rachel's wedding ring to Elizabeth. Jackson was also instrumental in obtaining a West Point appointment for the eldest Blair son, Montgomery.

Blair's place at the pinnacle of national power was secure as long as Jackson was president, and he stood in good stead under the general's Democratic successor, Martin Van Buren. When the Whigs captured the presidency in 1840, Blair became editorial leader of the opposition.

But the election of Van Buren's intraparty rival James K. Polk in 1844 proved a turning point in the fortunes of both Blair and the party's northern wing. Blair held onto the editorship of the *Globe* until 1849, but President Polk had a different vision of the party than Blair, and the pro–Van Buren *Globe* was displaced as the administration organ. Blair lost his government printing contracts and was shut out of policy discussions. He would spend much of the next decade trying to reclaim the mantle.

Those efforts would prove unsuccessful, as radically proslavery southerners grew stronger and stronger within the party. When northern Democrats were decimated in the election of 1854 following passage of the Kansas-Nebraska Act, Blair joined those disaffected Democratic losers, Whigs in search of a new party, and Free Soilers in attempting to organize a new coalition.

At first, Blair had hoped to form a splinter Democratic Party—much like Weed and Seward had hoped to hold the Whigs together shorn of their southern branch—but soon came to realize that was not going to be a viable option. In a widely circulated letter published December 1, 1855, Blair called on all northern Democrats to leave their party, as he had done, and join with Republicans to repudiate the abandonment of the Missouri Compromise. "The extension of Slavery over the new Territories would prove fatal to their prosperity," he wrote, "but the greatest calamity to be apprehended from it, is the destruction of the Confederacy, on which the welfare of the whole country reposes." To avoid such a calamity, unity was necessary, and achievable if those of like mind "can be induced to relinquish petty differences on transitory topics, and give their united voice, in the next Presidential election, for some man, whose capacity, fidelity, and courage, can be relied upon." Blair had just such a man in mind already.

The defection of such a distinguished Jacksonian as Blair—though it had been coming for a long time—caused a considerable sensation even among the cynics in Washington. The new Republican Association of Washington tried to recruit Blair to join its ranks, which the Democratic *Washington Star* described as "made up . . . for the most part, of newly imported Abolitionists from Yankeedom."

That was only partly true. But Blair steered clear of the group, which included several members of the staff of the abolitionist *National Era*, including Gamaliel Bailey, while "in the main" concurring in the association's aims.

Instead, Blair preferred, as always, to work behind the scenes. By the time of his December 1 appeal, he had already been at it for some months. Now he had brought five of the leading members of any potential coalition—including a couple of potential presidential candidates—to his home to discuss what to do next.

A WHOLLY DIFFERENT PLACE

The country these men hoped to lead was vastly different from the one in which they were born. At the turn of the nineteenth century, America had been an overwhelmingly rural nation. To the extent that it was tied together at all, it was by a barely serviceable system of post roads that linked the few major cities of the North and that had only begun to stretch into the even more agrarian South. A population of just over five million was squeezed in behind the Appalachians, except for a few thousand daring souls who had ventured over the mountains into Kentucky and Tennessee. Only those two and Vermont had been added to the original thirteen states by 1800.

Of the five million inhabitants, just under a million were enslaved blacks. But the political system cobbled together at the Constitutional Convention in 1787 had largely avoided the question of slavery, except to endorse its continued existence and to account for the population by assigning the value of three-fifths of a person to each slave for the purpose of calculating representation in Congress. Aside from these enslaved descendants of Africans, and the uncounted Native Americans who still populated large swaths of the South, America was mostly a white Protestant country, English and Ulster Irish in makeup (with a smattering of German Protestants), dedicated to the idea of religious tolerance without having to deal with much religious pluralism in actual practice.

By the middle of the century, the Founders' America was a wholly different place. Middle-aged voters had grown up in a country where 90 percent of the people lived on farms or in small towns. By 1856, more than one in four lived in cities. The population had soared to more than 23 million in 1850, and was probably about 28 million by 1856. The number of slaves had grown to 3.2 million. The number of states had almost doubled, to thirty-one, with the admission of California in 1850, as the United States spread across the continent in pursuit of Thomas Jefferson's dream of an "Empire of Liberty." In doing so, the government had, for the most part, emptied the East of Native Americans, pushing them beyond the Mississippi River—often in cruel forced marches during which thousands died.

As the population increased, so did its ethnic and religious diversity. Waves of immigration from Catholic Europe—especially Ireland and Germany—had remade the demographics of America's eastern cities. Resentment among working-class Protestants had sometimes flared into violence against the aliens, who would work for less money and who practiced a religion the white Protestant natives detested.

The diverging elements of the national consensus—and, as it happened, the Whig coalition—could be encapsulated in one event in 1856: the founding of the State Industrial School for Girls in Lancaster, Massachusetts, about fifty miles west of Boston. On one hand, the country's first female reform school was a classic example of evangelical/Whiggish reform, an attempt to save girls and young women in dire straits from a sinful existence and, in the words of Boston Brahmin Charles Eliot Norton, a "sea of ignorance." On the other hand, it reflected a growing fear among polite society of the largely foreign-born urban poor. The people who ran the school were overwhelmingly Protestant. The inmates were overwhelmingly Catholic.

At the same time, Protestantism itself was undergoing a revolution, as the Second Great Awakening democratized American religion and broke the domination of the Calvinist orthodoxy that had reigned over the populace since the time of the Puritans. New sects sprang up, many teaching a kinder, gentler form of Christianity and invoking a social conscience that would have a dramatic effect on American society, most notably in the causes of temperance and abolitionism. And the first indigenous American religion—Mormonism—had established what amounted to a theocratic kingdom in the Utah territory that had been won in the war with Mexico. That kingdom, too, became an engine for immigration from Europe, gathering thousands of converts of the new religion to their Zion, and its doctrines—particularly plural marriage—posed novel challenges to the political system.

At least as dramatic as the religious awakening had been the revolutions in transportation and communication. In 1800, simply delivering a message from the new city of Washington to Baltimore, just forty miles to the north, had been an arduous, time-consuming task of a day or more. By 1856, much of the East was strung with telegraph lines that made instantaneous communication possible. Railroads moved people and goods from place to place at a rate ten or twenty times that of horse or oxen. These revolutions abetted and intertwined with others. The expansion of manufacturing that accompanied the Industrial Revolution was boosted by improvements in the technologies of transportation and communication, which in turn contributed to a market revolution that spread goods across the fast-growing country. More people had more access to more food, which made them healthier, which increased population growth, which sparked more westward immigration. And so on and so on in a prosperous circle that Americans by midcentury had come to think of as their God-given inheritance, their Manifest Destiny to spread that good fortune across the continent and the world.

"SOMEONE WHO WOULD INCARNATE OUR PRINCIPLES"

The six white, Protestant men who gathered at Francis Blair's home did not reflect many of the changes that had swept across the nation in the previous five decades. But having lived through them, they recognized that even more change was afoot and were trying to confront it.

They agreed on the easy things—for instance, naming Pittsburgh as the location for a proposed national organizing convention that would begin work on a statement of principles and make plans for a nominating convention in late spring or early summer. (Ohioan Chase, however, preferred Cincinnati, but he lost the argument.) And before any national meeting anywhere could be called, all agreed that the question of who would be Speaker of the House had to be settled, preferably in favor of their member Nathaniel Banks. The haggling had already gone on for almost the entire month, and no resolution was yet in sight. They must stand fast behind Banks if they were to have any chance of becoming the dominant faction in a coalition that included nativist North Americans and disaffected Democrats.

Blair, who was just getting over a bad cold, made a raspy pitch for unity on the harder things that fell largely on deaf ears. Bailey had made plain—publicly and privately—his opposition to making common cause with the nativists, although the abolitionist editor didn't mind collaborating with Blair, who owned more than a dozen slaves. None of the others in attendance had gone as far as Bailey in their objections to joining up with the North Americans—Seward would have, but he wasn't there. Only Chase joined Blair in sounding the clarion call for fusion, which Chase had already been doing for months.

Chase had some Know Nothing support, but he had also won backing from the less virulent Know Somethings, and he wanted to bring all the anti-Nebraska elements to bear on the cause. The man who had once written, "I cannot proscribe men on account of their birth. I cannot make religious faith a political test," now seemed willing to apply just such a test—in the service of a greater cause, of course.

"It seems to me that we can only carry the next Presidential election by making the simple issue of Slavery or Freedom," Chase had argued two months earlier. "We shall need the liberal Americans and we shall also need the Anti slavery Adopted Citizens. Neither of these great classes can be spared without imminent danger of defeat."

It was that kind of talk that had kept Seward away from Silver Spring.

To drive home the point, Chase also suggested that the Pittsburgh meeting should include an equal number of Republicans and American Party members. Preston King called it the Ohio Plan, and all present seconded it, with varying degrees of enthusiasm—except Bailey, who belittled it as the "half and half" plan. Like Seward, he didn't want to be seen in the company of those people. But Seward was politic enough to let others do the dirty work of creating a party broad enough to win elections and from which he hoped, eventually, to benefit. Bailey, on the other hand, not only didn't want to be seen with those people, he didn't want to be in the same party with them.

Chase had been down this road before. In 1848, he was among those attempting to organize free soil Democrats, conscience Whigs, and other disaffected supporters of the Wilmot Proviso into a united front in opposition to the expansion of slavery into the territories. The political differences among New York Barnburner Democrats, New England Whigs, and Liberty Party abolitionists were, if anything, even greater than those the anti-Nebraska forces now faced. Many hardline abolitionists refused to join the Free Soil Party, which rose up in opposition to the major party candidates, Democrat Lewis Cass and Whig Zachary Taylor, because it limited its platform to restricting the extension of slavery rather than its elimination. But, unlike the Liberty Party in 1840 and 1844, the new Free Soilers—united behind the ringing endorsement of "Free Soil, Free Speech, Free Labor and Free Men"—had managed to persuade major political figures to lead their ticket: former Democratic president Martin Van Buren, and Charles Francis Adams, a Whig and the son and grandson of presidents. Chase had played a key role in drafting a centrist platform that helped bridge the differences among the factions. Now here he was again, eight years later, trying to herd the same collection of political cats into an even larger corral.

There was one difference this time around: Chase was out front, a possible candidate himself, not simply an organizer.

Finally the Blair group got around to discussing potential presidential candidates. At least two—Banks and Chase—were in the room. If Chase was true to form when his name came up, he waved such thoughts away, asserting forcefully that he cared not a whit for personal ambition; it was the cause that mattered. If a better man than he could be found, that man should carry the standard. If not, then he would be prepared to do his duty.

Supreme Court justice John McLean, a New Jersey–born Ohioan who had also been mentioned—and dismissed—as a Free Soil candidate in 1848 and a Whig candidate in 1852, evoked little enthusiasm. He had voted the Know Nothing line in 1854 and "hailed with unmeasured satisfaction" the party's successes. But he had also carefully avoided any overt anti-Catholic or anti-immigrant rhetoric of his own. He had some support among the more conservative elements of the anti-Nebraska forces, including Abraham Lincoln, but none that night in Silver Spring.

Thomas Hart Benton, a longtime ally of Blair, was mentioned and quickly ruled out. All acknowledged that, as one of the two southern Democrats to oppose the Kansas-Nebraska Act, Benton had been a stalwart on the issue of nonextension. But he had lost his grip on his home state and was considered to be a man whose best years were long since past. It had been a rough few years for the aging Benton. Having been driven from the Senate in 1850 over his refusal to support the potential extension of slavery into New Mexico and Utah, he was elected to the House the following year, only to lose his seat in 1854 because he voted against the Kansas-Nebraska Act. Just before the election, his wife, Elizabeth, died. A few months later, his Washington, DC, home—and the nearly completed manuscript of the second volume of his memoirs—went up in flames. He was, in the words of his daughter Jessie, "that lonely old man." And he seemed the least likely person in the country to abandon the Jacksonian party that had been his home for three decades. A new party, the argument went, should be looking forward, not backward.

This had to be something of a disappointment to Francis Preston Blair. As with Jackson, the Blairs had established a close relationship with the Bentons over the years. Montgomery Blair had practiced law in Thomas Hart Benton's Saint Louis office and done legal work for Benton's son-in-law, famed western explorer John C. Frémont, in a complicated land case in California. And Benton's daughter, Jessie Benton Frémont, was among the closest friends of Blair's own daughter, Elizabeth Blair Lee. John and Jessie had named their last child Francis Preston Frémont.

But Blair recognized all along that Benton was an extreme longshot. So he had a backup plan, one that had been brewing for months. John C. Frémont had been courted by the Democratic Party early in 1855 as a potential presidential contender. He and Jessie had canceled plans to travel back to California, instead settling in New York, where they moved into a townhouse at 176 Second Avenue, between Tenth and Eleventh Streets in Manhattan, across from Saint Mark's Church and near the home of Whig senator Hamilton Fish. There they awaited developments. While John shuttled from New York to Philadelphia to Washington tending to business and politics, Jessie had removed to Nantucket in August, ostensibly to rest and recuperate from the difficult birth of little Frank, but also to escape what she sensed was a simmering hostility from her father. At some point, daughter Lily remembered, "it became more pleasant to visit Washington than to live there."

The offer from the Democrats was intriguing. Edward Carrington, a nephew of Virginia governor John B. Floyd and a cousin of the Benton side of the family, was part of a group that was fed up with Pierce and trying to bring southern Know Nothings and Democrats into a coalition. Frémont had espoused some nativist positions in the past: he supported a twenty-one-year residency before being allowed to vote, for example, and thought it might be time to limit immigration. And, perhaps best of all, Frémont's scant public record—he had served less than a year as one of California's first senators—offered little in the way of ammunition for the opposition to attack. Carrington engaged Frémont in a series of political discussions over the summer when the explorer was in Washington, which led to Floyd, Carrington, Frémont, and Banks getting together at New York's Saint Nicholas Hotel in the early autumn of 1855. Frémont had enjoyed the free-for-all discussions in the capital, but knew he was not a good fit for the aggressively anti-Catholic Know Nothing faction. As for the Democrats, the southerners laid down the law for Frémont in New York. Over three days of discussion, they let it be known that they would support him for the nomination—if he wholeheartedly backed the Kansas-Nebraska and Fugitive Slave Acts.

At this, Banks exploded. Like Frémont, he was a former Democrat who had abandoned the party over the extension of slavery. Banks took after the southerners so violently "as to nearly terminate the meeting," Jessie recorded, telling Floyd that the Fugitive Slave Act "was the entering wedge which would divide the North and South, place them in arms against one another, and become the lever by which the institution of slavery would be overthrown." This must have disheartened the southerners greatly, but they nevertheless stayed long enough to ask Frémont for an answer. Frémont's

JESSIE BENTON FRÉMONT.
Courtesy of Library of Congress

natural reserve in interpersonal relations contrasted with his well-known rashness as a man of action. In this case, in contrast to Banks, the would-be candidate kept his own counsel.

He wanted to talk it over with his wife. Carrington took that as a good sign. "We Democrats are sure to win, and no woman can refuse the Presidency," he remarked.

It was tempting, to be sure. Jessie had fond memories of her childhood trips to Jackson's White House, where Old Hickory would stroke her hair while talking momentous policy with her father. When Frémont returned to Nantucket, the couple took a long sunset walk on the beach to weigh their options. The Democrats, they agreed, were likely to win. The opposition had spirit but was disorganized and feuding internally. It appeared unlikely that the factions would be able to coalesce in time to make a serious run in 1856. But, as Frémont had heard from Carrington, the price would be fealty to Kansas-Nebraska. On they walked and talked, into the darkness, past the Sankaty Head lighthouse at Siasconset. Joining the Republicans, they knew, would mean a complete break with Benton, with the rest of Jessie's southern relatives, with Missouri, with "all that had made my deep rooted pleasant life," Jessie wrote. But, they reasoned, joining the Democrats

JOHN C. FRÉMONT.
Courtesy of Library of Congress

would mean openly supporting slavery. Frémont's mild manner played a role in the decision making. "It is the choice between a wreck of dishonor, or a kindly light that will go on its mission of doing good," he told her. But he also knew that it was his wife, not he, who would be surrendering the most emotionally. The prospect of being part of a crusading campaign in a great cause, and of being First Lady, appealed to her. She was used to being at the center of things. But she would not surrender principle to stay there. "There was only one decision possible," Jessie concluded. The Frémonts were now Republicans.

Jessie Anne Benton Frémont knew her way around politics. Raised in Washington, schooled at the knee of her powerful father, she was intimately familiar with the uses of power and had developed an independent identity rare for a woman of the era, especially one with such an imposing father and husband. Jessie and Elizabeth Blair Lee served as unofficial aides-de-camp, stenographers, and go-betweens for their fathers, but both were happy for the occasional respite from matters of state. "Isn't it charming to relapse into small talk," Jessie wrote in a letter that included discussions of children's hats and flounced dresses, "after clerking it for the Heads of the People. I feel like a horse set free from harness." After another round of important business, she asked "Lizzy" to "write me a womanish letter next time."

"She is a noble spirited woman," Seward told his wife, Frances. "Has much character. I am sure you would like her. She is very outspoken."

Jessie Benton Frémont also knew her way around her father. "Mr. Frémont has under consideration so important a step, that before taking it he wishes for the advice and friendly counsel which have heretofore proved so full of sagacity and led to such success," she wrote to the man she called "Father Blair" in the summer of 1855. Their long family friendship was not the only reason the Frémonts were approaching Blair. They knew Blair's advice would serve as an antidote to any "shocks that Father with his different organization is dangerously apt to give."

Throughout the late summer and early fall, Francis Blair and Jessie Benton Frémont—joined by Nathaniel Banks—worked the back rooms. Banks had known Frémont since 1853. They were men of action, shared youth and good looks, and had similar feelings about slavery and restrictions on immigration and immigrants' rights. Banks was especially fond of Jessie, as were so many other men in politics. Eventually, multiple streams of conniving led Banks to Blair, and the concentric circles began to widen.

Blair prepared a preliminary platform that endorsed the compromises of 1820 and 1850 while criticizing northern personal liberty laws that interfered with enforcement of the Fugitive Slave Act. (He never mailed the proposal to Frémont.) Jessie reported to Blair that the efforts of Banks and a politically active Siasconset neighbor—Philadelphia Quaker Edward M. Davis—were yielding "all that could be wished and more" in terms of organizing support in Pennsylvania and the Northeast. Massachusetts senator Henry Wilson was on board. Key journalists, including John Bigelow and William Cullen Bryant at the *New York Post*, were also being recruited. Bigelow, exposing the typical journalistic cynicism, had to admit that Frémont "impressed me more favorably than I had expected" on their first meeting, a confab at the Metropolitan Hotel that included Joseph Palmer of Palmer, Cook & Company, the state banker for California and Frémont's largest creditor. Banks made the point that you couldn't beat anybody with nobody, and the party would never get organized "until we produced someone who would incarnate our principles; that the people could never be made to join a party or to be active in favor of a platform without a man on it." That man, Banks was certain, was Frémont.

Blair met with Benton in November but proved unable to sway him to support his son-in-law. Some of Benton's objections to Frémont were personal—he considered him too young, too rash, and too inexperienced—but he also objected to the Republican Party on principle, fearing that its sectional character would tear the country apart. Blair tried again with Benton later in the month, stressing Frémont's "brave and attractive" qualities, and pointing to the advantages of having a candidate "unconnected with past corruptions and misdeeds." Blair's persistence was admirable, but Jessie Benton Frémont knew better. "I know both my people too well ever to look for concession from either side," she wrote of father and husband. After a get-together at Christmas, she wouldn't hear from her Washington-based father for more than four months. "He always drops me that way when he is offended with Mr. Frémont," she told Elizabeth Blair Lee.

THOMAS HART BENTON.
Courtesy of Library of Congress

Blair hoped for better results with his post-Christmas guests, and after they dismissed Benton as a possibility, he steered the conversation to Benton's son-in-law. King was already all but on board, having been lobbied by Bigelow, Wilson, and others. Chase, like Benton, opposed Frémont as a new man, untested in politics and untried on slavery, but he raised no definitive objection. Nor did Bailey, whose reluctance to endorse Frémont was perhaps even stronger than Chase's, except Chase wanted the nomination for himself. When Blair suggested Banks—who was sitting in the room—for either the number-one or number-two spot on the ticket, to create balance between Republicans and Americans—no one raised an objection, either on grounds that they hoped to avoid entangling themselves too tightly with nativists or that both men were from the North, which would be an unprecedented step in American politics. No presidential ticket had ever included two northerners. Only one—Andrew Jackson and John C. Calhoun in 1828—had included two southerners (and Jacksonians argued that it was a westerner and a southerner).

Disagreements remained, but as the men departed Silver Spring, Blair believed he had achieved his main purpose. A loose national anti-Nebraska coalition was being formed into a national organization—it was not yet fully Republican, at least in Blair's mind—and John C. Frémont was emerging as the consensus choice to be its titular head.

"A History of Romantic Heroism"

The same traits that made Frémont an appealing and dashing figure also made him an easy target for accusations of recklessness and immaturity like those leveled by Benton and former president Martin Van Buren, who resisted Blair's efforts to sell Frémont as "a new man . . . brave, firm [with] a history of romantic heroism."

Frémont was, as Blair described him, a man of "capacity, fidelity, and courage." Philadelphia lawyer John M. Read, a former free soil Democrat and founder of the nascent Republican Party, correctly assessed that Frémont "is a man of great natural sagacity . . . unassuming in his manners" and in possession of "a firm and vigorous will." But Frémont had also proved himself impetuous, arrogant, and prone to ignore orders when they didn't suit him. Benton had witnessed—and in some cases enabled—all of these traits, good and bad, up close, for a decade and a half.

When the young army officer first laid eyes on the senator's daughter in 1840, he was smitten. And so was she. He was twenty-seven. She was fifteen. Frémont, whose late father was a rakish French Canadian ne'er-do-well, had no parents around to disapprove. His mother, Anne Beverly Whiting, had not properly disposed of her first husband, John Pryor, before running off with Charles Frémon (John added the t later) and thus was in no position to cast stones.

After that first meeting, John and Jessie would not see each other again for several months. When they did, the girl's parents noticed right away that something was afoot, and they interceded immediately. But all efforts to sway Jessie met with defiance, which should have come as no surprise to the senator, who had helped instill such stubborn confidence in her. Both young people were used to getting their own way, and they kept up a correspondence. On April 4, 1841, Frémont proposed. Thomas Hart Benton was a student of the classics, but on this occasion he instead reached into the Bible for a response. Like David sending Uriah off to war, Benton conspired with the Corps of Topographical Engineers to exile Frémont to a survey of the distant Des Moines River. That would keep him occupied for months, Benton reasoned, providing time for Jessie's ardor to cool and her attention to turn to other things.

It didn't work. Frémont returned in August of that year, and the two began planning an elopement, which was consummated on October 19, with an assist from the wife of Attorney General John J. Crittenden, whose home they used to meet in secret. It took another month for them to work up the courage to tell her parents. Benton, whose fits of rage were legend, stormed for a while longer, then surrendered. If he could not keep Frémont out of his family, he would make the best use possible of him.

And so Frémont became the instrument of Benton's policy of westward expansion, with his new wife as full partner. He went on five expeditions in the West, two of which yielded bestselling reports—edited beautifully by Jessie—and made him a national hero. When Jessie defied the US Army and aided John in taking a howitzer on his 1843–44 expedition by refusing to forward a message ordering her husband to return to Washington, her father bailed her out of trouble and shielded Frémont from reprisal. The incident cast a long shadow over Frémont's career, and the upper echelons of the army would forever remain suspicious of the non–West Point officer who seemed free to ignore the chain of command under the protection of powerful friends and family.

Subsequent events would only augment that reputation. When Frémont caused a ruckus in California just before the Mexican War, coming to the aid of a ragtag band of American settlers and disaffected Californios— Spanish-speaking residents and longtime white settlers—attempting to overthrow the Mexican government in the 1846 Bear Flag Revolt, Benton backed him up. When he defied orders during the war the following year, Benton implored President James K. Polk to intercede on his behalf. Frémont was court-martialed, but Polk offered to reinstate him. Frémont refused out of pride, arguing he wanted justice not clemency, and left the army.

He remained enough of a hero to Californians to be chosen by their legislature as one of the first two senators when the state entered the Union in 1850. He drew the short straw, so he had to serve an abbreviated tenure rather than the usual six years to keep the terms staggered. He took his seat on September 10, 1850, one day after California was admitted to the Union, and served until the end of the session the following March. In that short span, Frémont began to establish the underpinnings of a moderate antislavery record, voting for a ban on the slave trade in the District of Columbia and against tougher penalties for assisting runaway slaves, while opposing a measure from Seward to abolish slavery in the District altogether.

While Frémont and his wife enjoyed the Washington social scene, politics did not seem to suit the senator's reticent personality. He had support from the Californios who, much like himself, had questionable land holdings. But the mass of Gold Rush immigrants saw the landed natives as the opposition, and the sizable minority of proslavery Californians disagreed with Frémont's nascent antislavery stance. The California legislature couldn't agree on a replacement and adjourned in late 1851 without electing anybody, and Frémont's term expired. Jessie had enjoyed her time in Washington, but expressed relief at not having to make another dangerous trip across the malarial swamps of Panama—more hazardous but faster than the overland route—or stay behind while her husband left. "I would dissolve the Union sooner than let Mr. Frémont go away a year to Congress," she wrote.

Frémont turned his attention to making money. He speculated in real estate, supplied beef to Native Americans under a federal contract, and had high hopes for the gold mine on his property at Las Mariposas in the southern Sierra Nevada foothills. The mine yielded some returns for a while, and the Frémonts grew increasingly wealthy. But Congress had passed a law in 1851 barring confirmation of any California land titles that lacked ironclad written proof. Las Mariposas didn't fit that description, and years of legal wrangling ensued, in which Frémont was assisted by Montgomery Blair.

The returns grew spotty and the headaches unending. By 1852, Frémont was tiring of the venture, and his father-in-law was urging him to unload it. But when Benton found a buyer willing to pay $1 million for the property, Frémont balked. Benton was apoplectic. The relationship between the two men, forged in the fires of Manifest Destiny, would never recover.

At the time, the dispute between Benton and Frémont seemed to be a family matter without any political implications. But it cemented in the older man's mind the conviction that the younger was impetuous at best, and probably just as loose a cannon as his critics had long contended. Benton had defended him for a dozen years. He wouldn't anymore.

So when Frémont entered the national scene in late 1855, the armor that had protected him for much of his career was no longer in place. He had appeal as a national hero and a "new man," but Chase, Seward, and the other potential candidates—much more agile on the political playing field than Frémont—knew it was a long way to June and the Republican convention.

Two days after the Silver Spring meeting (having been briefed by Weed), Seward told Preston King that he would "distinctly protest against any combination with Know-Nothing" elements. While Seward's principles were flexible, to say the least, his instinct for self-preservation was not. Weed assured Blair that Seward was blowing smoke and would come around eventually. Chase didn't need any persuading. He was committed to bringing nativist voters into the fold and making common cause with all comers—but so were other candidates who were better liked and more widely trusted. As the election year unfolded before them, Seward and Chase would both be hard pressed to live up to their absolutist antislavery images. And the reality on the ground was that the value of the nomination was questionable. Factions were squabbling, big states that had to be carried were still barely organized, and—despite Blair's fondest wishes—there was no hope of any substantial support from the South. On the upside, the Democrats had plenty of problems of their own.

{ 2 }

"A FUGITIVE
FROM FREEDOM"

Everything seemed to come easy for Franklin Pierce.

The boy wonder of New Hampshire politics, son of a Revolutionary War hero who survived Valley Forge, Pierce had run off a string of "firsts" unmatched in his lifetime. He was elected to the statehouse in his twenties, as Speaker in his last term; to the US House in 1833; and to the Senate in 1837, at age thirty-two the youngest ever to enter the body at that point. He turned down an offer to become attorney general under President James K. Polk in 1845, citing the ill health of his wife, Jane, who hated Washington. But there was one appointment Pierce could not refuse. His service in the Mexican War was not particularly distinguished, but unlike many a political general, at least he did not make a fool of himself or get his men slaughtered.

Pierce was a likable fellow and counted among his college chums the novelist Nathaniel Hawthorne and the education reformer Calvin Stowe, husband of Harriet Beecher Stowe. In 1852 Pierce became the youngest man elected president to that time, losing only four states. He carried with him two-to-one Democratic majorities in both the House and Senate. And, by general consensus, he was the handsomest man ever to hold the office.

Pierce had led a charmed life, one that carried this amiable man with a sonorous voice and a great memory for names and faces to the pinnacle of American life.

Now he faced a problem that backslapping and glad-handing couldn't solve. The Kansas-Nebraska trap laid by Stephen A. Douglas into which Pierce had stepped in 1854 was about to slam shut on him.

At the insistence of David Atchison and the Kansas territorial legislature, Pierce had recalled the territory's governor, Andrew Reeder, in July 1855, after thirteen months in office, on trumped-up charges of land speculation. Reeder had indeed engaged in some shady practices, but so had pretty much everyone else in the territory—much of the dispute over slavery had its roots in disputed land claims between immigrants from free states and those from slave states. But "no one believed at the time that Reeder was removed for the cause alleged," the *National Era* reported, even if some of his deals were highly questionable. The real reason for his firing was that the Pennsylvanian had sided with free-state forces when he refused to certify the blatantly fraudulent results of the March 1855 legislative elections won by the proslavery forces. In that election, more than 6,000 votes were cast—90 percent for proslavery candidates—following a census that counted 2,905 eligible voters. Reeder's replacement, Wilson Shannon, was more sympathetic to the proslavery forces—he lost his seat in Congress after one term because of his vote in favor of the Kansas-Nebraska Act—although he was also interested in public safety. Shannon, like Salmon Chase, had been governor of Ohio; like Abraham Lincoln, he was a former one-term congressman. Just a few months after taking office in Kansas, in late 1855, he had brokered a peace to end a modestly violent stand-off known as the Wakarusa War, after the river where two thousand proslavery men had gathered to confront an equal number of free staters holed up in nearby Lawrence. But he was not looked on kindly by abolitionists, who called him "the miserablest doughface in all the North!"

Even before the killing on the Wakarusa in November and December, factions had been forming militias and guns were flowing into the territory. Pierce had received a telegram from Shannon on December 3, 1855—the day the new Congress convened—asking him to send the army to restore order. "When farmers turn soldiers they must have arms," declared Amos

A. Lawrence; the Massachusetts businessman had turned a philanthropic abolitionist, funding both immigration and arms for Kansas. All told, more than $43,000 was raised to buy weapons for free-state Kansans. Formerly peaceful abolitionists were converted to fighters. Charles Stearns, a reporter for the *Liberator*, wrote from Kansas that "my non-resistance has at length yielded. I am sorry to deny the principles of Jesus Christ, after contending for them so long, but it is not for myself that I am going to fight. It is *for God* and *the slaves*."

After Shannon certified the proslavery election victory that Reeder would not, free staters had gathered in late October to write their own constitution. Thirty-seven delegates met for almost three weeks, producing what came to be known as the Topeka Constitution. While invoking the rhetoric of the American Revolution, the delegates submitted to the voters not just a proposed free-state constitution but also a separate proposal to exclude free blacks from the territory. The split over rights for African Americans ran along regional lines: immigrants from New England generally opposed the proposal to abridge those rights; those from western states generally supported it. When free staters voted on December 15—most proslavery residents boycotted or ignored the contest—the constitution was approved with more than 97 percent of the vote. (A little more than seventeen hundred people participated.) The ban on free blacks carried the day with 74 percent.

Less than two weeks later, one day before the gathering of Republican leaders at Francis Blair's home outside Washington, the Topeka Constitution was declared in force and elections were called for January.

The antislavery men may have considered themselves the heirs of Washington and Jefferson, but to the duly constituted authorities in Kansas, they were troublemakers (as were Washington and Jefferson to the British). Governor Shannon wrote to Pierce that "the time has come when this armed band of men, who are seeking to subvert and render powerless the existing government, have to be met and the laws enforced against them, or submit to their lawless dominion." Pierce, at first, didn't agree. In the annual message he prepared for Congress, he acknowledged that things were not as calm as he would have liked but he saw no reason for presidential intervention. Pierce delivered that message on December 31, but it was written before the outbreak of the Wakarusa War and was delayed by the inability of the House to get organized (see chapter 3).

The president's resolve lasted less than a month. Free staters held their elections for territorial officials on January 15, and it was a remarkably peaceful affair, in part because armed parties—including fiery-eyed radical John Brown and his sons—protected many of the polling places. One man was killed: a free-state militia leader named Reese Brown (no relation). Charles Robinson, a bearded and balding advocate of nonviolence and a former Californian who had been one of Frémont's "most determined supporters in the California Legislature" in his unsuccessful bid for reelection to the Senate in 1851, was elected governor by a wide margin. In the wake of his victory, Robinson, joined by militia leader James Lane, appealed to Washington for federal troops to protect their followers. Instead, the reaction from Washington was swift and hostile.

On January 24, Pierce announced a new policy for Kansas. In it, he blamed the territory's troubles on "inflammatory agitation" and "propagandist immigration." He named no names and nominally held both sides culpable. But he accepted the proslavery legislature because the sitting governor did, and he endorsed its actions. He completely rejected the free soil argument that the legislature was illegitimate because it was chosen in a fraudulent election swarmed over by Missourians.

"Whatever irregularities may have occurred in the elections, it seems too late now to raise that question," Pierce declared. "For all present purposes the legislative body thus constituted and elected was the legitimate legislative assembly of the Territory." The establishment of a free-state government was more than "illegal," Pierce charged. It was "revolutionary." And, he wanted to make clear, "our system affords no justification of revolutionary acts." He threatened "to exert the whole power of the Federal Executive to support public order." Delivery of the message in the House was met with "screeches and screams . . . bawling and halloing like a parcel of wild Comanche Indians."

But Pierce wasn't done. If his first message wasn't clear enough, he followed up its slightly veiled threat with a more specific one on February 11, ordering the free staters to "disperse and retire peaceably" or face "the employment of the local militia" and "of any available forces of the United States." Secretary of War Jefferson Davis, refusing to tolerate defiance of federal authority, empowered Shannon to call on US troops at Fort Leavenworth if he deemed it necessary.

The response was immediate, loud, and determined.

The president, said Philadelphia lawyer John M. Read, was using the army "to stab freedom in the heart." Another critic called Pierce "a fugitive from freedom."

Writing from Washington to militia leaders in Kansas, Mark Delahay, the free-state party's shadow delegate to Congress, warned that "we are on the brink of a crisis of serious import." He hoped to impress upon those in Kansas that Pierce was not bluffing, but that there was "a full and matured determination to carry this intention out, on the part of the President and his party."

Former governor Reeder, also now in Washington, called Pierce's dictum a "low contemptible trickstering affair" and a "slander on the Free State Party," and about what one should expect from the likes of the man that others were calling "that ninney Frank Pierce." But, like Delahay, he warned his allies against organizing their free-state government. Both sensed the danger in such a provocation, as well as the desperation emanating from the White House.

Others outside the capital were also counseling patience. When Thomas Barber, a free soil Ohioan who had settled in Kansas, was murdered during the Wakarusa War, John Greenleaf Whittier responded with the poem "The Burial of Barber," urging his fellow abolitionists to remember that the final judgment would right all wrongs:

> *Patience, friends! The eye of God*
> *Every path by Murder trod,*
> *Watches lidless, day and night . . .*
> *While the flag with stars bedeck'd*
> *Threatens where it should protect,*
> *And the Law shakes hands with Crime,*
> *What is left ye but to wait,*
> *Match your patience to your fate,*
> *And abide the better time?*

Delahay, too, hoped "that there will be nothing done to invoke the rath of the General Govt upon our friends." In a similar vein, Amos Lawrence—who had counseled farmers to arm themselves—urged "a deadly tho smiling quiet." But some free staters gladly accepted the revolutionary label appended to them by Pierce. "We seek communion with the spirits of 1775–76," wrote John Brown Jr., who had been elected to the free-state legislature.

To assist that communion, Rev. Henry Ward Beecher—one of the most famous preachers in the country and brother of the author of *Uncle Tom's Cabin*—upped the ante on the arms race, raising money to buy Sharps rifles, boxing them up, and shipping them to free-state allies in crates marked "Bibles." Thus were born the "Beecher's Bibles" that the free staters would soon take into battle.

Congress, in typical legislative fashion, stalled. Lawmakers voted to form a commission, which would travel to Kansas to see what was going on and investigate the allegations of election fraud and violence. That slammed the brakes on Pierce's plans for a constitutional convention to prepare the territory for statehood. But it left a dangerous power vacuum in the territory itself. The men who stepped forward to fill the vacuum were not in the mold of the gentle poet Whittier.

Abolitionists were not hopeful. The ever-pessimistic William Lloyd Garrison wrote that his "own conviction remains unshaken, that Kansas will be a slave State, and the 'border ruffian' legislation will be enforced, if need be, by all the military power of the General Government." Pierce, the dyspeptic editor predicted, "is ready to do all that the Slave Power demands at his hands."

Stephen A. Douglas prepared a report that blamed all the problems on the antislavery New England Emigrant Aid Company, and on March 17, 1856, he introduced a bill that called for a territorial census, in itself a reasonable first step that would establish the necessary mechanism for electing a constitutional convention. Douglas's bill also would have authorized the formation of a state constitution and government when the population reached 93,420; at the moment it was about one-tenth of that, more than 8,000 white settlers and a bit fewer than 200 enslaved blacks. Almost half the whites were from Missouri.

The relatively small population was among the things that made the Kansas situation unique. Previously, the impetus for the organization of territories had come from settlers in the territories. But Kansas was at least as important to the politicians in Washington as it was to the settlers themselves, so with such a small cadre in Kansas, the movement for organization had begun in Washington, with the result that it became more of a political football. While awaiting the requisite population, the proslavery territorial legislature would continue to hold sway. No matter how reasonable some of the provisions might seem, Douglas's bill had no chance of being enacted, any more than the measure offered days later by William Seward to admit Kansas as a free state under the Topeka Constitution, a nonstarter as far as Pierce was concerned.

Senate debate on the Douglas bill began on March 20. Galleries were full, with a considerable number of women crowding into the press area to watch. Debate continued sporadically for several weeks. Seward took the floor on April 9 to pitch his alternative. One day, Harriet Beecher Stowe took a seat in the gallery to watch the festivities. She described Douglas's debating style as something akin to "a bomb which hits nothing in particular, but bursts and sends red-hot nails in every direction." But Douglas's participation receded as he turned his attention to wooing support for the presidential nomination and as it became clearer that there was no chance either Kansas measure could be enacted.

The Democratic Party had now dedicated itself to popular sovereignty—in a Kansas without federal protection for honest elections, that effectively meant proslavery. Still, many anti-Nebraska Democrats remained reluctant to leave the party they had been attached to their entire lives. Some were wary of the "extreme" elements coalescing in the new party. Others were willing to wait and see if the Democratic convention would ratify Pierce's decision.

Nothing, it seemed, would be settled until the party gathered in June in Cincinnati to renominate Pierce for president—or replace him with another candidate.

"I Will Kill Them All"

At the very moment Pierce and the Democrats were warily eyeing each other ahead of their gathering, a quite different group was preparing to gather in Cincinnati, described by abolitionists as "a place where the great question of human liberty is so often brought up and where the friends of freedom are so few and so much needed."

The Queen City was home to about 140,000 people and growing rapidly, in large part owing to a rush of immigration from Germany. Of the total, about 3,500 were free blacks. Cincinnati was the sixth largest city in the country (but would soon fall to seventh, behind New Orleans) and one of the least hospitable to abolition in all of Ohio, the most proabolition state in the Union outside New England. While the abolitionist Salmon Chase was winning statewide in his race for governor the year before, he got less than 20 percent of the Hamilton County vote. Almost half the city's population had moved there from slaveholding states.

But for all of its hostility, Cincinnati had one thing going for it: it was directly across the Ohio River from Kentucky. Its sandy banks meant freedom.

On Sunday, January 27, three days after Pierce condemned Kansas to existence under slavery, eight people all too familiar with such an existence were readying themselves to throw off their yokes.

Maplewood, the plantation of Archibald Gaines, was in Richwood, in Boone County, Kentucky, crooked into the corner of the Bluegrass State abutting both Indiana and Ohio. Maplewood was anything but the idealized image of a southern plantation, with a simple two-story house and a profitable but unsentimental hog producing business. The Gaineses were well off, but not *that* well off. By 1856, they owned about a dozen slaves, including twenty-two-year-old Margaret Garner and her four children, three of whom were considerably lighter-skinned than the fourth and oldest, Thomas, age six. Margaret was also pregnant with her fifth child. That Archibald Gaines was more likely than not the father of her three younger children—Samuel, four; Mary, two; and Cilla, nine months—and of the one she was now carrying, might well have played a part in their decision to flee.

Archibald Gaines's brother, John P. Gaines, had been governor of Oregon Territory, a job he took in 1849 after Lincoln turned it down. John Gaines, a Whig, was friends with Thomas Hart Benton; the two men had even traveled together to Washington when Gaines served in the House of Representatives. When he left for the West Coast in late 1849, he sold the plantation and its slaves to his younger brother. That same year, Margaret married Robert Garner. With his parents, Simon and Mary, Garner was the property of Gaines's neighbor, James Marshall.

In January 1856, the coldest winter ever recorded in the Ohio Valley had turned the river into a solid block of ice. Nighttime temperatures approaching twenty below zero followed one after another. On the heels of the cold blast, a blizzard hit that Saturday, January 26, dropping another five inches of snow and smoothing the winter-rutted roads of northern Kentucky that had been snow-covered since Thanksgiving. The conditions were ideal for escape, and dozens had already attempted over the past two months. More would be coming.

Sunday dawned warmer, and foggy. By midday, that fog had turned to sleet; by afternoon, to snow. Slaves in "abroad" marriages often got to spend Sundays together, and the Garners did on this day, at Maplewood. But Robert returned to Marshall's plantation by early evening, leaving his wife and children behind.

Sometime before midnight, Robert hitched "two good horses" to a "large sled," bundled his parents into it, and set off for Maplewood. In the master's house, no one awoke. Stopping near the church where they had worshipped earlier in the day, hidden from the house at Maplewood by two knolls that rose on either side, he was joined by Margaret and the children, who had made a similar silent escape on foot.

From there, crowded together in the sleigh, the eight headed north in the darkness, silhouettes of sycamores, oaks, and locusts lining the road. The snow had abated, and the darkness was no problem. Robert had often driven the route to sell hogs in Cincinnati. He knew the way well, and the snow cover made for easy passage, even with the heavily burdened sleigh.

They passed through the small town of Florence, then began the steep downhill drive to the city of Covington, directly across the river from Cincinnati. There, at about three in the morning, they left the sleigh and the exhausted horses just across the street from a livery stable. Robert Garner might have wished to flee his master. But, as the finest chronicler of the Garner saga notes, he bore no ill will toward the animals that had served him so well this night.

A crease of dawn appeared on the horizon. Huddling together as they moved, the group slipped down the steep slope to the bank, then started across the frozen river, at first tentatively, then with greater confidence and speed as they found their footing. Robert carried little Mary. Margaret carried the baby, Cilla. The boys held hands with their grandparents.

Safely ashore on the Ohio side, they made their way uphill through winding, snow-clogged streets, bound for the home of Elijah and Mary Kite, former slaves and relatives of Margaret, in the southern section of town not far from the river. Mary Kite prepared breakfast while the fugitives peeled away a layer of clothes and tried to warm themselves by the fireplace. It was now getting light outside, about 5:30 AM. Elijah Kite knew he had to move quickly, for the safety of the fugitives as well as himself. So, leaving his charges behind with his parents, Joe and Sarah, he slogged his way three miles through the snow to the corner of Sixth and Elm Streets, to the store of Levi Coffin, a businessman, Quaker, and leading figure in the city's Underground Railroad.

By now it was almost 7 AM. Coffin's counsel was to get the family out of that part of town as fast as possible and move them to the west side, where a considerable number of free black families lived. They would be much less conspicuous there, Coffin said, and he would come later in the evening to "make arrangements to forward them northward." Back at the Kite home, the Garner children were taking a well-earned nap, while their parents kept watch by peeking occasionally through windows shuttered against both the cold and prying eyes.

Kite returned about 8 AM and began explaining the plan Coffin had laid out. But it was too late. No sooner had he begun than they heard a ruckus outside. Someone yelled, "They are coming, they are coming." Glancing furtively through the windows, Kite saw what he feared most: well-dressed men he suspected were the slave masters come to reclaim their property, accompanied by a handful of police officers and a collection of ragtag-looking men most likely hoping to catch a bit of reward money or simply torment a fugitive, perhaps a dozen men in all.

Having risked all to come this far, Robert Garner was not about to surrender his family without a fight. Neither was Margaret, who took up a large carving knife and retreated to the back room of the cabin with the children.

The men outside called out to be let inside the house. Garner and Kite answered with pounding and hammering, barring the doors and windows with whatever they had at hand. For several minutes the sound of banging was the only answer the posse got. Then Robert Garner shouted out to the men surrounding the house that they were not letting anyone inside. Around the perimeter, a crowd of neighbors began gathering to watch.

The restive crowd made the posse nervous. Would they attempt to effect a rescue? Would they interpose themselves between law enforcement and the fugitives? Deputy US marshal George Bennet, in command, wasn't going to hang around to find out. Five of the men used some stacked firewood to smash holes in the door and shuttered windows. As the morning light came shining into the cabin, Robert Garner, who in addition to the sleigh and horses had taken a pistol from his master, opened fire. His first three shots stalled the attack, but not for long. Then a fourth shot hit one of the deputies in the hand and face. That man staggered backward, but the rest of the men regrouped, using the firewood like a battering ram to crash through the door. One of the intruders was Margaret Garner's master, Archibald Gaines—the slight man went immediately for Robert Garner, attempting to wrestle the gun away from the much larger, stronger, and younger man, and somehow managed to get it out of his hand. The others moved quickly to assist Gaines, pinning down Garner and dragging him out of the house. The deputies noticed that Garner, though not shot or even seriously injured, was covered in blood. Where had it come from?

As the men in the cabin had begun pounding on the door and shutters, Margaret Garner had taken the carving knife and in one sharp motion sliced the throat of two-year-old Mary with such ferocity that it nearly decapitated her. As the babe crumpled to the floor, blood "spouting out profusely" from a throat now unable to make a sound, Margaret turned to her mother-in-law and the child's namesake, Mary Garner, with a plea

"The Modern Medea," a Margaret Garner engraving. *Courtesy of Library of Congress*

in her eyes. "Before my children shall be taken back to Kentucky, I will kill them all," Margaret told her. The women could hear if not see the increasing commotion from the next room. Margaret knew time was running out. But Mary told her daughter-in-law, "I cannot help you to kill them." Robert, hearing the wailing of his children, came to investigate. Seeing the corpse of his daughter, he scooped her up and held her tightly, drenching his own clothes with her blood. But he quickly placed her back on the floor and, with his father, spent some moments "pac[ing] the room and groaning." He soon returned to the front room, where the battle was about to commence.

Knowing she was on her own, Margaret picked up a coal shovel and lunged toward her other children, intending the same fate for them. They crouched on the floor, wailing, not sure whether they should be more afraid of the men outside trying to come at them with guns or their mother coming at them with a shovel and a knife "dripping with gore." Sarah Kite, Elijah's mother, wrested or talked the knife out of Margaret's hand, but Margaret continued on with the shovel, slamming it on Thomas and Samuel, who were—barely—old enough to defend themselves against the blows. They suffered cuts and bruises on the head and neck, and blood "trickled down their backs and upon their sleeves," but nothing life threatening. As the posse burst into the house and attacked her husband, Margaret turned on her baby, bashing the shovel into the infant's face. Before she could deliver another blow, a pile of men were on top of her, jarring the shovel from her hand and wrestling her to the floor. Miraculously, the baby survived.

"THEY WILL GO SINGING TO THE GALLOWS"

US commissioner John Pendery opened his courtroom at 3 PM on January 28 to dicker with federal marshals over whether there was sufficient documentation to immediately return the Garners to Kentucky. Pendery was commissioner for the Southern District of Ohio, a sort of under-judge who worked for federal court judges and Supreme Court justices, handling jobs such as taking depositions and processing other paperwork. But commissioners also were empowered by the Fugitive Slave Act to preside over cases. Pendery performed this duty in southern Ohio, a federal judicial district that was under the direction of Supreme Court justice John McLean, the same man the plotters at the Blair home had considered for the Republican presidential nomination a few weeks before.

Pendery decided there was not sufficient evidence to quickly send the fugitives back to Kentucky and ordered the family held overnight in a local lockup but in the official custody of US marshal Hiram Robinson, who was not only a marshal in Cincinnati but also editor and part owner of the *Cincinnati Enquirer*, a Democratic proslavery newspaper. His dual roles would be reflected in the events that followed. While Robinson, who was rushing back to the city from Columbus on January 28, would be busy doing everything in his power to send the Garners back to Kentucky, his newspaper would cover the case with an antiabolition fervor. Meanwhile, Hamilton County sheriff's deputies went to probate court judge John Burgoyne's bench to demand custody of the Garners, arguing that impending state murder charges should take precedence over the federal fugitive slave warrant.

Burgoyne hesitated. He was antislavery, but confusion still reigned over rightful custody and what charges might or might not be filed. The coroner's inquest was likely to result in a finding that a murder had been committed, but nothing had been decided yet. With the Garners essentially in dual custody for the night, Burgoyne left for Columbus—he might have passed Robinson coming the other way—to consult with Governor Chase, who told the judge that the state would support whatever ruling he handed down. But Chase stayed in Columbus, tending to state business, rather than rushing to Cincinnati, where a display of solidarity might have made a difference. Chase was not a man given to expressing regret over political decisions—his sense of self-righteousness always found the fault in others—but this was a decision he probably knew, later, was the wrong one, even if he couldn't admit it to himself.

Early the next day, as more snow fell, a coroner's inquest ruled that Margaret killed baby Mary. Robert and Simon were named as accessories. On January 30, Pendery ordered that the two fugitive slave claims—by Gaines for Margaret Garner and her children, and by Marshall for Robert, Simon, and Mary Garner—be considered separately. And he ruled that Marshall's case would be heard first, most likely to give himself and the court system more time to sort out the ramifications of the state murder charges that seemed certain to come.

Even without the governor around to stir the pot, the case was getting a lot of attention, from both the local newspapers and the antislavery press.

Outside the courthouse, the weather remained frigid, but the crowd was heating up. Blacks and whites were gathered together in the street, and "a wild and excited scene presented itself," with some rough talking and scuffling. Two black men were arrested, but there were no serious altercations. Organized forces were beginning to get their acts together. Attempts to hire a hall to hold a rally of support for Garner failed, however, when proprietors who were approached demurred, saying they feared violence might ensue.

"My brain burned at the thought that anybody could for one moment weight the safety of property in the scale with that which might have secured LIBERTY to those who have proved so well that they deserve it," Cincinnati abolitionist and women's rights activist Lucy Stone wrote.

Before the day was over, warrants were issued—although not yet served—on murder charges against Margaret, Robert, Simon, and Mary

Garner (although the coroner had not named Mary as an accomplice). It seemed as though another weight had been added to their burden, but in fact the state murder charges arrived as a possible salvation. In a move rich with irony, the Garners' lawyers welcomed these charges, which they would argue should take precedence over federal fugitive slave charges. State charges would keep the Garners in jail on the north bank of the Ohio. For Margaret Garner, who in any case might have preferred death, jail meant freedom.

Lead counsel for the Garners was John Jolliffe, the son of a slaveholder who had devoted his adult life to the antislavery cause. A lapsed Quaker, the stout, five foot eight, fifty-two-year-old beardless lawyer still dressed in the simple black frock and boots of his Friends ancestors. He made a modest living writing wills, handling divorces, and dealing with the usual detritus that drifted through the legal system. But his heart was with the cause, and he devoted considerable time to working on fugitive cases. He had worked with *National Era* editor Gamaliel Bailey, an attendee at Francis Blair's Republican soiree, when Bailey lived in Cincinnati in the 1840s. He had argued cases with James Birney, the Liberty Party presidential candidate in 1840 and 1844, and with future president Rutherford B. Hayes. He had even run unsuccessfully for Congress in 1852.

Jolliffe, who was also a former prosecutor, felt certain that no northern jury—even one in Cincinnati—would convict Margaret Garner of first-degree murder. So, after a day of desultory fencing over motions to postpone, attempts to gather witnesses, and arguments over federal vs. state custody, Jolliffe laid bare both the strategy of the defense and the mindset of the fugitives. "It might seem strange that as attorney for these people I should demand that they be given up on a charge of murder, but each and all of them has assured me that they would go singing to the gallows rather than be returned to slavery," he said.

The courtroom was filled to overflowing on those first days, and would remain so throughout the unprecedented four weeks of the trial—although at first not with the city's black residents, who were denied entry. On the second day of the proceedings, black citizens held a public meeting to protest their exclusion. Hundreds gathered outside the courthouse, demanding to be let in. Four hundred special federal deputies—many of whom were recruited from local Irish militias—were employed to keep the peace, with varying degrees of success. Marshal Robinson had rushed to Washington in an attempt to get President Pierce to empower him to declare martial law, but he met with no success. There was more scuffling, some rocks and snowballs were thrown, and more blacks were arrested. When lead counsel Jolliffe inquired about the absence of black citizens from the courtroom, Pendery pleaded ignorance, stating that the "court had made no such order" barring anyone. Perhaps, he suggested, it had been the marshal. Jolliffe made some inquiries and discovered that it had indeed been Robinson and his special deputies who were barring African Americans from entering. After some back and forth between Pendery and the marshal and Pendery and Jolliffe, the courtroom was at last integrated.

Jolliffe called witnesses to testify on behalf of the Garners, stressing the fact that they had been to the city on numerous occasions, and that their presence on free soil made them free. "The moment the party touched our soil the slave fell, and the free woman stood," he told the judge. But the slaves could not tell their own stories. The Fugitive Slave Act barred the escapees from testifying on their own behalf. It also barred appeals. The murder charges, however, introduced a wild card into the proceedings. Never in the six-year history of the law had there been competing state murder charges. Pendery had no precedent to guide him in such a circumstance.

Unlike Jolliffe, Francis Chambers, the attorney for the slaveholders, had bushy sideburns and a belligerent countenance. He called witnesses who testified to Marshall's ownership of the Garners, a point Jolliffe wasn't contesting. In his rare cross examinations, Jolliffe successfully got entered into the record the two points he wanted to make: that the Garners had been to Ohio, and that a homicide had taken place. "I wish to show," he told the judge, "that [the Fugitive Slave Law] had driven a frantic mother to murder her own child, rather than see it carried back to the seething hell of American slavery."

For most in the sizable audience, the trial was a welcome distraction from the continuing snowfall and freezing temperatures. Aside from the lawyerly arguments, they also would have observed the pathos of the family, usually huddled all together with their lawyers to the right of the judge (as the audience viewed the scene), separated from the onlookers by a row of federal marshals.

Another scene that occurred early in the proceedings combined comedy with menace. Levi Coffin, the Quaker leader of the Underground Railroad in the city who had tried to help the Garners to freedom, made an appearance. In his plain clothes and quiet demeanor, he was barely noticeable. But one of the deputy marshals noticed that Coffin, as a good Quaker, kept his hat on. This offended the sensibilities of the deputy, who ordered him to remove it. Coffin politely responded that "I shall not pull off my hat to accommodate thee. It is not my habit nor the habit of my people to make obeisance to men." No sooner had Coffin finished speaking than the deputy raised his cane and swatted the hat off Coffin's head, knocking it to the floor. Coffin didn't flinch, and he didn't make a move toward the hat. A low-grade rumble came from the spectators, who were now glaring at the deputy. For several minutes, the hat sat on the floor. Finally, the deputy retrieved it and put it on the end of the table where the Garners were sitting. Coffin still did not move, and the audience responded with more hissing and more defiant stares. After a few more moments, the deputy picked the hat up off the table and gently put it back on Coffin's head.

February 3, a "clear, cold beautiful Sunday," offered a break from the courtroom but not from the elements, with morning temperatures well below zero. The onslaught of local news coverage and trumpeting from the antislavery press quickly turned the Garner case into a national affair. The captives had a visit from a local minister, a former South Carolina planter who had freed his slaves, moved to the North, and turned to the ministry. The Western Anti-Slavery Society used the occasion of the case to petition the Ohio state legislature "to take preliminary steps for the withdrawal of Ohio from the Federal Union." Within days of her capture, Margaret Garner would be the most famous black woman in America.

On February 6, Jolliffe delivered his closing argument in the Marshall case. In three hours, he made a claim that was legally irrelevant to the question at hand but would redound through the year and into the next—that Margaret Garner should be a free woman, along with her children, because her owner had brought her to free soil in Ohio. It was a dubious argument and he knew it. Ohio case law was split on the matter, and in a notorious case from 1837 a teenage girl who had been importuned by Cincinnati abolitionists to apply for her freedom had taken her case to court and lost. Her lawyer was Salmon Chase. Jolliffe also made a constitutional appeal, arguing that those who aid escaped slaves are protected by the First Amendment right to the free exercise of religion, when their Christian duty called on them not to send a fugitive back into bondage. "Can you do it and keep your conscience void of offense?" he asked. "Can you do it and maintain for the people of the US the right of religious freedom?"

"The Constitution expressly declared that Congress should pass no law prescribing any form of religion or preventing the free exercise thereof. If Congress could not pass any law requiring you to worship God, still less could they pass one requiring you to carry fuel to hell," Jolliffe stormed. These ringing words "called forth applause from all parts of the court-room," said a witness. "It is for the Court to decide," Jolliffe concluded, "whether the Fugitive Slave Law overrides the law of Ohio to such an extent that it cannot arrest a fugitive slave even for the crime of murder."

Jolliffe was barking up a dubious constitutional tree in large part because the authors of the Fugitive Slave Act knew what they were doing. "The law of 1850, provides that no warrant in any event shall be served upon the fugitives in case they are remanded to the custody of their owner," the proslavery *Cincinnati Daily Gazette* reminded its readers. This is what made the question of custody crucial.

Nevertheless, that day a Hamilton County grand jury indicted Robert and Margaret for murder of their daughter, and baby Mary's grandparents, Simon and Mary, for accessory to murder. Sheriff Gazoway Brashears kicked US marshal Robinson and his federal deputies out of the courthouse and took custody of the fugitives.

The next day, February 7, Francis Chambers, attorney for Marshall, made a five-hour closing argument. In closing, he asserted that the Garners "have no rights except such as their master chooses to give them." At almost the exact same moment, 550 miles away in Washington, DC, John C. Frémont's friend Montgomery Blair filed a brief with the Supreme Court in the case of Dred Scott, a Missouri slave, arguing that Scott should be set free because his master had carried him into the free state of Illinois.

With the nation's eyes riveted on the Garner case, hardly anyone paid attention to Blair's brief.

Pendery said he would rule on Marshall's claims after hearing the fugitive slave claim against Margaret and her children. While local officials now held physical custody of the Garners, Pendery maintained his Solomonic finding of dual custody, ruling that the federal marshal still had *legal* custody of the prisoners.

The next few days would be among the most extraordinary in the history of enforcement of the Fugitive Slave Act.

They didn't start out that way. Temperatures had eased somewhat, and the persistent snow had turned to rain. Because of the ongoing battle over custody of the prisoners, Margaret and the children did not appear in court on the first day of their fugitive slave case. On the second day, Saturday, February 9, they did. Along with them were dozens of women, a majority of those in attendance that day, including Lucy Stone.

That day and the next, witnesses for Archibald Gaines confirmed his ownership of Margaret and thus of the children as well. But Jolliffe wanted to make a larger point. When it was his turn, he asked one witness if Robert Garner was the father of Margaret's children. Chambers quickly objected, noting that they had never contested that fact. Anyone looking at the two younger children, or who had seen the murdered baby, could see that their father was almost certainly a white man. The judge sustained the objection, but Jolliffe had made his point. Gaines, the short, slender man with the heavily lined face who wore simple clothes but still managed to exude the air of a country gentleman, was not only a slaveholder but also in all probability a rapist.

The light-skinned Margaret Garner herself was likely the progeny of just such a relationship, the kind southerners tried desperately not to talk about. She was about five feet three inches tall, "rather stoutly than delicately made," with an attractive face marred by two scars, an old one on the left side of her forehead and a newer one on her left cheekbone. "White man struck me," she said in response to a journalist's question about where the scars had come from. In court she was dressed in "dark calico, with a white handkerchief pinned around her neck, and a yellow cotton handkerchief, arranged as a turban, around her head."

On February 11, oral arguments began in the US Supreme Court in the *Dred Scott* case, following on Montgomery Blair's brief. In Cincinnati, likely for the only time in the history of the Fugitive Slave Act, an enslaved person was allowed to testify. Pendery would not let Margaret testify on her own behalf, but against Chambers's strenuous objection, she was allowed to take the stand on behalf of her children.

After recounting some of her travels—including a trip to the free soil of Cincinnati in June 1840—how she came to be in the Gaines home, and how she was sold, she made perhaps the simplest yet most poignant point of the trial: "As far as I understand old Mr. Gaines owned me." Referring to Mary Gaines, her "mistress," Garner continued: "I lived with her; often heard her say, when Mr. Gaines was by, that I was her servant; never heard him deny it; never heard him say it was so." The court probably paid little heed to her evidence, but before a packed and sympathetic courtroom, it was nevertheless a scene like no one had ever witnessed. And, again, Jolliffe made his point: Margaret Garner was a human being, a mother, and as such had a right to be heard. When he was done with his examination, Jolliffe turned to Chambers, indicating that it was his turn to question her. Waving his hand as if to dismiss even the notion as absurd, Chambers said, "I've nothing to say to her."

All that remained were the closing arguments. Southerners were confident in the outcome; abolitionists were predictably outraged by the proceedings. But some in the North noted a particular irony. Those in the South who had come to argue that slavery was an absolute good might have to adjust their thinking in the wake of a mother willing to kill her child to escape it. "Our Southern friends who extol the delights of servitude will have to revise their theory, or leave events like these out of the account," opined the *New-York Tribune*.

Jolliffe was not feeling well, so he left much of the closing argument to his less eloquent assistants. Chambers's remarks were equally mundane, as if both sides had run out of gas, or words, after the two-week trial. (Fugitive slave cases usually lasted only a day or two.) But Chambers did manage to get his hackles up one last time, accusing Lucy Stone of attempting to slip a knife to Margaret Garner while she was being led back to jail. He then accused Jolliffe of helping her. Jolliffe immediately rose to deny the charge, dismissing it as ridiculous and saying his only regret was that "Mrs. [Stone] was not present to answer the attack the gentleman had made upon her."

Lucy Stone had indeed visited Margaret in jail and written of her as "the heroic mother [who] killed her child." She also had talked with Jolliffe about what might happen to the children if Margaret were to be jailed in Ohio on the murder charge. She had even spoken at some length to Archibald Gaines about the possibility of buying the fugitives' freedom.

When apprised of Chambers's accusation, Stone asked for a chance to respond. But, not wanting to participate officially in a process she considered illegitimate, she asked for permission to speak after the proceedings were concluded. Most of those who had gathered for that days' session stayed to listen.

"I am only sorry that I was not in when Colonel Chambers said what he did about me, and my giving a knife to Margaret," Stone began, taking a place behind the judge's desk. "When I saw that poor fugitive, took her toil-hardened hand in mine, and read in her face deep suffering and an ardent longing for freedom, I could not help bid her be of good cheer. I told her that a thousand hearts were aching for her, and that they were glad one child of hers was safe with the angels. Her only reply was a look of deep despair, of anguish such as no words can speak." Stone denied giving Margaret Garner a knife, while conveying that she didn't necessarily object to the idea. "I thought the spirit she manifested was the same with that of our ancestors to whom we had erected the monument at Bunker Hill—the spirit that would rather let us all go back to God than back to slavery." A knife with which to fight, Stone urged, not to submit. "The faded faces of the Negro children tell too plainly to what degradation female slaves must submit. Rather than give her little daughter to that life, she killed it. If in her deep maternal love she felt the impulse to send her child back to God, to save it from coming woe, who shall say she had no right to do so? That desire had its root in the deepest and holiest feelings of our nature—implanted alike in black and white by our common Father. With my own teeth I would tear open my veins and let the earth drink my blood, rather than to wear the chains of slavery. How then could I blame her for wishing her child to find freedom with God and the angels, where no chains are?" And she delivered a final message to Pendery, who had not stayed to listen: "I know not whether this commissioner has children, else I would appeal to him to know how he would feel to have them torn from him, but I feel that he will not disregard the Book, which says: 'Thou shalt not deliver unto his master the servant which is escaped from his master unto thee: he shall dwell with thee, even among you, in that place which he shall choose in one of thy gates, where it liketh him best.'"

Democratic papers in the North lambasted Stone as a "fanatical female" espousing "very foolish but very mischievous" ideas. But Stone's argument, and its echoes across the abolitionist North, had weighed into the closing argument for Archibald Gaines. Defending Gaines against Jolliffe's charges that he "comes into this Court with hands dripping with warm blood and seeks to tear the mother from her child," attorney Francis Chambers insisted that "if there is guilt resting upon anyone besides its mother, it is upon those who invited the mother to do the deed—telling her to take its life, that it might be laid upon the altar of freedom and help the glorious cause. What matter though she might go to the gallows, it would help, and promote the cause of freedom."

The arguments were over. On February 22, Salmon Chase came to Cincinnati for the first time since being elected governor, to participate in the day's Washington's Birthday celebrations. With the weather warming a bit and the trial still on everyone's lips, Chase spoke for more than two hours. He never mentioned Margaret Garner or even alluded to the case.

For nearly two weeks, lawyers continued to argue over custody of the prisoners. Judges for different jurisdictions issued conflicting writs, with federal marshal Robinson finally winning physical custody, largely by promising Judge Burgoyne that he would not hand the Garners over to Gaines without first returning to his court. That proved to be a dodge. Marshall quickly turned to federal district court to obtain a writ of habeas corpus, essentially overriding Burgoyne's order.

He was back in court on February 26, arguing to keep the Garners in his custody. That same day, Pendery issued his decision on the fugitive slave claims. In the end, Pendery's ruling was not complicated by considerations of morality. "The question is not one of humanity that I am called upon to decide," he announced in his ruling. "The laws of Kentucky and of the United States make it a question of property. It is not a question of feeling, to be decided by the chance current of my sympathies. . . . We conceive that our highest moral obligation in this case is to administer impartially the plain provisions of the law." And the law was on the side of slavery. "It is the essence of the institution that the slave does not possess equal rights with the free-man."

Jolliffe's (and Montgomery Blair's) argument that the fact of the slaves' mere presence on free soil should free them carried no weight. "Had the slaves asserted their freedom, they would have been practically free, but they voluntarily returned to slavery. In allowing them to come to Ohio, the master voluntarily abandoned his claim upon them, and they, in returning, abandoned their claim to freedom," the commissioner ruled.

Pendery stayed his ruling that the slaves be returned to Kentucky until the district court ruled on Ohio's claim to custody under the murder charge, which in any case would not apply to the children.

Arguing for custody so he could return the slaves to Kentucky, Marshal Robinson asserted simply that the local authorities had no jurisdiction because the fugitive slave case overrode all others. Jolliffe, knowing this to be accepted practice under federal law, asked Judge Burgoyne to declare the Fugitive Slave Act unconstitutional, both as a violation of the free exercise of religion and on the Tenth Amendment grounds that trying the murder case was a right reserved to the states. Burgoyne said he would ponder the question, and he ordered that the Garners stay put for the time being.

But time was running out for the Garners. Part of the reason Pendery had stayed his ruling was so the Garners could be moved quickly after all the other courts had a chance to do their business. On February 28, the presiding federal district court judge found for Marshal Robinson in the custody case and ordered that the Garners be taken to Kentucky. That was the final piece of the judicial puzzle, and events now moved swiftly.

All seven of the "unsuccessful heroes," as Frederick Douglass called them, were handed back to Archibald Gaines, who hurried them in an omnibus to the riverfront in the lengthening shadows of late afternoon, to catch the ferry across the now-thawed Ohio River to Covington. The spectators who had followed the trial, and a few more who joined in off the street, trailed sullenly behind. But the atmosphere at the dock was quite different, where Gaines's Kentucky supporters were in a celebratory mood, "and there was great rejoicing among them," Coffin remembered. Without slowing, the omnibus drove straight onto the ferry, which was cut loose from its moorings as soon as the vehicle rolled to a stop on the boat.

Two days later, with the seven slaves back in bondage in Kentucky, Burgoyne refused to quash the habeas writ on the murder charge and ordered the federal marshal to return the fugitives to Ohio, or return to court by March 7 to explain why he couldn't. Anticipating this, Archibald Gaines has already begun the process of separating the Garners and sending them to the plantations of friends and family, playing what one historian termed a great "shell game" with the lives of his captives.

On March 4, Chase sent a lawyerly and lengthy request to Kentucky Governor Charles Morehead seeking to have the Garners returned to Ohio to face that state's charges.

On March 6, Morehead replied in officious, almost sarcastic terms, but nevertheless issued an order that they be returned to Ohio. "I cannot allow myself to doubt for a moment," he wrote, "if any of these slaves should be acquitted of the charge against them, that the proper tribunals of Ohio in obedience to the dictates of honor and of justice will restore them to their owners with the same promptitude with which I have issued my warrants for their apprehension, and removal to your state for trial."

But it was too late. News of Chase's request had been leaked, and before Morehouse could even consider it, much less respond, the Garners had been literally sold down the river.

From there, farce followed on farce, and tragedy ensued. Knowing of Chase's request and suspecting that Morehead might comply, Gaines sent the Garners to Louisville, accompanied by Covington sheriff Clinton Butts, who put them aboard the steamboat *Henry Lewis*, headed down the Ohio bound for Arkansas. When Chase's delegation arrived at the Louisville jail to pick up the Garners, they were already well under way. Returning to Burgoyne's court, Robinson told the judge he could not produce the Garners, pleading obeisance to federal law requiring their return to Kentucky.

In the wee small hours of March 8, near Troy, Indiana, the *Henry Lewis* collided with another steamboat, the *Edward Howard*. Rushing from the cramped steerage section to escape the wreckage, carrying the infant Cilla in her arms, Margaret reached the deck. There, witnesses' stories diverge.

Perhaps she tossed the baby into the river. Perhaps she tried to jump onto the other boat in a desperate attempt to escape. Perhaps she tried to kill both Cilla and herself. In any case, both ended up in the icy Ohio, and the baby was never seen again. Later, reporters wrote that Margaret "displayed frantic joy" on hearing that Cilla had drowned.

Two days later the surviving Garners reached Gaines Landing, Arkansas, at the cotton plantation of Archibald's brother, Benjamin, safely away from the clutches of prying Ohio abolitionists. But Archibald Gaines was not yet through with his shell game. He had decided that he wanted Margaret back at Maplewood, and sent the ever-faithful Sheriff Butts to retrieve her once more. By April 3, Margaret was back in jail in Covington. Despite orders from Ohio authorities to produce her, Gaines told no one about her presence until April 8. On that day, he telegraphed Chase that Margaret was in custody in Covington, but threatened to move her once again if she was not taken by April 10. Enjoying his petulant game, Gaines assumed Chase could not get anybody to Covington that quickly. But, taking no chances, he removed her late in the evening of April 9, less than a day ahead of the delegation Chase had sent—once again too late—to retrieve her. She was in leg irons, aboard a steamer bound for New Orleans. She would never be free again.

Gone from the headlines, Margaret Garner would soon mostly disappear from the public consciousness. But those few who remembered pondered if the country's political institutions, including its newest one, were up to the task of answering the questions her disappearance aroused.

"I wonder if the news of the triumph of the Republican party . . . would carry one throb of joy to the heart of poor Margaret Garner," abolitionist and women's rights activist Lucy N. Colman would write later.

It was a legitimate question. But first the Republicans had to triumph.

{ 3 }

THE FIRST NORTHERN
VICTORY

The loud and crowded anti-Kansas-Nebraska Congress that had been
elected in late 1854 and through the spring and summer of 1855
finally convened on December 3, 1855. The confusing coalitions led to
immediate disarray, abetted by the overflowing crowds in the galleries and
lobbies. In the year since the sweeping anti-Nebraska victory of November 1854, a number of members elected as Know Nothings had become
Republicans; some Whigs had become Know Nothings; some fusion ticket
winners were even harder to pin down. Somehow, all these factions had
to come together to elect a Speaker, but each had its own candidate and
none were ready to quickly give way.

Even sorting out who was aligned with whom was no easy task. The
Washington Star made a valiant attempt on January 31, but even its list
failed to account for all the fluctuations, continuing to identify the multi-
affiliated Speaker of the House candidate Nathaniel Banks of Massachusetts
as a Know Nothing, for example, and attaching no affiliation whatsoever
to several other members.

Though the anti-Kansas-Nebraska forces were in the majority, they were
divided—not so divided that a Democrat was likely to slip in, but divided

enough that it looked like it might take weeks if not months to choose a Speaker. Whichever faction came out on top in the Speaker's contest had a running head start on dominating the new party and choosing its first presidential nominee. By rough count, the House included 79 Democrats, 118 anti-Nebraska men, including conscience Whigs, Democrats, Republicans, and free soilers, and 37 proslavery Whigs.

Things were somewhat clearer in the Senate, where 42 Democrats, 15 Republicans, and 5 Know Nothings jostled for authority. But Republicans saw the race for Speaker of the House as their path to supremacy in the anti-Nebraska coalition. With the speakership came the power to organize the House, appoint committee chairmen, and set the legislative agenda. Ohio abolitionist congressman Joshua Giddings asserted that the Speaker "exerts more influence upon the destinies of the nation than any other member of the government except the President." Republicans wanted to be sure it was they, and not the Know Nothings, who were exerting that influence.

William A. Richardson of Illinois, a "tall, firmly built, coarse featured man, who stoops slightly"—still a close ally of Stephen A. Douglas—was the Democratic candidate, chosen in a caucus that had made the strategic blunder of formally condemning the Know Nothings while telling the southern branch of the movement that it could accept Richardson or lose to the Republicans. As it turned out, these "South Americans," as they were styled, had other ideas.

American Party leaders favored Solomon G. Haven of New York, former president Millard Fillmore's onetime law partner, or Henry Fuller of Pennsylvania, a Princeton-educated lawyer from Wilkes-Barre. Anti-Catholic, antislavery fusionists among the Know Nothings were divided regionally. Westerners and former Whigs backed Lewis D. Campbell of Ohio, who had been a crucial ally in Salmon Chase's victory in the Ohio governor's race just two months earlier and now expected Chase to return the favor. Easterners and former Democrats were supporting Frémont's friend and ally Nathaniel Banks.

Southern Know Nothings quickly abandoned Haven in favor of their own favorite-son candidates, reflecting the existing regional split in the party and dooming their party's chances of choosing the leader. Campbell was the early front-runner among the antislavery prospects, and he assumed the North and South Americans would eventually come around. He was wrong, and it wasn't the last serious miscalculation he would make. They continued to divide their support by region, even by state, and Republicans managed to organize an effective anti-Haven bloc, based on the fear that his close ties to the Ohio Know Nothings would damage the Republicans' chances of emerging as the stronger alternative to the Democrats.

On the first ballot, seventeen anti-Nebraska candidates received votes. Richardson led all candidates; Campbell was the leading anti-Nebraska man with 53 votes, but he was more than 20 behind the Illinois Democrat and a full 60 away from the 113 needed for victory. Banks garnered 21. Three more ballots on the first day resolved nothing.

The anti-Nebraska forces caucused the next day and decided to see how high they could push Campbell, who was anathema to the Democrats in their ranks. Assuming he would peak well short of a majority, they would then dump him and proceed with Banks, the next man in line. If that didn't work, they would switch to New Jersey Whig Alexander Pennington. "The present determination of the Republicans is to press Campbell's cause until he is elected," the *New York Times* reported, "or until they are satisfied he cannot be."

On December 5, Campbell got as high as 81 votes, almost all of his gain coming at Banks's expense. But that was still 32 short of the number necessary to be elected Speaker, and he could go no higher. The next day he crashed to 46.

Party affiliation meant a great deal. Whigs and Democrats had torn at each other's throats, sometimes literally, for two decades. It was asking a lot for them to set aside those differences now in the interest of unity. "It is a difficult matter to harmonize a new party, made of men who have been for a life-time engaged in political strife with each other," observed the *New York Times*, "and it could scarcely have been expected that the elements of the Republican Party in Congress would fuse at once and without trouble."

There were shades of gray in how each potential candidate expressed his antislavery bona fides. Regional loyalties mattered too, as did the various personalities of the competing candidates. The ex-Whig Campbell couldn't attract Democratic votes, but the truth was that even among his fellow ex-Whigs, he was none too popular. He had the support of Thurlow Weed, among others, but nobody much liked him on either side. His argumentative nature rubbed some potential supporters the wrong way, and given the opportunity, they began looking elsewhere. And he was none too clear about his stance on slavery in the territories, which alienated others. Among this latter group was Chase, who unceremoniously dropped Campbell.

Campbell was as bewildered by Chase's abandonment as he had been by his loss of Know Nothing support. But Chase was hanging back, fearing that betting on a losing horse now would hurt him later, when the party got around to choosing a presidential candidate. Campbell was incensed by what he considered ingratitude, if not an outright double-cross, but there was little he could do about it.

But just as Campbell began to fade, some of Banks's supporters got cold feet and began backtracking, fearing that to try their man now and fail would doom his candidacy. So they suggested switching the order and making a move with Pennington, a West Point graduate and lawyer who was new to Congress and had little to recommend him beyond his availability as an anti-Nebraska Know Nothing. The proposal stoked heated debate, which ended with an agreement to ride Campbell a little further. That proved to be a nonstarter, and Campbell, with undisguised disgust at the process, at his colleagues, and at Chase, withdrew from the race.

Campbell's exit renewed the confidence of the anti-Nebraska forces, who were now convinced "this will decide the question."

If so, it wasn't immediately apparent. On the first roll call after Campbell's withdrawal, Banks garnered a mere 40 votes. That sparked another long night of caucusing—and perhaps some soul-searching. When the House returned on December 8, Banks jumped to 86 votes, and then 100. On December 10, he stood at 107, just 6 votes short of a majority.

And there he stayed.

The numbers bounced around a little, but Banks could not get to the finish line. He hovered around 100, with Richardson at about 70 and Fuller at 30, give or take on a particular ballot, with a smattering cast for lesser lights. Pennington's nativist supporters stepped back into the fray, arguing that Banks had run his course and now it was their man's turn. And on the other flank, Fuller was about to cause more trouble.

The North Americans, realizing they held the swing votes, offered to support an antislavery, pronativist candidate—either Pennington or John Wheeler of New York. Republicans rejected Wheeler out of hand, but Pennington had some latent support. When the Republicans caucused, that support surfaced, but the Banks forces maintained their discipline and voted him down. The Republicans, for better or worse, would stick with Banks; the onetime temperance lecturer had been elected as a Know Nothing, but he was not really much of a nativist and had never been a participant in the affairs of the secret Order of the Star Spangled Banner, the anti-Catholic organization that evolved into the American Party. His moral flexibility, however, made it easy for him to shift his loyalties in whatever direction best suited his prospects. Banks's opportunism was a perfect match for the Republican/Know Nothing fusionists' desire to coalesce around a single candidate. And his rise from humble beginnings fit with the emerging party's notions of the virtues of free labor and the "self made man . . . a boy of 15 years, working 16 hours a day in the machine shop of the Boston Manufacturing Company," as one glowing tribute put it.

Banks, like President Pierce, was an affable, handsome man who was well liked even by political opponents, and was once described as having "a genius for being looked at." He was Speaker of the Massachusetts House when he decided to run for Congress in 1852. He defied calls by Pierce loyalists that he disavow antislavery support and won a narrow victory when the Free Soil candidate withdrew.

Something similar happened two years later. Banks had some support from Know Nothing elements, but the party ran a candidate against him anyway. Fortunately for Banks, the Reverend Lyman Whiting, who also had the backing of what was left of the Whig Party, withdrew from the race, fearing politics might soil his reputation.

Banks's success in leading a fusion ticket of northern Democrats, Free Soilers, and elements of the American Party, combined with his pliable ideology and his ability to make friends, cast him immediately into the swarm seeking to lead the House, which in December 1855 looked much like Banks's muddled constituency—a mishmash of nativists, Republicans, conscience Whigs, and disaffected Democrats, with no single group even close to wielding a majority on its own. Building a coalition to elect a

Speaker and run the place called for a unique combination of skills. Henry Clay was dead. Someone else would have to be found.

Banks's muddled ideology helped him along the way, but as the Speaker's race dragged on, some of his past comments and current attempts at clarification caused consternation among potential allies. A year earlier he had suggested in a speech that the Union might be better off if disaffected southern slave owners took their states and left. Now he backed away from that, insisting that he was "for the Union as it is, and not for dissolution under any circumstances." When some of his antislavery supporters balked at his reversal, Banks reassured them by citing the antislavery bona fides of his district. He also seemed to imply that he had no problem with interracial marriage, then backtracked on that and added for good measure "that there was an inequality of capacity and the condition of the races." But the Republicans were committed for better or worse. "It is a point of honor with us who have thus sustained Mr. Banks, and identified him as *the* Anti-Nebraska candidate for speaker, not to yield," wrote former New York senator John Dix, who concluded that "if we desert him, we ought to be deserted by hope in our hour of trial."

"THE ELECTION . . . HAS GIVEN GREAT HOPES TO OUR ENEMIES"

If the Republicans were sticking with Banks for better or worse, it didn't take long to get to the worse.

"The third week of the session is gone and no Speaker yet," Howell Cobb, a Georgian who had served as Speaker during the debate on the Compromise of 1850, wrote to his wife. "As usual the town is full of rumors that we will elect tomorrow but I do not see that there is any better prospect for it now than there has been all the time." Cobb sadly reported that "the last hope of spending Christmas with you is gone."

Christmas presents might be hard to come by, too. With Congress not yet organized, nobody was getting paid. "The House of Representatives is like the moon," William Seward, used to the more gentlemanly decorum of the Senate, later commented. "It shines brightest and smoothest at a distance." New York diarist George Templeton Strong supposed the lack of a Congress wasn't necessarily a bad thing. "The House of Representatives is trying hard to get a Speaker and organize," he wrote the week before Christmas, "but as yet in vain. I don't perceive that the country suffers much."

Strong's cynicism aside, the restlessness was reaching beyond the halls of Congress. President Pierce was eager to send up his annual message, but he could not do so until the House was organized, proving correct one analysis that suggested the delay "threatened to clog the wheels of government," if not quite reaching the level of "seriously [testing] the strength of our Federal compact."

John C. Frémont noted that the extended balloting reminded him of the "hundred and forty odd ballots" in the California legislature that failed to reach a decision and cost him his Senate seat in 1851.

The *National Anti-Slavery Standard* reported on an incident that took place on a crowded train traveling between Washington and Baltimore involving:

[a] Bostonian, as remarkable as any other in this city for his subserviency to the slaveholders, and a lady, admired beyond most others in Washington society for the brilliancy of her wit and the intelligent interest which she takes in public affairs. The conversation, of which she was the centre, turning on the great contest in the House, she expressed her decided sympathy for the Republican side, exulted in its prospect of success, and complimented Mr. Banks in the highest terms. This was too much for the Bostonian, who expressed his surprise that a Southern lady should countenance such a demagogue as Banks, and such an enemy to Southern institutions. The lady replied, "I can relieve your surprise in regard to myself, sir, for my husband, Col. Frémont, is a Free Soiler; but let me express my surprise, that you, sir, a northerner and a Bostonian, should oppose Mr. Banks in behalf of Southern institutions!" As the Bostonian who met with this terrible rebuke was candid enough to tell the story on his return, we forbear to give his name, in the hope that it has made him a wiser and better man.

Desperation drove lawmakers to sometimes silly extremes. One proposed that no member of the House "be allowed to indulge in the use of meat, drink, fire, or other refreshments, gaslight and water only excepted, until an election of Speaker shall be effected." More practically, some suggested longer sessions and weekend work, limits on debate, and election by plurality—a proposal made fifteen times.

The House held an all-night session on January 9–10; through eighteen hours of desultory speeches and roll call votes, nothing changed. The canteen almost ran out of food. Democrats toyed with the notion of supporting a plurality winner in the hope that Richardson and Fuller could reach an accommodation, but nothing came of it.

The American Party, meanwhile, was committing political suicide in the North by refusing to support Banks and insisting on Fuller. It was their refusal to recognize political reality as much as anything that caused the process to drag on. Anti-Nebraska lawmakers had long ago coalesced around Banks. After Fuller refused to renounce the repeal of the Missouri Compromise or support abolition in the District of Columbia, popular northern sentiment shifted dramatically in Banks's favor. But Fuller's pronouncements, which came during another extended session in which the candidates were quizzed about their positions on key issues, solidified his position with pro-Nebraska Know Nothings, and his holdouts refused to budge.

In fact, they were emboldened enough to make an offer: a plurality winner in exchange for Banks's withdrawal. It was a moment of truth for the anti-Nebraska men. And they did not blink. The proposal was voted down. The only casualties were Richardson, whom the Democrats dumped in favor of South Carolinian James L. Orr, and Horace Greeley, who was assaulted near the end of January by the sponsor of the plurality resolution, Arkansas Democratic congressman and future Confederate general Albert Rust, a recent target of Greeley's vituperative coverage of the Speaker contest. Greeley was leaving the Capitol at the end of the day's session when a large man he did not recognize, six feet tall and over two hundred pounds, came up to him.

"Is your name Greeley?" the man asked in a slight southern accent.

"Yes," the editor replied.

"Are you a noncombatant?" the man asked, attempting to ascertain if Greeley would accept a formal challenge of a duel.

"That," Greeley responded tentatively, "is according to circumstances."

And on "-stances," Rust clubbed Greeley "a stunning blow" on the right side of his head, and quickly followed with three more before Greeley could even get his hands out of his coat pockets. The New Yorker staggered back against a fence but did not fall to the ground. Regaining his senses, he stood up, and several people hurried in between the two.

"Who is this man?" Greeley demanded. "I don't know him."

"You'll know me soon enough," Rust replied, then turned and walked away as abruptly as he had appeared, west from the Capitol toward Pennsylvania Avenue.

One of the bystanders who had interposed himself between the men told Greeley that his attacker was Rust.

Injured and angry, Greeley began pursuing his assailant from some distance behind, and eventually came to the National Hotel at Sixth and Pennsylvania, where a "huddle of strangers" was gathered—mostly southerners, Greeley surmised, by their look and their presence at the National, generally considered the city's southern hotel (the Willard, eight blocks to the west, was known as the northern hotel, but it accommodated all comers, especially in its restaurants and bars). Among them was Rust. "Do you know me now?" Rust asked as Greeley approached.

"Yes, you are Rust of Arkansas," Greeley answered.

Rust, described as "one of the most powerful men in Congress," spat out another challenge, and was visibly unhappy that Greeley refused to accept. Swiftly he raised his heavy cane and swung it hard toward Greeley's head. The editor blocked it with his left arm, and Rust pulled back for another attempt. Again, a crowd rushed in to separate the two men.

Retelling the tale for publication, a bruised but unbowed Greeley wrote that "I presume this is not the last outrage to which I am to be subjected." The story got around fast. In an ominous precursor of the year ahead, some northern lawmakers began showing up for work with pistols. Visitors in the galleries grew conspicuously more armed.

All the while, the Banks forces worked ceaselessly to hold their bloc together. Antislavery Know Nothings Anson Burlingame of Massachusetts and Schuyler Colfax of Indiana were the key regional players, meeting every night with leaders of the other factions—anti-Nebraska Democrats,

former Free Soilers, and conscience Whigs—to plan strategy, recruit supporters back home to deluge Congress with telegrams and letters supporting
Banks, and make promises of committee assignments left and right. Banks,
naturally, disavowed any knowledge of such commitments but joined in to
bolster the grassroots efforts.

As February approached, everybody was growing weary of the end-
less balloting. Democrats, in charge of the White House and the Senate,
began to admit—at least in private—that they might be better off with a
Republican-led House than with no House at all. On January 30, North
Carolina's Thomas Clingman again brought a plurality resolution to the
floor. This one called for four more votes—three to see if anyone could
gain a majority; then, if no one did, a fourth on which the top vote-
getter would be Speaker. Five weary Democrats joined Clingman and
the Banks men in supporting the resolution, which failed, 106–110. The
next day they tried again, and again it failed, 108–110. But the trend
looked clear, and worried southern Democrats quickly began hatching
yet another proposal.

The idea came from Georgia's Alexander Stephens, who relished par-
liamentary maneuvering almost as much as he abhorred the possibility of
an anti-Nebraska Speaker of the House. Democrats would acquiesce in
the plurality rule, Stephens proposed, run through two futile roll calls,
and on the third—assuming the pro-Nebraska Americans would not vote
for the antinativist Orr—substitute William Aiken, a white-haired planter
from South Carolina and friend of the administration who had been polling better than Banks in some of the recent ballots. Aiken's advantage, as
Stephens saw it, was that he had played no role in the Democratic caucuses
that had condemned the Know Nothings. Perhaps he could draw enough
of them back into the fold to steal the race.

Unfortunately for Stephens, his well-laid plan was undone by a pair
of overeager supporters, who on February 1—before the plurality resolution was adopted—made a motion to elect Aiken as Speaker. Without the
resolution in place, this required a majority, which Aiken failed to get,
falling 8 votes short. And it spoiled Stephens's surprise, giving Banks's
forces time to secure their lines.

The next day, February 2, 1856, the House was jammed. Members crowded the floor, the galleries were packed with spectators, and journalists and hangers-on filled the lobbies. Samuel A. Smith of Tennessee made the motion to adopt the four-step plurality plan. This time the motion carried, 113–104, raising a ruckus among Banks's opponents, who cried out for adjournment. But they were gaveled down, and the first roll call began.

The surprise having been spoiled, the Democrats cast their lot with Aiken from the start. The totals looked familiar: Banks 102, Aiken 93, Fuller 14, and 6 spread among a handful of other candidates. Twenty of Fuller's former supporters switched to Aiken, and Fuller took to the floor to insist he was not a candidate. Nothing of substance changed on the second ballot, and another motion to adjourn was voted down. On the third ballot, it was the same. The anti-Banks forces hollered for adjournment. Again they were voted down.

After two months, it had come to this. The House was about to hold its 133rd roll call vote in search of a Speaker. Aiken gained strength. Having received assurances that Aiken was not antinativist, seven pro-Nebraska Know Nothings came over. But he needed more than that, and a handful of Fuller supporters who the day before had backed Stephens's proposal now ignored Fuller's plea and stuck with him rather than switch to Aiken, incurring the wrath of southern extremists who wanted to read them out of the party. Threats were hurled about. Pleas were made. One Fuller man was asked to vote for Aiken at the risk of black Republicans sweeping the House and destroying the Union. "I'll be damned if I do!" he shouted back. Southern men hung their heads, and the clerk shouted out the result above the din, inspiring "the wildest excitement": Banks 103, Aiken 100, Fuller 6, Campbell 4, Daniel Wells 1.

Nathaniel Banks was Speaker of the House. Aiken escorted him to the dais, where the tall, white-haired, stern-faced Joshua Giddings awaited him. An abolitionist and advocate of true equality, Giddings must have cringed at some of Banks's earlier statements on the inequality of the races. But there was no hint of ambivalence now as he boomed out the oath in his stentorian tone. "You do solemnly swear that you will support the Constitution of the United States, so help you God?" In a somewhat quieter voice, Banks responded "I do," and it was done.

Then, standing before the House, Banks delivered a "brief and neat speech" accepting the post. True to his highly flexible ideology, Banks announced that "I have no personal objects to accomplish."

And indeed, Banks's victory was less a personal triumph than a political imperative. Preston King of New York, who had been at the late December meeting at Francis Blair's home with Banks, argued now that his election as Speaker was "indispensable" to the unification of the anti-Nebraska forces into a cohesive party. It was a sentiment echoed by other allies, and by not a few potential enemies.

Through two months of balloting Banks did not receive a single vote from a southern lawmaker, making his victory entirely sectional. "The election of Banks has given great hopes to our enemies," Georgia's Robert Toombs concluded.

Toombs was right, but it was an amorphous sort of hope. While Banks's victory had served as an organizational weapon for the Republicans, the practical effect would be more symbolic than substantive. "We cannot admit Kansas as a State," Greeley acknowledged. "We can only make issues on which to go to the people at the Presidential election."

And despite the singular display of unity it took to elect Banks, the nativist press, while not exactly overjoyed at his elevation, was not particularly worried about it either, expressing confidence that he would not "listen for an instant to the prompting of [antislavery] fanaticism, or be counseled into measures tending to disunion."

But the Know Nothings were dazed, and would never really recover. The Republicans had bested them on an organizational level, crucial to forming a national party in which antislavery and not nativism would be the driving force. They had done it by converting what was essentially a regional and personal battle among anti-Nebraska congressmen into a national fight over slavery. "This was the first victory of importance achieved by the Free-Soilers," newspaperman and Frémont supporter John Bigelow noted later, "that could not fail to have very great influence upon the . . . presidential election."

Just as important, the Republicans now had one lever of power in Washington with which to drive events. In short order, they began driving them toward Kansas, with a detour through Pittsburgh. "Hell is uncapped," wrote one southern newspaperman, "& all its devils turned loose—to howl until next November."

"An Able ... Argument for the Freedom of the Plaintiff"

"Amidst the political excitement consequent upon the protracted efforts to organize the House of Representatives, little attention seems to have been given to a case which was last week argued before the Supreme Court," the *National Era* reported, "in which are involved highly interesting legal and constitutional principles, touching Slavery and the rights of free colored people." And, once again in the freezing winter of 1856, a Blair was playing a central role.

While much of the political and journalistic world was oblivious to the case, the abolitionist press and a few others were paying close attention and grasped the stakes. "The public of Washington do not seem to be aware that one of the most important cases ever brought up for adjudication by the Supreme Court is now being tried before that august tribunal," the *Washington Star* reported after the first day of oral argument.

Salmon Chase had been following the case since 1854, when he received a pamphlet from supporters of the Missouri slave named Dred Scott who had sued his master for his freedom. Chase had offered to help Montgomery Blair prepare the legal case before the Supreme Court, but Blair demurred, perhaps preferring to keep the case out of the political spotlight, which he assumed Chase would bring with him.

Montgomery Blair was not an abolitionist, nor was he a believer in equal rights or the notion that black and white Americans could live together in peace and harmony. He was, like his father, opposed to the extension of slavery, and favored gradual emancipation followed by colonization— sending the newly freed slaves to Africa or some other foreign destination. He was brought into the case by Roswell Field, who had handled Scott's federal appeal in Missouri. Field felt he needed a higher-profile attorney before the Supreme Court, and knew Blair through his Saint Louis connections. Gamaliel Bailey agreed to help raise the money to defray Blair's costs. Leaders of the abolitionist movement were not consulted.

This quiet little case would soon explode into the national consciousness.

Dred Scott was born a slave in Virginia, somewhere near the beginning of the nineteenth century. His master, Peter Blow, moved his family to Alabama and then, by 1830, to Missouri. Blow and his wife, Elizabeth, had seven children. Elizabeth died within a year of their move to Saint Louis, and Blow in 1832. Before his death, Blow sold Scott to John Emerson, an army doctor.

On November 19, 1833, Emerson left Saint Louis with Scott in tow for Fort Armstrong, Illinois, built after the War of 1812 for frontier defense on Rock Island, in the Mississippi River. Emerson and Scott were there for three years. Under the Illinois constitution, slavery was forbidden. In 1836, Emerson and Scott moved on to Fort Snelling, another Mississippi River fort, in the Wisconsin Territory. Wisconsin law was governed by the Missouri Compromise of 1820—which, like the state constitution of Illinois, prohibited slavery.

Shortly after arriving at Fort Snelling, Scott married Harriet Robinson, the teenage slave of Major Lawrence Taliaferro, Wisconsin's Indian agent, who performed the ceremony. Soon after, Emerson became the owner of his slave's new bride.

On October 20, 1837, Emerson was finally granted a long-held wish, for transfer back to Saint Louis. But ice on the Mississippi prevented steamboat travel that far north, so he had to make the trip by canoe, forcing him

DRED SCOTT AND HARRIET SCOTT. *Courtesy of Library of Congress*

to leave behind most of his property, including Dred and Harriet Scott. The slaves were hired out until Emerson could arrange to bring them to Missouri. If the thought ever occurred to them to flee to Canada or seek legal recourse to gain their freedom, they never acted on it.

Almost as soon as he arrived in Saint Louis, Emerson was transferred again, to Fort Jesup, Louisiana. He would be there less than a year, but it was an eventful few months. He met and married Eliza Irene Sanford, a Saint Louisan who was visiting a sister. A couple months after that, on Emerson's request, Dred and Harriet Scott joined the couple in Louisiana. Then, in September 1838, all four steamed back up the Mississippi to Saint Louis, where they stayed for a short visit before returning to Fort Snelling. On the way back to Wisconsin aboard the steamer *Gipsey*, north of the Missouri Compromise line of 36-30, Harriet gave birth to a daughter, named Eliza.

The Emersons and the Scotts stayed at Fort Snelling until May 1840, when Emerson was ordered to Florida to serve as a medical officer in the war then raging against the Seminoles. He dropped his wife and the Scotts off in Saint Louis and proceeded on to his new post.

Irene Emerson's father, Alexander Sanford, lived on a plantation outside Saint Louis, where he owned four slaves. Dred and Harriet Scott were hired out for the next two years, until Emerson returned from Florida in August 1842. Unable to revive his medical practice, he and wife Eliza moved to Davenport, Iowa, in the summer of 1843. In November, Irene gave birth to a daughter, Henrietta. A little over a month later, John Emerson died. So in 1844, Irene Emerson packed up Henrietta and moved back to Saint Louis to live with her father.

Two years later, in April 1846, Dred and Harriet Scott filed suit against Irene Emerson in Saint Louis circuit court seeking their freedom. Their claim: that John Emerson's taking them to the free state of Illinois and the free territory of Wisconsin made them free, under the same principle that Margaret Garner's lawyers would argue unsuccessfully in her fugitive trial. A Missouri Supreme Court ruling in 1824 had established the principle of "once free, always free," but the Saint Louis circuit had effectively negated the ruling by ignoring it. In the two years preceding the Scotts' suit, twenty-five such cases had been heard; twenty-four plaintiffs had been returned to slavery.

The children of Scott's former master Peter Blow stepped up to provide financial support for the Scotts' legal battle, but the winds of change in Missouri were blowing against them. At trial, which began on June 30, 1847, no one disputed that the Scotts had long lived in free territory, or that Missouri law should view them as free under those circumstances. But on a technicality—there was dispute over whether Irene Emerson actually owned the Scotts—they were ordered to remain in slavery.

The Scotts' lawyers moved for a new trial, but the prosecution filed a bill of exceptions to the motion, which sent the case on appeal straight to the Missouri Supreme Court. Before the high court could hear the case, however, the Scotts' motion for a new trial was granted. The supreme court demurred, sending the case back to trial. Meanwhile, the Scotts were placed in the custody of the sheriff of Saint Louis, who continued to hire them out under the authority of Irene Emerson.

A series of delays pushed the new trial back to January 1850. The confusion over Irene Emerson's ownership was cleared up, and the state argued that because John Emerson was under military authority, civil law should not apply in the case of his slaves (an argument that had been tried—and failed—in the Missouri Supreme Court in 1837). This time, the jury found for the Scotts. Emerson appealed the verdict to the state supreme court, which separated the cases of husband and wife and agreed to hear Dred Scott's.

At the March 1850 high court hearing, the arguments did not change. But the decision makers had: Though the proslavery justices pushed the case back until October, Scott's fate was already decided. He was ordered back into slavery as the court tossed out a generation's worth of precedent with a unanimous decision. At this point politics intervened. The deciding judges were voted off the court, and new members agreed to rehear the case. On March 22, 1852, in a 2–1 decision, the court again held that Scott remain a slave. The freedom afforded in northern states by the Missouri Compromise did not apply within the state of Missouri, the judges ruled. They did not dispute that presence in a free state afforded the opportunity for freedom, but wrote that the status of slave reattached once the bondsman was back in slave territory.

Scott and his wife remained in bondage. In November 1853, friends helped him file a federal suit challenging the Missouri Supreme Court decision. Attorney Roswell Field agreed to carry the case onward, free of charge, and another player entered as well. John Sanford, Irene Emerson's brother, now claimed ownership of Scott. In May 1854, the federal court found in favor of Sanford, and Field appealed to the US Supreme Court. A transcription error resulted in the case being misnamed, and at Field's behest Montgomery Blair filed his brief in *Dred Scott v. Sandford* on February 7. Oral arguments began February 11 and lasted four days.

Representing Sanford were Senator Henry S. Geyer of Missouri, who now held the seat filled for thirty years by Thomas Hart Benton, and Reverdy Johnson, a former senator from Maryland and attorney general under Zachary Taylor and Millard Fillmore and widely considered one of the best lawyers in the country. They attacked the constitutionality of the Missouri Compromise, which had not previously been at question in the original case or its lower-court appeals. Until now, this had simply been the latest in a long line of cases considering whether presence in a free state emancipated an enslaved traveler. Now it was more, encompassing the central political issue facing the nation in a presidential election year. With the lawyers in charge and politics in the forefront, Scott almost ceased to matter. Blair's client was the Republican Party. Johnson's was the South.

Most observers considered Blair's performance adequate. "We had not the pleasure of listening to the argument of counsel," the *National Era* reported, "but an inspection of Mr. Blair's *brief* satisfies us that he presented an able and irrefragable argument for the freedom of the plaintiff." But the perpetually dissatisfied Horace Greeley took a different view. Getting his information secondhand—he also did not attend oral arguments—Greeley moaned that "able counsel would have volunteered in behalf of Freedom had they had the least intimation that they were wanted."

Greeley's skills as a legal talent scout notwithstanding, Blair's argument was cogent and firmly grounded in precedent. His—and Scott's—problem was not legal nicety. It was the makeup of the court, which included among the nine justices five southerners and two northern men sympathetic to the South.

Greeley's powers as a prognosticator left much to be desired as well. His newspaper reported after oral argument concluded that "it is expected the judgment of the Court will be rendered within a fortnight." It would take somewhat longer than that.

There were jurisdictional issues to be sorted out, but the substantive issues before the court were:

- If a slave is taken by his master to reside in a free state, then brought back into a slave state, does his previous presence outside the world of slavery make him free? Like Margaret Garner's lawyers, Blair argued it did, and pointed out that until the Missouri court changed its mind in 1852, this had been the law even in that slave state.
- Are free blacks citizens of the United States? This was a hotly debated topic inside and outside the court. Blair pointed to case after case in which states recognized blacks as citizens.
- Was the exclusion of slavery from northern territory by the Missouri Compromise constitutional?

The court seemed ready to issue a narrow decision with a narrow, sectional majority. Justice Benjamin Curtis wrote to a relative the first week of April that "the Court will not decide the question of the Missouri Compromise line—a majority of the judges being of the opinion that it is not necessary to do so."

But Chief Justice Roger B. Taney, a Marylander who had grown ever more virulent in his defense of slavery since his appointment to the court in 1836 by Andrew Jackson, seemed intent on pushing for a broader decision, one that would go beyond a narrow 5–4 vote. To do that, he would have to enlist one or two of the northern justices.

That would take longer than Greeley's fictional fortnight. It was time that Supreme Court justice—and Republican presidential aspirant—John McLean, who was planning a scathing dissent in hopes of impressing the Republican bigwigs about to gather in Pittsburgh, could not spare.

{ 4 }

"Not a Mere Aggregation of Whigs, Know-Nothings, and Dissatisfied Democrats"

Gamaliel Bailey was just the sort of all-or-nothing fanatic who drove practical politicians up the wall. The editor of the *National Era* had not softened his antislavery position in the intervening year since the free soil coalition's victory in the 1854 election, and he was determined not to go "into any association with Republicans *and* Know Nothings with members of two Parties, with men trying to serve two masters." If the North Americans wanted to abandon their objectionable antipathy to foreigners and join the antislavery crusade, he would welcome them. But he refused to join a party that tried to smooth over the hypocrisy of demanding freedom on the one hand and endorsing bigotry on the other. When he lived in Cincinnati Bailey had been a close ally of Salmon P. Chase, but the two men were growing apart over the governor's blossoming relationship with the Know Nothings. Chase saw this as simple politics. He needed allies to get elected and do the things he and Bailey wanted to get done. Bailey saw it as cozying up to a "detestable organization" and unfavorably compared Chase's stand to William Seward's.

Bailey's antipathy was shared by many, but as winter closed in, the antifusionists appeared to be in the minority. Winning was what mattered, and not only to the professional politicians. John Greenleaf Whittier urged all to keep their eye on the ball—"forget, forgive, and unite"—in the cause of antislavery.

Chase was similarly unmoved by Bailey's importunings. Bailey tried to delay the date of the Republican organizational meeting planned for February 22, 1856, in Pittsburgh, to give him more time to block Chase's "Ohio Plan" for a 50–50 split in Republican and Know Nothing representation at the conclave. He found some allies, including Joshua Giddings, but Seward declined to sign on. Mostly, supporters of the early date argued, it was important to get together before the Know Nothings nominated their presidential candidate in a convention planned for the same week, so they could prove they weren't kowtowing to the nativists. If things worked out as Chase planned, the already existing rift in the nativist movement, which had been revealed the previous summer but since papered over, would be ripped open again, all to the Republicans' advantage.

The meeting went forward as planned, the festivities getting under way at 11 AM on Washington's Birthday. Two dozen states were represented— all the free states plus Maryland, Virginia, Kentucky, Missouri, Delaware, Texas, Tennessee, and, most surprisingly, South Carolina. The Kansas, Nebraska, and Minnesota Territories also sent delegates. About half of the eight hundred people crowded into Lafayette Hall, at the downtown corner of Fourth Avenue and Wood Street, were delegates. After Owen P. Lovejoy of Illinois opened the proceedings with a prayer that asked God to "enlighten the mind of the President of the United States," John King of New York, son of Rufus King, who had served in the Continental Congress, was chosen temporary chairman. Committees on organization and resolutions were appointed, although the fruits of their labor had largely been cooked up beforehand by a group of Washington and New York insiders. Freezing cold temperatures and a bad snowstorm—some of the same weather that had assisted the escape of Margaret Garner and her family—delayed the arrival of many delegates. Chase had sent surrogates to act on his behalf. But Horace Greeley, Joshua Giddings, and Owen P. Lovejoy showed up on time and were among the first speakers. The usually caustic Greeley and Giddings were relatively tame, with Greeley appealing to Know Nothings "to act with us in the great struggle for which we are now preparing," and promising to "be careful to do or say nothing which would render such action difficult or embarrassing." But Lovejoy let loose, thundering that "the places of those patriots who were about to be shot down in Kansas would be supplied by other freemen" and that he was "willing to go either as a captain or private. [I] would rather be there sweltering in blood than to see a set of drunken ruffians take the government out of the hands of the people of Kansas."

After the introductory speeches, Francis P. Blair was presented as the permanent chairman. The irony of a slaveholder presiding over the public coming-out of the antislavery party was noted by some, but no one objected and his appearance was greeted with a loud, enthusiastic demonstration. Blair and Giddings had traveled together to Pittsburgh by train, an unplanned symbolic conjoining of the two wings of the antislavery movement. Blair was seen as a unifying force for the party's disparate elements, a man who reached back into American history, an ally of Andrew Jackson, who had evolved as the nation evolved and now stood right on the central issue of the moment.

Now Blair gave the first public speech in his long—although virtually entirely behind-the-scenes—career. Noting that he was not an orator, he introduced a paper he had written—"Address of the Southern Republicans"—which quietly but forcefully made the case for union and freedom. In it, he was appealing less to the people in the hall than to the people of the South, and to his fellow border-staters, where he still believed a core of Jacksonian nationalism survived.

His old Democratic allies called Blair a bitter old man, derided him as a traitor, and hinted that he might be going senile. "That Blair should, at his time of life and with his knowledge of the world, venture to palm off on his abolition brethren such a roorback, is evidence merely of the desperation of his determination to die striving to get revenge for his loss of the national organship of the Democratic party," the *Washington Star* opined. (*Roorback*

was a term for an untrue but damaging political attack, with roots in a libel
of James K. Polk during the 1844 campaign in which the candidate was
accused of using a branding iron to mark his slaves, a story that appeared
in a bogus volume supposedly written by a Baron Roorback.) Blair didn't
care. He retorted that he was the true heir to Jefferson and Jackson, and
those fomenting disharmony betrayed the general's devotion to the Union.

But the critics were right about one thing: Blair had too much confidence in some of his fellow slaveholding southerners and border-staters.
The essence of Blair's message, read later in the day, was that Republicans
could build a national rather than a sectional party, if they stuck to the
core goal of restoring the Missouri Compromise. This was the path to kin-
ship with the border states such as Missouri, where his son Frank Jr. was
attempting to build an antislavery party, and the way to isolate secessionists
and nullifiers. Some in the hall grasped at the hope. Others, like Indiana
abolitionist congressman George W. Julian, felt Blair's sentiments "were
too conservative in tone to satisfy the demands of the crisis." Conversely,
in the South the speech was denounced as "ultra in its sentiments."

After that, it was a roll call of politicians providing the usual platitudes. However, Joshua Giddings received a thunderous response when he
took the dais and joked that "for the last twenty years I have been called
a fanatic so often that I almost now believe it myself." His humor had a
point. As Giddings looked out over the sea of like-minded delegates, he
grew poignant. "Had I been told that I should have lived to see a sight
like this, I would have called my informant a fanatic."

After the first day, an optimistic *New-York Tribune* reported that "it is
all harmony and enthusiasm." And, to a certain extent it was—but largely
because the spirit of Blair's appeal had ruled the day and anything that
might provoke consternation was laid to the side so as not to interfere with
the more urgent business of simply getting organized.

Such Whig-like avoidance of the task at hand could not continue indefi-
nitely. Republicans still had not fully organized in several states they would
have to win to capture the presidency, namely New Hampshire, Rhode
Island, Connecticut, New Jersey, Indiana, Illinois, Iowa, and California.

When the convention reconvened at 9 AM the next day, the committees
that had been appointed the previous day were ready to present their work.

George W. Julian's panel on organization had come up with a plan for a national committee that would include one member from each state; that group would be empowered to add members as it saw fit. It would also play a role in establishing party organizations at the state, district, county, and town levels. To lead the group, ex-Whig Edwin D. Morgan of New York was named interim chairman—the committee's main function would be fundraising, and Morgan was well connected to the moneymen on Wall Street. And, with Blair seeming to drive events in Pittsburgh (assisted by Chase's surrogates), Morgan was a handy way to reach out to Seward and his acolytes, although the chairman had been privately committed to John C. Frémont since meeting him at the home of New York journalist John Bigelow at the end of January.

Morgan's appointment was not the only move the delegates took that bedeviled Chase's plans, although that was not necessarily their intent, for he had considerable support in the hall. The Ohioan wanted the national nominating convention to be held in Cincinnati—where he happened to be on the day of the Pittsburgh meeting—supposing that having the gathering on his turf would supply a home field advantage (as it would, four years later, for Lincoln). But most of the delegates preferred either Harrisburg or Philadelphia, hoping to give the party a boost in the crucial state of Pennsylvania. They settled on Philadelphia and chose the symbolic date of June 17, the anniversary of the Battle of Bunker Hill.

The presentation of the resolutions committee was, if anything, even less controversial than the organization committee. They succeeded by keeping it simple. Proposals to take a stand against nativism and to assist the armed resistance in Kansas were loudly voted down. Three broad items were approved: repeal of the Kansas-Nebraska Act and any other law that might allow slavery to spread to new territory; admission of Kansas as a free state; and a proclamation that the party intended to defeat Pierce and the Democrats in November.

And that was it.

As much as anything, the meeting in Pittsburgh accomplished the task of making the attendees feel like they were actually a political party, a whole rather than the sum of several parts. "It was quite manifest that this was a *Republican* convention," wrote Julian, "and not a mere aggregation of Whigs, Know-Nothings, and dissatisfied Democrats."

Outside the hall, though, abolitionists were not yet reconciled to the Republican Party's temperate free soil position. Contemplating a potential career in elective politics, Henry B. Blackwell, husband of women's rights activist Lucy Stone, opined that he would "never be found crouching & whining to slaveholders, or doughfaces. I believe in aggressive, frank, energetic political action. No truce with slavery. No parleying with crime. No courtesy with man stealing, woman-whipping, & child-selling!" Bailey moaned to Chase about the "conceding and conceding, diluting and diluting."

Wall Street entrepreneur and abolitionist Lewis Tappan had been among those who noted the irony of the slaveholder Blair presiding over the antislavery party's convention. But when Tappan, Frederick Douglass, and others called soon after the Republican meeting for a convention of antislavery men to nominate candidates of their own, William Lloyd Garrison was derisive. "Can anything more ludicrous than this be found inside or outside the Utica Insane Asylum?" And he was just as caustic when it came to the Republicans, whose "tone . . . is becoming more and more feeble and indefinite, in order to secure a large vote in the approaching Presidential struggle."

Among the professionals, the dilettantes' complaints fell on deaf ears. Charles Sumner was happy with the declaration of principles, which he described as "strong and yet moderate, conservative and yet progressive." John Bigelow, editor and co-owner of the *New York Evening Post* and a recent convert to Frémont, said victory was within their grasp "if anything like the same discretion and singleness of purpose are exhibited by the Republican nominating convention which shall meet in June as were exhibited by that which has just adjourned at Pittsburgh."

Around the country, antislavery men who were not tied to the antipolitical wing of the abolition movement saw more than a ray of hope in the focus on fighting the expansion of slavery while setting aside other contentious issues that might tend to derail the coalition. One attendee of the Iowa Republican convention, held the same week as the Pittsburgh meeting, rejoiced that "the proper spirit of concession was manifested on all minor subjects, while there was no shrinking from responsibility on the mighty subject that brought us together." That mighty subject: "The doctrine that *Freedom* is national, and Slavery sectional, that the General Government should prohibit Slavery wherever it has national jurisdiction; that Slavery should be circumscribed to States where it now exists."

Inside the hall, the politicians had been around long enough to remember the fate of the Liberty Party in 1840 and 1844, and the Free Soil Party in 1848. They meant not to repeat those noble but lost causes. They meant to win.

To win, they needed a candidate. While there was "little said about Presidents or Presidential candidates" during public sessions, according to one reporter who was there, behind the scenes the usual hobnobbing was going on.

"Had the Pittsburgh convention been a nominating convention, you would have had the nomination for the Presidency by two to one," an Ohioan wrote to Chase. Considering Chase's inability to steer the meeting toward his desired end of a Cincinnati convention in June, that conclusion might have been more enthusiasm than analysis. In any case, Pittsburgh was not a nominating convention, and Chase didn't secure the party's support.

The attendees had, however, rejected proposals to shun the Know Nothings, which could have devolved to Chase's advantage. Unfortunately for Chase, most of the political class was beginning to clamber aboard the Frémont bandwagon and were already thinking about who might fit well with him. Indiana congressman Schuyler Colfax was not alone in suggesting after Pittsburgh that an anti-Nebraska Whig with nativist sympathies needed to be attached to the ticket if, as Colfax and many others in the know assumed, Frémont was to be the candidate. This was not yet a public notion, although the time for that was fast approaching.

Chase's other signal problem was that a number of Ohio delegates supported Supreme Court justice John McLean. This reflected their wariness of Chase and the overriding power of party: former Whigs found it difficult to unite behind former Democrat Chase. Some were also annoyed that he had ultimately supported Banks for House Speaker over fellow Ohioan (and former Whig) Lewis Campbell. "Judge McLean is more popular with the moderate men of the Republican party—the Whigs among them, especially—than any other prominent man," the *Washington Star* adjudged, although McLean's devotion to the new party was suspect.

The *Washington Star* was correct in surmising that Blair and his allies had "put out of joint the nose of Governor Chase" by not supporting his

JUSTICE JOHN McLEAN.
Courtesy of Library of Congress

candidacy, but the paper was on the wrong side of the family feud in supposing that it was Thomas Hart Benton who was the object of Blair's affection in Pittsburgh. The major Democratic organ in the nation's capital had not yet caught on to the smoke-filled-room machinations for Frémont.

Seward continued to publicly demur, which was disheartening to the more fervent antislavery members of the coalition. But for those who worried that Frémont might not be fully committed to the cause of freedom, there were signs—although none that the ever-reticent Pathfinder freely flashed about—that he might be more radical in his thinking than some supposed. Earlier in the month, Frémont and his thirteen-year-old daughter, Lily, enjoyed an evening in Philadelphia with women's rights activist Lucretia Mott and her husband, James, both of whom were abolitionists of the first order. Appearing in public with the Motts at such a sensitive political moment was a mark of Frémont's willingness to abjure political niceties, and a hint that his campaign would be different from any that had gone before.

SALMON P. CHASE.
Courtesy of Library of Congress

Another indication was that his wife was front and center in promoting his candidacy. One visitor observed that "Jessie Benton seemed to be far more interested in his success than he, in fact she bore the principal part of the conversation" and was "full of her father's resoluteness."

She was ready for the battle. "I'll go, my chief," was a favorite—and apt—saying, from a boatman in Scottish poet Thomas Campbell's "Lord Ullin's Daughter," in which the lord's daughter and her betrothed are forced to flee across a stormy sea to escape the father's wrath after their elopement. The story had obvious personal meaning for Jessie. But if she thought she had experienced her father's wrath in the past, she would soon enough be introduced to an entirely new level of Bentonesque thunder.

"HE BELONGS TO THE UNION"

In 1852, Pope Pius IX contributed a block of Italian marble to the United States, for use in building the Washington Monument. The gift—from the ancient ruins of the Temple of Concord—stirred a firestorm in anti-Catholic circles. A little more than a year later, a US visit by the papal nuncio, Gaetano Cardinal Bedini, sparked riots and threats of assassination. The resulting agitation helped consolidate the previously amorphous nativist movement into a political force. The cardinal was burned in effigy. Rallies were held, pamphlets were distributed, and funds were raised to purchase a "Protestant" marble block that would sit next to the Pope's Stone in the obelisk then under construction to honor the first president.

The outrage gave way to absurdity on the night of March 5, 1854—as Congress was debating the Kansas-Nebraska Act—when nine men broke into the base of the monument, tied up the night watchman, and spirited the Pope's Stone away, rolling it several blocks to a boat in the Tidal Basin, breaking it into smaller pieces, then hauling them into the Potomac River, where most of the pieces—some were kept as souvenirs and would turn up decades later—were dumped.

It was a nineteenth-century Keystone Cops operation, but it served as a rallying point for nativists. The culmination was the convention of the American Party in Philadelphia on February 22, 1856, the same day the Republicans were getting organized across the state in Pittsburgh. Unlike with the Republican confab, the Know Nothings were there to nominate candidates and write a party platform. But while the Republicans were feeling a growing sense of unity of purpose, the Know Nothings were on the verge of disintegrating.

The nativist movement preceded the kidnapping of the Pope's Stone by a decade. It grew out of anti-Catholic organizations founded in response to a wave of Irish and German immigration, which swelled to massive proportions after 1845 and the advent of the potato famine. Three million Irish and Germans arrived between 1846 and 1854, most of them Catholic. But even before that, in local controversies over state-financed parochial schools and the use of Catholic Bibles in public schools, passions rose and violence flared. Every time it did, more recruits were brought to the nativist banner.

A pair of riots in the spring and summer of 1844 rocked Philadelphia, sparked by another battle over the use of Bibles in schools. Opportunistic politicians seized on the controversy, rival rallies led to violence, and gun battles broke out in May and July that resulted in dozens of deaths. One of the leaders of the nativist movement, Lewis Levin, was indicted for inciting to riot. He was never convicted, but he was elected to Congress. That winter, the Order of United Americans was founded in Philadelphia.

A larger, more effective organization was founded about 1850 by Charles B. Allen, in New York. It was Allen who created the Order of the Star Spangled Banner, the secret society dedicated to quiet action to reduce the political influence of immigrants. Its secrecy sometimes reached ridiculous extremes. Staying hidden in places like New York and Philadelphia was not that difficult. But in some smaller cities and towns, where secrecy was hard to come by, members would gather in cornfields to stay out of sight. Whatever one thought of the American Party's policies, some saw this aspect of the movement as downright un-American. "Secrecy is the natural covering of fraud, the natural ally of error and the enemy of truth," railed Robert Toombs. It was not yet a political movement, but it was skulking around the edges. Philadelphia nativists, some of whom were likely members of the Order, attempted to recruit Daniel Webster to lead a presidential campaign in 1852, but the great man died soon after and the movement splintered in the absence of an immediate crisis.

Then the Pope's Stone arrived. Suddenly everything was about politics. New York merchant James W. Barker took control of the Order. He was a better organizer than Allen, and steered the group toward a more open activism.

By the end of 1854, the Order of the Star Spangled Banner was evolving into the American Party, and claiming more than one million members. The movement was no longer a secret, but it preserved one element of its former being: its members became known as Know Nothings—most likely as a result of the members claiming to "know nothing" of any secret organization of nativists. The transformation from secret society to political party was greatly aided by the impending collapse of the Whigs, who were devastated in the election of 1852.

While the movement was inspired by anti-Catholicism, its rapid growth owed a great deal to the related issue of temperance, as well as to antislavery—many antislavery and temperance northerners viewed the movement as something of a halfway house between their Whig and free soil Democratic pasts and their Republican future, as soon as the Republican Party got itself organized. Joshua Giddings called the movement "a screen—a dark wall—behind which members of old political organizations could escape unseen from party shackles, and take a position, according to the dictates of judgment and conscience."

That was not, however, immediately apparent in 1855. Even after Banks won the speakership, it was by no means certain that the Republicans with their focus on antislavery, rather than the Know Nothings with their emphasis on anti-Catholicism, would become the primary alternative to the Democrats. It would take a Whig-like suicide to confirm that, and the Know Nothings appeared willing to oblige.

When the American Party gathered for its convention in June 1855—in Philadelphia, like the party's gathering the following February—many of the leaders hoped to skirt past the question of slavery. It had been a year since the Kansas-Nebraska Act, emotions had cooled somewhat, and they seemed to believe they could emphasize nativism and temperance. They were wrong. "The moment the new party begins to act in the domain of National politics it must be on one side or the other," the *New-York Tribune* reminded Know Nothings three days ahead of their convention.

Southern Know Nothings would have none of it. While preferring silence, some were willing to accept the old Whig solution of separate planks for North and South. But under no circumstances would they countenance an antislavery plank. When fusionists like Schuyler Colfax of Indiana and Henry Wilson of Massachusetts, who dreamed of uniting the two antislavery movements, insisted on a strong statement against the extension of slavery to the territories and the Fugitive Slave Act and for abolition in the District of Columbia, southerners—and some frightened northerners—balked. The convention adopted a majority report that declared current law "conclusive . . . in spirit and substance."

That was too much for the antislavery wing, and they bolted, leaving behind a rump group of southerners and ex-Whigs from New York that was solidly behind the Union-at-all-cost wing led by former president Millard Fillmore. The alienated antislavery group began drifting ever more certainly toward the Republicans. That movement became evident most obviously in Fillmore's home state of New York that fall, when William Seward's fixer, Thurlow Weed, orchestrated the merger of the conscience Whigs and the nascent state Republican organization under the Republican banner.

Seward, who had equivocated about joining the new party, noted of the same-day state conventions held in Syracuse in September 1855 that the Whigs and Republicans would enter through two doors, but they would exit through one. And that's just what happened.

In the eight months since the June 1855 Philadelphia meeting, the situation had stabilized a bit, but the differences had not disappeared. The northerners who had not abandoned the party the previous June were back in Philadelphia in February 1856, but in a preconvention platform-writing session, they got no more satisfaction, again losing on the slavery question.

When the convention proper opened at National Hall on Market Street on February 22, the same day the Republicans assembled in Pittsburgh, they were determined to get their candidate, even if they couldn't get their issue. Two New Yorkers were vying for the party's presidential nomination, which would be decided by 227 delegates from twenty-seven states—Georgia, Maine, South Carolina, and Vermont were not represented. Fillmore was the favorite of old-line Whigs, southerners, and those Yankees who wanted to steer clear of slavery altogether. And while some talked of Sam Houston of Texas, who had been approached the previous year by some of the Republicans who eventually moved on to Frémont, Fillmore's main competition was George Law, a wealthy, self-made industrialist, former Democrat, and much more sincere nativist than Fillmore. He was, in the words of correspondent Murat Halstead, "a silly old fellow with a long purse . . . who wishes to be a great man."

When Millard Fillmore left the White House in March 1853, he assumed it was the end of his political career, although at fifty-three he was still a relatively young man. But, like Abraham Lincoln, Fillmore returned to politics in 1854, spurred not by policy but by grief. His wife, Abigail, had died only a few weeks after Fillmore's presidency ended. Then, less than a year and a half later, in July 1854, his beloved daughter, Mary Abigail, died suddenly at age twenty-two. Fillmore thought politics might take his mind off his heartbreak, and he threw himself back into the storm. The results of the 1854 elections told Fillmore that Whiggery was dying and nativism could be a rallying point for a new national party—unlike antislavery, which would only exacerbate sectional tensions. He joined the

Order of the Star Spangled Banner in early 1855, then almost immediately left the country.

"It is better to wear out than rust out," he said as he prepared to depart for a tour that would take him to England, Ireland, France, Italy, Egypt, Turkey, and Prussia, "and as my political life has unfortunately deprived me of my profession, perhaps I can do nothing better than to diversify my pursuits by travelling."

When he got to Rome, Fillmore had an audience with Pope Pius IX, but only after being reassured he would not have to kiss the pontiff's ring or kneel before him, lest he risk his standing with the anti-Catholic nativists who had always made up a large part of Fillmore's constituency and dominated the party he was now hoping to lead. And indeed he did not have to kiss or kneel as he met with Pio Nono under the "radiant pictures of Raphael, of Murillo, Titian, and Guido," whose subjects gazed down on the necessarily abbreviated ceremony—Fillmore spoke no Italian, and His Holiness no English. Fillmore also sat for a bust by the noted sculptor Edward Sheffield Bartholomew.

Fillmore was still in Europe when the nominating convention convened, "the cause of unfeigned admiration on the part of every European with whom he came in contact," wrote one correspondent covering his travels. Law's forces had come to Philadelphia believing they were in command. Fillmore's supporters concurred in that opinion, and had unsuccessfully sought a delay of several months to drum up more votes. They needn't have bothered. When all the delegates were assembled in Philadelphia, Fillmore's superior position quickly became obvious, and it was now Law's organizers who were stumping for a delay. They were no more successful than Fillmore had been.

Before they got around to nominating candidates, though, the northern bloc tried one more time to add an anti-Nebraska plank to the platform. The ruckus caused by the northerners stirred up "boldly proclaimed" threats of a bolt by the southern members on the convention's second day. Virginia delegate John D. Imboden pleaded with his colleagues not to leave, suggesting that the difficulties would be smoothed over, and if they weren't "perhaps in a few hours" he and others might leave the hall with the disgruntled. After a long day of mostly pointless speeches, "amid a scene of wild confusion," the delegates agreed to adjourn until Monday, February 25.

The Monday session opened with a motion to bar the convention from nominating any candidate not in favor of reinstating the Missouri Compromise line and thus barring slavery north of 36 degrees, 30 minutes. When that failed on a vote of 141–59, thirty northerners walked out of the hall to hoots of "good riddance," "glad you are gone," and "Black Republicans." The remaining delegates then quickly moved to nominate a candidate. On an informal nominating ballot, Fillmore led with 71 votes, followed by George Law with 27. John McLean and Sam Houston got some attention as well. But it was clear that Fillmore commanded the hall. The delegates then took a short recess. When they returned, Fillmore got 179 of the 241 votes cast, and another large group of antislavery delegates departed. All told, about seventy left, and they took tens of thousands more with them in spirit. The bolters were led by Chase's Ohio allies, who were determined to unite with the Republicans behind a Chase presidential ticket and quickly called for a separate North American convention to assemble in June, just ahead of the Republican convention.

For vice president, the remaining delegates selected a Democrat to balance the Whig Fillmore, and he was one with a glorious party pedigree: Andrew Jackson Donelson, nephew and confidant of Old Hickory, who must have been spinning in his grave at the thought of his beloved kin joining forces with a Whig. "He labors under the worse hallucination of supposing that the mantle of Jackson has fallen upon his shoulders," a Tennessee critic noted, "and that he could do whatever Old Hickory accomplished." Donelson argued that Jackson (and Henry Clay and Daniel Webster) would have approved of the ticket, dedicated as it was to preserving the Union. But Jackson had done so by asserting national power and standing up to nullifiers. Donelson paid lip service to such sentiments, accusing Pierce of "professing the Union doctrine of Jackson" while serving as "the instrument of the Abolitionist and Nullifier." A good many delegates concurred in the sentiment of one who, when Donelson said, "I left the Democratic Party," shouted back, "It left you." But there was no indication that the Fillmore-Donelson ticket was prepared to face down southern extremists; on the contrary, appeasement was built into the party platform and Fillmore's very being. The platform commended "the perpetuation of the Federal Union as the palladium of our civil and religious liberties, and the only sure bulwark of American independence." The message was clear: union, and peace, at any price.

Southerners, for their part, seemed satisfied, if not excited. Southern Know Nothingism was less virulently anti-Catholic than the northern variety, and rested largely on a demographic argument that would have been familiar to John C. Calhoun. Continued unchecked, immigration that added to the population of the North vastly more than to the South would eventually swamp southern rights as northern states—and electoral votes—commanded the nation. Worse, from the point of view of slavehold- ers in the Deep South, the South's share of immigrants mostly landed in the border states, where their numbers could soon begin to affect electoral outcomes. Within just a few years, both Delaware and Missouri would have more foreign immigrants than slaves. To the extent that Know Nothing- ism developed any following in the Deep South, it was as an antidote to the perceived unreliability of northern Democrats, a position vehemently protested by the likes of Georgia lawmakers Alexander Stephens and Howell Cobb, who continued to insist that the best protection of southern rights was a national Democratic Party. "To Divide the South is to Betray her, and to Imperil the Union," opined Georgia's *Augusta Constitutionalist*, in endorsing that sentiment.

"The American Party are the first in the field, with an unexceptionable candidate, and there is really no use in the Democrats putting up one, unless they really want to elect a Black Republican," the *Richmond Whig* predicted. But being first out of the box had its drawbacks as well. "The best feature in this Fillmore nomination is that it has to stand eight months of wear and tear," prophesied Thurlow Weed.

Technically, Fillmore was not the first candidate into the field. New York congressman Gerrit Smith—philanthropist, abolitionist, and heir to a vast fur-trading fortune—had won the nomination of the new Radical Abolition Party at a convention in Syracuse the previous June. Fillmore was first of practical significance. Smith was a reluctant nominee who did no campaigning, and the only speeches he delivered were ones he likely would have made anyway in support of his many reform causes.

Fillmore's friends understood the danger of prolonged exposure and hoped to keep their candidate under wraps as much as they could. They were aided in this endeavor by his absence from the country. His stateside advisers urged him not to officially accept the American Party nomination until he was back on American soil, while publishing a pronativist letter he had written the year before and spreading the word that he had joined the Order of United Americans. At the same time, New York's state council of the Order endorsed him, and the group's national president threatened to sweep out any state council that refused to go along.

The threats worked, but Fillmore's nomination nevertheless pointed the Know Nothing movement in a new direction, one less stridently antiforeign and more focused on preserving the Union. "We do not say Millard Fillmore of New York," the party's *Daily American Organ* proclaimed, "because he has shown that he belongs to the Union." Likewise, Georgia's branch of the American Party called the Fillmore candidacy "an insurrection of the honest masses against the despotism of party and party leaders—a rebellion, like that of our revolutionary sires, against the tyranny and corruption of their rulers." In some ways this made sense, both practically and as a matter of political evolution. The movement's claims to being antiforeign or anti-immigrant had always been something of a misdirection. Some local organizations included foreign members—Protestant Irish who hated their fellow immigrants' Catholicism, not their Irishness. But Fillmore would temper to some degree even the anti-Catholicism, in favor of stressing that any way but his way would lead to disunion. The bolters who were already planning their own convention for June issued a manifesto making the same point, in considerably less laudatory terms, calling Fillmore's nomination "an utter betrayal of the American movement" and "a traitorous attempt to wrest it from its purpose."

Fillmore was trying to build a coalition that could counter the Republicans. He had no delusions of winning. But the Know Nothings thought they might be able to throw the election into the House of Representatives by winning enough electoral votes to deprive any other candidate of a majority. Harking back to the just completed election for Speaker of the House, they knew that bargaining might produce almost any result.

Republicans understood the danger. They spent the next several weeks trying to get organized nationally, and the wording of the call for the June 17 convention sparked more disputes between the practical politicians like

Chairman Edwin Morgan and the antislavery and antinativist absolutists like Gamaliel Bailey.

Greeley, with a foot in both camps, got to the heart of the matter. "Our real trouble is the K.N. convention on the 12th prox," Greeley wrote of the bolters' planned June 12 meeting. "I can't see around that corner."

{ 5 }

BLEEDING NEBRASKA

A s political violence began to erupt in Kansas, violence of a different nature was already under way in Nebraska. The war about to
envelop Kansas would start because of a disagreement over human freedom.
The one in Nebraska, though also political, was blamed on a cow.

The vast wasteland of the "Great American Desert" was now pitched as
a paradise, transformed not only by the popularity of the Frémonts' *Report of
the Exploring Expedition* but also by the legislative power of Congress to point
a finger at a place and call it civilized. White settlement was encroaching ever
farther westward, which is one reason Stephen Douglas and others wanted
to get the territories organized. On a bluff above the Missouri River, the site
where in 1804 Lewis and Clark lost the only member of their expedition,
Sioux City, Iowa, was founded in 1855. From across the river, tales sprung
up of towering timbers, flowing streams, and coal-choked seams ready to
be exploited. None of that was true. But there was land to be had for next
to nothing, and that always drew a crowd. The Pawnee, Otoe, Omaha, and
Ponca tribes had been shoved aside, and Thomas Hart Benton and other
expansionists were certain the army could move the rest of the natives out
of the way with relative ease. George W. Manypenny, the commissioner of
Indian Affairs, interpreted the relevant treaties and current political situation
differently, but hardly anyone was listening to him.

The 1851 Treaty of Fort Laramie had defined rough boundaries for several Plains tribes, established a $50,000-a-year annuity for fifty years (amended to ten by the Senate), and allowed the US Army to garrison troops at forts along the Overland Trail for the protection of Oregon- and California-bound immigrants. The treaty was honored in the breach by the Plains tribes, who didn't have the same conception of hierarchical authority as the white men they were treating with, and honored not at all by those white men, who year after year failed to come across with the full amount of the annuity. And each year, more pioneers were making their way across the land, using up the grass, killing the buffalo, and spreading deadly diseases such as cholera.

On August 18, 1854, fifteen hundred Lakota Sioux of the Brule, Oglala, and Miniconjou subtribes were camped along a three-mile stretch of the south bank of the North Platte River, about eight miles east of Fort Laramie, waiting for their annuities to be delivered. That day, a Mormon train bound for Utah came through. Amid the dust and wagons and crowds of commingling Scandinavian Mormons and natives, a cow wandered away from its owner and into the Brule camp, where a visiting Miniconjou named High Forehead caught and slaughtered the animal and treated the village to a rare feast. The Mormons continued on to Fort Laramie.

Once there, the immigrant who lost the cow lodged a complaint with US Army lieutenant Hugh Fleming, who sent for Conquering Bear, the nominal chief of the village where the cow was slaughtered. Under the treaty, the Native Americans were liable for any stolen property, and several offers of restitution were made, including replacing the cow with one supplied as part of the annuity. Conquering Bear also offered the immigrant a horse from his own supply. Trader James Bordeau offered to pay ten dollars for the lost cow, just to help keep the peace. The Mormon thought it was worth twenty-five dollars.

Then Lieutenant John Grattan intervened. The West Pointer would be happy to volunteer to go the village and arrest High Forehead if that would satisfy the Mormon's demand for justice. That was not the way the system was supposed to work. Tribal responsibility was outlined in the 1851 treaty; individuals were not to be held personally liable. That didn't matter to Grattan, who was known as something of a blowhard, a heavy drinker, and an officer who had little appreciation for the martial abilities of Native Americans. He would soon be disabused of this last notion.

Bending to Grattan's suggestion, Fleming ordered Conquering Bear to return to the village, arrest High Forehead, and bring him to the fort. Conquering Bear patiently explained to Fleming that it didn't work that way. He had no authority over High Forehead, who was not even a member of his band. Fleming waved away the objection, and Conquering Bear finally had to tell the officer that if he wanted to arrest the miscreant, he would have to use the army to do it. He would guide the troops, he would even point out the man they wanted, but the Brule leader would not attempt to arrest a Miniconjou. The army would have to do so. Fleming said that was just what would happen, and he should expect the soldiers to be there the next day.

Conquering Bear sensed trouble. On his ride back to the camp on the river, he shared his fears with Oglala and Brule leaders. It was decided that one more attempt would be made to reach an accommodation, and a thirty-five-year-old Oglala leader, Man-Afraid-of-His-Horse, volunteered to go to Fort Laramie in the morning and attempt to dissuade the army from trying to arrest High Forehead.

But he was too late. By the time he arrived, Fleming had already given Grattan his orders, and there was a flurry of activity as men prepped for battle. Grattan took twenty-nine volunteers and two howitzers, leaving the already undermanned post with just ten men available for duty—thirty-two were outside the fort gathering wood and cutting hay. He also took along Lucien Auguste, a drunken bully who spoke Lakota, though not very well, as an interpreter. It would prove to be a fateful choice. The small force headed out of the fort at 3 PM, headed for the Brule village about eight miles down the river. It was a hot, humid, dusty day as the men, horses, and mules, which were enlisted to pull the gun carriages toting the howitzers, moved slowly east along the bluffs above the North Platte. As they made their way, Man-Afraid-of-His-Horse left the fort unnoticed and trailed along a short way behind.

Two hours of sweaty marching brought them to a fur trading post about halfway to the Brule camp. Grattan ordered a halt to rest and water the animals and for the men to load their weapons. Some of the traders there tried to dissuade Grattan, but he would not be moved. At least, they warned, send the already drunken interpreter Auguste back to the fort. He would, they warned, cause nothing but trouble. Again, Grattan refused. When the force saddled up and resumed the march, a handful of traders rode along with them, hoping against hope that they might be able to intervene before shots were fired.

Another two miles of marching brought the troops to a bluff overlooking the Native American villages below. Grattan stopped to survey the situation. What he saw must have given him pause—directly below him were three hundred Oglala lodges; further down the river were a Brule camp of two hundred lodges and a smaller Brule encampment of eighty lodges, then a couple miles further was Bordeau's trading post and the destination of the venture, the Miniconjou camp consisting of twenty lodges. All told, Grattan's men were riding into almost six hundred lodges housing approximately forty-eight hundred Native Americans. Fully twelve hundred of those were men of fighting age.

Obridge Allen, a trader and trail guide who had joined the group at the trading post, rode up to Grattan. "Lieutenant, do you see how many lodges there are?" he asked. Grattan saw, but there would be no changing his mind at this point. "Yes, but I don't care how many there are," he replied. "With thirty men I can whip all the Indians this side of the Missouri." Sensing, though, that the traders' concerns might have filtered down to—or even originated with—his men, Grattan called them together on the bluff to reassure and inspire them. After telling them that High Forehead must be taken at all costs, he told them they could "fire as much as you damn please," and then he dismounted to take personal command of the artillery, because no one else in the small contingent was qualified. Man-Afraid-of-His-Horse came up to talk with Grattan, who asked him in a peremptory manner to ride into the Oglala village and tell them to "have nothing to do with this business" or "I will crack into them." The Oglala leader chose not to deliver the threat.

As Grattan led the force down into the valley, he could see dozens of mounted warriors following along beside. This was the first moment when Grattan's determination began to waver. As he rode along and more and more Sioux made quick charges toward his column, he decided to stop at Bordeau's and seek a second opinion. How, he asked the trader, could he extract High Forehead without sparking a battle? Bordeau told him he should seek out Conquering Bear, enlist his help, then be patient while the elders dealt with the situation. While Grattan was listening to this sound advice, outside the post Auguste was taunting Sioux warriors, telling them, among other things, that the soldiers had come "to drink your blood and eat your liver raw."

Bordeau said he could arrange things with Conquering Bear, but only if Grattan could get Auguste to shut up. Grattan ordered the drunken fool to desist, but it did no good. He kept up his shouting; Grattan refused to order him back to the fort. Within a short time after the troops' arrival at the trading post, Conquering Bear arrived with two other Brule leaders. These three met with Man-Afraid-of-His-Horse, Grattan, and Bordeau to talk things over, even as Auguste lingered a short distance away, continuing to irritate the many warriors who had gathered around. Grattan insisted that High Forehead be turned over, and Conquering Bear insisted he had no authority over the Miniconjou. It was a useless reprise of the original debate at Fort Laramie, and accomplished exactly the same thing. Bordeau tried a few different tacks, but nothing worked. Then a rider arrived from the village bearing a message from High Forehead himself, telling all the talkers that he would rather die fighting than give himself up to the army.

That was that. Grattan decided to go, and asked Bordeau if he would accompany him as the column moved toward the Brule village. Bordeau refused, called Grattan a damn fool, pointed out High Forehead's lodge, and went back inside the post. This time, none of the civilians rode along.

The quiet light of dusk enveloped the valley as Grattan stopped about forty yards from the Miniconjou camp. There, he placed the howitzers in the center of his line and waited. His men rested on the ground. Conquering Bear, joined by Man-Afraid-of-His-Horse and some other Brule leaders, came out to talk. A staggering Auguste attempted to translate. As before, Grattan demanded they turn over High Forehead. Again, Conquering Bear said he couldn't do it. Some of the others went to High Forehead's lodge and asked him to give himself up. His response was to gather a group of armed friends outside his lodge and shout that he would sooner die than be taken by the white men. Even as the soldiers and the Native Americans began moving into position for battle, the talks continued for almost an hour. But they proved as fruitless as before. Both sides were repeating themselves and had nothing new to offer. The soldiers pointed the artillery at the lodges. Behind the camp, in a depression that hid the movement from the troops, a young warrior named Spotted Tail led four hundred men on a flanking movement around Grattan's right. Oglala warriors crept down a dry creek bed on the left. Another group of Oglalas led by Red Cloud were filtering into position. The thirty troopers were surrounded and didn't even know it.

As the sun neared the horizon, Grattan called a halt. Ostentatiously looking at his watch, he announced, "It is getting late and cannot wait any longer."

A disgusted Conquering Bear replied, "I have done all I could. You are the solider. Since you will have him, now push on and take him." With that he turned and left, and Grattan did the same.

By the time Grattan got back to his men, the shooting had started. Some troopers had spied Spotted Tail's men on the right and fired at them. Grattan hurried back to the gun placement and ordered the crew to fire into the village. They did, and it was then that Grattan's inexperience proved decisive. With properly placed artillery, he might have held hundreds of warriors at bay for hours. But he had placed his guns too close to the enemy, less than half a football field away. There was no way his inexperienced crew could reload the guns before the mounted Native Americans swooped in and overwhelmed both the gunners and the infantry.

And that is exactly what happened. "After the cannon was fired, the first Indian I saw fire was the one that killed the cow. He shot a soldier, which staggered some distance and fell. All the other soldiers threw themselves on the ground and when they raised, they commenced getting into the wagon," a Brule named Big Partisan recalled. Free from any worry of another artillery blast, Spotted Tail's men then rushed in firing arrows. Several soldiers were killed immediately. Grattan was hit by "twenty-four arrows, one of which passed through his head," according to one report. Survivors retreated in good order but were hit by Red Cloud's men as they broke out of the hills into a flat area. They were wiped out. The few troops still standing were scattered around the village and didn't last long. All were killed; Conquering Bear, who was hit three times by rifle fire, was mortally wounded.

The Grattan fight—the army called it the Grattan Massacre—created disorder just where Franklin Pierce didn't need it: next door to Kansas, where there was already plenty of disorder. Emboldened, the Sioux conducted a series of hit-and-run raids in the following weeks and months, attacking trading posts and travelers on the Oregon Trail. In the worst incident, a group of Brule warriors attacked the Salt Lake City stage about twenty miles east of Fort Laramie, killing three men and making off with $10,000 worth of gold.

Officially, the army blamed the Grattan fight on the Native Americans, of course, claiming they had killed the cow to deliberately ignite an incident. That version of events was supported by many eastern newspapers, which duly reported that "it appears to have been a pre-concerted plot, on the part of the Indians, to waylay and murder the party." That nonsense was disputed by the Indian Affairs Bureau, particularly Commissioner George Manypenny, but the Pierce administration accepted it and agreed to increase the size of the army and sanction a punitive response. That position was popular on the frontier, where newspapers blamed the massacre on "the want of adequate military force at the garrison." During Senate debate, Sam Houston of Texas questioned the army's conclusion, and Thomas Hart Benton belittled the officers, including the martyred Grattan, as "schoolhouse officers and pot-house soldiers." Benton also pointed out that the cost in blood and treasure would be "a heavy penalty for a nation to pay for a lame runaway Mormon cow." He was right. The Grattan fight lit a fuse that would burn for three decades. But the dissenters were overwhelmed. Just as Stephen A. Douglas was hoping to organize Nebraska for white settlement, the government was declaring war on the territory's nonwhite residents.

On October 26, 1854, Secretary of War Jefferson Davis wrote to his old friend Colonel William S. Harney, who was visiting family in Paris, asking—not ordering—him to return to the United States to lead an expedition against the Sioux. Two months later, on Christmas Eve, Harney boarded a steamer bound for home. He was being asked to do the impossible. The jurisdiction of the army's newly established Department of the West stretched from the Mississippi to the Rockies and from Texas to

Canada. The tall, rugged Harney, who had been a soldier for thirty-five years, was to patrol and garrison this vast expanse with seventeen hundred men. Davis was asking for more men, with justification beyond the Grattan Massacre and the threat on the Plains. The army was also fighting Native Americans in Florida, Texas, New Mexico, and the Oregon country of the Pacific Northwest. But there was no guarantee Congress would see fit to fund a larger army, and no chance it would do so before summer.

"THE MOST SANGUINARY PUNISHMENT"

In the wake of the Grattan fight, most of the confrontations between Native Americans and whites were taking place far from the frontier of settlement. While southerners had poured into Kansas, Nebraska was being settled by northerners from Ohio, New York, Pennsylvania, Indiana, Illinois, and Iowa. Almost all of them settled within shouting distance of the Missouri River, which formed the boundary between the new territory and Iowa. In addition to real farmers, a goodly number of land speculators had set up shop. There also was a settlement of Mormons six miles north of Omaha: the town of Florence, which the saints used as their jumping-off point for treks to their Zion in Utah. By the mid-1850s Florence was "flourishing . . . alive with business, and houses rising all around as if by magic." And a few brave souls had ventured a few miles westward up the Platte River. About thirty-five miles beyond Omaha, surveyors had laid out a small town of about twenty plots and named it Fremont, in honor of the famous hero of western exploration.

When Colonel Harney arrived back in the United States to oversee the Department of the West, he met with Secretary Davis, who handed him a brevet promotion to brigadier general and told him to make his first expedition "short and decisive." And he gave him twelve hundred men—about 10 percent of the entire army—to secure ninety thousand square miles of his new command. Harney didn't protest and left for Saint Louis, arriving April 1, 1855. His staff was delayed by outbreaks of cholera and smallpox already stalking the trail.

It took three months to get organized. Harney blamed Indian Affairs for most of the problems, including his inability to hire scouts from the

Delaware tribe. Manypenny had told them they would lose any annuities due to them if they aided Harney. That was a lie, but the commissioner justified his dishonesty by citing his conscience, which bound him to try to stop the expedition any way he could. On July 3, Harney received orders to move out, and on July 18 he reached Fort Leavenworth and began to gather the forces from Fort Pierre up the Missouri River and those scattered along the trail. On August 4, he started out with six hundred men for Fort Kearney, up the Platte.

While Harney was moving, a former army officer turned Indian agent, Thomas S. Twiss, was at Laramie dividing up the Native Americans. Attempting to sort the guilty from the innocent, he declared the North Platte the line of demarcation and sent four thousand pacified Arapaho, Cheyenne, and Sioux south of the river. All of the Miniconjou and some of the Brule and Oglala stayed on the north side, camped on Blue Water Creek. The creek, twenty feet wide and two to three feet deep, was a clear-watered tributary of the North Platte, about 150 miles east of Fort Laramie and less than five miles from the Oregon Trail. On the western bank of the sandy, rock-bottomed stream that flowed south, about 250 Native Americans had set up their lodges. Twiss was convinced there was not "a single hostile Indian" to be found anywhere in Nebraska.

News reports made no distinction between the Native Americans camped on the north and south sides of the North Platte. The *Kansas Herald of Freedom* reported in July that the Brules, Cheyennes, Arapaho, Kiowa, Minneconjou, and even Comanche were "assembling at Ash Hollow to the number of three thousand warriors, and are eager for a fight." Ash Hollow, long a favorite spot for immigrants to stop and rest on the way to Oregon and California, was described as "a great stronghold for the Indians," a natural fortress with a narrow and winding road through the hills, with plenty of rocky outcrops and canyons to provide cover.

One of the officers traveling west to east to hook up with General Harney was Captain John B. S. Todd, a cousin of Mary Todd Lincoln. At first, Captain Todd—like the Sioux—was unpersuaded that anything would happen. "The probability is there will be nothing done with the Indians this summer or fall and that another year will elapse before they are punished for their depredations," he noted in his journal.

Before long, though, Todd was disabused of this notion. Harney had fought in the Black Hawk and Seminole Wars, against the Comanche in Texas, and in the Mexican War. He believed that the Plains Indians "must be crushed before they can be completely conquered," and he was as ready to fight as any man in the army. His combativeness filtered down through the ranks. Todd soon came around. On August 23 he noted that "tomorrow the 'Sioux expedition' has a beginning in earnest."

Other officers less well known than Harney—but destined to become known—were just as ready. Among them were John Buford, Alfred Pleasanton, G. K. Warren, and Henry Heth, all of whom would meet again at Gettysburg.

For days at a time, the weather was dry and the troops moved swiftly. Warren used the journey to apply his engineering talents. He had an eye for detail, measuring barometric pressure and humidity daily, as well as noting the types and amounts of clouds and taking soil samples. Twice in his own report he cited the reports of John C. Frémont for comparison and reference. The August 23 crossing of the Platte "gave us no trouble, as it was no where more than 1 foot deep, and spread out over its bed, here a mile wide," Warren recorded.

At other times, it rained a lot and progress was slow. The end of August saw "one of the heaviest thunder storms I ever knew," Todd recorded in his diary. But two days later they crossed the South Platte—seven hundred yards wide, eighteen inches to two feet deep—and pushed through to the "very sudden" descent into Ash Hollow on a long, hot march, falling exhausted in a fireless camp near the confluence of the North Platte and Blue Water Creek. The next day would prove to be "a busy and exciting day for us but a bloody and disastrous one to the Sioux."

Most of the ash trees that had given the place its name were gone from Ash Hollow, consumed in more than a decade's worth of campfires by California- and Oregon-bound immigrants, but it remained an oasis. "We arrived near their camp just at daylight," one of the soldiers reported, "which was in a valley between the hills, and the Blue Water running through the centre, the most lovely place I ever saw."

As with the Grattan fight, the army and the Native Americans parleyed under overcast skies. In this case, both sides were merely stalling. Little

Thunder, a Brule chief, wanted a delay so he could move his women and children to safety. Harney needed more time to bring up his infantry. When enough time had elapsed that both men felt they had honored the niceties and served their own purposes, they heard a shout from behind the line of lodges that the cavalry had been spotted. All hell was about to break loose.

Cavalry units stormed through the camp, and the infantry laid down a withering fire. Native Americans of all ages scattered, but there was nowhere to run to. When the shooting ceased, eighty-five Native Americans lay dead, mostly women and children. Another five dozen or so were taken prisoner. The attack on the Brule camp "very nearly, if not quite, 'rubbed' it out." Four soldiers were killed outright, and four more would die from their wounds.

"The Indian Slaughter at Blue Creek . . . will make the white man of civilized life blush for his race, and the American for his countryman," the New-York Tribune opined.

But neither Harney nor his superiors back in Washington were blushing. "The result was what I anticipated and hoped for," Harney reported. The Saint Joseph Gazette in Missouri reported that "the Indians have become convinced that Gen. Harney will not trifle with them, that they must submit to such terms as he may dictate or have the most sanguinary punishment visited upon their heads." One senior officer said Harney has "produced more terror and consternation among the Indians and their fiendish coadjustors than was ever thought or dreamed of before." Another concluded that "the punishment inflicted on the Brules and Ogalalas at Blue Water has taught them a useful lesson, which they will not soon forget." Harney put an exclamation mark on the terror by marching straight through Sioux territory, from Fort Laramie to Fort Pierre with 425 men in late September and early October. "The scenery is exceedingly solitary, silent and desolate, and depressing to one's spirits," wrote Warren, but Harney's political and military point was made. As the soldiers collected fossils in the Badlands, the Sioux retreated to the Black Hills.

From that position of strength, as Francis P. Blair organized his post-Christmas political party at the end of 1855, Davis empowered Harney to negotiate a new treaty. By March 1, 1856, almost five thousand Plains Indians had gathered at the run-down Fort Pierre. Thomas Twiss, still opposed to the war policy and feuding with Harney, advised the Oglala not to attend, and they stayed away. But most other Sioux bands were represented. Among the attendees were Little Thunder of the Brule and Sitting Bull of the Hunkpapa. Harney refused to shake hands with any of them.

He brusquely told them that "every nation must have laws and the people must obey them." The treaty would require the Native Americans to turn over to the army anyone who killed a white civilian and to return any stolen property. High Forehead would have to be surrendered. (Presumably the already-eaten Mormon cow was exempt from the returns policy.) The Sioux would be required to stay clear of the immigrant road and to stop attacking wagon trains. Horses and mules could no longer be traded. And peace must be made with the Pawnee. If all that was agreed to, the United States would ensure that Sioux would be protected from violence by encroaching settlers and immigrants, prisoners taken at Blue Water Creek and elsewhere would be released, and annuity payments—halted when the fighting started—would resume.

Harney also tried to revive the old and failed policy of naming chiefs to police restive elements among the Sioux. He "appointed one principal Chief and nine under Chiefs, and one hundred warriors, to prevent further trouble, and be responsible if any occurs." The Native Americans accepted the treaty terms—at this point they had little choice—and shrugged at the white man's absurd attempts to once again impose an alien political system on the Plains Indians. After five days of talk—mostly by Harney— the general finally shook hands with the men he had selected as leaders of his defeated foes, and the treaty was signed. Six weeks later, the Oglala belatedly joined in.

Hopeful journalists reported that the treaty "will insure a general pacification of almost all the tribes east of the mountains and south of the Missouri," and noted particularly the provision requiring all Native Americans to stay away from the immigrant roads, "an important step towards preventing future collisions."

Pierce and Davis backed the treaty, but the US Senate—egged on by complaints from Twiss and Manypenny—refused to go along. The annuities were too generous for the politicians to live with and it was never ratified.

Harney, also with the blessing of Pierce and Davis, knew that ragged old Fort Pierre would not do, so he scouted out a new site to house the army he envisioned would keep the peace.

In Warren's opinion, "Military occupation is essential to the safety of the whites, and the military posts should be such positions and occupied by such numbers, as effectually to overawe the ambitious and turbulent, and sustain the counsel of the old and prudent." He also believed the posts "should be placed well in the country whence the marauders come, as well as on the frontiers and lines of communication they are designed to protect." And he recommended a new site in the vicinity of the dilapidated Fort Pierre. "A permanent establishment here, with the occasional movement of troops between it and Fort Laramie, must entirely drive the disaffected and dangerous Dacotas from all the country south of this route."

Fort Randall was built at the spot that marked the change from prairie to plains, about thirty miles north of the confluence of the Missouri and Niobrara Rivers. The first troops would arrive June 26, 1856, just weeks after the Democratic and Republican parties met to nominate their presidential candidates, to lay out the post, situated about a quarter mile from the Missouri, at a point where the mighty river was a thousand yards wide. The first permanent detachment to be garrisoned there would come in August. The first sutler serving the fort was former captain John B. S. Todd.

"ALL THE SAINTS WHO CAN, GATHER UP FOR ZION"

Two weeks after Harney concluded the treaty with the Sioux, one thousand miles to the west the legislature of the Mormon-dominated territory of Utah adopted a constitution, hoping that it would lead to statehood. Voters approved the document on April 7.

The Mormon immigrant who had lost the cow that led to the Grattan fight was part of a hegira, a mass movement of a people. The "Gathering of Zion" envisioned by the founder of the Church of Jesus Christ of Latter-Day Saints, Joseph Smith, and accelerated by his successor, Brigham Young, was an international effort that was bringing immigrants by the thousands from across the United States and Europe. It had been going on since the first Mormon pioneers trekked to Utah in 1847, and was now gathering steam as Young rushed to boost the population and make a push to join the Union.

The new constitution was the second the territory had approved. The first had been signed in 1849 and had met with widespread opposition in Washington. The 1849 constitution would have named the state Deseret—a name derived from the word for honeybee in the Book of Mormon, representing industry and cooperation—and included Utah, most of Nevada and Arizona, and parts of California, New Mexico, Colorado, Wyoming, Idaho, and Oregon, a total of 265,000 square miles. Church leader Almon Babbitt, who had once served in the Illinois House of Representatives, was sent to Washington, DC, as the House member in waiting, but wait was all he did. Congress refused to consider Utah's petition for statehood. Brigham Young even considered uniting with California to gain admittance as a state then splitting off later. Instead, as part of the Compromise of 1850, a much smaller Utah Territory was created (along with the New Mexico Territory), with both given "popular sovereignty" to decide the question of slavery for themselves. Young was appointed territorial governor and superintendent of Indian affairs by President Millard Fillmore, and most of the territory's other officials were also Mormons.

Utah's 1856 constitution endorsed popular sovereignty, although Young was confident that slavery would gain no foothold. "Our constitution is silent upon the subject of slavery, leaving that question where Congress has left it with the People, but neither our climate, soil, productions, nor minds of the people are congenial to African slavery," he wrote. "Our past experience in this Territory exemplifies the fact that it cannot exist with us as an institution." Young pointed out that while many southerners had come to Utah with their slaves, hardly any stayed. Almost all of the slaves left after a short time as well. Probably fifty were in the territory in 1856.

But a lot had happened between 1849 and 1856, not least of which was the public acknowledgment by the church hierarchy of polygamy, or plural marriage as the saints called it, in 1852. So even though Utah had a larger population than Kansas—approaching forty thousand, although Young claimed nearly eighty thousand—and almost as many as Oregon, Oregon's statehood was by far a more popular cause. And even it couldn't achieve statehood, because of the sectional controversy. Mormonism, already anathema for many Americans, was made more so by the offense of polyg-amy. Young seemed not to understand the size of the obstacle presented by plural marriage. Republicans would soon be explaining it to him.

During the congressional struggle over the Kansas-Nebraska Act in 1854, Young had endorsed a transcontinental railroad as an aid to emigra-tion. "It should be a national work, and constructed without delay; the Magnetic Telegraph should also precede it," opined Young. It became clear soon enough, though, that politics was going to get in the way of progress. "The miserable Nebraska-Kansas Measure has spoiled" any movement on the Pacific railroad, Thomas Kane, a leading non-Mormon supporter of the church, told Young.

There was more than a touch of irony in the Mormon desire to join the Union. The saints had fled westward in 1846–47 to escape the United States, in large part because the federal government refused to intervene on their behalf when state and local governments persecuted them. The governor of Missouri had issued an infamous "extermination order," and the murderers of Joseph Smith went free in Illinois. But their chosen destination did not stay out of American hands for long. After Utah and considerable other territory was ceded to the United States as part of the settlement of the Mexican War, Utah was at least partially back under the thumb of non-Mormons. The move for statehood was motivated, in part, by the Mormons' desire to elect their own officials rather than be governed by hostile outsiders appointed by the president. "We strongly desire to become a state," Young wrote in 1856.

"What think you," Young inquired of Kane a week after voters approved the constitution, "will our admission be favorably received, and acted upon? Shall we gain admission into the Union this session of Congress, in time to vote for President of the United States next November?"

Young fundamentally misunderstood the political moment, and had a surprisingly tenuous grasp on the depth and breadth of anti-Mormonism in the capital and across the country. Others worked hard to clarify the situation for him, including John M. Bernhisel, the territorial delegate to Congress, who informed the governor in April "that there is a poor pros-pect of our coming into the Union at present." If Young didn't grasp the totality of that feeling in the spring, action in Congress and the summer political party convention season would leave no doubt.

In the House, the Committee on Territories approved a bill by Justin Morrill of Vermont "to suppress polygamy in Utah." The Republican Morrill saw polygamy in the light of popular sovereignty, and he wanted to end that practice both in terms of slavery and plural marriage. And though southerners were of course friendlier to popular sovereignty than the antislavery Morrill, they held no truck with Mormon practice and "are yet scarcely prepared, owing to sectional influences, moral social & religious prejudices to stand up in defense of Polygamy." Pushing the issue now, Bernhisel warned Young, would end with "the abolition of our Territorial Government, the division of the Territory, and the annexation of it to the adjacent Territories for judicial purposes."

Young still hoped to build up the population of the territory as a way toward statehood, but he had other reasons as well to encourage the Mormon hegira. He feared—correctly as it turned out—that statehood or no, direct federal intervention in the affairs of Utah was coming sooner rather than later, and he needed more men on hand if resistance became necessary. The local economy had suffered greatly the previous year, a result largely of an infestation of grasshoppers that destroyed much of the harvest. He also hoped an infusion of new blood might aid in his desire for a religious awakening among the saints.

The difficult economy had, unfortunately, depleted the resources of the Perpetual Emigrating Fund, or PEF, established in 1849. In effect, the fund—with capital supplied by church members—was a kind of bank. It paid for all or part of a saint's travel to Utah. The immigrant was then expected to repay the fund through work or financial contributions. The system worked well enough during prosperous times, and when a small proportion of new immigrants needed assistance. With the faltering economy and an influx of destitute European immigrants expected in 1856, another plan was needed.

Franklin D. Richards had been appointed in March 1854 to coordinate all of the European missions, including the fertile recruiting grounds of Britain and Scandinavia. Until 1855, the church had brought European immigrants through the port of New Orleans. In an effort to shorten the journey and, hopefully, reduce both costs and the incidences of "ship fever" and avoid the cholera outbreaks that were regularly striking the Mississippi Valley, the decision was made to switch to a northerly route. Richards decided to conduct a test run to see which US port would be most efficacious, and that year he sent ships to Boston, New York, and Philadelphia. The result of the experiment was that New York provided the best facilities for sending immigrants along their way to the west, although the 1856 ships would unload their saintly cargo in both New York and Boston.

But an even more significant change came courtesy of Brigham Young himself. First he wrote to Richards in September, near the end of the 1855 migration season, telling him of the plan to use handcarts for the 1856 migration. Young wrote that the plan would "save this enormous expense of purchasing wagons and teams—indeed we will be obliged to pursue this course, or suspend operations." Then, on October 29, 1855, the prophet publicly directed "all the Saints who can, gather up for Zion and come while the way is open before thee; let the poor also come, whether they receive aid or not from the Fund, let them come on foot, with handcarts or wheelbarrows; let them gird up their loins and walk through, and nothing shall hinder or stay them." Young made sure that all understood what was being asked of them—that "they are expected to walk and draw their luggage across the plains, and that they will be assisted by the Fund and in no other way." Undiscouraged, thousands upon thousands answered the call. Richards put out the word to members of the church in Britain just before Christmas. The plan he called "the device of inspiration" drew a wildly popular response.

From 1847 to 1855, a total of 150 wagon train companies made their way to Utah. But as far back as the California Gold Rush, Young had considered using handcarts for the migration instead. If clodhoppers bound for the gold fields could walk from Missouri to California, he reasoned, surely saints motivated by the Holy Spirit could do it as well. Though the saints stuck with ox-powered wagons in the absence of a compelling economic reason to rethink them, when the cost became prohibitive, Young decided to roll out the handcarts. It was a fateful decision.

Franklin Richards's immigration roster for 1856 was truly international: England, 2,231; Scotland, 401; Wales, 287; Ireland, 28; France, 75; Denmark, 409; Sweden, 71; Norway, 53; Switzerland, 15; Italy, 15; Germany

14. The total, including an additional smattering from other countries, came to 3,629. The vast majority were destitute.

From its inception in 1849 through the 1855 emigration, the PEF had helped pay for 3,411 saints to reach Utah. But it was now $100,000 in debt and faced the prospect of thousands of 1856 emigrants wholly unable to pay their own way. A serviceable wagon cost about $100; the three yoke of oxen it took to pull it cost about $200. This $300 was well beyond the means of a growing number of European emigrants, and the PEF was going broke. The church could not afford to supply them all with fully outfitted wagons, and these were not yeoman farmers from the Midwest who could bring their own. They would need transportation across the Atlantic, a train ride to Iowa, and supplies to get them on to Zion. Something had to give. What gave were wagons and oxen.

Sea journeys via steamship were no longer the hazardous undertakings of old, but they still involved a degree of peril. Fresh in the minds of Mormon immigrants would have been the recent disappearance of the SS *Pacific*, a mystery followed closely on both sides of the Atlantic. The ship had set a new trans-Atlantic speed record in 1849, making the crossing in just ten days. But sometime in late January or early February 1856, it went missing on a journey from Liverpool to New York, with 196 people on board. British and Americans dispatched search parties, but no trace of the ship was ever found. (In 1861, however, a message in a bottle washed ashore in the Hebrides claiming the *Pacific* had sunk after striking an iceberg.)

Fortunately for the saints, their sailings proved to be relatively smooth, although every company reported their share of seasickness and other maladies.

For the 1856 migration, eight ships carrying more than 4,400 Mormons sailed from Europe (including about eight hundred not accounted for by Richards's roster). About 2,400 of them expected to get on the train for Iowa and press on through to Utah. The rest would stay behind in the states for a year, a practical necessity but still one Young frowned on, because the rate of apostasy was much higher for those saints who didn't quickly proceed to Zion. Fully 2,000 of the 2,400 Utah-bound saints were traveling entirely on the PEF's dime. Low-cost handcarts were their only hope of reaching the Promised Land.

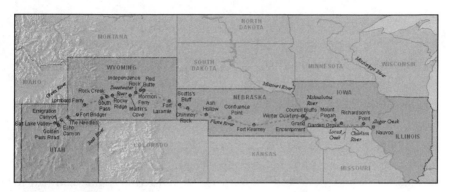

MORMON TRAIL MAP. *Public domain*

The handcart-bound immigrants came over in four ships, whose sailings were delayed by storms. The first, the *Enoch Train*, weighed anchor in Liverpool on March 23, followed by the *S. Curling* on April 19, the *Thornton* on May 4, and finally the *Horizon*, which departed May 25. By that date, most of the non-Mormon immigrants bound for California and Oregon were already on their way up the trail.

After landing in New York or Boston, groups of immigrants made their way across the country by train (and occasionally steamboat), a thousand miles to Iowa City, the end of the Rock Island Line. From there, it was 270 miles across Iowa to the frontier town of Florence, the jumping-off point for the final thousand miles to Salt Lake City, with only three intervening oases of civilization, loosely defined, in between: Forts Kearny, Laramie, and Bridger.

Entrusting their journeys to handcarts was justifiable, considering the number of immigrants involved, the widespread desire to make the journey, and the cost of moving them. But the planning left much to be desired. Trouble getting the ships hired caused delays in England. Rail transport was not smoothly organized. Supply stations that were supposed to be set up along the route were never finished. In Iowa City and Florence, not enough seasoned lumber was readied, carts were not built, and those that were tended to be made with green wood by people unused to building such things.

The carts were made of hickory or oak, with two wheels, each about four and a half feet around. The axles were made of hickory, a harder wood that theoretically would stand up better to the rigors of the trail. The interior box of the cart typically measured three feet by five feet. Empty, the cart weighed about sixty-five pounds. The trade-off in weight, of course, made the cart more likely to break down.

Each immigrant was limited to seventeen pounds of personal belongings—clothes, bedding, cooking utensils, and any personal items such as toys and books. For a typical family, with their share of the communal allotment of flour, bacon, and other supplies, and invariably a small child or elderly member of the family who grew too tired or twisted an ankle and had to ride part of the way, the carts could weigh more than two hundred pounds.

The saints would follow the route taken by Brigham Young and the original Mormon pioneers who had fled the previous Zion of Nauvoo, Illinois, in the winter of 1846, hoping to make it all the way to the Salt Lake Valley. That group had to put up for a year on the western bank of the Missouri River, a site north of Omaha they called Winter Quarters, before proceeding on in April 1847, along the trail surveyed by John C. Frémont. Young carried with him the expedition report written by John and edited by Jessie.

Now, a decade later, the first handcart company departed Iowa City on June 9, under the captaincy of Edmund Ellsworth, a farmer, returning missionary, and son-in-law of Brigham Young. The next two companies followed hard on their heels, led by Daniel D. McArthur, like Ellsworth a native New Yorker and Mormon missionary, and Edward Bunker, who was a veteran of the Mormon Battalion's long march to California in 1846.

John Jaques, a missionary who joined the fifth and last handcart company bringing up the rear of the 1856 migration, likened the Iowa City–to–Florence portion of the trip to a new sailing vessel's shakedown cruise. "This first part of the journey will just get the saints used to travelling, without a great deal of toil all at once," he observed.

But even this relatively short 270-mile journey across gentle terrain was trying for some. On June 14, twelve-year-old William Lee died of consumption. It was the first fatality for the 1856 handcart companies on the migrant road.

Traveling through Iowa roughly along a line that is now US 34, the immigrants alternated between searing heat and ferocious thunderstorms, with an occasional day of rest mixed in. They passed through small towns and across tracks of prairie, with the occasional rise breaking the view. Some parts of the trail were quite hilly. These English and Scots had never seen anything like it before.

The first company, led by Ellsworth, with 280 people, 56 handcarts, and 3 wagons, crossed the Missouri River on July 8 and spent much of the next week in Florence getting fully outfitted and repairing the carts, many of which were already breaking down. Sand and dust got into the axle mechanism and ground the wood. Immigrants experimented with various solutions. Some wrapped their axles in leather. A few used bacon grease. Others forfeited cooking utensils to use the tin to protect the hickory.

The third handcart company, led by Bunker, comprised mostly natives of Wales, many of whom did not speak English. This group landed in New York, traveled by rail to Saint Louis then by steamship up the Mississippi, and left Iowa City on June 28. The immigrants made the trip to Salt Lake in a brisk sixty-five days, but still needed the supplies sent eastward from Utah to complete their journey.

While the McArthur and Bunker companies were close behind Ellsworth, the train carrying the fourth company, led by James G. Willie, a native of Hampshire in England, didn't reach Iowa City until June 26. The group would stay there for three precious weeks, "engaged in making yokes, handcarts &c., and the Sisters in making tents. For the want of these latter articles immediately on our arrival, we had several soakings with rain, which the Saints bore with becoming fortitude," Willie reported.

As all of the companies that passed through before them had also experienced, "many strangers seemed to take considerable interest in our proceedings." Most were merely curious. "Only one drunken man made a little disturbance," Ohio-born saint Levi Savage, another veteran of the Mormon Battalion, noted in his journal. One Good Samaritan who "seemed to be influenced by a sincere desire to do good" gave the company fifteen pairs of children's boots, Willie wrote. Across Iowa "considerable opposition was shown towards us by the people from time to time, and threats of personal violence were sometimes made use of, though never carried into effect." Sometimes, when a town's rowdies got out of hand, the more genteel among the non-Mormons would chastise them back into good order.

The Willie company, with 500 saints, 120 handcarts, 5 wagons, 24 oxen, and 45 beef cows, would not reach the jumping-off point in Florence, Nebraska, until August 11. The fifth and final handcart company, led by Lancashire native Edward Martin, was even farther behind.

{ 6 }

A MONTH OF VIOLENCE

Democratic representative Philemon T. Herbert—the congressman from John C. Frémont's own California district—was a regular in the dining hall at the Willard Hotel, a gathering place for politicians of all stripes at the corner of Fourteenth and F Streets in Washington.

At about 11 AM on May 8, 1856, Herbert arrived at the Willard with a companion, hoping to catch a late breakfast before heading on to the Capitol for the day. It was after the usual time for breakfast, but Herbert demanded he be served anyway. The waiter, a young Irish immigrant named Riordan, told Herbert he would have to wait while Riordan checked to see if the kitchen could prepare a breakfast at that hour.

Unused to such insolence from a mere waiter, the Alabama-born congressman told Riordan to "get my breakfast, damned quick." The raised voice drew the attention of a more senior attendant, Thomas Keating, another Irish immigrant, who came to Herbert's table to see what the problem was.

Herbert, still focused on Riordan, screamed, "Clear out, you Irish son of a bitch" at the youngster. Noticing Keating, Herbert turned his fury on him. "And you, you damned Irish son of a bitch, clear out, too."

No fool, Riordan fled to get permission in the office to fill the late breakfast order, which was standard procedure at the hotel. Keating then said something to Herbert, and Herbert rose and struck him in the back of the neck with his pistol. Keating circled around a neighboring table and picked up a plate. He faked a couple of throws, and Herbert responded by throwing a chair at the waiter. Keating then threw the plate at Herbert. They came around the table to meet each other, jostled, and broke some dishes.

Pat Keating, a kitchen employee and Thomas's brother, heard the commotion and rushed out to help. Seeing that Herbert had drawn a pistol, Pat Keating grabbed hold of it, and the two men struggled for a few moments. Herbert's dining mate then grabbled Pat Keating, causing him to lose his grip on the gun.

Seeing this, Thomas instinctively threw his hands up in front of his chest, but it was too late. Herbert fired one shot at almost point blank range. Thomas Keating fell to the floor, bleeding to death.

Herbert walked out of the hotel, got into a hack, and rode to the police station, where he turned himself in.

He was taken to the guard room at the city jail, where he appeared before two justices of the peace and an "anxious and excited assemblage of citizens, Californians, members of Congress, &c." Those unable to get inside jammed the doorway or peered in through the barred windows. After five and a half hours of testimony from more than a dozen witnesses, Herbert was held in the custody of the US marshal.

He stayed there through the weekend. The justices of the peace heard arguments from counsel on whether to grant release, but declined to rule and left it to DC Criminal Court judge Thomas Hartley Crawford. Crawford entertained arguments on Saturday, May 10, and two days later released Herbert on $10,000 bond with a warning not to leave town. His trial was set for the third Monday in June. In setting bail, Crawford offered up the unsolicited opinion that "it is quite clear to my mind that a conviction of murder should not take place," although he failed to explain why he thought this except to imply that he believed manslaughter was the more likely charge.

It was an inauspicious beginning to one of the most violent peacetime months in American history.

"The Harlot, Slavery"

Two weeks before Congress convened in December, former New York governor Washington Hunt, clinging to Whiggery, predicted "high words and stormy scenes" from Republicans deliberately trying to provoke southerners into rash acts that would assist their own party-building efforts.

Some Republicans seemed to agree with Hunt. "We have before us a long session of excitement, & ribald debate," Massachusetts senator Charles Sumner had forecast as the Kansas debate got under way in March.

Senator Sumner was self-righteous, overbearing, utterly convinced of his own superiority, and intolerant of others' opinions. He suffered fools not at all, and to Sumner, almost everyone who disagreed with him was a fool, or worse. He described Stephen Douglas as "a brutal vulgar man without delicacy or scholarship." If that wasn't personal enough, he also said the Little Giant "looks as if he needed clean linen and should be put under a shower bath."

Douglas didn't think much of Sumner, either. But even many of the people who considered themselves Sumner's friends weren't all that fond of him. One told him that "you appear in the eyes of your friends as

CHARLES SUMNER.
Courtesy of Library of Congress

a demagogue." Another made a familiar observation about self-described idealists: "Sumner is so much occupied with thoughts of how the world is to be made better, that he does not pause to consider and observe what the world really is."

Sumner lost a lot of friendships over political disagreements. "His solitude was glacial and reacted on his character," Henry Adams wrote. "He had nothing but himself to think about."

He was also utterly humorless. When a young acquaintance noted that he had never heard a joke in one of Sumner's speeches, Sumner replied, "Of course you never did. You might as well look for a joke in the book of Revelations." And there would be no humor—at least none that the listeners could detect—in his upcoming speech "The Crime Against Kansas." "My soul is wrung by this outrage and I shall pour it forth," Sumner wrote to Salmon Chase of the Kansas-Nebraska Act.

Sumner was sincere in his outrage, but he also had another reason for wanting to "pour it forth." The publishers compiling a collection of his speeches were pushing him to provide "something they can *call* a last speech" that would help them market the book. Sumner promised the publishers and his political allies that he would deliver. "I shall pronounce the most thorough philippic ever uttered in a legislative body," he told abolitionist minister Theodore Parker.

Sumner had been hearing directly from antislavery settlers in Kansas, who wrote to him that "preparations of the most warlike kind are in progress" (after the New England Emigrant Aid Company had disingenuously described their number as those "whose only weapons are saw-mills, tools, and books"). And they begged for Sumner to come to their assistance. Sumner harked back to the 1854 debate on the Nebraska bill to inspire him. Then, attacks on Douglas, Andrew P. Butler of South Carolina, and James M. Mason of Virginia had proved popular, if not especially effective, and he took care to single them out again. To ensure he could not be upbraided for misquoting a source, rather than work from memory he checked out a copy of *Don Quixote* from the Library of Congress.

Sumner wrote the entire speech out by hand, then had the congressional printer typeset it—the printed version came to 112 pages. He worked on the rhythm and cadence, memorized all 112 pages, and recited the whole thing to William Seward and his wife, Frances, both to get feedback and to practice before a live audience. Seward, though cautious in private, projected a public persona of audacity, and he had taken considerable grief on occasion for the use of outlandish language. He suggested Sumner avoid or at least tone down the personal attacks. Frances Seward was even blunter. "I would on no account have you suppose that I objected to the general tone of all that you read," she wrote to Sumner. . . . "I objected only to the cutting personal sarcasm, which seldom amends, and is less frequently forgiven." Sumner heard them out, but changed nothing.

Sumner's speaking style has been described even by admirers as condescending. His movements and gestures were stiff and rehearsed. Henry Wadsworth Longfellow, a close friend, said Sumner's oratorical pose was "like a cannoneer . . . ramming down cartridges." But what his carriage denied, his passion employed. Sumner spoke from a sense of outrage that most of his listeners could barely fathom.

And on May 19, there was a horde of listeners. The capital knew something special was coming, and the galleries drew an unusually large crowd. Not just newspapermen and interested citizens but House members as well surged into the gallery. On the floor, almost every senator was in his seat for the performance, although not all of them were paying close attention. Stephen Douglas and Robert Toombs made a great show of being too busy writing letters to tune in. Others talked loudly at the back of the chamber. But when Sumner's voice moved up a notch just after 1 PM, they turned toward his desk, quieted down, and leaned in.

"Mr. President," he began, "you are now called to redress a great transgression. Seldom in the history of nations has such a question been presented."

He would go on for three hours that day, and resume the next.

Employing the copy of Cervantes he had borrowed from the Library of Congress, Sumner used some of the harshest language ever heard in the Senate. And he took direct aim at Douglas and Butler, "who, though unlike as Don Quixote and Sancho Panza, yet, like this couple, sally forth together in the same adventure." Butler wasn't in the chamber, and Sumner noted his absence. "I regret much to miss the elder senator from his seat; but the cause, against which he has run a tilt, with such activity of animosity, demands that the opportunity of exposing him shall not be lost." Butler might not be there to defend himself, but Sumner was going to let him have it in any case.

"The senator from South Carolina has read many books of chivalry, and believes himself a chivalrous knight, with sentiments of honor and courage," Sumner went on, rising to the fury he promised Chase he would release from his soul. "Of course he has chosen a mistress to whom he has made his vows, and who, though ugly to others, is always lovely to him; though polluted in the sight of the world, is chaste in his sight—I mean the harlot Slavery."

No one rose to appeal to the chair to shut down the venom, and it continued. But Douglas was in the rear of the chamber, pacing back and forth, and quietly suggested "that damn fool will get himself killed by some other damn fool."

And that was before Sumner had turned his attention to the Little Giant. If Butler was the knight errant, then Douglas was his "squire of slavery, its very Sancho Panza, ready to do all its humiliating offices."

The next day he came back for more, with two different targets.

Mason, he bellowed, "represents that other Virginia, from which Washington and Jefferson now avert their faces, where human beings are bred as cattle for the shambles."

Lewis Cass, the senior man in the body, rose to chastise Sumner, calling the speech "un-American and unpatriotic." Mason, sounding a more-in-sorrow-than-in-anger tone, was "constrained to hear here depravity," but supposed he would have to put up with it because he and Sumner were, as senators, political equals. But outside the legislative chamber, the proper response would be to "shun and despise" such a man. When Mason finished, he turned to reporters prowling the floor and told them "the senator is certainly non compos mentis."

Then Douglas's turn came. "Is it his object to provoke some of us to kick him as we would a dog in the street," Douglas asked of Sumner, "that he may get sympathy upon the just chastisement?"

Sumner refused to let Douglas get the last word, and told him "that no person with the upright form of man can be allowed . . ."

"Say it!" Douglas interjected.

"I will say it," Sumner shouted back. "No person with the upright form of man can be allowed, without violation of all decency, to switch out from his tongue the perpetual stench of offensive personality. . . . The noisome, squat, and nameless animal, to which I now refer, is not a proper model for an American senator. Will the senator from Illinois take notice?"

"I will, and therefore will not imitate you, sir," Douglas retorted.

"Mr. President, again the senator has switched his tongue, and again he fills the Senate with its offensive odor," Sumner concluded, then took one closing jab at Mason. Douglas got the last word: "I will only say that a man who has been branded by me in the Senate, and convicted by the Senate of falsehood, cannot use language requiring reply, and therefore I have nothing more to say." With that he walked out and the chair gaveled the chamber into adjournment.

Abolitionists praised Sumner for his "inspiring eloquence and lofty moral tone." Longfellow called him "the greatest voice on the greatest subject that has been uttered."

But others were less sanguine, and not all of those were Sumner's ideological opposites. Sumner's former Senate colleague Edward Everett, a Massachusetts Whig, said he had "never seen anything so offensive." Republican New York lawyer George Templeton Strong termed the speech "rather sophomorical."

Sumner's enemies were, predictably, even less gracious. "Mr. Sumner ought to be knocked down, and his face jumped into," a Tennessee law-maker presciently said. If Sumner really was trying to foment violence against himself, as Douglas said, he succeeded beyond anything he might have imagined. Sumner's friends were worried, but he would have none of it. When friendly colleagues offered to escort him out of the Capitol, he brushed them aside. "None of that," he said, and traipsed home alone in the pleasant May evening.

"To Stop This Coarse Abuse"

Congressman Preston S. Brooks of South Carolina was, in the context of his home state's representation, considered to be something of a moderate, although that reputation was based on a very small sample in a state rich

with fire-eaters. Where Senator Sumner and those fire-eaters were generally humorless men, Brooks had a sly streak. In the midst of the Kansas-
Nebraska debate he had proposed—in jest, or at least that's what most
people thought—that members of Congress should be required to check
their firearms in the cloakroom before being allowed to enter the chamber.
This was a matter of honor, Brooks pointed out. If you're going to start
a fight, be enough of a man to deal with your opponent without aid of a
firearm, the carrying of which onto the House floor was an "unmanly and
pernicious habit." Brooks's proposal was "greeted with much applause and
laughter." In a more serious vein, he had been criticized back home during
the Nebraska debate for not standing firm enough for southern interests.
But he had genuine friends among his colleagues, and was considered a
"cordial and agreeable" fellow.

Brooks came from a prominent family. His father was a well-known
and highly respected lawyer and politician. Somewhat hotheaded as a young
man—he had once engaged in a duel with future senator Louis Wigfall—
Brooks eventually overcame his tendency toward reactive violence to the
point that he had even once gotten in a fight in college over his refusal to
engage in a duel. He briefly served in the Mexican War, enjoyed success as
a planter, and served in the state legislature before being elected to Congress
in the Franklin Pierce–led Democratic sweep of 1852.

As pure an abolitionist as Gerrit Smith had referred to Brooks as "a
frank, pleasant man." The *National Era* called him "always a Southern
gentleman . . . of fine appearance, of good information and fair elocution."

The southern gentleman was in the Senate on the first day of Sumner's
speech and heard the remarks aimed at Andrew Butler, his cousin. Brooks
didn't come back for day two. Knowing that the fifty-nine-year-old Butler
would feel compelled to respond to Sumner once he got wind of the speech,
and that the enfeebled Butler—he was a year away from death—would be
no match for the buff forty-five-year-old Sumner, Brooks decided to take
it upon himself to defend the honor of his family and his state.

Brooks was not much more of a match than Butler. Sumner was an
impressive physical specimen: broad chested, standing six feet two inches
tall and weighing about 185 pounds. The slight Brooks was younger by
eight years but also two inches shorter and fifteen pounds lighter.

And Brooks knew from the start that this would be a physical confrontation. He was not interested in suing Sumner for libel. He also knew Sumner would not accept a challenge, so there would be no duel. But there was another consideration: Brooks did not consider Sumner his social equal, the usual ground necessary for an affair of honor. For Brooks, Sumner had no honor and so deserved to be treated, in effect, dishonorably. Instead of pistols, the weapon he chose was symbolic of that standard: a cane, the affectation of a gentleman. Women and working men did not sport canes. Brooks would use the emblem of his class to teach a lesson to the Yankee.

On May 21, Brooks sat outside the Senate side of the Capitol waiting for Sumner to arrive. Unable to sit still, he would rise, pace back and forth, resume his seat, then repeat the process. An expansion of the Capitol was under way, and the outside work was nearly done, but debris from the work that continued on the interior was strewn about. The old dome had been taken down. The new one was a skeleton, more theoretical than real, while Congress continued to debate whether to appropriate more money for the project. A colleague from Virginia, Henry A. Edmundson, intercepted one of Brooks's walking volleys, and Brooks asked him to join him. "It was time for southern men to stop this coarse abuse used by the Abolitionists against the Southern people and States," Edmundson remembered Brooks saying, "and that he should not feel that he was representing his state properly if he permitted such things to be said."

What, Edmundson asked, could he do to help? "I wish you merely to be present, and if a difficulty should occur, to take no part in it. Sumner may have friends with him, and I want a friend of mine to be with me to do me justice."

But Sumner did not pass by, and by midday the two men gave up and walked over to their side of the Capitol. That night, two more men were brought into Brooks's confidence—fellow South Carolinians Lawrence M. Keitt and James L. Orr, and Brooks and Keitt spent the night drinking and working each other up into a fury. Brooks was up bright and early the next morning to resume his stalking of Sumner.

But again he was foiled. Congress typically convened at noon, and Brooks was outside the Senate by 11 AM, watchful for Sumner's approach by coach or on foot. He had devised a plan to attack Sumner just as he entered the building if he was walking; if he came in a carriage, Brooks planned to race through the Capitol and intercept him on the back side, where drivers deposited their customers. But Sumner again failed to appear. At about noon, though, Edmundson came by to check on his progress. When Brooks filled him in on the details of his plan, Edmundson cast a dubious look at his slender friend. After running all the way up the steps and across the Capitol to chase down Sumner, Edmundson wondered, wouldn't Brooks be too worn out to confront his prey?

Brooks saw that Edmundson was correct in his analysis, and he headed for the Senate. Entering the chamber, he saw Sumner sitting at his desk and took up a position in the lobby, across the aisle from Sumner. Edmundson and Keitt had come over to the Senate and were standing in the vestibule, with a view of both Brooks and Sumner. Maybe, Edmundson suggested, they should leave. "No, I cannot leave until Brooks does," Keitt responded, and left Edmundson to talk to a constituent behind the tall chair at the front of the chamber where the presiding officer sat.

The Senate adjourned at 12:45, earlier than usual so members could attend a memorial service for a House member who had recently died. Most quickly scurried away, but a few stragglers stayed behind in conversation, and Sumner remained at his desk, stamping copies of "The Crime Against Kansas" to send to admirers.

Brooks was getting impatient, and he took a seat in the back row, three rows away and still across the aisle from Sumner. He was trying to calm his nerves, and to ease the pain in his hip, the result of a duel. Sumner's Massachusetts colleague Henry Wilson bowed toward Butler as he left the emptying chamber. Edmundson, freed of Keitt, joined Brooks in the back row and jokingly asked him if he was now a senator, but the humor bounced off Brooks. Pointing to a woman in an animated conversation standing at the side of the chamber, close to where Sumner sat, Brooks said he could not carry out his plan with women present. He caught the attention of the sergeant at arms and asked him to remove the woman. But because the Senate had adjourned, there was nothing he could do. Brooks had to wait some more.

But he couldn't sit still. Declaring that "he would stand this thing no longer," he returned to the vestibule and threatened to leave a note for

Sumner to, in effect, step outside for a moment. But again, Edmundson persuaded him otherwise; Sumner would only respond by asking him to come to the chamber.

So Brooks returned to the chamber, where Sumner was still stamping his speeches. But the woman conversationalist was gone. Brooks stalked down the aisle. Reaching Sumner's desk, he shouted "Mr. Sumner, I have read your last speech with care and as much impartiality as possible under the circumstances, and I feel it my duty to say that you have libeled my state and slandered my kinsman who is aged and absent and I have come to punish you for it." While still delivering his speech, he began beating Sumner on the head with his "large and heavy" cane while Sumner was still seated. Stunned, Sumner was trapped by his desk and couldn't get away. After several more blows, he was able to rip the desk out of the fastenings that kept it bolted to the floor. And still Brooks kept at it, "with great rapidity and extreme violence," as Sumner crumpled to the floor, a bloody mess.

Behind the assailant and his victim, the straggling senators, finally realizing what was happening, attempted to come to Sumner's aid. John J. Crittenden of Kentucky, upon seeing the attack, "immediately left my seat and went towards the parties for the purpose of interposing." But Keitt, also armed with a heavy cane, stood astride the aisle blocking anyone who might attempt to intervene. In less than two minutes, with about thirty blows having been delivered, it was all over.

BLEEDING SUMNER

The attack on Sumner was a demonstration for many in the North that the two sections could never be reconciled, and the voices that for some time had been saying "If the South wants to go, let the South go" began to grow a little louder.

"What is the Union good for if the Representatives of the different States meet, as enemies, not to deliberate and freely confer on matters of common interest, but to defy each other to mortal combat?" asked Gamaliel Bailey. "Better, far better, that both sections separate, agreeing on an amicable division of the public property, than bathe their hands in fraternal blood."

Others wondered if free speech itself had ceased to exist. "If we continue to laugh at them, or to question their logic, or dispute their facts, are we to be chastised as they would chastise their slaves?" the *New York Post* asked.

George Templeton Strong predicted the attack "will strengthen the Free-soilers and Abolitionists, and it's reasonable and right it should strengthen them." Secretary of State William L. Marcy of New York went Strong one better, forecasting that the Sumner-Brooks affair would cost the Democrats two hundred thousand votes in November.

After this series of violent indignities, some Republicans questioned the very name of the opposition party, and its devotion to democratic ideals. "Those who aid in the extension of human slavery cannot be democrats," wrote one Ohio editor. "Those who believe the murder of an Irish servant not worth investigating cannot be democrats. Those who would strike down, with bloody hand, freedom of speech in the halls of congress, cannot be democrats. If ever any portion of the true democratic spirit pervaded the party which has called itself the Democracy, it has utterly departed."

Republicans certainly tried their best to exploit the attack, distributing a million copies of "The Crime Against Kansas" and linking "Bleeding Kansas" and "Bleeding Sumner" together at every opportunity. Invariably, meetings in support of Sumner outdrew those aimed at protesting Kansas, and one played off the other. Bleeding Sumner was the physical manifestation of the slave power that dominated distant Kansas, something most northerners had no firsthand knowledge of. "Had it not been for your poor head," one supporter wrote Sumner, "the Kansas outrage would not have been felt at the North." The attack on Sumner, Indiana's George W. Julian reflected, "perhaps did more to stir the blood of the people of the Northern States than any of the wholesale outrages thus far perpetrated."

Reactions to the attack echoed the vote for House Speaker earlier in the year, divided purely by section. Though many politicians in the North criticized Sumner's intemperate language—Fletcher Webster, son of the late, great Daniel, suggested that if Sumner were going to "indulge in such attacks . . . he ought at least to take the precaution of wearing an iron pot on his head"—nearly every northern politician excoriated Brooks. Massachusetts congressman Benjamin Butler, passing through the capital on his way to the Democratic convention in Cincinnati, made a great show

of visiting Sumner and called him "a chivalric citizen of the Puritan commonwealth." Brooks, said Butler, was "a coward and an assassin."

Brooks, who was modest in his testimony before Congress, was less
reticent in communications with family, friends, and constituents. "Every
lick went where I intended," Brooks told his brother. And, Christ-like, he
claimed "the fragments of the stick are begged for as sacred relics." Stu-
dents at the University of Virginia sent Brooks a new cane with "a heavy
gold head . . . and also bear upon it a device of the human head, badly
cracked and broken."

Theirs was not the only one. "Four canes have already been subscribed
for in South Carolina and Virginia to present to Col. Brooks, of the House
of Representatives. On the first one, it is said, was engraved the words, 'Hit
him again,' and on the last, for which fifty dollars was raised at a meeting
in Clinton, S. C., is to be engraved, 'The knock down argument.'"

A few southerners were mildly critical, chastising Brooks for the pre-
cise manner of the attack, and for doing it in the Senate. Senator James
Mason of Virginia offered that while Sumner "did not get a lick amiss,"
it would have been better for appearances "had it lighted on him outside
the Chamber." But these were essentially tactical disagreements, not abhorrence at the violence.

Former Georgia congressman Junius Hillyer referred to the incident as
"some sport in the Senate," and asked Howell Cobb to "give my respects
to [Brooks] and offer him my sympathy and most sincere regard."

Toombs laughed that "the Yankees are greatly excited about Sumner's
flogging. They are afraid the practice may become general and many of
[their] heads already feel sore."

Invitations for Brooks to speak and be honored poured in. More than
one newspaper called for Brooks to be South Carolina's next governor, "not
as a reward, but as a testimonial of our high appreciation of patriotism,
firmness, dignity, and statesmanship." Others suggested he should be chosen
president of a future southern confederacy.

And Brooks's defenders condemned "freedom shriekers," those calling
for their man's head while supporting Frémont, who in 1851 had attacked
Mississippi senator Henry Foote, "an old grey-haired man of small stature,"
after a Senate speech critical of Frémont.

Sumner and his ilk "have been suffered to run too long without collars," declared the *Richmond Enquirer*. "They must be lashed into submission."

Northerners, of course, saw it differently, but even the British were appalled. *Blackwood's Edinburgh Magazine* weighed in with the opinion that the attack on Sumner was so "atrocious that we believe the veriest coalheaver in this country would have scorned to have perpetrated it."

Meetings were held in the North to demonstrate solidarity with Sumner. Sympathetic speeches were given, and some yielded memorials intended for delivery to Congress. In a shrewd move, Republicans encouraged the meetings without playing a large role in organizing them, making them seem less overtly political. As they hoped, many quickly evolved into Republican organizational meetings.

The attack on Sumner brought home the distant outrages in Kansas in a way newspaper reports of faraway atrocities never could. If people wondered about the accuracy of reports from Kansas or were inured to violence on the frontier, "Brooks has knocked the scales from the eyes of the blind, and now they see!" a Vermont Republican wrote.

Pennsylvania Republican activist Alexander McClure estimated that the attack "caused many scores of thousands of Democrats of natural antislavery proclivities to sever their connections with the Democratic party." Author Lydia Maria Child, a former editor of the *National Anti-Slavery Standard*, was ready "to mount the rostrum myself. I have such a fire burning in my soul," she wrote a friend, "that it seems I could pour forth a stream of lava."

When the Senate met to consider forming a committee to investigate the attack, Henry Wilson rose to speak in support of his home-state colleague, but deferred to "older senators, whose character . . . eminently fit them for the task," to propose creation of the panel. No Democrat stirred. It fell to Seward to introduce the resolution to launch the investigation.

The committee named to investigate included no Republicans and ruled May 28 that the Senate had no authority to discipline members of the House. The proximate cause of the attack, the report said, was "certain language used by Mr. Sumner in debate." During debate on the report on May 27, Benjamin Wade of Ohio was incredulous that the Senate would take no action in defense of one of its own. "If the principle now announced here is to prevail, let us come armed for the combat." Henry Wilson called the attack "a brutal, murderous, and cowardly assault," to which Butler, by now back in town, shouted "You are a liar!" Both men's comments were stricken from the record and cooler heads prevailed.

The House appointed its committee on May 23, with failed Speaker contender Lewis Campbell as chairman. Other than a few minor details, all the parties—witnesses, attacker, accomplice, and victim—agreed on what happened.

The committee released its report on June 2. Unlike the Senate, the majority ruled that the House did have jurisdiction; that the attack was not justified by the content of Sumner's speech, which in any case was protected by the Constitution (although it also noted as a mitigating factor that "there is no evidence beyond the character of the attack tending to show an intention on the part of Mr. Brooks to kill the Senator"); that Brooks, Keitt, and Edumundson should face varying degrees of discipline—expulsion for Brooks, censure for Keitt and Edmundson. The minority argued precisely the opposite. Referring only to the "alleged assault," the minority report—a good portion of which consisted of Howell Cobb recounting much of Sumner's speech, which the Georgian considered exculpatory evidence—said members could be punished only for acts conducted within the realm of their official duties, not what they did outside of Congress. It was a novel reading, to be sure, but indicative of the chasm that separated North from South.

"The Minority Report . . . goes against the idea of Members of Congress having any privileges at all," opined the *New-York Tribune*. "This is consistent with the system of violence which everywhere prevails where Slavery is concerned."

"The symbol of the North is the pen," cried the Reverend Henry Ward Beecher. "The symbol of the South is the bludgeon."

"BE CAREFUL AND COMMIT NO RASH ACT"

In Kansas, however, the march of violence had slowed during the winter of 1855–56, thanks as much to the frigid weather as to anything President Pierce had done. Temperatures were as cold as twenty-nine below zero. Ice on the ponds and streams ran eighteen inches thick. Snow covered the prairies and the freezing, nearly constant winds blew it into drifts that buried smaller homesteads. But the reduction in armed conflict had done little to create a sense of calm.

On April 19, Sheriff Samuel Jones rode to Lawrence to arrest some men who had been involved in violence earlier in the month, but a crowd of citizens confronted him and he rode away empty handed. He came back the next day with a volunteer posse, and was greeted with threats by the crowd that gathered in the street to confront the small band. On April 23, Jones was back in Lawrence again, this time accompanied by a party of dragoons. Much more reluctant to confront the army than they were to heckle men they saw as the hired guns of the proslavery territorial government, the townsmen stepped aside and Jones arrested six men—although not the man he was really after, lawyer S. N. Wood. So he set up camp on the outskirts of town and waited.

About 10 PM, while he was sitting in his tent, Jones was shot in the back. He survived, but the proslavery press had a field day decrying the antislavery forces as would-be murderers and traitors. While the antislavery press had much the better of the propaganda war, it was not alone in its ability to exaggerate for political effect, and Jones was back on his feet in short order. Free-state leaders in Lawrence condemned the attack, and the only real casualty was the congressional investigating committee, which had to pause because, until tempers cooled, potential witnesses feared retaliation.

When the free-state government that had been elected in January moved to organize in March, a grand jury issued indictments of the leaders, and several men, including would-be governor and Frémont supporter Charles Robinson, were arrested. The arrests in the first week of May played into Republican hands—another outrage committed by the insatiable slave power. But the grand jury, prompted by proslavery chief justice Samuel Lecompte, went further, ordering that two antislavery newspapers be shut down and that the Free State Hotel in Lawrence—actually more of a militia headquarters than a hotel—be torn down, on the grounds that it was a public nuisance. (The hotel's walls were two feet thick at the base and eighteen inches at the top, where they extended two to six feet above the roof and had covered portholes. For a hotel, it was a fortress.) US marshal

Israel Donaldson, acting in response to the grand jury, called for volunteers. Hundreds of proslavery men answered the call.

Fleeing the indictment, Robinson lit out from the territory but was nabbed by a Lexington, Missouri, "vigilance committee," which shipped him off to Leavenworth.

The politics of the wannabe state were growing increasingly unsettled, and they were about to get worse. On the same day Preston Brooks attacked Charles Sumner, Donaldson's posse, a force of about seven hundred men, set up camp on the outskirts of Lawrence. Citizens of the town appealed to the army for relief, but the local commanders simply passed along their concern to state officials, who were not inclined to help. For several days the two sides maintained an uneasy peace. A southern volunteer in the militia wrote home that "I expect before you get this Lawrence will be burnt to the ground."

On May 21, Sheriff Jones demanded that the proslavery men surrender their arms. They gave up the howitzer that had been stationed in town but kept their sidearms. Jones then told them that he would commence enforcing the grand jury's order to deal with the public nuisances, particularly the Free State Hotel. He gave them until 5 PM to remove anything from the building that they wanted to preserve. At that hour, the posse moved into position in front of the hotel, placed four guns to command the site and its approaches, and began firing. The bombardment lasted an hour, then the troopers placed kegs of gunpowder around the hotel and tried to blow it up. That blew out the windows but accomplished little else. So Jones's men set the place on fire, then scattered to loot nearby homes and businesses, including Charles Robinson's house and the newspaper office.

Through all this, the free-state forces stood aside. None were killed or even engaged in any fighting. The only casualty of the day of violence was one proslavery man, who had the misfortune of a portion of a ceiling falling on his head.

While the raid gave the proslavery forces something to do, it gave the free-state forces a priceless propaganda victory that was compounded by exaggerated reporting. Newspapers reported that the town was utterly destroyed and that many people had been killed. Missouri's David Atchison was falsely accused of stoking the flames by urging his fellow statesmen to "spring like your bloodhounds at home upon that damned abolitionist hole." He never gave any such speech.

The violence may have been exaggerated, but it was real. And, like the politics, it was about to get worse.

In December 1855, when Charles Robinson, then the Lawrence agent for the New England Emigrant Aid Company, was trying to negotiate a truce with the official state government, John Brown had been trying to muck it up by devising a plan to attack the proslavery militia encamped on the Wakarusa River. Robinson's argument, which made perfect political sense, was that thus far the antislavery side was winning the war of public opinion. Newspapers were filled with headlines accusing the proslavery forces of violence against civilians, of ignoring law and order, of raiding the border and stealing the election. What Brown proposed would serve no tactical or strategic purpose, Robinson told him, and would simply engender sympathy for men who deserved none.

Aside from the tactic of winning the propaganda war, Robinson was also playing the long game. While slave state emigrants had a head start, demographics favored freedom. More people from the North than the South were interested in coming to Kansas. The South still had massive amounts of land available for settlement, thanks largely to the removal of Native Americans tribes in the 1830s and 1840s. Restless southern farmers, if given a choice, would favor Alabama, Mississippi, Arkansas, and Texas over Kansas.

If Robinson's arguments did not sway Brown, he said, he would have his men forcibly restrain Brown and his followers. Brown, sensing Robinson's resolve, beat a tactical retreat. He supported Robinson as the free-state nominee for governor under the Topeka Constitution. But he had no intention of surrendering. The Second Great Awakening had opened up a universe of theological possibilities to Americans, but John Brown saw no need for a new light. His stern, old-fashioned Calvinism, which would have been at home in seventeenth-century Massachusetts, still shone brightly enough to illuminate his path, and his destination was clear as could be. Brown marshaled his forces and bided his time, knowing that eventually his moment would come.

Three days after the sack of Lawrence, it came with a vengeance. Lawrence had given the free staters yet another propaganda victory that their Republican supporters could put to good use. But this time Brown did not listen to the politicians.

John Brown Jr. possessed his father's name but had the softer facial features of his mother and a much more effective regulator on his passions. He was captain of the Pottawatomie Rifles, a militia unit that did not include his father. Hearing of the latest troubles, Brown had marched with some of his sons from their encampment in southeastern Kansas toward Lawrence. But the standoff ended before the militia could arrive. When John Jr. decided not to proceed on to Lawrence, the elder Brown and his unattached group split off, with Brown declaring he "would rather be ground in the earth than passively submit to pro-slavery usurpation and wrong." But it was the arrival of the news of Charles Sumner's beating that sent Brown over the edge—one witness said he "went crazy—crazy." As Brown left the camp, John Brown Jr. shouted after him, "Father, be careful and commit no rash act."

At 11 PM on May 24, Brown, four of his sons—Frederick, Owen, Salmon, and Oliver—and two other men approached the cabin of James Doyle and his family. Doyle was a proslavery settler from Tennessee who had lived in Kansas about six months. He owned no slaves—had in fact left Tennessee because of a feeling that black slavery was "ruinous to white labor." But once in Kansas, he became active in proslavery politics. When Brown's party knocked on the door of the cabin, they asked for directions to another homestead. Doyle stepped outside to show them the way. No sooner had he opened the door than the men pushed roughly past him into the cabin. Brandishing "pistols and large knives," they quickly subdued Doyle and told him and his two eldest sons that they were now prisoners. These three were dragged outside while Mahala Doyle and her four younger children were left inside under guard.

In the darkness, Brown's men struck quickly. A loud "whoop" preceded a pair of gunshots. Standing near the dirt road that ran a short distance from the cabin, Doyle was shot in the head and stabbed in the chest. One of his sons was repeatedly stabbed in the head and side. The other was stabbed in the head and chest, and his fingers and one arm were cut off as he raised his hands to defend himself from the attackers' broadswords.

Moving swiftly, the band of executioners hurried to the next cabin a half-mile down the road. A barking dog, perhaps disturbed by the wails of the murdered at the Doyle home, had awakened the residents, Louisa and Allen Wilkinson, another Tennessee couple, though they had been in Kansas a year longer than the Doyles. Soon after, a knock came at the door. Four men entered and demanded to know if Wilkinson was a southern sympathizer. Despite his wife's protests, the men pulled Wilkinson from the cabin, telling her that he was being taken prisoner.

He wasn't, any more than James Doyle. And like Doyle he owned no slaves, though Wilkinson was a member of the proslavery legislature. Again using swords, Brown's men hacked at Wilkinson, cutting his throat and gashing his head and sides. He was left in a brush pile about 150 yards from his home, where he was found the next day.

On they went. James Harris's cabin sat hard on Pottawatomie Creek. Brown's men rousted Harris and his wife and child. Three other men were also inside. One, Jerome Glanville, was taken outside and interrogated, then sent back into the cabin. They did the same with Harris—a close questioning about associates, who had been at the cabin, who might still be there, had he ever aided the proslavery cause. Soon, he too was sent back into the cabin. Then William Sherman was taken down to the creek by Brown while two others stood guard at the cabin. Sherman's answers apparently did not satisfy Brown as well as those of Harris and Glanville. Thomas Weiner and Henry Thompson used their broadswords to hack Sherman to pieces and threw him into the creek, where they then washed the blood off their weapons.

Five proslavery men were dead at the hands of free-state supporters, in especially vicious fashion. While Brown had used the cover of night to strike with stealth and escape unscathed, he made certain the result of the attacks would be seen in the light of day. The mutilated bodies, the rage with which the killings took place, sent the message Brown wanted to send: the sins of this land would be purged with blood.

The sympathy that had flowed toward Lawrence was now in danger, the politicians feared, because of Brown's fanatical action. The lack of free-state casualties, Robinson had predicted, might have a negative effect, a situation noted by abolitionist Thomas Wentworth Higginson, who would head for Kansas in early June only to be blockaded at the Missouri River boundary. "I almost hoped to hear that some of their lives had been sacrificed," he wrote, "for it seems as if nothing but that would arouse the Eastern States to act. This seems a terrible thing to say, but these are terrible times."

It was a terrible thing to say, but Higginson was right. To counteract the effect, reporters from Republican papers flooded the territory and filed ever more exaggerated reports of proslavery depredations. These were widely disseminated by the *New-York Tribune* and the *Chicago Tribune* and picked up by hundreds of small dailies across the North. The distorted reporting was accompanied by overwrought editorializing, as when Horace Greeley's paper wrote that Pierce was "sprinkled from head to foot with the blood of the Free State men of Kansas." While politicians and partisan journalists made hay from the tragedy, those on the front line suffered. "The lonely cabin and the unprotected settlement felt the full force of the merciless anarchy that followed," wrote Charles Robinson's biographer.

But it worked. "The doubtful hesitating men are the more excited now," reported Republican national chairman Edwin Morgan, "than those who took the right ground early." Nonviolence had always been more of a tactic than a strategy; now the tactics would have to shift. And with that shift, the full force of the federal government would be brought to bear on Kansas.

{ 7 }

"The Union Is in Danger"

After six national conventions in Baltimore, the party of Andrew Jackson was finally coming to the West. Democrats were convinced of two things as the 1856 convention in Cincinnati approached: Franklin Pierce could not be reelected, and anybody else they might nominate could not possibly lose. Their confidence rested on the assumption that the Republicans would never be organized in time to wage a serious campaign, and that none of the leading men of the new party would step forward to face certain defeat.

"Frémont bids fair to have no opponent for their nomination," the Democratic *Washington Star* reported, "as no man who believes he has a political future before him, will be induced to place himself in a position in which he will be so very badly beaten, as it is admitted their nominee must be." The newspaper predicted Frémont would fare no better than the 1848 Free Soil ticket of Martin Van Buren and Charles Francis Adams, which won a paltry 10 percent of the vote. A pessimistic George Templeton Strong tended to agree. The Democratic convention "may bring forth Pierce, Douglas, Buchanan, or somebody else, as our Southern rulers shall determine, and I doubt if the North be even yet sufficiently irritated to unite in defeating their nominee."

It had escaped no one's attention that Frémont could not even get his father-in-law to support him. Thomas Hart Benton remained loyal to the Democrats. He was in Cincinnati, holding court in a parlor at the Broadway Hotel, where the doyens of the party all came to call on the "lion of the town." He was "electioneering hard and hot" for James Buchanan, for much the same reason most other Buchanan supporters had lined up behind the Old Public Functionary: he had been out of the country—and thus out of the line of fire—during the debate on the Kansas-Nebraska Act. Pierce, Benton told anyone who would listen, "don't know his own mind for one hour." Douglas "is a political filibuster," in the nineteenth century meaning of the word—someone who acts like a military adventurer, without discipline. Nominating Buchanan, Benton asserted, would "restore peace." The Republican *New-York Tribune* concurred in Benton's analysis, although in considerably less complimentary tones. Buchanan would win, the *Tribune* asserted, "by virtue not of his own strength, but of the weakness and odiousness of his rivals." Benton worried about the opposite: "If the Democrats don't unite, they will have plenty to fear from those rag-tags now trying to form new parties."

Among the rag-tags were his daughter and son-in-law, and it pained Jessie to be caught in such a position. "It has been a sore thing to me to see Father and Mr. Frémont arraying themselves against each other," she told Elizabeth Blair Lee. She often compared herself to Portia, wife of Brutus, daughter of Cato, and liked to quote from Julius Caesar: "Think you I am no stronger than my sex, Being so father'd and so husbanded?"

An attempted rapprochement near the end of May ended in bitterness when Jessie came to Washington for a visit only to find that her father was gone. He had already left for Cincinnati, where the sentiment was strong to nominate "the strongest northern man sound on Southern principles."

Franklin Pierce remained in Washington, but his allies established a headquarters in the Customs House Retreat restaurant on Fourth Street, near the new customs house, the symbolic epicenter of federal power and patronage in the city. Former New Hampshire representative Harry Hibbard—tossed out of office for his support of the Kansas-Nebraska Act—was in charge of things for Pierce.

Patronage, however, was not one of Pierce's strong suits. He had made a mess of it in New York, where factional fighting was always a minefield for any Democrat. His base was in New England and the Deep South, except Louisiana, with some support in Arkansas, Kentucky, and North Carolina. He also had support in New York, but it wasn't clear yet which faction of that fractious state's Democratic Party would hold sway. The old Barnburner and Hunker factions had evolved into the Hards and the Softs. There were policy differences between the two, but most of the fighting was over personalities and patronage. Softs were for Pierce; Hards for Buchanan.

And Pierce's support of the Kansas-Nebraska Act and his ardent defense of the proslavery government in Kansas had soured many of his New England supporters. Concord, the New Hampshire capital that had once sent its conquering hero off to war on a magnificent horse paid for at public expense, now witnessed the hero's burning in effigy.

"The Kansas outrages are all imputable to him," Pierce's former secretary wrote, "and if he is not called to answer for them here, 'In Hell they'll roast him like a herring,'" quoting Robert Burns.

For Pierce, success depended on first uniting with Douglas to block Buchanan, then rallying Douglas men if it became clear the Little Giant could not be nominated.

JAMES BUCHANAN.
Courtesy of Library of Congress

STEPHEN A. DOUGLAS.
Courtesy of Library of Congress

If Kansas was a dead weight around Pierce's neck, Douglas could hardly be held blameless. The Kansas-Nebraska Act was more his than Pierce's. And, while he did not have the albatross of incumbency holding him back, Douglas had other problems. In the eyes of newspaperman Murat Halstead, who was covering the convention for the local *Cincinnati Commercial*, Douglas was "a foul-mouthed bully self-convicted of cowardice." This was not an opinion unique to Halstead; plenty of Democrats shared it, and they were determined to deny the nomination to Douglas.

The success of the Pierce-Douglas combination depended on coupling Douglas's western support with Pierce's southern backers. Solid Douglas delegations were Illinois and Missouri, with a scattering of support across Kentucky, Iowa, Ohio, and Wisconsin. The opposition of Lewis Cass, the party's presidential nominee in 1848, deprived Douglas of Michigan. All depended on the Illinoisan's ability to secure Indiana's delegation, where the people and the delegates were with him but which was in considerable doubt because Hoosier party leader Jesse D. Bright, competing with Douglas for western supremacy, was backing Buchanan. If Indiana fell to Buchanan, Ohio was likely to follow suit, and Douglas would be finished.

FRANKLIN PIERCE.
Courtesy of Library of Congress

In addition to the ever-loyal William A. Richardson, Douglas relied on former Ohio congressman David T. Disney and friend and one-time Illinois militia comrade James W. Singleton, a former Whig who had supported the Kansas-Nebraska Act. His chief financial angel was New York financier Edward C. West, who rented a suite of rooms in the Burnet House, Cincinnati's swankiest accommodations.

Senator Douglas, like the other candidates, stayed behind in Washington. Just days before the convention, he bumped into Buchanan in the parlor of the National Hotel. The senator and his "Young America" allies had been referring to Buchanan, twenty-two years Douglas's senior, as an "old fogy" since the 1852 convention. They felt no need to take advice from their elder, but Buchanan avuncularly offered it anyway. Douglas did not take it well. "I expect to choose my Constitutional advisers soon, and am most happy thus to receive your acceptance in advance," he told Buchanan.

Buchanan had not only been out of the country during the Kansas-Nebraska debate, he had somehow—despite a lifetime in electoral and appointive politics that extended so far back into American history that he had once been a Federalist—managed to be out of Congress during the great debates over the Missouri Compromise in 1820, the nullification crisis in 1833, and the Compromise of 1850 as well. Unlike Clay, Jackson, and even Douglas, he had, noted correspondent Murat Halstead, done nothing to earn "splendid ovations or national gratitude."

One could suppose that the unearned fruit and his string of luck were both bound to run out sooner or later. While in London, they almost did. As the US ambassador to the United Kingdom, Buchanan had to tread lightly, with Pierce's foreign policy putting the British in a difficult position. American aggressiveness in the Caribbean and Central America threatened British interests. The long-held dream of southerners to acquire Cuba was made concrete in Pierce's Ostend Manifesto, which laid out the reasons the United States should acquire the island and suggested that war with Spain would follow if a deal could not be worked out. In Nicaragua, American filibuster William Walker, with support from the Pierce administration, had seized control of the government. Pierce would recognize Walker's government less than a month after Buchanan's return to the States, two weeks before the Democratic convention. A disgusted George Templeton Strong feared "administration blundering" would mean war with England over "a quarrel about which no mortal feels interest enough to induce him to spend five dollars."

Still, as the convention approached, Buchanan enjoyed several advantages. First, Franklin Pierce still had to govern, and every telegraphic report from Kansas further dimmed his chances. Second, the moment called for calm and quiet, and Stephen A. Douglas was constitutionally incapable of keeping his mouth shut. The unemployed and naturally aloof Buchanan could sit back at Wheatland, his Lancaster, Pennsylvania, estate, and wait for the party to come to him. Buchanan had created an extensive network over his long career with multiple feints at the presidency in 1844, 1848, and 1852. He could call on it now to create a national campaign.

Buchanan had returned to the United States on April 24, the day after his birthday, following a calm crossing, and gave a brief speech from the Astor House balcony in New York, condemning without a hint of dough-faced irony the "arbitrary power" he had witnessed in the Old World. "I like the noise of democracy," he told a large crowd that had gathered below to serenade him. But he declined the invitation to a dinner, knowing full well that the fractious New York Democrats would bustle for the best seats and likely stir up controversy on his first day back. Buchanan preferred the quiet of his hotel room.

Back in Pennsylvania, things were a little louder. He was greeted by celebratory cannon fire in Philadelphia and Lancaster, and enjoyed a fireworks display, a parade, and a torchlight procession. But that was it. Buchanan closed the front door of Wheatland, began corresponding with allies, and left the dirty work to others.

His usual fixer, John Forney, had been temporarily attached to Pierce as editor of the *Washington Union*, the administration organ. He would soon be back in the fold, but in the meantime, a quartet of senators—John Slidell and Judah P. Benjamin of Louisiana, James A. Bayard of Delaware, and Indiana's Jesse Bright—had been working nonstop on his behalf. They were a diverse lot.

The white-haired, red-faced, arrogantly officious Slidell had been born in New York and migrated to Louisiana, where he demonstrated a gift for political corruption, helping to secure a victory for James K. Polk in the 1844 presidential contest by hauling Irish immigrants from place to place around the state to vote multiple times. Worried that Forney and J. Glancy Jones, a House member who served as Buchanan's other amanuensis, were not up to the rigors of a national campaign, Slidell—who was always certain he was the smartest guy in the room—swooped in to take over.

Bright, a paunchy Hoosier, was the personification of the Northern Man with Southern Loyalties, a common species in his native Southern Indiana. He was contesting the presidential nomination as a surrogate for his battle with Douglas over who would be the biggest fish in the medium-sized pond of Northwestern politics. David Disney had told Douglas that Bright was "acting in good faith toward you," but it wasn't true. Slidell had promised Bright control of patronage in the West if he joined with Buchanan, and Bright seized the moment.

Benjamin was as urbane and agreeable as Bright was rough-hewn and ruthless. The Louisianan was not always smiling, but the countenance of his face seemed to give that impression, and he was unfailingly polite. He was that rarest of political animals—a Jewish southerner—and that outsider status gave him a certain freedom.

Bayard brought a hint of eastern establishment to the group. He was the scion of a prominent Delaware family, a considerable advantage in a state so small, and he was both ideologically and temperamentally in sync with the prospective nominee from neighboring Pennsylvania.

Some southern men had their doubts about Buchanan, but there were prominent exceptions. Virginia governor Henry Wise, an old drinking buddy of Franklin Pierce, was solidly in Buchanan's camp, and considered a likely running mate. And Georgia senator Robert Toombs was at least open to his candidacy. "I saw Buck in London last summer and he talked to me very satisfactorily on the slavery question," he said, going on to note that he "will not support any man who is not clear, distinct and unequivocal on this subject." But early on Toombs was inclined to stick with Pierce, if for no better reason than "we cannot do much better than to run him." Thomas R. R. Cobb alerted his brother Howell, who was leaning toward Buchanan, to keep a watchful eye on Toombs and Alexander Stephens, who "are very warm for Pierce."

Toombs feared a replay of past conventions, where the leading men failed to prevail, prompting deal-making and a lesser light being chosen. "Buck and Douglas are the most prominent, and are likely to beat each other and give place to some incompetent outsider," he confided to former Georgia governor George W. Crawford. In the end, though, he supposed one of them might emerge victorious.

"The indications are so strong in favor of Buchanan that it is difficult to see how men can resist," noted prominent Georgia pol John E. Ward, who would be elected president of the convention. "Yet they do resist, and the intrigues to defeat him are disgusting." Ward's early take was that Buchanan was doomed, and that a dark horse was likely to claim the nomination as the three leading contenders ripped each other to shreds.

Buchanan forces set up shop at the home of Samuel L. M. Barlow, a Wall Street lawyer and Democratic rainmaker who had relocated temporarily to the Queen City to oversee completion of his Ohio and Mississippi Railroad. Joining the four aforementioned senators were New York journalist George Butler and Buchanan's former legation secretary in London, Dan Sickles. While Barlow's home was headquarters for private councils, Bayard, Benjamin, Bright, and Slidell took a suite across the street at the luxurious Burnet House for the purposes of wining and dining delegates and state party leaders. Their aim was to disrupt what they correctly feared was a Pierce-Douglas coalition aimed at depriving Buchanan of the nomination, deadlocking the convention, and combining their forces to win the two-thirds majority—198 votes—for one of their own.

"SPURNED BECAUSE HE IS KNOWN"

Far from February's freezing temperatures during the Margaret Garner trial, Cincinnati in June was a steamy, sweltering "great political exchange," populated by convention "buzzards and camp followers—pimps and prostitutes, political and other gamblers, that are inseparable from such events" as great party conventions. "Rumors of all kinds are flying in every direction," reported Murat Halstead, among the "multitudes that now swarm in the city."

Most politicians stayed at the Burnet House, several blocks from and high above the Ohio River. The five-story, domed, 240-room behemoth billed itself as the "finest in the United States." Entering the hotel required the often hefty visitors to climb a steep flight of steps to the entrance, where they huffed and puffed across a colonnaded porch to the lobby.

A short walk away was Smith & Nixon's Hall, a windowless, sweaty, "black-hole of Calcutta," as Benton called it. The convention hall had no street frontage and had to be entered via other buildings or a passageway from the sidewalk. Perhaps worst of all for the delegates, there were no drinking establishments nearby. And, as was so often the case, the hall was too small to accommodate all those who showed up and hoped to enter. Legal entry was limited to delegates and reporters. At about 10 AM, an hour before the doors opened, a large crowd began gathering outside, clogging Fourth Street between Main and Walnut, making it impossible for those who were actually allowed inside to fight their way through to the doors. The press was admitted through a back entrance, and delegates were left to claw their way through, which they began doing about 11 AM on June 2.

Democrats being Democrats, the convention opened with a disturbance, a fist fight, or a near riot—depending on who was doing the telling—when Frank Blair Jr. forced his way onto the floor with his free soil, pro-Benton Missouri delegation. After some "wild cursing and shouts," accompanied by a few raised fists and "excessive" profanity, along with some pleas of "Don't shoot" and "Pitch in," order was restored. William Richardson had the Missourians run from the hall. The Buchanan forces demonstrated their majority support by electing one of their own as permanent chairman, John Ward, and stacking the credentials committee. Thus, before the first ballot was even held, Pierce's chances of securing the nomination were dealt a mortal blow. The credentials committee deferred a decision on a dispute between the Hard and Soft factions of the New York delegation, raising the possibility that the state's 35 votes would be divided between them. Pierce needed all of the Softs to have any chance. Such a Solomonic decision would also be bad news for the Know Nothings' candidate; Millard Fillmore was counting on a wedge of disgruntled Hards defecting to his cause. If they were on the inside of the Democratic cage, that seemed much less likely.

The next day, the credentials committee officially barred the Blair delegation from Missouri, but it was not yet ready to decide on New York. And, as was traditional with the Democrats, nomination would require that two-thirds majority of 198 votes, effectively handing southerners a veto over the candidate. "This is the old story," Halstead opined, "a Northern man with Southern principles—a man from the North and a platform from the South."

Before they decided on the man, they would decide on the platform.

On June 4, the convention's third day, the platform committee brought its work to the floor of Smith & Nixon's Hall a little after 10 AM. The slavery planks, calling for "non-interference by Congress with slavery in the territories or in the District of Columbia" and declaring "that Congress has no power, under the Constitution, to interfere with or control the domestic institutions of the several states," were adopted unanimously and "given double rounds of stamping and cheers," although they hedged on whether popular sovereignty should be invoked before or after statehood, providing "an elastic platform susceptible of double reading" on that issue. And the candidate would provide no clarity. Buchanan himself interpreted it two different ways, saying early on that territories should be "perfectly free to form and regulate their domestic institutions in their own way," and later that sovereignty applied "when about to enter the Union as a State." It was a significant difference, and the distance between the two notions would add immensely to the problems that lay ahead for Buchanan. Douglas would continue to dance around the issue as well, inspiring Lincoln to note, "Douglas is a great man—at keeping from answering questions he don't want to answer."

Those anti-Nebraska Democrats who had held back from signing on with the Republicans until the convention wrote a platform now had their answer. It was time to decide.

Delegates agreed to adjourn until midafternoon, hoping that when they came back they would have a settlement of the New York question, allowing them to move on to nominating a candidate. When they returned, however, they found that not only were the Hards and Softs still at each other's throats but, almost literally, the sky was falling.

Actually, it was the roof. "Some enterprising individual" who did not have a ticket had found his way into the space between the ceiling and the roof of the hall, and in so doing had kicked loose some plaster, which began falling on the surprised heads of a few delegates. He was quickly found and escorted from his hiding place, but some delegates must have wondered if the roof caving in on them was an omen.

With the ceiling—if not for certain the sky—secure above them, the delegates proceeded to approve, plank by plank, the rest of the platform, endorsing a transcontinental railroad, US adventurism in Central America, and the acquisition of Cuba, although these provisions were not met with the unanimity that greeted the slavery planks. When that task was completed, they again agreed to adjourn until 9 AM on Thursday, June 5, when they would at last hear from the credentials committee on New York and begin voting on a nominee.

The credentials committee, striving to keep the peace, did indeed cut the New York baby in half, splitting the state's delegate votes evenly between the Hards and the Softs and dealing a death blow to Pierce's prospects.

With New York split, the voting could begin late in the afternoon. The hall was filled to the rafters, literally—some youngsters had climbed into the catwalks for a better view—and it was a stuffy, steamy room that reeked of perspiration and cigar smoke, the air still but for the "flutter of a thousand fans" that seemed to be having no effect. The roll call started with Maine—it was conducted not alphabetically, like modern conventions, but geographically—and moved down the coast and inland from there. The split New York delegation gave 18 votes for Pierce and 17 for Buchanan, a result that brought forth a "burst of applause followed by a storm of shrill hisses" and demands from the chair for order, which were slow to be heeded. When the first ballot was over, Buchanan didn't even have half the votes, much less the two-thirds necessary, with 135 votes to 122 for Pierce and 33 for Douglas. Lewis Cass of Michigan, the losing 1848 nominee whose introduction by Samuel Inge of California had elicited a "rattle of surprise" from the delegates, had 5 votes. Along with divided New York, Pierce's New England bloc was cracked right off the bat when Buchanan won a majority in Maine and swept Connecticut. Pierce's home base had already fallen apart, although he held a 74–34 lead over Buchanan among slave state delegates. In the northwestern corner of the hall, a telegraph clicked out the results of the first inconclusive ballot to the candidates back home and the nation.

And on it went, pretty much unchanged for five ballots, except Pierce's count was suffering a small but steady decline, as if his political life force could be seen slipping away in the numbers. Another omen distracted the delegates during the fifth roll call, when a large flag adorning the stage fell from its mounting and floated ignominiously to the floor. But it was a momentary blip. Attendants swooped in and gathered up the standard, and the sixth ballot was immediately gaveled in. Messengers scurried up and down the aisles, and the telegraph maintained a constant business. But there was no real news to report.

Through fourteen ballots no candidate mustered even a majority, let alone approached the two-thirds necessary for nomination. So after the fourteenth fruitless roll call, the convention adjourned Thursday night. That evening, Douglas and Pierce delegates hatched a plan that they hoped would break the deadlock. It had become clear that neither of their men was going to sweep the convention. Buchanan was too strong. So on Friday, June 6, one of Pierce's lieutenants, Harry Hibbard, took the floor. "The time has come when the New Hampshire delegation deems it a duty that she owes to her distinguished son and to the Democratic Party, to yield her cherished preferences for that statesman, and to withdraw his name from the convention," he said to polite applause. And then added, "New Hampshire desires to express her preference for her second choice—Stephen A. Douglas, of Illinois," which was met with considerably louder and more sustained applause.

"He was taken up, in the first place, because he was unknown," opined the *New York Times*, referring to Pierce's dark horse nomination in 1852, "and now he is spurned because he is known."

Most of Pierce's support went to Douglas, but not all of it. On the fifteenth ballot, Buchanan won 168 votes, to 118 for Douglas and 3 holdouts for Pierce. Douglas peaked at 122 votes on the sixteenth ballot—the second of the day on Friday—and his supporters realized he was not going to be nominated. Douglas might be the "very embodiment of pluck," as a fellow Illinois pol described him, but he knew the game was up. William A. Richardson, Douglas's staunch ally from the Kansas-Nebraska debate, then rose to read a letter the Little Giant had written two days prior. Greeted by defiant shouts of "No! No! Sit down—ballots! Ballots!" Richardson, in his "ample, yet far from melodious" voice, tried to silence the crowd so he could be heard, shouting "Mr. President," to get the attention of the chair.

"Sit down," came the reply from those around him. "We want the ballot and nothing else."

"I am far from advising," he began, but was then shouted down again with a roar of "Don't withdraw Doug. Stop!"

Gesticulating wildly to make room amid the crowd surging around him, Richardson shouted out "I shall say what I would and I am far from advising any man what he shall do at this hour. But I feel I have imposed on me a duty to—"

"Damn the duty," shouted someone in the Missouri camp, "sit down there."

"A duty to Stephen A. Douglas as well as to our common cause," Richardson continued. "As a friend of that statesman, that I cannot advance his interests or the success of the party, by continuing him in this contest."

Richardson then drew out a letter from his vest pocket and ceremoniously unfolded it, even as the combination of cheers and jeers rose ever louder around him. "I see in the telegraphic dispatches in the newspapers," he began reading, "that there is danger of an embittered spirit in your convention. I wish you and all my friends to remember that the ascendency of our principles is a thousand fold more important than my own elevation. If the withdrawal of my name will ensure harmony, I beg you not to hesitate to take the step. My highest wish is granted if the convention is unanimous for the platform that embodies the principles of the Democracy of the Republic."

A wild scene interrupted Richardson again, this time with cheers far outnumbering the few remaining jeers.

"If the nomination of Mr. Pierce or Mr. Buchanan, or any other of the Democratic statesmen named for the office can be secured by your aid," he resumed reading, "I beg that he may receive it."

The convention rose as one and cheered, and the demonstration lasted for a "prolonged" period. When order was restored, with some difficulty, a seventeenth ballot was ordered, and the roll call began. Each state in turn—even fractious New York—unanimously cast its votes for Buchanan.

The strategy was straightforward enough. Douglas was forty-three years old. Buchanan was sixty-five and seemed older. (Coincidentally, both men had been born on April 23, Buchanan in 1791, Douglas in 1813.) Douglas felt secure in stepping aside, confident that his magnanimity in 1856 would be rewarded come 1860, and Buchanan would be too old to stand in his way. Pierce would be forgotten. The depth of Pierce's failure as chief executive was reflected in the fact that he was the only nineteenth-century elected president to seek renomination and be denied.

"The Union Is in Danger"

When the *Columbus Enquirer* from Georgia suggested in the wake of the Nebraska debate the need for an all-southern presidential ticket, Alexander Stephens had reacted negatively. "This I am decidedly opposed to," he wrote to another newspaper's editor. "What we want is a sound national organization upon broad—national—republican principles. We want no sectional men or sectional issues." And then he added a qualifier: "At least so long as national men enough can be found to make a party on national issues and principles."

Having now nominated a northern man with southern principles for president, the convention broke for lunch before turning its attention to pairing him up with a southern man with national—not northern—principles. There were plenty of possibilities. Richardson noted that Buchanan had "forty candidates for Vice & will cheat them all."

Kentuckian Linn Boyd, a former congressman and recent Speaker of the House, was the first name tossed out. He was quickly joined by John A. Quitman, a member of the House, a former Mississippi governor, and a hero of the Mexican War, "the first to plant the victorious American flag on the famous Hall of the Montezumas," according to Thomas Harris of Illinois, the man who placed Quitman's name in nomination. A Louisiana delegate rose to name Kentucky's John C. Breckinridge, the man who had proved instrumental in coordinating the development of the Kansas-Nebraska Act. Key Democrats had been writing to Breckinridge since the beginning of the year concerning the vice presidency, including John Slidell and John Forney. On the evening of June 5, Pennsylvania delegates had visited Breckinridge to make a pitch for him to bring his loyalists into the Buchanan camp and join him on the ticket. Breckinridge thanked them for their interest but said he would be sticking with Douglas. With that option foreclosed, they reasoned, they could reopen the vice presidential bid. Breckinridge had just eaten lunch with Iowa delegate W. F. Coolbaugh, who told him he was going to push him for the vice presidency whether the Kentuckian liked it or not. But Breckinridge had already committed to Boyd, much his senior in Bluegrass politics. Boyd was fifty-five and boasted a career stretching back into the 1830s. Breckinridge had reached the constitutionally required age of thirty-five only a few months earlier. "I hold that unless there are very special reasons for having it otherwise," Breckinridge, standing on a chair, told the delegates, "promotion should follow seniority, and I beg leave therefore, most respectfully to decline to be a candidate."

Nearly a dozen others had their names entered in the contest, and none reached even 60 votes on the first ballot, with Quitman in the lead at 59 and Breckinridge, despite his demurral, second at 55. Boyd led the also-rans at 33.

When Vermont cast its ballot, delegate David Smalley shouted that "no Democrat has a right to refuse his services when his country calls," and cast the state's 5 votes for Breckinridge. When the second ballot began, Smalley's declaration inspired others, and Breckinridge swept to victory with 117 votes. The crowd surged around him in wild cheering, "hats and handkerchiefs waved in the air—all dignities and proprieties waived altogether," and cannons positioned outside the hall were fired off in celebration.

The youthful Breckinridge was a graceful man with delicate features. "Nature seemed to have favored him far beyond most men," a colleague once gushed. Even an unfriendly reporter noted that "on the whole there is a poetic glimmer about him."

When he rose to address the convention that had just elevated him and demanded a speech, he was "proud, defiant, and full of passion, tempered by educated discretion." He assured the delegates that "strong in the principles of Jefferson, enforced by the irresistible temper of Jackson, the people will entrust the men you have named for their government. I hope, in that event, I shall never forfeit the confidence of the Democracy of America."

In terms of uniting the party, Breckinridge served several purposes: He was a Douglas ally, and one of the Pierce administration's few strong defenders in the House. His youth blunted the "old fogy" charges against Buchanan. And he was a border-state man, not a man of the Deep South. The Democrats had, at least geographically, rejected the extreme and settled on two men of the middle to make their case that radicals were threatening to tear the country apart.

The most-radical southerners had lost Pierce, Quitman, and the Douglas platform plank on popular sovereignty, but the party knew that no matter how mad or disappointed the fire-eaters were, they had nowhere to turn. They certainly weren't going to vote for any Republican, and Fillmore and the American Party were almost as unacceptable.

The Republican *New-York Tribune* predictably derided "the studied equivocation, sonorous verbiage and diplomatic ambiguities" of the Democratic convention, but the response of Jeremiah S. Black, a Pennsylvania ally of Buchanan's and his future attorney general, was both more typical and an indication that the Democrats were hardly interested in democracy. "No greater service could be rendered to the cause of truth than by putting Greeley where he ought to be. He is a liar and the truth is not in him,"

Black spewed forth. "Shall this political turkey buzzard be permitted to vomit the filthy contents of his stomach on every decent man in the country without having his neck twisted?"

After the violence that had already rent Washington over the past several weeks, threats of more coming from a chief legal adviser to the leading party's candidate was not a sign of calmer days ahead.

The unhappy truth was that calm served neither party's interest. If Republicans were prepared to regale voters with stories of Bleeding Kansas and Bleeding Sumner until their own ears bled, the Democrats were just as ready to frighten voters with the specter of secession.

And it wasn't just rabid Garrisonians who provided the Democrats with ammunition. It was also Joshua Giddings, who had said, "I look forward to the day when there shall be a servile insurrection in the South" and called for "a war of extermination against his master." It was William Seward who had appealed to a "higher law" than the Constitution to justify resistance to the Fugitive Slave Act. Speaker of the House Nathaniel Banks had once suggested he was perfectly "willing . . . to let the Union slide."

In accepting the nomination, Buchanan took a swipe at the American Party, asserting that "no party founded on religious or political intolerance towards one class of American citizens, whether born in our own or in a foreign land, can long continue to exist in this country." That the Democratic Party was founded on just such a basis—to safeguard white property and political power against enslaved blacks—seems to have slipped Buchanan's mind. And little wonder that it would, as he went on to declare that on the subject of the late agitation over slavery, "we may safely anticipate that it is rapidly approaching a 'finality.'"

But not, he was certain, if the Republicans were victorious. "The Black Republicans must be, as they can be with justice, boldly assailed as disunionists, and this charge must be reiterated again and again," he wrote later in June. The cool, considerate Buchanan was making essentially the same argument the supposedly hotheaded abolitionists were making: elect me, or the other guy will wreck the country. "The union is in danger & the people everywhere begin to know it."

"Civil War Is Just Upon Us"

Back in Kansas, the arrest of the free-state leadership proved to be counterproductive. On the outside, Charles Robinson had possessed few means to slam the brakes on John Brown. Locked up, he had none. After Pottawatomie, Brown melted into the countryside, out of the reach of both the proslavery men who wanted to hang him and antislavery officialdom, which wanted to contain him.

On June 1, as Democrats were arriving in Cincinnati, Brown attached his band of ten men to the twenty-five-strong Prairie City militia. He was determined to gain the freedom of two of his sons—John Jr. and Jason— who had been taken into custody by territorial militia and handed over to the army.

The territorial militia, made up mostly of Missourians and commanded by deputy US marshal Henry Clay Pate, was camped at Black Jack Springs on the Santa Fe Trail, about halfway between Lawrence and the site of the Pottawatomie Massacre. Pate had been assigned to find John Brown and other free-state fugitives and arrest them. Unfortunately for Pate, Brown found him first.

The free-state forces attacked on the morning of June 2, while Democratic delegates were getting ready to convene and Pate's men were eating breakfast.

Black Jack was the first fight in Kansas between organized militia units, but that didn't make it any less of a disorganized brawl. Only a few dozen men were involved. Through about three hours of battle, the sides exchanged gunfire and tried without much success to outmaneuver each other. Four proslavery men were killed. Brown's men got pinned down in a ravine. In an attempt to assist his father, Frederick Brown rode in to save the day, shouting, "Father, we have them surrounded and cut off their communications!" Though a ruse, it was enough to persuade Pate that free-state reinforcements were on their way, and he raised a white flag. But Brown did not feel himself bound by the rules of war, and when Pate crossed into his lines to negotiate, Brown held him at gunpoint, marched him out to his own line, and ordered that the men surrender or Pate would be killed. Pate protested, but to no avail. "Had I known who I was fighting, I would not have trusted to a white flag," Pate said later. He surrendered his men to Brown.

Brown achieved his purpose, arranging a prisoner swap that freed Pate and regained the liberty of John Jr. and Jason Brown. Brown's sons were singled out in the "articles of agreement for the exchange of prisoners," a legalistic document the sides exchanged outlining the terms for the release of those held captive. "The sons of Capt. John Brown Sr., Capt. John Brown Jr. and Jason Brown are to be amongst the liberated parties (if not already liberated) and are to be exchanged for Capt. Pate and Lieut. Brockett respectively."

A list of the wounded prepared by Brown included his son Salmon, who was "accidentally wounded after the fight & liable to remain a cripple."

But Brown could claim a great moral victory, and more than one correspondent claimed that "civil war is just upon us." Northern newspapers hailed the triumph, while southern newspapers rushed to "correct" the record, claiming, "Northern papers have been filled with ridiculous misrepresentations." But it wasn't just abolitionist journalists stoking the flames. A North Carolina paper headlined its combined report on Pottawatomie and Black Jack with THE CIVIL WAR IN KANSAS and filled the story with sensational accounts of the "horribly mutilated" victims of John Brown and the torching of proslavery settlements.

The Democrats had their candidate, and now they had their cause. Republicans already had their cause. Now they had to settle on a candidate.

{ 8 }

"Free Soil, Free Speech, Free Men, and Frémont"

After their preliminary national meeting in Pittsburgh, Republicans around the nation were scurrying to turn the gathering's organizational promise into practical activity at the precinct level. They accomplished much. In the nearly six months between the post-Christmas conclave at Francis Preston Blair's home and the start of the Republican National Convention in Philadelphia, the party had gone from having no organizations in half the free states to having at least a bare-bones structure in all of them. This was no mean feat considering the competing interests that had to be massaged, if not reconciled. In some states, it was Know Nothings. In others, it was temperance advocates. In still others it was antislavery Germans. Balancing these often mutually exclusive groups took tact, time, and money, and fully embracing any one group risked alienating another. Some were more tactful than others. Indiana's George W. Julian, for example, essentially talked himself out of the party by harping on his refusal to cooperate with Know Nothings, who were a powerful force in his state's politics. He admitted that his contrariness—he called it his integrity—"has laid me prostrate, and precipitated me out of politics." Israel Washburn meant it as a complaint but got to the heart of the matter when he noted the party's "quest for as small a modicum of Republicanism as will answer, & as large an infusion of K.N.ism as will be safe."

Frémont backers kept their machinations under wraps through the late winter and early spring. They were aided financially by Frémont's old comrades in California, the state's bankers, and his largest creditor, Palmer, Cook & Company. But as March turned to April they were ready to go public, and the first major newspaper endorsement appeared in the *Cleveland Herald*. Jessie Frémont reported to Elizabeth Blair Lee that "just here & now I am quite the fashion—5th Avenue asks itself, 'Have we a Presidentess among us?'" In response to this less than spontaneous burst of popular acclaim, within the week William Seward was privately conceding that Frémont would almost certainly be the candidate. "Frémont is not the first choice of a majority," noted correspondent Murat Halstead, "but is the second choice of nearly everybody." Turning up the heat another notch a week later, a Frémont letter to Kansas's soon-to-be-arrested free-state leader Charles Robinson noted that "as you stood by me firmly and generously when we were defeated by the nullifiers in California, I have every disposition to stand by you in your battle with them in Kansas." The *New-York Tribune* ran the letter, dated March 17, on April 10, and it was widely published in other Republican journals.

Gamaliel Bailey, however, remained "apprehensive that the Republican movement is about to slip from the control of men of principle"—by which he meant himself—"into the hands of Place hunters and politicians," by which he meant virtually everyone else. He specifically cited Henry Wilson, Horace Greeley, Nathaniel Banks, and Schuyler Colfax, who were "demor-alized by a passion for immediate success." Looked at another way, Bailey was interested in making a statement; the others were interested in winning.

Bailey called the move to nominate Frémont "a regular plot." It certainly wasn't a secret plot, as Bailey had been aware of it for months. Nevertheless, complaining that stalwarts like Chase and Seward had been "thrust aside," Bailey held out hope that "the Frémont movement will exhaust itself by its own hot haste before the Philadelphia Convention."

Frémont's lack of a public record on slavery was a concern to Bailey, and the abolitionist editor could derive scant comfort from what little record there was—for instance, Frémont's decision as a senator to support the abolition of the slave trade in the District of Columbia but not the end of slavery itself in the District. Supporters were trying to make much of the fact that the California legislature had refused to reelect Frémont in 1851, alleging a slave-power plot against him. But the record revealed that Frémont was the victim of internecine politics in the new state that were only tangentially related to slavery. He may have evolved on the issue over the years, but in 1851 his Senate defeat did not make him a "martyr to the cause of freedom." Insiders debated whether Frémont should engage in the type of letter-writing that politicians did in those days in lieu of openly campaigning. Other than the letter to Robinson—in effect, his public declaration of candidacy—Frémont had been silent. Those counseling reticence—Frémont's natural state, in any case—won out. There would be no more letters until the convention.

Bailey had practical objections as well as ideological ones. He feared Frémont would not fare well in the crucial states of Pennsylvania, New Jersey, Indiana, and Illinois, and told Salmon Chase up front that he thought Seward would be the better candidate of the two in Pennsylvania and New Jersey, likely because Seward had done less to offend the growing immigrant populations in those two states.

Seward believed the same thing, and debated with Thurlow Weed about the best course. Weed consistently argued that 1856 was the wrong year to be the Republican candidate, and that Seward should wait until 1860. "We do not want [Seward] nominated for fun" was his refrain. More colorfully, Murat Halstead wrote that Weed wanted to keep Seward "nicely pickled away to turn up at some time auspicious to him." At the same time, Weed didn't want Seward to withdraw his name from consideration ahead of the convention, providing both flexibility and leverage. Seward's son Frederick believed that his father's "own feelings would have inclined him" to make the race. Weed, who had met Seward in 1824 when the newspaperman helped pull the politician's carriage out of a muddy ditch in Rochester, saw it as his duty to keep Seward out of this ditch and avoid the senator's getting stuck in a hole he couldn't escape.

Bailey acknowledged the likelihood of defeat in any case, no matter who the candidate was, but he argued that "with our principles themselves boldly proclaimed," the result of defeat "would not be disorganization and demoralization," as he suggested it would be under Frémont, but "the precursor of victory in 1860." Indeed, defeat with Chase or Seward running on a strong platform would be preferable to victory by Frémont with a weak platform, which would result in a "victory almost fruitless."

It was just this sort of thinking that had helped dissuade real politicians from engaging with the likes of Bailey in the past. They knew that defeat was not victory, and that you couldn't do anything unless you won elections. Some appreciated the esprit, but all of them could count.

Bailey opted to sit this one out unless he got his way. Frémont was "an amiable, honorable Gentleman, with a gift for exploration and adventure, but without the knowledge of Politics or political men, or the value and aims of our movement. Should he be nominated with a bold platform, and place himself Squarely upon it, it might become my duty to support him; but should he be nominated on a vague declaration respecting a mere transient question"—he meant Kansas statehood—"I fear I should be obliged to retire from the Struggle."

The "amiable and honorable" description of Frémont was half on the mark. He could be quite amiable, and he was certainly honorable within his own definition of the term. But he could also be petulant, rash, and prone to overdefensiveness when challenged. Those traits tended to materialize under stress, such as being trapped in a blizzard in the mountains. They were not immediately apparent in the parlors of Washington and New York. What was apparent was Frémont's startling naïveté toward politics, at least as it was practiced by the men running the Republican Party. "I am afraid several volumes might be filled with what he don't know about the first elements of Politics," Horace Greeley warned.

How Frémont was viewed often involved a generation gap. Men in their forties, like Greeley, were more suspect than those in their thirties, like New York journalist Charles A. Dana, who enthusiastically supported Frémont as "the true metal." Frémont's best biographer contends that this quality was a kind of dynamic "aloofness [that] also helped to preserve a long-burnished charisma," and in one-one-one meetings, "he projected an impressively dashing, commanding presence."

Seward was publicly ambivalent about being Bailey's sacrificial lamb in 1856 to make victory possible for someone else in 1860, and Weed was dead set against it. While Seward had said that he did not want to "bear the responsibility of such a disaster" as he supposed defeat would bring—a staggering miscalculation—he also spent considerable time working with a writer on a campaign biography and having his speeches printed in pamphlet form, just in case. He was also feeling abandoned by both Weed and Greeley, whom he said had "struck hands with enemies of mine, and sacrificed me for the good of the cause." For the moment, the New Yorkers were ready to acquiesce to Frémont, however unenthusiastically, as an act of self-preservation. "Thurlow Weed says he is contented with Frémont, and if so, of course Seward is," newspaperman John Bigelow reported. Weed was considerably more contented than Seward, who at a minimum wanted to make the magnanimous public gesture of stepping aside himself rather than be disgraced by a public rejection at his own party's first convention.

Support for Seward among the rank and file was wide and deep. If he contested the nomination, he would have almost unanimous support from Michigan, one of Weed's minions reported back, and other western states looked good for him as well. Bailey, though formally backing Supreme Court justice John McLean at least in part because he believed Seward was not a candidate, wrote to Julian that "Seward is by all odds the strongest man we could run"—meaning strongest antislavery man. At the same time, Bailey feared Seward would lead the party to defeat. In any case, he believed McLean offered the greater chance to win in the battleground states.

Seward seemed to think that the attack on Sumner was having a salutary effect on northern voters, a result that was beginning to worry the elected men of the South. "The excited sensibilities of the North have served to alarm the Southern politicians in the slavery interest," he told his wife. The New Yorker was not sure about the outcome, but he was sure it didn't involve him. Just days before the convention began, he wrote to his wife that "the nomination of either the California candidate or the Ohio judge is regarded as a foregone conclusion."

Despite concerns about Frémont's youth and inexperience, Horace Greeley endorsed him in a series of editorials in the days leading up to the convention, mostly because he considered him the most electable. "There is no name which can find such favor with the masses," he asserted, and suggested that inexperience might not be such a bad thing. "We have had enough of third-rate lawyers and God knows what rate generals." The always mercurial editor hedged some in private, though, suggesting the possibility of a Banks-Frémont ticket, or even a Banks nomination with Kentucky abolitionist Cassius M. Clay, a cousin of the immortal Henry Clay, in the number-two spot. Seward praised Greeley's efforts on Frémont's behalf, saying "he has done the very best thing in the rightest way."

Though Weed worried that defeat was inevitable for a party so new and unorganized, the enthusiasm he witnessed among voters was beginning to alter his view. As June approached, he still leaned toward waiting for 1860, when, he believed, the stench of nativism would be greatly reduced and Seward would be more acceptable to a wider swath of the electorate. But he wasn't entirely certain, and so opted to wait until Philadelphia to decide for sure.

As for Justice John McLean, his case for Republican nomination rested, ironically, on the same foundation as James Buchanan's case for the Democratic nomination. At seventy-one, he was acceptable to conservatives, nativists, and former Whigs, had been around forever, and had a similarly extensive if undistinguished record of public service as a member of Congress, postmaster general under James Monroe and John Quincy Adams, and as a Jackson appointee to the high court. The movement to nominate him was fairly described as an attempt "to reorganize the defunct Whig Party under a thin disguise of Republicanism."

That helped explain why former Whig and Republican latecomer Abraham Lincoln was in the McLean camp. "The news of Buchanan's nomination came yesterday," Lincoln wrote shortly before the convention to Lyman Trumbull, the man who had bested him in the Senate race the year before, "and a good many whigs, of conservative feelings, and slight pro-slavery proclivities, withal, are inclining to go for him, and will do it, unless the Anti-Nebraska nomination shall be such as to divert them. The man to effect that object is Judge McLean. . . . I think they would stand Blair or Frémont for Vice-President—but not more." Lincoln made clear, though, that this was simply his impression of others. "I think I may trust you to believe I do not say this on my own personal account. I am *in*, and shall go for any one nominated unless he be '*platformed*' expressly, or impliedly, on some ground which I may think wrong." Lincoln was not playing hard to get, but no one knew the importance of words more than he did, and as late as June 7, just ten days before the convention, he still couldn't bring himself to say "Republican," referring to the prize about to be awarded as "the Anti-Nebraska nomination." That did not bode well for a united November front in the crucial state of Illinois.

Fellow Illinoisan Orville H. Browning told Trumbull that "many, very many, tenderfooted Whigs could readily support McLean, but were fearful of Frémont."

Most Republican members of Congress leaned toward McLean, asserted Ohio's Ben Wade—of the serious candidates, he was best known to them, was part of the Washington scene, and had been around politics and government the longest. The group had some regional diversity and included members from Indiana, Ohio, Vermont, and Maine. But McLean had opposed Chase's successful bid for governor the year before, fearing that he was too strident in his antislavery sentiments. Wade, like Lincoln, was simply assessing the field. He was among those who did not fondly remember McLean's dealings with the Fugitive Slave Act, and believed that "if McLean is with us at all it is but timidly and feebly."

McLean, like Chase, had his home-state problems, in part created by his opposition to Chase. "I think our U.S. judges are the worst men we have," wrote William C. Howells, a prominent newspaper editor and Chase supporter, and the father of author William Dean Howells, "and the last to whom we should entrust our liberties; and he is a particularly obnoxious specimen," referring to McLean, whom Howells compared unfavorably even to President Pierce.

Thurlow Weed was also not a fan, fearing that McLean would turn on his party, as John Tyler and Millard Fillmore had done when they inherited the presidency from dead Whigs William Henry Harrison and Zachary Taylor, respectively. He considered the Ohioan a "white-liver'd hollow-hearted Janus-faced rascal."

Aware that his antislavery credentials were questionable, McLean had hoped to use the Dred Scott case to prove his bona fides with the new party. He knew how the court was going to rule, and he had prepared a dissent blasting the majority decision. When the case was argued in

February, it had seemed set for a quick and simple resolution. But on May 12, little more than a month after Justice Benjamin Curtis had suggested such an outcome was likely, the court ordered that the case be reargued in December. Republicans—particularly supporters of McLean—cried foul. The party wanted the case decided before the election. The McLean wing wanted it decided before the convention. Robbed of that opportunity, the day after the postponement was announced, McLean wrote to Lewis Cass, the father of the doctrine of popular sovereignty—clearly with the intention that the letter would be published—that "I never doubted that Congress had this power [to prohibit slavery in a territory], and I could never have expressed doubt on the subject." He also called for "the immediate admission of Kansas as a State into the Union under the [free-state] Constitution already formed." But this craven display helped him little with strong antislavery men, who remembered his rulings from the bench in support of the Fugitive Slave Act.

Release of the core argument of his pending dissenting opinion was a breach of judicial etiquette even in those days, but McLean was getting desperate. He had hoped his dissent would make him the leading voice in Washington on the nonextension of slavery. Foiled, he had no qualms about finding another way, however unethical, to get his case before Republican delegates.

The oddest coupling was McLean and Gamaliel Bailey. The *National Era* editor was an abolitionist, pro-immigrant, and had long been associated in the public mind with Chase as the leading antislavery voice in national politics. Now, in Chase's hour of need, his old friend abandoned him, ostensibly over Chase's acceptance of fusion with the nativists. Then Bailey began canvassing for McLean, who had never joined the Order of the Star Spangled Banner but enthusiastically endorsed the Know Nothing platform, voted for Know Nothing candidates, and made a play for the Know Nothing nomination.

"Bailey worked among anti-slavery men for McLean," Hiram Barney, a New York abolitionist who would cast his delegate vote for Sumner, told Chase. Bailey's reasoning was sound if his judgment was suspect. If the simple criterion was "availability," as the Frémont men seemed to argue, then McLean was the strongest "available" man. Bailey could also cite Frémont's father-in-law, who had once said of McLean that he was "abolitionist enough for anybody outside of a mad house—& his wife is abolitionist enough for all those who ought to be in one." In fact, that would have been a fair description of Benton's daughter and her husband, as well.

But Bailey was not the only strong antislavery man in McLean's corner. Pennsylvanian Thaddeus Stevens said McLean was the only potential candidate who could carry his state, and he warned that Frémont not only couldn't carry Pennsylvania in the presidential contest but would deliver the state elections to the Democrats as well. Joshua Giddings, another whose antislavery credentials could not be questioned, similarly worried over Pennsylvania without McLean on the ticket.

Greeley's Frémont-friendly *New-York Tribune* had a slightly different take, expressing confidence that the "young man of energy and action, of tried courage, and of a nice heroic sense of honor" could prevail in Pennsylvania, and rejoicing that he was not—presumably like McLean—"soiled or washed out by the foetid turbidness of office-hunting." That analysis came after the nomination was firmly in Frémont's grasp. Only the month before, Greeley, who changed his mind like other men changed their shirts, had told Colfax that "if McLean is the man for Pennsylvania and New Jersey, then I am for McLean." In the intervening weeks, he apparently decided that McLean was not the only man for the mid-Atlantic.

McLean's backers were not quite ready to give up, however, and they made an eleventh-hour push as Republicans began gathering in Philadelphia, focusing on those delegates—including Abraham Lincoln—who liked Frémont but considered him more vice presidential material than presidential. This was a sentiment shared by many in Washington, but it was a nonstarter as far as Frémont was concerned, and he instructed Francis Blair to so inform the Pennsylvanians and anybody else who suggested the idea.

In the end, much of the opposition to McLean came down to personalities. The contrast between the contenders could not be starker. If Frémont was infused with "a history of romantic heroism," in Blair's phrase, McLean was anything but: an "old fogy"—the same epithet Douglas men used for Buchanan—and a "marrowless old lawyer," in the words of Frémont supporter Charles Dana. Just as had been the case at Francis Blair's home in December, the new man had it over the old fogy.

This kind of thinking troubled Chase. "Our only danger is in the policy which some men seem to have fallen into of taking up an untried man for President," Chase warned a scant two months before the convention. But that was not the only danger he was worried about. He also feared a divided front. "The Abolitionists proper are determined to organize. . . . Whoever may be the Republican nominee they will have a man in the field." If the Republicans were to nominate someone who had been tested on the issue and tried in public office—someone like, say, Salmon P. Chase—a rump abolitionist candidate would hardly matter. "But if they nominate new men, discarding the tried, thousands of antislavery men will be alienated & lose confidence, and, in my judgment, defeat is certain."

But as governor, Chase couldn't even control the Ohio delegation, many of whom were supporting McLean. Former Whigs in his state revolted against him for supporting Nathaniel Banks and for a decade of Democratic politics. Some Democrats who had elected him to the Senate in 1849 still resented his self-serving methods in that contest. Germans, a sizable constituency in the state, were wary of his ties to nativists.

Chase had been running for president almost from the moment he was elected governor in October 1855. The men trying to form a national Republican Party were happy to let him do much of the grunt work of organizing, in the confidence that when the time came, they could easily shunt him aside in favor of someone less threatening. "While he is the ablest and truest Jeffersonian Democrat alive, and a gentleman spotless in private life," a home-state journalist observed, "nearly half the people imagine that he is a pirate."

As late as mid-June, even while acknowledging that victory in November was likely out of the question, Chase still thirsted for the nomination (while of course disavowing any interest except in advancing the cause of freedom). "It seems to me that if the unvarnished wishes of the people could prevail I should be nominated," he wrote, then qualified the claim—"this may be a delusion." Suggesting that Seward was leaning toward Frémont because of his ambivalence toward becoming a sacrificial lamb, Chase chided Seward and Weed as running the risk of setting a bad example by "preferring a new man to one who has seen service." If that theory was good enough to justify Frémont in 1856, it might be good enough to counter Seward four years hence.

On the eve of the gathering, the Democratic *Washington Star* ignored the other contenders and focused their fire indirectly at Frémont and directly at the entire Republican enterprise, attributing to Benton—without quoting him directly—the sentiment that "the triumph of their schemes will be the certain and speedy destruction of our present government." And, the paper continued, if the Democratic press or Benton were willing to absolve Frémont of any ill convictions, neither would provide the same quarter to his party compatriots, who were committed "1st. To the establishment of a state religion; 2d. To the disfranchisement of all foreign born citizens; and 3dly. To the abolishment of slavery throughout the country." That none of that was true mattered not at all. The election season was in full swing, and neither side was going to start being careful with the facts at this late date.

"A Pretty Long Finger in the Pie"

Republicans were divided over how to handle the impending meeting of the antislavery North Americans who had split from the Know Nothings at their February convention. The North Americans were set to convene in New York five days before the Republicans met in Philadelphia. Some Republicans, like Blair, wanted to take the extreme step of enlisting dissident Democrats in a subconvention in Cincinnati, to nominate Frémont and pressure the Know Nothings into accepting him. Benton threatened to disrupt any such conclave, and the nomination of Buchanan squelched any notion that there would be large numbers of Democratic defectors. Others thought Blair's idea was a bad one even before the Democrats made it moot. Why invite Benton to go public with his wrath toward Frémont before the Republican convention? They felt sure they would hear enough of it after.

For their part, the North Americans were having a hard time deciding how to proceed as well. Some were for immediate fusion, a "joint stock arrangement with Republicans," in one reporter's description. Others wanted to extract some concessions before giving in, particularly a promise on the vice presidential nominee.

But when delegates assembled on June 12, it quickly became clear this was to be a mostly Republican-friendly gathering. The smallish convention hall was not filled, and the speeches leaned away from Know Nothingism and strongly toward Kansas and Sumner, free soil and Frémontism. One early speaker hailed Frémont as "the man who had grit to climb the Rocky Mountains, half-starved, half-naked, and on his hands and knees."

A phalanx of senior Republicans circulated on the convention floor, looking to tamp down any uprisings. And though the recognizable Weed was not among them, "Thurlow Weed and his set have a pretty long finger in the pie," reported the *New York Herald*, until recently a basher of all things antislavery and now a convert to Frémont's cause. Their plan, surmised Murat Halstead, was to "melt the whole mass down and pour it into the cauldron of the Quaker City."

Weed enlisted an ally, former Pennsylvania governor William F. Johnston, to keep an eye on things for him. Johnston was happy to do so, expecting in return that he would wind up as Frémont's running mate. In conjunction with Weed's covert operations, Republican chairman Edwin Morgan sent an official message to the Know Nothing meeting, inviting them to confer. George Law, the man vanquished in February by Millard Fillmore, was named the chief correspondent.

And for two days, while the bigwigs talked in private, the delegates sat around listening to speeches. Bored, probably a little put off by being treated like ribbon clerks, the delegates decided they would vote for a nominee. Most favored Frémont. Weed and his cohorts went into action. They blocked the sending of a letter, above Frémont's signature, asserting that he could not unconditionally accept the nomination. The operatives wanted Frémont free of the taint of Know Nothingism when they went into their own convention in three days, but they didn't want to risk offending Know Nothing voters. It was a delicate balance, and inaction seemed to be the best way to preserve it.

What Weed and the others needed to do was persuade the delegates to nominate a candidate who would then readily step aside for Frémont *after* the latter had already secured the Republican nomination. This idea was the brainchild of Isaac Sherman, a New York financier who was friends with both Banks and Frémont. There were only two possibilities: McLean and

Banks. Nobody trusted McLean, and they were right not to. He disdained Frémont, and it is unlikely he would have gotten out of the way for him. Banks was not exactly known for his moral rectitude, but he was a more reliable politician than McLean, was the party's leader in the House, and had been considering the possibility for more than a month. With some trepidation, he was ready to go.

The details were left to a group of less experienced North Americans led by a rubber magnate, Horace Day. In one of those delicious ironies that make politics so interesting, Day had sold Frémont an inflatable boat in 1843 that proved to have a leaky valve. Frémont and a small party using the craft to explore Great Salt Lake almost went under when it began to take on water. Luckily for Frémont, Day managed the Banks movement more successfully.

Day spread some of his considerable wealth around. A few Republican-friendly delegates voted for McLean on the first ballot to throw suspicious Know Nothings off the scent. It worked for a while, but Republicans overplayed their hand and spread the false rumor that if the North Americans waited until Monday, Banks would be nominated by the Philadelphia convention. The wiser among the Know Nothings smelled a rat and bolted, led by New Jersey's Robert F. Stockton, "another old fogy, with more money than brains," as a reporter described him, who had served in controversial fashion with Frémont in California. Out of time, Day and the Republicans pushed forward with the vote, nominating Banks for president and Johnston for vice president. A committee was appointed to go to Philadelphia for the Republican convention, scheduled to start the next day. The operation had not run as smoothly as they had all hoped, but the result was what they had planned for. Now, all they had to do was put the pieces together in the City of Brotherly Love.

"THOSE TWIN RELICS OF BARBARISM"

Delegates began making their way early on June 17 to Philadelphia's Musical Fund Hall, a former Presbyterian church at the corner of Locust and Darien Streets. Renowned for its fine acoustics, the historic building was the site of an 1825 reception during the Marquis de Lafayette's final tour of America. It was a large space—106 feet long, 60 feet wide, and 26 feet high, with more than two thousand seats—and it would need every inch of that room over the next few days.

There were 565 delegates in attendance from all the free states plus Delaware, Maryland, Virginia, and Kentucky. Another 100 free soil Democrats from New York were allowed entrance to the hall but had no vote in the proceedings.

Hotels were filled to the brim, including the Lawrence, where the Ohio delegation was in nearly constant conversation about the state's two potential candidates, and reaching no consensus. Caucuses had been held somewhere "nearly every hour in the last twenty-four" as the convention began. While the crowds outwardly resembled those in Cincinnati, the differences were stark and reflected the disparate natures of the two parties. "The crowd here is nearly as large but not so noisy," one observer wrote, and also noticed considerably smaller quantities of liquor being consumed and profanity being hurled.

As delegates entered the hall, they found copies of the morning's *Pennsylvanian* newspaper, with a front-page notice:

> It is proposed, if Colonel Frémont's friends succeed in procuring him
> the nomination for the presidency, to head their ticket thus:
> > For President
> > col j. Frémont, son-in-law of
> > Thomas H. Benton.

It was worth a chuckle, "the palpable imitation of the Andrew Jackson Donelson joke," a reporter noted of the ever-striving nephew of the great general, while pointing out that "the fun of it is that Benton is supporting Buchanan."

Inside the jam-packed Musical Fund Hall, former Whig Henry S. Lane of Indiana was named chairman. Country lean with no front teeth, he set up shop with a sizable chaw in his cheek and his boots on the head table. When something happened that he liked, rather than applaud, he clacked his heavy cane on the floor, "small eyes glistening like those of a wild cat."

To get the delegates' attention, he would "fling his arms in wild gesticulation . . . smacking his fists horribly at the close of every emphatic period."

Aside from Lane's entertaining antics, the first day was consumed by speech making, most of it unremarkable. But one man, Philip Dorscheimer, a German miller's son and Democrat-turned-Republican who owned hotels in Buffalo, New York, provided a brief respite from the usual platitudes tossed out by the likes of Henry Wilson and Owen Lovejoy. "I am a plain old German—no politician," he explained to the still-unsettled delegates, "but I can tell this assembly that I know my countrymen, and they will vote for no one more cheerfully than for John C. Frémont, who is well known to them as the pathfinder, and the one who first planted the Stars and Stripes on the face of Mexican California." With his "pronounced Rhenish Bavarian accent," it's likely that few fully grasped what Dorscheimer was saying. The gist must have come through, though, for he was "immensely cheered" at the conclusion of his presentation.

On June 18, a steamy day with a slow and steady rain, the platform committee, headed by David Wilmot of Pennsylvania, handed in its product.

Wilmot, like Judah P. Benjamin at the Democratic Convention, seemed always to be wearing a smile, and he read the platform to a wildly cheering audience. For Wilmot, who had "attained a fair prospect for immortality at a very cheap rate" by attaching his name to the amendment he sponsored to bar slavery in any territory obtained in the Mexican War, there was plenty to smile about.

"We deny the authority of Congress, of a Territorial Legislature, of any individual, or association of individuals, to give legal existence to Slavery in any Territory of the United States," declared the platform, which also called for the admission of Kansas as a free state, condemned the Ostend Manifesto as a "highwayman's plea" for stealing the territory of Spain, endorsed a Pacific railroad, and declared it "the right and imperative duty of Congress to prohibit in the Territories those twin relics of barbarism—Polygamy and Slavery," a phrase greeted with "rapturous enthusiasm" by the delegates.

It was a remarkable departure from the stultifying vagueness of Whig platforms, and it stood squarely for the notion that freedom was national and slavery sectional. "It includes denationalization of slavery entire," Chase crowed. Having feared a weak platform plank on slavery, abolitionists were pleasantly surprised that it took a forthright stand in favor of freedom, at least in the territories. "It is go for the principles although we may not approve the nominee," wrote Joshua R. Giddings.

But that was as far as the party would go. "The conservative Democrats and Whigs in the party did not want to go to extremes; the few Abolitionists present, on the contrary, were for a general declaration of war against all slavery," but the anti-Nebraska Democrats "ruled the Convention," wrote one of those Democrats.

To that end, the platform did not mention anything specifically about overturning the repeal of the Missouri Compromise, repealing the Fugitive Slave Act, or abolishing slavery in the District of Columbia. The party hoped to appeal to working-class whites with a pitch that slavery was as bad for them as it was for the enslaved blacks, and that the expansion of slavery into the territories would spell doom for free white settlers who wished to move west and make a better life. The platform also dodged temperance, on the logical premise that the issue was too volatile, with too many regional variations, to be of any use. Better to remain silent and let local candidates deal with it in their own ways. The plank on immigration was as hedged as the plank on slavery expansion was forthright, opposing only legislation that would adversely affect "liberty of conscience and equality of rights among citizens." An original draft that had called for opposing "all proscriptive legislation" was rejected.

The platform's reference to slavery and polygamy as the "twin relics of barbarism" was no mere rhetorical device, although it was highly effective on that score. For Republicans, the issue of slavery in Kansas and polygamy in Utah—and statehood for both territories—were inextricably linked by the Democratic insistence on popular sovereignty. Republicans tied slavery and polygamy together as moral wrongs. Through their condemnation of popular sovereignty, they hoped to link Democrats to the even more widely unpopular Mormon practice by arguing that leaving such decisions as slavery in Kansas to the will of the territory's residents would mean that the will of the Mormons in Utah would rule on plural marriage.

Seward had earlier argued on the floor of the Senate that granting statehood to Kansas under slavery or Utah under polygamy "will bear heavily, perhaps conclusively, on the fortunes of the entire conflict between Freedom and Slavery."

Tacitly acknowledging the logic of the Republican argument, Democrats sensed the danger and struck back. Finessing the moral question, popular sovereignty made sense on slavery, they reasoned, because it already existed in several states. Polygamy existed in none. Benton, who had long represented the jurisdiction most hostile to the saints, told a Saint Louis crowd that Mormon polygamy in Utah was indicative of a "state of things at which morality, decency and shame revolts."

Perhaps most remarkably, the Republican platform accused friends of the Pierce administration of "murders, robberies, and arson"—clearly aimed at proslavery Kansans—and promised to bring them to justice.

Having created a platform upon which to stand, the Republicans now moved to nominate a candidate who would do the standing. The fix appeared to be in for Frémont. But emotions matter in politics, and Seward held an emotional grip on the hearts of antislavery men, even if he was hemming and hawing about whether to be a candidate. Pro-Seward delegates pestered Weed about why the New Yorker remained on the sidelines. On the first day, Henry Wilson had given a routine speech designed to say something nice about each possible candidate. When he referred to Seward as "the foremost statesman of America," bedlam ensued, the first real demonstration of the convention. Weed, who had already wavered in the face of Republican enthusiasm, wavered a little more.

Seward was still being buffeted by contradictory advice. A friendly newspaper editor in attendance in Philadelphia wrote Seward that "one word from you will give the country its candidate," and if that didn't interest him, "*you* can say *who* shall be nominated." At the same moment, another friend, former New York Congressman John Schoolcraft, echoing Weed, told Seward that "nomination now would be unwise and unsafe, on the ground that the election would be impossible." In making the case to another supporter, Schoolcraft laid it on the line. It was "better that Frémont be sacrificed than Seward."

And that was the conclusion Seward reached. His reputation as something of a radical on slavery belied a cautious nature, and he would not feel fully armored going into battle without Weed fully invested. The pair's half doubts added up to a whole, and Seward sent a letter on the first day of the convention refusing to allow his name to be placed in nomination. The foremost historian of the early years of the Republican Party wrote that Seward "would unquestionably have been the first Republican standard bearer" had he gone before the delegates. With his withdrawal, it seemed a certainty that Frémont would claim that mantle.

Just before the voting was to begin, a supporter of Justice McLean from Ohio read a letter from the candidate withdrawing his name, necessary to achieve "a hearty and vigorous cooperation of all the elements of the party." The announcement "caused a fierce sensation in the Pennsylvania and New Jersey delegations," and Thaddeus Stevens jumped to his feet to plead that McLean, as the only man who could win Pennsylvania, remain a candidate. Then another Ohio delegate rose to declare that Chase, too, would not be a candidate, and he read a letter from Chase asserting that "it would ill become any true friend of liberty and justice to allow any personal considerations whatever to stand in the way of that complete union which is essential." Chase's letter sparked another eruption, calls from Frémont supporters that their man be nominated by acclamation since there were now no other entrants in the field. McLean men objected to this and begged for time to regroup. After a period of confused turmoil, Chairman Lane put down his cane, slipped his chaw out of his mouth, and gaveled the convention to an adjournment until 5 PM.

At five, the hall was filled to the rafters and a damp, humid air hung over the room. It was still raining outside, but inside the air was stifling. "It was enough to knock a man down to draw his breath," one attendee wrote. Pennsylvania's insistence that McLean—despite his official withdrawal—was still a candidate prevailed, and his withdrawal was withdrawn. Chase and Seward remained withdrawn. Rather than rushing immediately to an official roll call, however, an informal poll was conducted, in which Frémont received 359 votes to McLean's 190. Frémont dominated in New England, New York, the upper tier of northern states, and California. McLean was strongest in Pennsylvania and New Jersey. They were closely divided in Ohio, Indiana,

and Illinois. Frémont backers again shouted out for a nomination by acclamation. Clearly, they said, their man was the choice of the convention. But
McLean's men wanted a roll call, so they got one. Frémont won 520 votes,
to 37 for McLean. A motion was then made to make it unanimous, and a
thunderous shout from the badly ventilated hall confirmed that.

After the final vote was cast, a giant FOR PRESIDENT, JOHN C. FRÉ-
MONT banner was unfurled amid raucous cheering. People leapt up on
their chairs and tossed their hats in the air in celebration. The band rose
to new heights of noisemaking, as did the deliriously shouting delegates
and hangers on, both inside and outside the hall, in support of "Free Soil,
Free Speech, Free Men, and Frémont."

It was an act of faith in an untested candidate, a man who had achieved
great things outside the world of politics by overcoming adversity and
confronting death itself. Many of the faithful believed that a military man
with that kind of courage was going to be needed soon. The evangelical
nature of the Republican movement, "borrowing the self-forgetting devotion
and dedicated zeal of a religious conversion," as George W. Julian put it,
demanded a romantic figure to lead it. Now it had one.

The selection of Frémont's running mate was another of those balancing acts that the party leadership had thus far managed to finesse. Ideally,
they wanted a serious person who would appeal to the North Americans
without giving too much offense to the men like Bailey and Seward who
rejected nativism. The Know Nothings were still sitting on hold in New
York, waiting for the Republicans to do the right thing.

After Frémont's nomination, Republicans and North Americans
appointed committees to hash it out. The North Americans wanted their
vice presidential candidate, Pennsylvania's William F. Johnston, to join
the ticket with Frémont. But he was unacceptable to the Thaddeus Stevens faction of Pennsylvanians, and so he was blocked. Johnston's faction
objected to Wilmot. Pennsylvania was believed to be the key to winning
in November, but the small men of the large state could not set their petty
differences aside. It would not be the last time Pennsylvania factionalism
would get in the way of victory.

The obvious choice, Nathaniel Banks, was not interested and could
not be made to be interested. Here is where a savvier candidate than

Frémont could have stepped in, told his friend that he was needed for the good of the country, and pieced together a formidable coalition. Instead Frémont favored Simon Cameron, another factional Pennsylvanian who had made a fortune in banking and railroads and who, like Banks, possessed a flexible ideology. But Cameron had too many enemies, and the wrong ones—including Francis Blair—and the two committees threw up their hands in defeat.

The decision left to the convention, a handful of men were considered. All had something to offer, but none seemed to bring any particular spark of interest or inspiration to the ticket.

McLean's men pushed William Dayton, a conservative Whig from New Jersey who was nominally a Know Nothing. Though New Jersey was a must-win state for Frémont, it paled in importance next to Pennsylvania. To his credit, Dayton had voted against the Fugitive Slave Act and had attempted to amend the bill to provide for trial by jury, but he was unremarkable in both presentation and accomplishment.

A caucus of Illinois delegates thought a western man would be preferable to Dayton, and quickly began organizing an alternative.

Lyman Trumbull, not a delegate and only very recently a Republican, was at the caucus and suggested they select a candidate "of decided Whig antecedents." That pointed toward Abraham Lincoln, and he endorsed the opponent he had bested for the Senate seat in 1855 as a "very good man."

Illinoisans worked through the evening of the eighteenth to solicit support from other delegations for Lincoln, and focused particularly on neighboring Indiana, looking to create a western bloc to oppose New Jersey's Dayton. Congressman William Archer was the main mover. He worked with Schuyler Colfax to bring Indiana aboard, and he solicited another House colleague, John Allison of Pennsylvania, to place Lincoln's name into consideration.

Joshua Giddings had tried without much success to recruit Lincoln earlier in the year as a party organizer in Illinois. Like several other cautious free soilers in the state, Lincoln continued until very late to consider himself a Whig. Elected in May as a delegate to the Republican convention, he chose not to attend. Now he was under consideration for the Republican Party nomination for the second-highest office in the land. Illinois was a battleground state, and Lincoln was considered an effective speaker, but he had never won anything larger than a state legislative district.

On the morning of June 19, after Allison nominated Lincoln, Archer, a "grey-haired old gent, slightly bent with age," jumped a foot and a half off the floor to make the case for Lincoln, shouting out "Will he fight?" and then answering his own question with a resounding "Yes!" This inspired a "tremendous yell" from the delegates, but Archer stepped on his own applause line by continuing on. "Why, he's from Kentucky, and all Kentuckians will fight." A hall filled with antislavery northerners needed no exhortations about southern manhood, and the moment of maximum excitement passed quickly.

Judge John M. Palmer of Illinois, who had played an instrumental role in Lincoln losing the Senate seat to Trumbull in 1855, said "we can lick Buchanan anyway, but I think we can do it a little easier if we have Lincoln on the ticket."

After the speeches, an informal ballot showed Dayton with the highest vote total, 259, to 110 for Lincoln, 43 for Wilmot, and the remainder scattered across thirteen candidates, a result that prompted announced withdrawals via the Massachusetts delegation for Nathaniel Banks, Henry Wilson, and Charles Sumner. They understood that "Bleeding Sumner" was more valuable as a martyr than as a candidate. An Ohio delegate rose to remove from consideration Lieutenant Governor Thomas Ford, one of the most active fusionists at the Know Nothing convention. Thaddeus Stevens took Wilmot out of the running. With all the noncandidates now safely on the sidelines, the balloting began for the nomination, and Dayton was the nearly unanimous choice.

The Frémont men hoped Dayton would act as "a poultice on the sore just opened" with McLean. He would prove to be more like a festering wound.

Back in New York, the rejection of Johnston and the nomination of Dayton, not even a member of the Order of the Star Spangled Banner, did not sit well with the rank-and-file North Americans. Leaders, who understood they had few real options, tried to calm the troops. They readily agreed to dump Banks and accept Frémont, but refused to give way on the vice presidency, the only crumb they felt they had claimed for their troubles.

FRÉMONT-DAYTON BANNER. *Courtesy of Library of Congress*

The North American ticket would be Frémont and Johnston. Dayton had been kept in the dark about the swap plan. When he was informed, he made it clear that he would not go quietly, if at all.

"GIVE US JESSIE!"

The vanquished responded in different ways.

Chase pouted for a while, calling the party's rejection of him "an act of positive injustice." But he was soon out on the stump, crisscrossing Ohio and the Northwest in support of the ticket. Seward did less. It would be almost four months before he would lift a finger to help Frémont. Weed fumed at Seward's insolence but did nothing to spur him to action. McLean did nothing at all, except for complaining about Frémont's shortcomings and "desponding for the future," certain that North and South were "rapidly approaching a dissolution of the Union." Although he didn't speak publicly, he was privately disparaging of Frémont, whom he judged "not fit to discharge the duties of an auditor." He had "no hope of good coming from Frémont's election" and asserted that the candidate had "no qualifications for the office."

Francis Preston Blair reported to his congressional candidate son Frank in Missouri on "a vast deal of enthusiasm" post-convention, "which I think will continue to rise and to spread until it carries him to the Presidency. But you know my sanguine temperament, I never think a good cause can fail."

He wasn't the only one. Lincoln believed that "if we can get rid of the Fillmore ticket, we shall carry [Illinois] for Frémont." And Seward sensed an "alarm" among the Democrats amid the postconvention euphoria of the Republicans.

Publicly, Democrats belittled Frémont as a soldier who had never fought a battle and a politician who had never made a speech, but some of the more astute among them worried about overconfidence. Alexander Stephens warned of "the fusion ranks of Black Republicanism which now seriously threatens to sweep the entire North." Secretary of the Treasury James Guthrie feared defeat should they lose a single southern state.

Other southerners were less worried, including one of Jessie Benton Frémont's estranged cousins, Sally McDowell, who called Frémont's candidacy "the greatest farce upon earth" and "a burlesque on human nature." And Jessie's own sister, Eliza, and brother-in-law, William Carey Jones, sided with Benton over Frémont.

New York's George Templeton Strong had no qualms with Frémont personally; he simply feared the North was not up to the task. Maybe "ten years hence" enough southern degradations would have an effect, he believed, but for now the "Republican Party is a mere squirm and wriggle of the insulted North, a brief spasm of pain under pressure and nothing more."

In formally accepting the nomination on July 8, Frémont anticipated Lincoln's reliance on the Declaration of Independence as the foundation for "freedom national" as the guiding light for American government. "Nothing is clearer in the history of our institutions than the design of the nation, in asserting its own independence and freedom, to avoid giving countenance to the extension of slavery," he wrote. It would be his only substantive statement of the campaign. From there, he turned it over to others, chiefly his wife.

A least five substantial books were written in support of Frémont's campaign, including one by Emma Willard, a leading light of the women's rights movement. Tens of thousands of copies were sold, and hundreds of less ambitious works were produced. Poet George S. Burleigh published a volume of poems about Frémont's exploits. They weren't very good, but Burleigh freely acknowledged that artistry was not his point. "If this writer could flatter himself that his effort would in some degree . . . strengthen the force that would repel the aggressions of Slavery, he could easily forego the hope of a permanent value in his work," he wrote in the preface.

Ever the editor, Jessie Benton Frémont took great care in seeing that the various campaign biographies were up to her high standards. When Charles Upham wrote of her and Frémont's elopement, Jessie was quick to respond. "There was no 'dash' in our marriage," she corrected him after reading page proofs. "It was done in sober sadness on my part and as sober judgment on Mr. Frémont's." Various other fixes followed throughout June as pages and letters flowed back and forth between Upham and the Frémonts in New York.

Newspaperman John Bigelow wrote the best campaign biography of the candidate, *Memoir of the Life and Public Services of John Charles Frémont*, and again Jessie lent her skilled hand to the final product, writing the opening chapters and detailing a distant—and perhaps dubious—familial relationship between Frémont and George Washington through Frémont's mother. Frémont met with Bigelow on several occasions, regaling the author with tales of his travels in the West. Bigelow's work had appeared in serial form on Saturdays beginning May 18 in the *New York Post*, but publication in book form was a slower process and lagged behind some of the other biographies being produced. And it was a different kind of product. Bigelow included a retelling of Frémont's court martial in California, arguing that a thorough examination would allow supporters to put the lie to the exaggerated claims of the Democrats. Bigelow even mentioned the two times Frémont issued challenges for duels, including once while he was in the Senate. Some Frémont partisans blanched, but neither the candidate nor his wife objected to Bigelow's skilled framing of the controversies.

Jessie used her opening chapters to turn one criticism of Frémont—his bastard birth—against southern critics. In her travels to Virginia, she found no record of a divorce, but cleaned up the story of Anne Whiting's flight from her first husband and subsequent elopement with Frémont's father, saying that "twelve long years of wedded misery" came to an end when the unhappy couple agreed to separate. Whiting, wrote her daughter-in-law, was a victim of arrogant Virginia aristocrats who forced her to marry a much older man she didn't love. It was a subtle reminder for northern voters of the way the slaveocracy treated as chattel anyone not a member of their club, and of how the egalitarian Republicans were different. And while Jessie was happy to defend John's mother, she would not attack her own father. Some other Frémont biographers did: Samuel Schmucker cited Thomas Hart Benton's objections to the young army officer as indicative of backward southern attitudes toward self-made men.

The biographies were huge sellers. Upham's sold thirty thousand copies, Bigelow's forty thousand. The *National Era* called Bigelow's tome "the only biography which contains an adequate account, not only of the public services but of the private history of our candidate" and recommended it to all Republicans as "an efficient weapon" with which partisans should "arm themselves" for debate.

The books contained illustrations, but new photos were also hot items. Matthew Brady's New York studio was selling photographic portraits of Frémont at three dollars a pop; Jessie regretted that the black-and-white images were not able to display her husband's handsome blue-gray eyes.

Hagiographical campaign biographies were as old as the republic. What was new was the role that women—not just Jessie—would play in the Frémont campaign.

The organizations of the Benevolent Empire—the interlocking reform groups that grew out of the evangelical fervor of the Second Great Awakening—gave women their first real opportunity to participate in American civic life. They seized the moment, leading the way on temperance, education, and a host of other causes. For many, antislavery was seen as a particularly female concern, for it was only women, the reasoning went, who could put themselves in the place of someone like enslaved mother of four Margaret Garner and "imagine her place to be hers." The experience thus gained, when the Frémont campaign provided the moment to step onto the partisan battlefield, they were ready. "All Ladies have politics now," an Ohio abolitionist wrote to a friend.

Elizabeth Cady Stanton, whose husband worked for the Republican Party in New York, "attended all the Republican meetings" preceding the state elections in 1855, and was not alone. Told at one crowded event that "we do not wish to spare any room for ladies," she determined to push her way in, and "found a dozen women already there."

Whigs had brought women into the arena in a small way during William Henry Harrison's 1840 campaign; they sewed banners and rode atop floats, and voter participation soared. But women were now taking on a host of new tasks: speaking before mixed audiences, raising money, and writing in political journals. With Harriet Beecher Stowe as an example, others felt free to join in the fray. Lydia Maria Child, the abolitionist author spurred to action by the attack on Senator Sumner, corresponded with Jessie Frémont and wrote a serialized novel, *The Kansas Emigrants*, that would appear in the *New-York Tribune* in the last two weeks of the campaign.

Republicans were not shy about making direct appeals to women, even though they couldn't vote. John Frémont's heroic persona was a sharp selling point, and the fact that he had possessed the fortitude to scale the Sierra Nevada in winter was nothing next to the courage he had shown in "dar[ing] to run away with a senator's daughter. . . . It shows a manliness, it shows courage, it shows determination and virtue," proclaimed one speaker.

It was clear almost immediately that the star of the campaign was going to be not the candidate, who by tradition would make few or no public appearances, but his wife, lauded in print as "noble young Jessie the flower o' the land."

When well-wishers flocked to the Frémonts' New York home a week after the convention, cries of "Give us Jessie" echoed through the night air. The crowd had marched as one from a rally at the New York Tabernacle, which had featured speeches by Lyman Trumbull and Robert Emmet, son of the famed Irish rebel of the same name, to the Frémonts' house on Ninth Street, where they had moved in May. Filling the street and crowding together against the brisk night air, the throng refused to leave until "the flower o' the land" herself appeared. Even a portion of a stone balustrade from the house crashing to the street did not deter them—they cheered the fact that no one was injured and considered it a portent of more good fortune ahead. John Frémont appeared and made a few inconsequential remarks, but few in the thousands below could hear anyway, and another roar arose demanding "Mrs. Frémont!" and "Give us Jessie!" One of Frémont's entourage thought such a request was undignified and pleaded with the crowd to offer one more cheer for the candidate, then call it a night. They would have none of that, and again called for "our Jessie." After another short interlude, she came out and stood with her husband, the young, handsome, dashing hero, his skin "sun-burnt and frost-blistered in his adventurous journeyings, that though he has lived some time in the shade, it looks as if excessively bronzed by recent exposure." On his arm, Jessie glowed just as brightly.

"Is Jessie a candidate for the presidency?" the anti-Frémont *Richmond Dispatch* wondered, while acknowledging, "We would rather be under Jessie than her spouse."

The Democratic paper in Janesville, Wisconsin, wrote simply: "FOR PRESIDENT. john c. Frémont, husband of JESSIE BENTON."

Her name even became a verb, at least among critics, who scolded women who got involved in the campaign as "jessying" around the country.

Newspapers readily promoted the idea, blaring headlines reading FRÉMONT AND "*HIS JESSIE*," GIVE 'EM JESSIE, NO BACHELOR FOR JESSIE, OUR JESSIE, and MRS. FRÉMONT AND HER HUSBAND.

This was going to be a campaign like no other in American history. Just as women were involved in a serious way for the first time, men of the arts took up the cause, and abolitionist poet John Greenleaf Whittier penned a stirring campaign song that invoked the violence in Kansas and the heroism of Frémont.

> *Sound, sound the trumpet fearlessly!*
> *Each arm its vigor lending,*
> *Bravely with wrong contending,*
> *And shouting Freedom's cry!*
> *The Kansas homes stand cheerlessly,*
> *The sky with flame is ruddy,*

The prairie turf is bloody,
Where the brave and gentle die.
Sound the trumpet stern and steady!
Sound the trumpet strong and high!
Country and Liberty!
Freedom and Victory!
These words shall be our cry,—
Frémont and Victory!

The contest was thus joined, "unparalleled in bitterness and violence."

"THE MOST PAINFUL DUTY OF MY LIFE"

Franklin Pierce may have been unaware that a civil war was already looming, but foreigners had noticed. *Blackwood's Edinburgh Magazine* reported that "a civil war rages in the State of Kansas, which has become the battlefield of the Slavery and Anti-Slavery parties."

The commission that the House sent to Kansas in the spring delivered its report July 1. William Howard of Michigan chaired the three-man delegation and the report bore his name, but John Sherman of Ohio wrote most of it. The Howard Report could effectively have been an appendix to the recently approved Republican Party platform. Sherman laid out the rampant intimidation and terror imposed by the proslavery government and associated militias on antislavery settlers and voters. He documented the invasion of Missouri voters who contributed to the electoral victories by the proslavery forces, and declared the territorial legislature illegitimate. The report was carefully documented and was a valuable tool in refuting Democratic allegations that Republicans were wildly exaggerating the state of things in Kansas. But it was nevertheless a Republican document, and thus it viewed those events from that angle. Mordecai Oliver, a Missouri Democrat, added a minority report that dissented in almost every particular.

Certainly, southerners and Democrats were not buying it. The congressional committee returned with the proof of fraud that "they were sent by their abolition friends in Congress purposely to obtain," one North

Carolina newspaper opined. "Who will place any faith in the truth or honesty of their report?"

Not the president, as it turned out.

During the long cold winter, John Brown had written to his wife that "we hear that Franklin Pierce means to crush the men of Kansas. I do not know how well he may succeed; but I think he may find his hands full before it is over." Pierce did have his hands full, but he had also been fighting with one tied behind his back. Now he would bring it to bear.

Governor Wilson Shannon was an empty suit, with no control over the Missourians and no credibility with free staters. Army colonel Edwin V. "Bull" Sumner, late of the Sioux expedition in Nebraka, had been dispatched by President Pierce and Secretary of War Davis to rattle the federal sword in Kansas. When Shannon went on a trip to Saint Louis, he left acting governor Daniel Woodson to deal with the impending meeting of the Topeka legislature, scheduled for July 4. Colonel Sumner at first sent Major John Sedgwick to bust up the free-state legislature before it could assemble, but Woodson did not want an underling performing the task. So Sumner took his five companies of cavalry and his field guns to Topeka. A thousand men in arms showed up in the town. But for once in this "three-cornered" war, the militias took a backseat. Sumner was no fan of the Pierce administration's strategy in Kansas. Rather than aim the armed force of the United States exclusively at those opposing the existing—and dubious—territorial government, Sumner would have preferred to disarm all parties. But Pierce and Davis saw it differently, and Sumner was a loyal soldier.

The legislature gathered, but almost immediately after the roll was called, Sumner mounted the speaker's platform and announced "the most painful duty of my whole life," ordering the lawmakers to disperse. He had written orders from President Pierce and Governor Shannon to back him up. But the real backup was outside—a thousand troops and several cannons. "God knows I have no party feeling and will hold none so long as I hold my present position in Kansas," Sumner declared. "I have just returned from the borders where I have been sending home companies of Missourians and now I am here to disperse you. I now command you to disperse. I repeat that this is the most painful duty of my whole life. But you must disperse."

Someone, not a member of the legislature, shouted a question, asking if they were to be "dispersed at the point of the bayonet?"

"I shall use the whole force under my command to carry out my orders," Sumner replied.

Seeing that he was serious, the free-state men left the building. As Sumner was departing behind them, a man from the gallery shouted down "Colonel, you have robbed Oliver Cromwell of his laurels."

But Sumner got few thanks from Washington for his effectiveness. Why, the skittish politicians in the Pierce administration wanted to know, did he threaten force so publicly? Couldn't some quieter way around have been found?

Sumner's show of force gave the free-state leaders and their supporters in Congress the justification they needed to argue that the army was little more than a supplemental militia for the proslavery territorial government. And it gave abolitionists a golden opportunity to say "I told you so."

Joshua Giddings had predicted Pierce would not use troops "to shoot the citizens of Kansas." He was right, but just barely. While no one had been shot, the troops were perfectly prepared to do so if needed. Garrison's prediction in March that "the 'border ruffian' legislation will be enforced, if need be, by all the military power of the General Government," had come to pass. "Freedom," he now said, "lies trodden in the dust, or wanders as an outlaw."

With a serious threat of federal force in place, a tense—and temporary—calm settled on the territory. The party conventions had slowed consideration of the Kansas statehood measures, but Congress got back to work on them after the Republican meeting.

Alexander Stephens worked with Robert Toombs to write a new Kansas measure to replace the one Douglas had unsuccessfully advanced earlier in the year. Its chief aim was to undercut every Republican objection and serve as a platform on which to contest the presidential election. Starting in the Senate, where prospects of passage were infinitely greater than in the Republican-led House, Toombs announced on June 23 that his new bill would authorize the president to appoint a five-member commission to oversee a new census in the territory, register voters, and hold an election that would be restricted to bona fide residents. The bill called for holding that election—for delegates to a constitutional convention—on the same day as the presidential election, on the theory that Missouri ruffians would stay home and vote in their own state rather than stampeding into Kansas. When Republicans objected that many free soil men had been chased from the territory by violence and might not be eligible to vote under the terms of the bill, Toombs changed it to allow any who had done so to return by October 1 to register. The delegates so elected would meet in December to draw up a constitution.

The measure was designed to placate both Kansas and the voters, while robbing Republicans of their most potent political weapon. Toombs, Douglas, and their allies had no illusions that the bill would get through the House and become law. But they wanted to get Republicans on the record opposing what appeared by most accounts to be a reasonable proposal.

"Douglas and others are scared by the storm their selfish folly has raised," wrote George Templeton Strong, who was moving ever closer to active participation in Republican politics. "Should things be compromised and smoothed over, the Northern party will accomplish little next November." Still, as a worried New Yorker with business interests, he was hoping "the mischief may be so far repaired as to make a sectional contest unnecessary."

Greeley spotted the trap. Fearful that Congress might actually do something to address the violence in Kansas and steal the issue from the Republicans, he wrote a worried letter to Schuyler Colfax. "Do you want some nasty fix-up or compromise on Kansas—one that will be hailed by the whole Fillmore and Buchanan press and parties as a settlement of the Kansas question?"

Greeley need not have worried. The bill went to the floor June 30 and debate continued with few breaks for more than two days. Lyman Trumbull of Illinois repeatedly offered amendments aimed at clarifying when the decision to allow or not allow slavery could be made, by granting the territorial legislature that authority. It was a ploy—Trumbull didn't want to give the Kansas legislature that authority, he merely wanted to put duplicitous Democrats on the spot. They had been dodging the issue for years, and they continued to do so now, voting down Trumbull's amendments and arguing that provisions related to what a territorial legislature can do were irrelevant on a bill concerned with statehood. In truth, Democrats were so divided on the issue that they wanted to avoid it at all costs, hoping the Supreme Court would eventually bail them out.

The final vote on the bill came early in the morning on July 3, after a nonstop twenty-hour session, and the measure passed easily, 33–12. The next day Sumner laid down the law to the free-state legislature.

But the Nathaniel Banks–led House refused to consider the Toombs bill, in part because Republicans feared their majority was shaky. "Our difficulties are numerous, and those we have to contend with are able and resolute," noted Banks. Even more importantly, they feared—probably correctly, given the recent imposition of military power against the antislavery forces in Kansas—that Pierce would not name a balanced commission or enforce the other provisions fairly. Based on his performance over the past two years, they had no reason to believe otherwise, despite assurances from Michigan's Lewis Cass during Senate debate that Pierce would appoint men from both parties. "No man who has the least regard for the rights or dignity of the free states at heart, will consent to put liberty under the guardianship of our present President," argued Ohio Senator Ben Wade. Instead, as Sumner emptied the Topeka legislative chamber, the House passed its own bill that would admit Kansas as a free state under the Topeka Constitution.

Douglas promptly took up the House bill, substituted the Toombs bill, and got it passed again in the Senate, then shipped it back to the House once more, where once again it died.

During Senate debate, Douglas had castigated the Republicans for stonewalling. "All these gentlemen want is to get up murder and bloodshed in Kansas for political effect. They do not mean that there shall be peace. Their capital for the presidential election is blood. We may as well talk plainly. An angel from heaven could not write a bill to restore peace in Kansas that would be acceptable to the abolition Republican Party previous to the presidential election." This elicited a roar of laughter and applause from the gallery, and a round of heavy gavel pounding as the chair tried to restore order. When calm returned, the Little Giant delivered what he surely believed was the coup de grâce, charging Republicans with attempting to "gather political capital from the blood of your fellow citizens."

Douglas was making political hay of his own, but he nevertheless precisely described the new party's strategy. Violence in Kansas might be bad for Kansans, but it was a terrific recruiting tool. That was true as far as it went, but there was more. Defeat of the Toombs bill was the substantive manifestation of victory at the polls in 1854 and 1855, and of Banks's election as speaker. The antislavery men felt the North had caved to southern blackmail in the Missouri crisis of 1820, the nullification crisis in 1833, the Compromise of 1850, and the Kansas-Nebraska Act in 1854. Now that they controlled the House and had visions of winning the presidency, the caving was over. Republicans were not going to abandon their principles, and their new party, to placate Stephen A. Douglas.

"Suppose we abandon the Republican party for its short-comings," posited William Seward. "Will freedom then have any party left; and if so, what party and where shall we find it? Certainly no other party but the Democratic Party, of which Franklin Pierce and Stephen A. Douglas are the Apostles. But that is the party of Slavery."

After the failed back-and-forth on the Toombs bill, John Sherman—author of the Howard Report—offered an amendment to an army appropriation bill to bar the use of the military for enforcing laws enacted by the proslavery Kansas legislature. If Pierce was going to use the army to defend slavery in Kansas, the Republican House would refuse to fund it. This would also have the ancillary effect of boosting free-state public relations. Though fighting the territorial government made it easy to get good press, fighting the army was a tougher sell to voters. Republicans hoped to prevent that by removing the army from the equations. The House adopted Sherman's proposal overwhelmingly, but the Senate refused to concur in the amendment, and three conference committees failed to reach an agreement on a final version. Congress adjourned in mid-August without funding the army, and Pierce called them back into special session in the last week of the month. After several more days of pointless back-and-forth, the House passed a clean spending bill, the army got its money, and Congress went home to campaign.

Congress had washed its hands of Kansas for the time being, but that didn't stop the trouble. John Brown had continued his depredations, launching attacks at Osawatomie and in Douglas County. Other free staters killed half a dozen in an attack on Franklin. The newly funded army was deployed to disarm the militias and blockade armed immigrants. Predictably, this drew protests, while also inspiring those hoping to reach Kansas to improvise, adapt, and overcome. One way they did this was to mingle with other immigrants headed west; a few attached themselves to Mormon companies making their way across Iowa and bound for their jumping-off place north of Omaha. Among those slipping into Kansas through the back door was an army of several hundred men, with artillery. This force attacked a Missouri militia at the end of August, though no advantage was gained by either side. The major battle of August, though, was fought at Fort Titus, when about forty free staters attacked the garrison ten miles west of Lawrence, using ammunition cast from the melted-down remains of type used by the destroyed *Herald of Freedom* newspaper, wrecked during the sack of Lawrence in May. The free-state victory at Fort Titus was avenged a fortnight later when four hundred proslavery men on the trail of John Brown assailed Osawatomie. Unable to capture Brown, they had to settle for killing his son Frederick, who had saved the day at Black Jack, and torching the town. (Brown, of course, would never face justice in Kansas but would be hanged in Virginia in 1859 following his failed raid on Harpers Ferry.)

The propaganda value of Kansas was obvious to everyone, including James Buchanan. Through intermediaries, the Democratic candidate begged Franklin Pierce to do something to take the pressure off. Bending to reality at last, Pierce acted. He recalled Sumner and replaced him with Brigadier General Persifor Smith, an old colleague from the Mexican War viewed by men on both sides as less partisan and better suited to the task at hand. Pierce also sent word that he wanted Charles Robinson and the other free-state officials who had been jailed released on bail. Finally, he appointed John W. Geary to replace Wilson Shannon as governor. The hulking Geary, who wore an Old Testament beard and stood over six feet five inches tall, radiated authority. Another Pennsylvanian, he saw the challenge in Kansas as a problem to solve rather than a situation to exploit. But he was no fool. He knew he was "carrying a Presidential candidate" from his home state on his back.

The moves didn't temper Republican criticism. "Jefferson Davis especially thirsts for blood. His instructions to General Smith not to be too squeamish about how he sheds it, are characteristic and significant," the *New-York Tribune* reported. But when Geary reached the proslavery capital of Lecompton on September 11—the day Robinson and the other free-state prisoners were released—he moved with alacrity to shut down militia activity by both sides. He sent armed Missourians home, while warning Democratic politicians that another incident like the sack of Lawrence would spell doom for their ticket in November. The most effective free-state militia leader, James Lane, retreated into Nebraska. Geary's evenhanded approach proved somewhat successful in his task of "carrying a presidential candidate," which he said he "labored night and day" to achieve.

Soon after the prisoners were released, Republicans brought them east to campaign for Frémont. They talked about the human cost, the three dozen people killed, the millions in property destroyed. And they blamed the Democrats. In a speech in New York, Robinson called Buchanan an "accessory after the fact" to Pierce's "treason" against the people of Kansas. Though former governor Andrew Reeder, until very recently a Democrat, had escaped arrest, he too endorsed the Republican, lending further credence to the party's Kansas cant. Reeder was such an effective spokesman that Buchanan henchman John W. Forney suggested violence might be the proper response. "He must be met and brained," Forney urged the candidate.

Another Buchanan adviser had suggested the solution to the problems facing a country embroiled in violence from coast to coast was more violence. It was little wonder, then, that more violence is what ensued.

{ 9 }

"THE SEVEREST
DEADLIEST BLOW UPON
SLAVERY"

Negotiations between Republican and North American leaders in the days and weeks after the two parties' conventions yielded few results. Republican vice presidential nominee William Dayton was immovable, vowing to remain in the race "for good or evil." The Know Nothing supporters of William F. Johnston were just as intransigent. Some North Americans were incensed that Republicans had reneged on what they believed was an ironclad guarantee that Johnston would be the fusion VP nominee, and they were in no mood to give way. Party leaders and the rank and file were unsure about each other. And Johnston himself seemed even less certain.

Following the conventions, North American state councils in New England voted to insist on Johnston. But again there seemed to be a split between what the prideful party leaders wanted—some kind of victory they could claim over the Republicans—and what most of their voters wanted: a united ticket that could win in November. The argument for Johnston was made more difficult by the factional nature of Pennsylvania politics; it was not at all clear that Johnston would do much to help the ticket in the state. And he was sending signals that he would be happy with some other job, perhaps in the cabinet. When almost a thousand delegates attended separate Republican and North American state conventions in Hartford, Connecticut, on August 6, the Know Nothing leadership—"a mere clique of office holders," one Republican called them—folded under pressure from their own delegates, who demanded unity. That solved the problem in Connecticut and paved the way for a final resolution, although not without a few remaining bumps. Desperate, the North American leadership suggested that both VP candidates step aside and a new man be chosen. Johnston accepted the idea, but Dayton rejected it, as did the Republican leadership, who sensed that they now had the Know Nothings in a bind. National chairman Edwin Morgan seized the opportunity to be magnanimous, telling Johnston that "the past we cannot recall, but for the future something may be done." That was good enough for Johnston, who met with Frémont and followed that up with an August 29 letter of withdrawal.

At last, the ticket was set and the campaign could get under way.

In the nineteenth century, parties—like government—were very much an affair of the states, and united into a national organization only for the purpose of contesting presidential elections. For the Republicans, in their first national campaign, this was doubly true. That lack of coordination would have severe consequences in some of the most closely run states.

On the other hand, Republicans had to organize only in the North. What little activity there was in slave states received virtually no attention from the national party apparatus. But the argument that the Republicans were a "sectional" party rang hollow with some, who correctly pointed out that it was the people who *opposed* the Republicans who were being sectional. Republicans would have been happy to win support in the South; the fact that none was forthcoming made southerners sectional, not Republicans.

"A party is not national merely because interest or ambition may lead some in the proscribed portion of the country to its support," wrote New York Whig Hamilton Fish. "Neither is it sectional because fear or prejudice may deter any or all in one section from its advocacy."

The Radical Abolition Party's presidential candidate, Gerrit Smith, expanded on Fish's point. "I admit that Col. Frémont is a sectional candidate; and I also admit that I am sorry for it. It is wrong that he should be a sectional candidate. But is he to blame for it? Not at all. The South makes him a sectional candidate by refusing to vote for him."

Republicans could not match the Democratic organization at the national level, and in most cases not at the state level. But nineteenth-century politics being largely a state-by-state affair even in presidential election years helped minimize the wide disparity in resources—human and capital. Buchanan was known to everyone, so Democrats had less need to introduce their man to the electorate, but they were nevertheless sending out forty thousand pieces of campaign literature a day. Frémont was famous but a political blank slate; Republicans spent enormous sums of time and money on pamphlets and other paper introducing Frémont the explorer as a potential national leader. At the same time, they missed an opportunity to make the best use of such materials. While the multiple biographies of Frémont highlighted his compelling life story and romantic adventures, other campaign materials did not. Instead, banners, buttons, tokens, and the like focused almost exclusively on the issue of slavery extension, with barely a mention of Frémont's heroic exploits. (The most frequent exceptions to the slavery focus were the materials that mentioned Jessie.) Even larger presentations, such as parade floats, which could have been used to display mountainous scenes of exploration, tended toward dismal depictions of violence in Kansas and the like.

Those running the show did so with little help from the man for whom they were running it. John C. Frémont was a babe in the woods when it came to politics. To his credit, he had enough sense not to act like he knew more than he did. But in the process, he "was so extremely cautious that he evaded the most ordinary expressions relating to the conduct and prospects of battle," one Pennsylvania pol remembered.

So the men of the national committee did the only thing they could in such circumstances: they turned to a woman. Jessie Benton Frémont was not cautious, and she was no babe in the woods. She joined three men on the committee informally assigned to make sure the candidate didn't do or say anything stupid—an unlikely concern, since Frémont was not apt to say much of anything. The campaign had an official headquarters at 34 Broadway in New York, an office occupied by Frémont's California business manager. But the real hub was the Frémont home at 56 West Ninth Street, a three-year-old rowhouse just off Fifth Avenue. Here, mail was sorted and answered, newspapers were scoured, and visitors were entertained. Jessie did the sorting on a dining room table heaped with market baskets filled with fruit, mail, and newspapers, in a room where the aroma of coffee filled the air as if in a High Sierra camp. She enlisted thirteen-year-old daughter Lily in the campaign, teaching her to clip and file newspaper stories. Lily remembered that stories were "blue penciled by my mother" before Frémont got to read them. While Jessie, John Bigelow, Francis Blair, and others tended to business, Frémont stayed out of the way and out of the public eye. Having always been a man of the outdoors, he spent most of his time during the campaign there—fencing, riding his horse, and taking long walks through what was then still not an entirely urban landscape.

"Quite at the beginning I asked that all mail should pass through me and the few friends qualified to decide what part of it needed to reach Mr. Frémont," Jessie noted. She handled the "personal and friendly letters," while Bigelow dealt with political correspondence and Isaac Sherman focused on New York matters. Some inside the campaign criticized Frémont as being too delicate to face all the criticism. But that wasn't it. Jessie was his "second mind," and they were so much in sync that she knew what he needed to know and didn't need to know, and he trusted her implicitly to separate the wheat from the chaff. He was known to be thin-skinned, but the man who had survived winter in the Sierra Nevada was not afraid of a snide newspaper columnist. What the politicians couldn't countenance in Frémont was his inwardness, his refusal to engage in small talk, his lack of a sense of humor with anyone but Jessie, and his refusal to play the game by their rules. He judged people quickly, and some of them came up on the short end of his assessment. He was not always right, but he was right often enough to make the pros uneasy. He was not one of them, and they did not know what to make of a man who showed no desire to become one of them.

In addition to her organizing and clerical duties, Jessie received guests. The Frémonts lodged in a hilltop farmhouse on Staten Island in July to escape the heat of Manhattan and the crush of visitors but took a boat back to the bustle daily. The Frémont home was a constant hive of activity.

"This house has people pouring in from all quarters from 6 oclk in the mng until late at night," Elizabeth Blair Lee reported during a visit. One rude visitor sat down across a table from Jessie and proceeded to grill her about her supposed ownership of slaves, whether she read racy magazines on Sunday, the obedience of her children, and how English her manners seemed. Jessie took it all in good form, and the skeptic eventually wrote a glowing newspaper article about the candidate's wife.

One of the first visitors to the Ninth Street house was Rev. Henry Ward Beecher, who came to tell the Frémonts of his plan for a campaign speaking trip across several states. Beecher also passed along that half the women in his congregation were mimicking Jessie's hairstyle. This was something of a trend across the country. Women everywhere were adopting her favorite color, violet, for their outfits, and wearing the flower in their hair and belts. Letters came to the Frémont home from every northern state with birth announcements for little Jessie Annes. "Nearly all the girl babies that have made their appearance of late, in these parts, are called Jessie," the *Indiana American* was already reporting in late July.

The campaign's strategy was straightforward. To reach the 149 electoral votes necessary for victory, a way had to be found to win Pennsylvania (27 electoral votes) and one or two of the other three middle-tier northern states: New Jersey (7 electoral votes), Indiana (13 electoral votes), and Illinois (11 electoral votes). New England (41 combined electoral votes) and New York, the single largest prize with 35 electoral votes, seemed reasonably secure if the Know Nothings could be held at bay. The upper states of the Old Northwest had quickly turned into the Republican base: Ohio (23 electoral votes), Michigan (6 electoral votes), Wisconsin (5 electoral votes), and Iowa (4 electoral votes). Despite Blair's early optimism, there was no chance of winning anything on the Middle Border or the South (despite an endorsement from Texan Sam Houston, who said, "There will be neither bustling, bayonets, nor secession, if Colonel Frémont shall be elected by a majority of the people"). Much to Frémont's chagrin, California (4 electoral votes) looked like a Democratic bastion.

The division of labor for the opposition seemed clear enough as well. Democrats had to compete everywhere, in line with their claim of being the only national party. The Know Nothings would pin Democrats down in the South, ensuring they could not devote all their resources to the four targeted northern states. So the Democratic strategy was to render Fillmore unviable, leaving southerners and northern doughfaces nowhere to turn but their party.

The tent revival enthusiasm of the Republican convention carried over into the campaign. An estimated sixty thousand people attended a Republican parade in Indianapolis, which featured what had quickly become a staple: thirty-two girls dressed in white representing the states of the Union, and one in black representing "downtrodden Kansas." Fifty bands played along the route, which took five hours to complete and was secured by twenty-five marshals and a thundering cannon.

A rally in Beloit, Wisconsin, involved hundreds of Republicans in the small city of about three thousand inhabitants. The partisans attended planning meetings, served on committees, and prepared food for volunteers and visitors, who poured in from eight counties in Wisconsin and five from Illinois. All told, about twenty-five thousand people crowded into town for a parade and speeches. Women sold meals for twenty-five cents each, and the proceeds were contributed to relief efforts for antislavery settlers in Kansas. They cleared $600; all the provisions had been donated.

Among those stumping Illinois was the runner-up vice presidential candidate. Abraham Lincoln spoke before thirty-five thousand people in the riverfront city of Alton, where two decades earlier the newspaper publisher Elijah P. Lovejoy (brother of Republican firebrand Owen Lovejoy) had been murdered by proslavery zealots. Just to kill time while waiting to deliver a speech in the small town of Oregon, about halfway between Rockford and Dixon, Lincoln counted more than seventy nursing babies on hand "to receive their political christening," as one of his fellow speakers noted.

Lincoln ventured out of Illinois only once (although he had other invitations). In late August in Kalamazoo, Michigan, site of a giant gathering that featured parades, eight bands, the Battle Creek Glee Club, and four stands with speakers orating simultaneously all afternoon, he cut to the heart of the matter. "The question of slavery, at the present day, should be not only the greatest question but very nearly the sole question." Responding to charges that a Frémont victory would result in secession, Lincoln scoffed. "How is the dissolution of the Union to be consummated? They tell us that the Union is in danger. Who will divide it? Is it those who make the charge? Are they themselves the persons who wish to see this result? A majority will never dissolve the Union."

Such denials were crucial to and an integral part of the evangelical fervor that enveloped the Republican campaign. But every time one was made, the word "dissolution" was entered once again in the ledger. For Buchanan, it confirmed his worst fears and most fervent hope. "I have always had a pretty firm conviction that the danger to the Union would eventually make us stronger in the North than our friends have imagined," he crowed.

"Put Her Up for President"

In Missouri, John and Jessie Frémont's quarrel with Thomas Hart Benton had direct electoral ramifications.

Jessie's father, having been deposed after a thirty-year Senate career because of his opposition to the spread of slavery then unceremoniously dumped after one term in the House, was running for governor. Frank Blair was running for Congress in Saint Louis as a free soil Democrat. Benton and the son of his old comrade quarreled over Benton's insistence that Blair not do anything to overtly support Frémont's candidacy.

A few months earlier, Jessie had believed that once her husband secured the nomination, Benton would change his mind about him. "Success, if it comes, gives a more graceful position to be friendly from and if it should be so I think Father cannot resist the influence of it all," she optimistically contended. But he could and he did. Just two days after Frémont secured the Republican nomination, Benton assured a Democratic audience in Missouri, "I am above family and above self, when the good of the Union is concerned."

In speeches throughout June and July, Benton railed about the "fractional parties," who were to blame for the "violence and disorder which overspreads the land." He—and, by extension, Buchanan and the Democrats—represented "the principle of peace—of order, law, and justice."

"We are treading upon a volcano that is liable at any moment to burst forth and overwhelm the nation," he warned. Referring to Frémont specifically, Benton said in Missouri that "there was nothing which a father could do for a son which I have not done to carry him through his undertakings, and to uphold him in the severe trials to which he has been subjected." This was true. But in this latest adventure, Benton would stand against Frémont. "I told him at once that I not only could not support him, but that I would oppose him."

In a similar vein, Martin Van Buren, the former Democratic president and 1848 Free Soil Party candidate—whom Elizabeth Benton had urged her daughter to marry instead of John C. Frémont—endorsed Buchanan, who had escorted Jessie to Washington functions only a year before she married Frémont. Van Buren insisted that "all must admit it to be certain that there never was a period in the history of this Republic when sectional animosities were so rife, or had, to so great an extent, inflamed the masses of the people."

Frémont at least enjoyed the endorsement of one male Benton, Jessie's cousin Tom, who lived in Iowa and "has come out from the corruption of the Pro-Slavery faction, and declares himself openly for Frémont and Freedom."

Jessie Benton Frémont was not the only interested party in the presidential election to be deserted by family. The mainline Know Nothings' vice presidential candidate, Andrew Jackson Donelson, was abandoned by his brother Daniel, a loyal Democrat, and his cousin Andrew Jackson Jr., the adopted son of the late president whom Donelson had served so devotedly.

In August Frank Blair was elected to Congress from Missouri as a free soil Democrat. In the governor's race, Benton won Saint Louis County but trailed badly elsewhere and finished third with less than 25 percent of the vote. It was the end of the line for Benton's long and glorious career. But even more, it was the end of the line for the antislavery movement in statewide Missouri Democratic politics. When Blair showed up at the US Capitol to take his seat, it would be as a Republican.

Benton's defeat left him momentarily bereft, "very much thinner and so still," Jessie wrote. "It seemed as if sadness and silence were so fixed upon him that he could not shake them off." But silence and Thomas Hart Benton were not well acquainted, and he would snap out of it quickly and continue his campaign against Frémont or, as he would term it, for the Union.

Although there could be no doubt which way Benton was blowing on the presidential canvas, he could still be hot tempered and evasive on the subject when cornered. On a campaign swing through Ohio, a fellow passenger walked through the train and polled the occupants of each car. When he got to Benton, whom the "officious individual" failed to recognize, and asked how he planned to vote in November, Benton let loose: "Sir! By what authority, sir, do you ask me for whom I shall vote? Sir, I will answer that question at the ballot box, not to you."

While Benton was losing, Frémont's campaign was gathering steam. Along with fundraising and distribution of campaign literature, managing the speakers' bureau was one of the central functions of the national party, which worked in conjunction with state and local organizations to find orators and schedule events. Chairman Edwin Morgan relied on a shifting circle of outside advisers for this task. Henry Stanton of New York was in charge, but advice came from men across the regional and political spectrum, including Schuyler Colfax, Thurlow Weed, Simon Cameron, John Bigelow, Preston King, and Frémont's closest political friends, Francis Blair and Nathaniel Banks.

Stanton complained that there were simply not enough good speakers to go around, and with the focus the campaign was placing on Pennsylvania, other states often went begging. On the other hand, New York, a relatively safe state for Frémont, had a surfeit of speakers, because so many available men lived there or nearby and were happy to participate without having to travel too much.

Banks urged the Frémonts to visit Pennsylvania in person. It would have been unprecedented for a candidate to make such a trip. For a candidate's wife, it would have been unthinkable. The candidate was not especially tempted; the wife was. She sought Francis Preston Blair's advice, and in the end, neither went. "I want to fight with stronger weapons than courtesies," she wrote to Elizabeth Blair Lee from Staten Island in August, "and I will do mischief if I am let loose among opponents. I am better on my island here where I can get over indignation by myself."

One source of enthusiastic campaign orators was Kansas. Alerting Frémont in late July that a mutual friend—"an excellent Stump Speaker"—was traveling east from Kansas to join the campaign, would-be free-state governor Charles Robinson had provided a lay of the territorial land while he was still being held a prisoner. "Affairs here are as bad as they can be. Tyranny rules with a rod of iron. It is unknown as yet whether Pierce has fully decided to hang us or not. However, if our hanging can change this infernal administration they will not make much by the investment."

Also coming from Kansas was Cyrus Holliday, one of the founders of Topeka and a regimental commander during the Wakarusa War. A group of Pennsylvanians had invited Holliday, a native of the Keystone State, to speak at a series of Frémont rallies. Holliday, who was traveling east at the time anyway to bring his family back to Kansas, accepted the invitation, and ended up delivering 130 speeches on behalf of Frémont. He didn't get his family back to Kansas until the election was over.

Philadelphia lawyer John M. Read pointed out in a long speech delivered in his hometown at the end of September that a similar "speech in favor of Frémont in Kansas would place the speaker in the penitentiary, or rather condemn him to the ball and chain," because of restrictions on freedom of expression written into the "pretended laws of Kansas" enacted "by force, fraud, intimidation, and violence."

Another source tapped by Stanton was women, who were hitting the hustings for Frémont in a way never before seen in American politics. But Stanton missed out on one obvious opportunity. Elizabeth Cady Stanton frequently accompanied her husband to the events he helped organize. As hard up for stump speakers in crucial states as he was, he never seemed to consider the dazzling speaker who had thrilled the New York Women's Temperance Society as its president and most popular public figure. "To think that all in me of which my father would have felt a proper pride had I been a man, is deeply mortifying to him because I am a woman," she wrote. "That thought has stung me to a fierce decision—to speak as soon as I can do myself credit." But she would not make it onto the stage in the 1856 campaign. "Henry sides with my friends who oppose me in all that is dearest to my heart."

Kansas emigrant Julia Louisa Lovejoy was another woman who supported Frémont, although she rejected the very idea of "these gadders abroad" like Lucy Stone, "these women lecturers who are continually at the old theme, 'women's rights.'" She believed women could be just as effective if they would "exert their individual and associative influence over their husbands and brothers in favor of freedom and Frémont." Sometimes the movements were in competition. A New York women's rights convention originally planned for October was rescheduled for late November "in view of the absorbing interest in the Presidential question."

Stone was on the stump that summer, but she was not overtly participating in the Frémont campaign, although with her antislavery rhetoric she sounded much the same as those who were. During a July 4 speech in tiny Viroqua in the Kickapoo River valley of southwestern Wisconsin—thought to be the first women's rights and antislavery speech ever made by a woman in the old Northwest, in a state where a women's suffrage measure had been introduced only four months earlier—the stage on which she was speaking collapsed. No one was seriously injured, and Stone seized the moment to make a larger point to the crowd gathered to listen. "So will this country fall unless slavery is abolished," she declared.

Stone herself was suspicious of the Republicans and cautioned her comrades to be wary as well. Her sister-in-law, Antoinette Brown Blackwell, the first American woman ordained as a minister, took the opposite view on partisan political activity, and had been an enthusiastic advocate of the Liberty Party. Susan B. Anthony wrote that "had the accident of birth given me a place among the aristocracy of sex, I doubt not I should be an active, zealous advocate of Republicanism."

Kansan Clarina Howard Nichols, a veteran journalist and "lady lecturer" who had called for the "impeachment of the tyrant" Pierce, traveled to Connecticut, Pennsylvania, and New York at the behest of *New-York Tribune* editor Horace Greeley, one of those advising Stanton, delivering five lectures a week at the rate of ten dollars a talk. "If old Penn. is to be carried by only a few votes & I could change the votes of that few to Frémont, nothing would induce me to leave the field I am now in," she wrote.

"Everywhere the Republicans had said that there would be seats reserved for ladies at their meetings," said Lucy Stone, "as when Mr. Frémont was to be seen in New York, there was no peace among the people until Jessie came out too. They all recognized woman's right to have something at least to do with politics."

Just as women had always been excluded from American political life, so had African Americans. In 1856, that changed. In the North, free blacks were a public part of the campaign in states where abolitionist sentiment was strongest. The *National Anti-Slavery Standard* reported in August that a "Frémont Barbecue is to be held in Charles River Grove, ten miles from Boston, on Tuesday next, when an ox is to be roasted whole! Music by the steam calliope. The caterer for the occasion is the well-known coloured artist, J. B. Smith."

And even in the South, among the enslaved population, blacks clandestinely held meetings and spread the word about the possibilities presented by the Frémont campaign. Mississippi slave William Webb later wrote of slaves who "held great meetings and had speeches among themselves, in secret." At these meetings, some of the younger men talked about "rebelling and killing," while older men cautioned that it would be better to "wait for the next four years," in the certain hope that the "next president would set the colored people free."

Inevitably, word of the secret meetings leaked out, and the backlash was violent. Across the South in 1856, from Texas to Virginia, vigilantes hired by slaveholders (or acting on their own) beat, tortured, and hanged slaves whom they suspected of believing that "Frémont was at the head of a large army, and was only waiting for them" to rise up so he could lead that army against the South.

Estimates vary and records are scarce, but as many as thirty-three slaves were lynched during the campaign, more than were killed following the Nat Turner rebellion in 1831. Some of this was paranoia on the part of southerners who often saw such conspiracies where none existed, but the fear was not entirely fatuous. Slaves were indeed getting together to talk about the campaign and to try to figure out what, if anything, they could do to help Frémont.

Ironically, Democrats were largely to blame for the slaves' inflated hopes of liberation. Republicans consistently asserted that they had no intention of interfering with slavery where it already existed. But when Democratic stump speakers visited Democratic counties, exaggerated accounts of "abolitionist Black Republicans" filtered down to the slave population, providing a distorted view of Republican intentions and inadvertently inspiring hope among the enslaved.

One group of slaves in Texas conspired to arm themselves and escape to Mexico. Southern newspapers accused Republican operatives of egging them on, supposing that slaves "had got hold of some indistinct and vague ideas about obtaining their freedom" from such agitators. Unable to do anything about supposed Yankees in their midst, Texans took their rage out on the slaves, beating dozens—two to death—and hanging three others.

The fear spread quickly after the incidents in Texas in September. Similar "plots" were uncovered in Arkansas, Missouri, Louisiana, Kentucky, and Tennessee, again "led on by white men" and linked to the election campaign. "Fred Douglass and Joshua R. Giddings, leading off the whole Frémont party are busy instigating these negro insurrections," an Ohio journalist surmised.

In Arkansas, two white men accused of "distributing fire-arms among the negroes" ahead of Election Day were killed by mobs. Four slaves owned by Tennessee senator John Bell were ordered hanged by a judge while Bell was in Washington. Five more were killed by a mob.

"The negroes manifested an unusual interest in the result . . . and attended the political meetings of the whites in large numbers," noted a Tennessee editor, who concluded, "This is dangerous."

The mere presence of slaves on the periphery of such meetings was deemed ominous, even though they had no votes or voice. But one former slave did have a voice, and he was now ready to employ it on Frémont's behalf.

On August 15, Frederick Douglass announced in the newspaper that bore his name—Seward had quietly provided some of the working capital for the paper—that he was switching his support in the presidential contest from the Radical Abolition Party's Gerrit Smith to John C. Frémont. While acknowledging that the move would be "an unwelcome surprise" to many of his readers, it was time for practicality to trump absolutism—without principle being abandoned. "The name of Gerrit Smith has long been synonymous with us as genuine, unadulterated Abolitionism," Douglass wrote. "Of all men beneath the sky, we would rather see this just man made President." Alas, it was certain that he would not be. And it was becoming evident that Frémont might. "Anti-Slavery consistency itself, in our view, requires of the Anti-Slavery voter that disposition of his vote and his influence, which, in all the circumstances and likelihoods of the case tend most to the triumph of Free Principles in the Councils and Government of the nation. It is not to be consistent to pursue a course politically this year, merely because that course seemed the best last year, or at any previous time. Right Anti-Slavery action is that which deals the severest deadliest blow upon slavery that can be given at that particular time." Now, Douglass was saying, was the time to begin.

Douglass had come to believe what fire-eating southerners also understood: the claim by Republicans that they were steadfastly opposed to the expansion of slavery but would not interfere with it where it existed was a dodge. Those who spoke of "higher law" and "irrepressible conflicts" would not be satisfied with halting slavery's advance, and their plan for doing so was clearly intended to squeeze slavery in on itself, surround it with freedom, and drive it to eventual extinction. "While the Republican Party has not at this point adopted the Abolition creed, it has laid down principles and promulgated doctrines, which in their application, directly tend to the Abolition of Slavery in the States," he wrote. This was not

FREDERICK DOUGLASS.
Courtesy of Library of Congress

Douglass's preferred method, but it was a method, and for the first time a national political party was advocating something that could lead to the eradication of slavery. Douglass could not miss this opportunity in the name of loyalty to a friend or dedication to a higher calling. He could not let the perfect be the enemy of the good.

"The greatest triumphs of Slavery have been secured by the division of its enemies," Douglass wrote, and he would no longer play into their hands. "All men will agree, that, generally speaking, the point attacked, is the point to be defended. The South has tendered to us the issue of Slavery Extension; and to meet the Slave Power here is to rouse its most devilish animosity. It is to strike hardest, where the Slaveholders feel most keenly. The most powerful blow that could be given at that point would in our judgment, be the election to the Presidency and Vice Presidency of the Republic the Candidates of the Republican Party . . . the admitted and recognized antagonists of the Slave Power."

William Lloyd Garrison had some sympathy for Douglass's position. "As between the contending political parties, my feelings and wishes are with the Republican party, of course, because it occupies a position relatively anti-slavery," he said. And, albeit grudgingly, he granted the Republicans more respect than he ever had the Liberty Party, largely because he had a softer spot for politicians striving to be moral than for moralists striving to be politicians. But he doubted the proposition that any political party would deliver more than it promised, and nothing could pull Garrison into the maw of electoral politics under a Constitution that permitted slavery. He would not be part of the revolutionary movement of which Douglass dreamed and that Frémont represented.

Abolitionist Wendell Phillips echoed Garrison, questioning Frémont's antislavery bona fides. "I know he has battled with nature; with the frost and the snow, with starvation, with want—all of that; but when has he battled as the unflinching advocate of an unpopular idea? When? Where is his life tossed into angry turmoil by the opposition of minds that he has roused against him?" the orator wondered. He did know of one example. "Never, but when he stole his wife! For once, he opposed a MAN. I think he did well," a line that drew applause from his audience.

But Garrison and Phillips were not the entire abolitionist movement. While New Yorker George Templeton Strong had dismissed the Republican Party as "a mere squirm and wriggle of the insulted North," he also acknowledged that "it calls out many who have long eschewed politics." Some of those now entering the fray were Garrisonians.

Abolitionist author Lydia Maria Child had come to believe that "if the Slave-Power is checked now, it will never regain its strength." Though she couldn't vote, she declared that she would "come and rap at the ballot box," and urged all like-minded women to do the same. "I was never bitten by politics before; but such mighty issues are depending on *this* election, that I cannot be indifferent." She promised to dress up in her husband's slouch hat and overcoat and vote in his stead if he didn't return in time from a business trip. Harriet Beecher Stowe never formally endorsed Frémont, but referred to "we" in writing about the Republicans. Massachusetts Senator Henry Wilson credited Stowe with "the rich fruitage of seed" that *Uncle Tom's Cabin* provided to the Republican movement.

And no less a figure than Gerrit Smith came to the defense of his Republican rival for the presidency, through Jessie. "Mrs. Frémont told me that her mother taught her to hate Slavery, and she did hate it. She said she would never own a slave, nor permit one to do her work. She did her own work, rather."

Rev. Henry Ward Beecher at first used the pulpit of his Plymouth Church in New York City to raise money for the campaign and urge parishioners to action. He was devoting so much time to Frémont's cause that eventually the trustees of the church decided to grant Beecher a leave of absence for the duration of the campaign, and he traveled throughout the Northeast making stump speeches. Thousands attended, usually standing, sometimes in foul weather, to listen to the bombastic preacher regale them with rhetoric that "abounded in side-splitting fun and pathos alternately."

But Frémont's wife remained his most popular and effective advocate by far. Wendell Phillips, who had wondered at Frémont's qualifications, had no such qualms about his wife. "If Jessie is an abolitionist, put her up for President," he said to rousing cheers. "But do not put her husband up, while he allows himself bound by a Constitution that makes slavery in the Carolinas safe from the interference of the United States government."

"Isn't it pleasant to have a woman spontaneously recognized as a moral influence in public affairs? There's meaning in that fact," wrote Lydia Maria Child.

Still, there was the ever-present pain of opposition from Jessie's father, which seemed to be growing louder and even bitterer. In a public letter in mid-August, Thomas Hart Benton recalled his early problems with Andrew Jackson and compared them with his present family situation. "There are cases in which public duty rises above personal considerations," he wrote, "though there are a great many people who cannot conceive it possible. Thus, when I supported Jackson (with whom I had been on ill terms) thirty years ago"—he had shot Jackson during a running gunfight in a Nashville hotel in 1813—"the sordid motive of office was assigned for it; now, when I support Buchanan (with whom I am on ill terms), and support him against a member of my own family, the same class of persons can see nothing in it but falsehood and treachery. Incapable themselves of anything disinterested and patriotic, they believe others to be equally so."

While Benton was quick to defend his own motives, he neglected to defend the honor of his son-in-law—and, indirectly, his daughter—against critics who called Frémont a Catholic, a bastard, and a slave owner. "Father's silence when he has always been so prompt to do battle for the right hurts me literally to the heart," she poured out to Francis Preston Blair, who also must have wondered about the moral backwardness of his old friend. "I hoped I might have served as hostage for at least his being just but I see he is with them altogether."

The opposition had some fun with what they considered the circus-like atmosphere that surrounded Jessie Benton Frémont's appearances. In a lengthy diatribe shortly after Frémont's nomination, a Saint Louis Democratic paper derided "the feminine partner in the business." Recounting a recent rally at the Frémonts' home in New York City, the paper belittled the "pretense of holding back—a sham coyness—in the matter of complying with the request of the gentlemen who wanted to 'see Jessie.' . . . When Harrison ran for the Presidency, something was said about his being a 'petticoat candidate.' But that aspersion was intended in a very different sense from anything which can attach to the use which it seems Frémont's managers intend to make of Frémont's wife." Suggesting that showman

P. T. Barnum must have had a hand in organizing such a ridiculous spectacle, the paper "supposed that Frémont had in his own person gunpowder glory enough to suffice for all the clap-trap which would be needed by these managers. But they evidently think otherwise, since they have turned his wife—'our Jessie'—in as a part of his electioneering stock in trade."

Another wag set new words to the tune of "Oh Susanna."

I've climbed the Rocky Mountains,
And traveled far and wide;
But after next election
I know not where I'll hide.
I tried to catch Americans,
But they were all too shy;
They somehow knew too much for me
Yet Jessie don't you cry.

That contrasted with the supporters, who importuned:

Ah Jessie! Sweet Jessie!
Bid the hero speed—
Let the people find him true
In their time of need!

Not all the criticism was quite so lighthearted. One stern foe suggested "these demented females would much better form sewing circles, bread, pudding, and knitting circles, spanking-bad-children-and-putting-them-to-bed circles, than to be Jessying around the country whilst their husbands starve and their brats hollow murder at home."

Another happily remembered that "luckily, they have no votes, and must content themselves with a continual caterwauling in the garrets and about the eaves of public places, shocking the nerves of the community, and provoking irritable people to throw brickbats among them, now and then, but doing no further disadvantage."

Even without votes, women continued to push themselves into the process, and Jessie was the touchstone.

Frémont events invariably included a banner reading FRÉMONT AND OUR JESSIE, JESSIE'S CHOICE, and JESSIE FOR THE WHITE HOUSE.

"At an impromptu gathering of Frémonters up town, the other evening, an enthusiastic advocate of the Rocky Mountain candidate put it to the crowd, whether it were not better to send a man to the White House who had completed his humanities by marrying an accomplished woman, than to send there such a rusty old bachelor as Buchanan, whose domestic hospitalities could only be seasoned with the doubtful graces of some hired housekeeper? At this interrogatory, a gentleman present, who remembered the maiden name of Mrs. Frémont (Jessie Benton), shouted 'WE'LL GIVE 'EM JESSIE!' This felicitous double entendre only needs to be published to become the watchword of the campaign," reported *Frank Leslie's Weekly*. "Beautiful, graceful, intellectual, and enthusiastic, she will make more proselytes to the Rocky Mountain platform in fifteen minutes, than fifty stump orators can win over in a month."

But she was more than a symbol. An Ohio Republican said out loud what many must have been thinking: that Jessie "would have been the better candidate."

As the reaction of figures like Wendell Phillips and Gerrit Smith suggests, Jessie particularly helped to buttress her husband's antislavery credentials. "I would as soon place my children in the midst of small pox," she wrote to Lydia Maria Child, "as rear them under the influences of slavery." A favorite and frequently repeated story involved the pre-statehood debate over slavery in California, during which a group of southern women who had moved to the territory urged Frémont to come out forcefully in favor of the peculiar institution. Without slaves, they asked, who will cook, clean, and tend the children? "Rather California should be a slave state, I would do my own work and be my own servant," she told them.

Working and worrying herself to a frazzle, and with baby Frank coming down with a fever, by the end of August Jessie was ordered by her doctors to take it easy—"no newspapers, no ideas, no excitement of any kind." As part of her respite, Jessie visited Washington for a week in early September with elder son Charley and daughter Lily, and joined her father for dinner with the Blairs in Silver Spring, where she chose to take the optimistic view despite the haggard appearance of Benton. She continued to believe, despite all evidence to the contrary, that "one of the good things in Mr. Frémont's success would be the enlivening of Father."

Even with her forced downtime, Jessie's influence was felt in ways large and small, all across the country. Portraits of Jessie labeled "Head of his 'kitchen cabinet'" were sold by New Englanders. Women's groups sprang up across the North. The Republican women of Fall River, Massachusetts, organized a "JessieCircle." There were the "Sisters of Jessie" elsewhere in the Bay State, "Jessie Clubs" in the mining towns of California, the "Tribe of Jessie" in Ohio and New York, and the "Ladies' Jessie Club" in Pennsylvania. And women were turning out in huge numbers for rallies. One reporter commented that "some 400 ladies" attended a Frémont rally in Buffalo.

The sense of empowerment felt by Republican women was trickling down, out of politics and into everyday life, even among women who would not dream of supporting John C. Frémont. Henrietta Baker Embree of Bell County, Texas, attended a trial, an experience she imagined was more regular elsewhere than in her home state. "Ladies attending court is to me something novel. I suppose it is quite common in the North," she wrote.

Still, politics was not of interest to everyone, and most women were not taking to the streets. Another Texas diarist noted with relief that the menfolk "will not hinder me from writing for they have gone out in the gallery and discussing politics, Manlike."

"Given Over to Fatal Delusion"

Buchanan's allies in Congress were doing what they could to aid their own candidate. Pennsylvania senator William Bigler tried to launch an investigation of Frémont's financial dealings at his Las Mariposas property in California and his actions during the Bear Flag Revolt in 1845, when he arrived on the scene in the midst of a local uprising and was elected by a small band of insurrectionists to be president of the short-lived California republic.

Bigler's efforts served as another spear in Jessie's heart. Her father "could by one line set right this Bigler movement," she complained as Thomas Hart Benton remained silent while his son-in-law was slandered by one of Benton's former colleagues. "I am blazing with fever from the sudden anger I felt last night on reading Mr. Bigler's motion in the Senate." But she did not directly confront Benton on the subject, and Frémont took no action. Instead, Jessie railed in confidence to Elizabeth Blair Lee, concluding that "the best answer will be in the triumph of our party." Soon after, she learned that Benton had, at least in private, stood up for Frémont's character, if not his politics.

Buchanan didn't campaign, of course, but that didn't keep him from soliciting support in whatever ways he could, including poking the hornet's nest of southern fears. "Should Frémont be elected, he must receive one hundred and forty-nine Northern electoral votes at least, and the outlawry proclaimed by the Black Republican convention in Philadelphia against fifteen Southern states will be ratified by the people of the North," he wrote.

Buchanan assigned John Breckinridge, his Kentuckian vice presidential candidate, the task of putting the Bluegrass State in the Democratic column, where it had not been since Andrew Jackson bested John Quincy Adams in 1828. One of the primary pieces of ammunition was a pamphlet produced by the national committee titled "Old Line Whigs for Buchanan and Breckinridge," which included endorsements from such leading lights as Henry Clay's son, James B. Clay. The literature was aimed directly at the heart of potential Fillmore voters; despite Francis Preston Blair's fondest wishes, Buchanan had nothing to fear from Frémont in Kentucky.

He had little more to fear from Fillmore. Some disaffected wags had suggested voting for Fillmore for president and Breckinridge for vice, and concocted complicated plots in which the election would be thrown into the House, which would be unable to reach a decision, leaving the Senate to elect Breckinridge as vice president and thus having him succeed to the vacant presidential chair. "If we cannot get the head of the ticket, I am perfectly willing to take the tail," opined Tennessee's Andrew Johnson. But it was all smoke and mirrors. Democrats swept away the Know Nothings' congressional majority in Kentucky in the August election. With Kentucky apparently secure, Breckinridge turned his attention toward Indiana. Breaking with tradition, he accepted an invitation to speak at a rally on the old Tippecanoe battlefield, chosen as a site for the giant gathering as a sentimental sop to old-line Whigs nostalgic for the days of William Henry Harrison, who won his most famous battle there. That opened the floodgates, and

Breckinridge soon decided to make a tour of it, through Indiana, Michigan, Ohio, and Pennsylvania. The Tippecanoe event, northeast of Lafayette, Indiana, was billed as the largest ever held in the West, and was attended by Stephen A. Douglas, Lewis Cass, James B. Clay, presidential son John Van Buren, and dozens of lesser dignitaries. A separate stage was set up so German voters could be addressed in their own language by Douglas ally Francis J. Grund. But Breckinridge was the featured speaker, and he delivered the party's fearmongering message to the assembled thousands in unfiltered form. "He must be blind indeed," he told the throng, "and given over to fatal delusion, who does not see that the union of the states is in imminent peril."

"I Know Only My Country"

Millard Fillmore had given in to a political delusion or two during his long career, including the Compromise of 1850. But he was guiltless on this latest count. He agreed that the union of the states was in peril.

Like Buchanan, Fillmore had been out of the country for more than a year. After fifteen months touring Europe, he arrived in New York City on June 22 aboard the *Atlantic*, which fired its guns to herald the former president's return to his native soil. He was met by a multitude of Know Nothing admirers who offered their own fifty-gun salute that lit up the warm night sky. Two or three thousand people swarmed the docks to cheer Fillmore as he disembarked. With the assembled crowd primed and ready, Fillmore gave them his first speech of the campaign, tying together the two great themes the party faithful expected him to carry through to November and the White House. "If there be those either North or South who desire an administration for the North as against the South, or for the South as against the North, they are not the men who should give their suffrages to me. For my own part, I know only my country, my whole country, and nothing but my country."

But there would be much more to be heard in the coming weeks on the sectional conflict, and very little on Americanism. Fillmore would deliver twenty-seven speeches on this campaign swing; in only three did he make an overtly nativist pitch. The word "Catholic" passed his lips only once.

"We see a political party presenting candidates for the presidency and vice presidency, selected for the first time from the free states alone, with the avowed purpose of electing those candidates by suffrages of one part of the Union only, to rule over the whole United States," he said.

Lest anyone mistake this for a Whig campaign, Fillmore stressed that he had moved on and it was time for everyone else to do the same. In a speech to the New York City Whig General Committee the day after his arrival, Fillmore declared that the "canker worm that has been gnawing at the very vitals of that party has at last, I fear, destroyed it." But, he assured his listeners, "a phoenix . . . has arisen from its ashes that is yet to save the country." This phoenix, he said, must embrace all "true Whigs" and "true-hearted Democrats."

The faithful were satisfied enough that the speeches Fillmore delivered as he traveled north from New York City to his home in Buffalo were gathered into a pamphlet and distributed as campaign literature.

Fillmore and his running mate had a clear division of labor. While Andrew Jackson Donelson castigated his former Democratic mates as nullifiers—"my idea throughout the canvass has been that it was our policy first to kill off Buchanan"—Fillmore went after Whigs-turned-Republicans with equal fervor.

Vitriolic criticism of Frémont himself, particularly the canard that he was Catholic, was left to others for the most part. One of the more outlandish charges alleged that Frémont was the pawn in a vast conspiracy led by Thurlow Weed, William Seward, and New York archbishop John Hughes to elect a Catholic president. The story was ridiculous, but the accusations were taking their toll.

Back on the firmer ground of Planet Earth, Fillmore, like Douglas, accused the Republicans—with some justification—of exaggerating the violence in Kansas for political purposes. His supporters also questioned—with less justification—whether Charles Sumner was really injured as badly as had been reported.

Massachusetts Whig Robert Winthrop, a onetime Speaker of the House, spelled out the Republican recipe in a speech at Boston's Faneuil Hall: "One-third part Missouri Compromise repeal . . . one-third Kansas outrages by Border Ruffians . . . one-third disjointed facts and misapplied figures, and a great swelling of words of vanity, to prove that the South is, upon the whole, the very poorest, meanest, least productive, and most miserable part of creation." But Winthrop, like many old-line Whigs, couldn't swallow Buchanan and the Democrats either. "The best safety of the Union is to be found in the defeat of both of them. . . . Nothing remained but to support Fillmore," he concluded.

Fillmore didn't give up entirely on nativism. "Americans should govern America," Fillmore told an audience in Newburgh, New York. "If we value the blessings which Providence has so bounteously showered upon us, it becomes every American to stand by the Constitution and the laws of his country, and to resolve that, independent of all foreign influence, Americans will and shall rule America."

It was an appeal that worked better in some places than others. Nativism remained a vivid fact of life in the Northeast but barely resonated in Georgia, for example, where fewer than 2 percent of the population was foreign born and only eight Catholic churches existed in the entire state. Still, the American Party perceived an unexpected opportunity in Texas, where some German immigrants of recent vintage had voiced opposition to slavery. This was by no means a majority opinion—the first wave of Germans who had come to the Republic of Texas before statehood were generally more establishment-oriented and had even opposed annexation in 1844. But the next large wave, which came in the wake of the European revolutions in 1848, were of a more liberal bent and agitated against the peculiar institution, declaring "that slavery is an evil, whose final removal is essential to the foundation of democracy." This didn't sit well with Anglo locals or the more established German immigrants, and some of the more vocal antislavery Germans were threatened with violence. The controversy gave the nativist Know Nothings a chance not only to demonstrate their proslavery bona fides and perhaps make a little political hay in a strongly Democratic region, but also to point their fingers at the foreigners and say "I told you so."

Such broad-based response filled the party's candidates with hope. They fully expected to win in New York, Maryland, Kentucky, Tennessee, Louisiana, and California. They were particularly optimistic that if the Pennsylvania state elections in October went against Buchanan, the South would rush to Fillmore to avoid the possibility of a Frémont victory.

But before Pennsylvania went to the polls, there would be one more piece to slide into the puzzle. As the Whig Party disintegrated, its multiplicity of factions—straight, old line, old guard, conservative—grew ever more attached to the sometimes minute but always deeply felt differences among them. Those differences made organizing a response to the Know Nothing nomination of Fillmore difficult. Some pushed to quickly call a Whig convention for summer, to give the party imprimatur to Fillmore and "rally multitudes of the solid & conservative men of the country."

The goal for these Silver Grays, so called because of their tendency to be rather older gentlemen (like Fillmore) with shocks of distinguished-looking hair atop their heads, was less to unite with the Know Nothings than to preserve the form of the party. They were sure it would be needed after the temporary storm of Republicanism—the "ephemeral factions of the day," as the *New York Commercial Advertiser* put it—blew through. But there was little if any dissent from the notion that the nomination of

MILLARD FILLMORE. *Courtesy of Library of Congress*

the American Party should be confirmed. No one was looking for another presidential candidate to carry the Whig banner. Quite a few, however, were unhappy with Andrew Jackson Donelson as the number-two man.

How to go about calling a convention presented a practical problem. With no real bloc of members remaining in Congress or in state governments, no one was sure who was empowered to do so.

Leading southern Whigs such as Archibald Dixon, Robert Toombs, and Alexander Stephens had decamped for the Democratic Party soon after Nathaniel Banks's election as Speaker. "The truth is the Southern Whigs must strike out a lead for themselves," Stephens had written in 1854, after passage of the Kansas-Nebraska Act. "They cannot afford either for their own sake or that of the country to fall into the ranks of either of the great nominal parties as they are now organized and constituted." Now that the parties were no longer "organized and constituted" as they had been just two years before, Stephens had to find a new home. It would not be with Fillmore.

When "pure" Whig endorsements came flowing in from state parties, Fillmore at first recalled his "phoenix rising from the ashes" metaphor from June, rejecting them as coming from "men who cannot see what is passing around them and do not know that the idea of reviving the Whig party by its name is utterly hopeless." But Fillmore was ultimately reduced to begging Whig holdouts to join him. Some, notably Edward Everett and Robert Winthrop, came aboard, swayed by Fillmore's prediction that "Civil War and anarchy stare us in the face," if either of the other parties claimed the presidency. Others, such as New Yorker Hamilton Fish, did not. But the joiners were of little help. Everett was largely retired from public life and spent much of the year traveling the country delivering speeches on George Washington. One Whig critic characterized them as "the fossil remains of too low and ancient a strata to stir up the surface in the least now."

To gather the flock, Fillmore decided it was necessary to acquiesce to a Whig convention and accept the party's separate nomination at a convention in Baltimore on September 17. It was a desultory affair described by one observer as "a Historical Society or Congress of Antiquarian Associations, rather than a practical political assemblage, for the Whig Party is dead, decomposed, and disintegrated." Most states sent only a few delegates, and they were anything but the leading men, although future attorney general Edward Bates represented Missouri, and 1860 presidential candidate Senator John Bell was there for Tennessee. Nine states—Maine, New Hampshire, Vermont, Rhode Island, California, Wisconsin, Michigan, South Carolina, and Texas—sent nobody. Almost half of the 144 delegates were from Fillmore's home state of New York.

The party platform was a classic edition of Whig pablum: "Without adopting or referring to the peculiar principles of the party which has already selected Millard Fillmore as their candidate, we look to him as a well-tried and faithful friend of the Constitution and the Union." But it was an equal-opportunity slammer of the opposition parties, "one claiming only to represent sixteen Northern States, and the other appealing to the passions and prejudices of the Southern States," and concluding that "the success of either faction must add fuel to the flame which now threatens to wrap our dearest interest in a common ruin."

It was by no means clear that claiming the Whig nomination did Fillmore any good. But it did supremely annoy the nativists in his new party. Lewis Levin of Pennsylvania, who had been indicted for inciting to riot following 1844 nativist violence in Philadelphia, told Fillmore that "your pretended friends have destroyed you!" Actually, it was worse than that. As one reporter for a Republican paper described the Whigs' denial of reality, "These gentlemen are evidently incapable of the idea that the process now going on in the politics of the United States is a *Revolution*."

William Seward made that clear in simple terms, while answering Fillmore and those in his own party who counseled common cause. "The question now to be decided is, whether a slaveholding class, exclusively, shall govern America," he said in a speech in Detroit. "This is not the time for trials of strength between the native-born and the adopted freeman."

At the same time, fear of the Republicans drove potential Fillmore voters—especially the kind of old-line Whigs who had championed the Compromise of 1850—into the Buchanan camp. "We cannot divide our fire," was the fearful cry. "We must defeat the Republicans. Better to sacrifice Fillmore by throwing our weight behind Buchanan who is safe on the sectional issue than by our division permit Frémont to win." Former Whig senator Rufus Choate of Massachusetts, a onetime ally of Daniel Webster,

LINCOLN'S PATHFINDER

said the primary duty of all Whigs was to defeat the Republicans. If their old comrade Fillmore had to be sacrificed in the name of union, so be it.

And Georgia Democrat Howell Cobb predicted that southern men would come to their senses and ignore Fillmore. "Every day makes it more and more manifest that he has no showing and that a vote given to him only strengthens Frémont," he told Buchanan, "and this conviction will ensure for you every Southern state."

Republicans did what they could in the North. The strategy in Pennsylvania was summed up by Simon Cameron, the man Frémont wanted but didn't get as his running mate: "Convince the people that Frémont can be elected and that Fillmore, as is the truth, has not the shadow of a chance."

Fillmore supporters saw this as further evidence that he was the only man who could save the Union. "The Republican leaders have been successful in keeping the attention of the community directed towards Democratic iniquities"—violence in Kansas and support for slaveholders' rights—"until, taking advantage of a combination of things, a deep seated and almost vindictive antipathy has been concentrated over the entire North towards the South."

"Hit 'em Again"

It wasn't as if the North needed much convincing to feel more antipathy toward the South. And helping to keep the attention on Democratic iniquities were the further iniquities that resulted from the violence of May.

Because the man murdered by Congressman Philemon T. Herbert at Washington's Willard Hotel in May was Irish, the capital city's Know Nothing newspaper saw the killing as little more than "material for mischief" for Archbishop John Hughes. In the fevered minds of the nativists, Hughes was the secretly Catholic Frémont's "coalition" partner. When Herbert's fellow Democrats opposed his expulsion from the House, it "afforded Hughes a good pretext to assail the Democratic party and to draw off from it the foreign vote and to throw its influence in favor of Frémont's nomination." Such were the paranoid political implications of Herbert's killing of Thomas Keating.

The local politics were less fevered. Herbert had been released on bail May 12. On July 2, a grand jury indicted the Alabamian-turned-Californian on a murder charge—the charge Judge Thomas Crawford had said was not warranted when he released Herbert on bond in May—and the congressman was rearrested.

The trial began a week later. It took all day to select a jury, and the questioning of witnesses began on July 10. Prosecutor Philip Barton Key, son of the man who wrote "The Star Spangled Banner" and nephew of Chief Justice Roger Taney, was personal friends with Herbert. He did not throw the case, but his prosecution was perfunctory. The worst thing anyone said about Herbert during the trial was that he "is disposed to defend himself always against insult," which should have been obvious to everybody by that point.

If Key was just doing his job in prosecuting his friend, Judge Crawford was doing his best to aid him. After instructing the jury, Crawford chatted with the lawyers, loud enough for jurors to hear him say that he "looked upon the act as a clear case of self-defense." Even Key took umbrage at that, responding "that is the business of the jury to determine."

The jury began deliberations on Saturday, July 12, and kept at it until Tuesday, when they came back into court at midday and informed the judge they were hopelessly deadlocked: seven for acquittal, five for conviction on a lesser charge of manslaughter.

A second trial began the next day. To speed things up, a jury of only eight was seated. Another week of testimony carried the case to July 23. This time jurors did not need three days. They retired at 8 PM. Less than an hour later, they came back with an acquittal.

The next day, Herbert went back to work in the House.

Congressman Preston Brooks wasn't there. After his attack on Charles Sumner, Brooks faced three trials, and nearly a fourth: one in court, one in Congress, one back home in his district, and almost one on the field of honor. He won them all.

Brooks was arrested after the attack but freed on $500 bail almost immediately. A grand jury indicted him, and his case went to a bench trial on July 8 in DC circuit court before the same Judge Crawford who tried Herbert. Crawford was a Polk appointee and notorious to abolitionists as the presiding judge in the case of the *Pearl*, in which a shipload of slaves attempting to escape to freedom were returned to bondage. Philip Barton Key again was the prosecutor. His southern sympathies were well known, and his prosecution of Brooks was, again, uninspired.

There was no jury. Crawford found Brooks guilty of simple assault and fined him $300. He would spend no time in jail.

In the meantime, the House voted 121–95 to expel Brooks, well short of the two-thirds necessary for removal. As for the fellow congressmen who served as his accomplices, Lawrence Keitt was censured, while Henry Edmundson faced no punishment. Brooks delivered a valedictory filled with humorous references and legal analysis, and he was listened to with respect by members and spoke through "several interruptions from the gallery" including both "applause and hisses." More than once the chair threatened to clear the galleries if the demonstrations were repeated. Brooks paradoxically argued that he had breached only the privilege of the Senate, not the House, and that the Senate "had no right . . . to prosecute me in these halls." He claimed no intent to kill Sumner, merely an "unalterable determination to punish him."

"He was welcomed, as he left the House in his majesty, by the congratulations and embraces of Southern 'gentlemen' and the kisses of Southern ladies, who crowded the galleries and rushed into his arms," recorded a disgusted George Templeton Strong. Echoing Amos Lawrence's reaction to the Anthony Burns fugitive slave case and the Kansas-Nebraska Act, Strong concluded, "I fear I shall come out a 'damned Abolitionist' after all."

It was all too much for Representative Anson Burlingame of Massachusetts, a Know Nothing–turned–Republican facing a difficult reelection. He delivered an address ostensibly intended to defend the honor of the commonwealth. His true aim was to bolster his reputation at home and to tweak Brooks, who took the bait and responded by challenging Burlingame to a duel. "If we are pushed too long and too far, there are men from the old commonwealth of Massachusetts who will not shrink from a defense of freedom of speech, and the honored state they represent, on any field, where they may be assailed," Burlingame said. But, to be safe, he insisted the affair take place outside the United States, on the Canadian side of Niagara Falls. Brooks, with some justification, pointed out that any trip through the North would be hazardous to his health. So the thing died, and Congress was spared another violent confrontation. But Burlingame's gambit paid off. His challenge to Brooks revived his prospects, and made him one of the most popular stump speakers for Frémont.

Brooks, meanwhile, returned to South Carolina a hero.

Secretary of War Jefferson Davis turned down an invitation to attend a public dinner given on Brooks's behalf but used the occasion to "express to you my sympathy with the feeling which prompts the sons of Carolina to welcome the return of a brother who has been the subject of vilification, misrepresentation, and persecution, because he represented a libelous assault upon the reputation of their mother."

"I felt it to be my duty to relieve Butler and avenge the insult to my State," Brooks had told his brother immediately after the assault, but the message was aimed at the folks back home.

Not that he needed to worry. Although the House had failed to expel him, Brooks decided to resign and seek a renewed mandate from the voters of his district. On July 28, Brooks was reelected without opposition, the general temper of his home reflected in laudatory newspaper accounts that claimed "his whole constituency sympathise with and applaud his spirited course of conduct. . . . She says to her member—'Well done good and faithful servant;' If necessary she would add—'Hit 'em again.'"

The man once seen as something of a moderate and lauded as "one of the most magnetic and widely admired men in the capital" was now a symbol of Southern resistance, and he eagerly played the part. Speaking to a crowd in Ninety Six, a town in South Carolina, Brooks declared that in the event of a Frémont victory, "the only hope of the South is in dissolving the bonds which connect us with the government—in separating the living body from the dead carcass."

Some northern conservatives had predicted that southerners would repudiate Brooks. When that didn't happen, such men were shocked—and they were also shunned by a northern populace who, in effect, said "We told you so."

Conservative Whigs like Robert Winthrop and Edward Everett grasped the significance of the attack and the reaction. "You can have little idea of the depth & intensity of the feeling which has been excited in New

England," Winthrop wrote to fellow Whig John J. Crittenden of Kentucky. Everett noted that news of the attack "produced an excitement in the public mind deeper and more dangerous than I have ever witnessed."

Bleeding Kansas mattered more in Washington. But Bleeding Sumner mattered more in the country.

{ 10 }

"THE HARDSHIPS THAT WE SHOULD HAVE TO ENDURE"

T he first Mormon handcart company, led by Edmund Ellsworth, reached Fort Laramie on August 26, 1856.

Ten days west of the fort, on September 5, the company encountered the first snowfall of the year. "We remained in camp today owing to the inclement state of the weather[.] it rained & snowed alternately for the whole of the day that we could not cook hardly anything," the company journal reported. But that early snow proved no barrier, and the company made good time across Wyoming. The Ellsworth company reached Salt Lake City on September 26.

Hard on their heels was the company led by Daniel McArthur, which arrived later the same day, and Edward Bunker's company of Welshmen, which reached the city six days later. They had suffered many travails and witnessed some death—though only slightly more than was typical for the journey—but were now safely in the bosom of their fellow saints.

The final two handcart companies, led by James G. Willie and Edward Martin, were still far back along the road. Their travails were just beginning.

The Willie company reached Florence, Nebraska, on August 11. The next day the saints began to take sides on whether it was prudent to go on. "To day we commenced preparing for our jour[ney] and acertaining who wishes to go on this fall and who wishes to remain here," wrote Levi Savage. "Many are a going to Stop, others are faltering, and I myself am not in favor of, but much opposed to taking women & Children through destitute of clothing, when we all know that we are bound to be caught in the Snow, and Severe colde w[e]ather, long before we reach the valey."

Unlike the European emigrants who were strangers in this strange land, Savage had been here before. Born in Ohio, he had moved with his convert parents to Nauvoo and on to Utah. While serving in the Mormon Battalion in the Mexican War, he'd marched west to California, and he knew the terrain. He had seen the snow-capped mountains of summer. He wanted no part of them in winter.

At a meeting on August 13, "Brother Willey Exorted the Saints to go forward regardless of Suffering even to death." Savage rose and asked to speak. "I then related to the Saints, the hard Ships that we Should have to endure. I Said that we were liable to have to wade in Snow up to our knees, and Should at night rap ourselvs in a thin blanket. and lye on the frozen ground without abed; that was not like having a wagon, that we could go into, and rap ourselves in as much as we liked and ly down. No Said I.—we are with out waggons, destitute of clothing, and could not cary it if we had it. We must go as we are." He was not condemning the handcart project itself. "The lateness of the Season was my only objection."

Savage was not the only one urging caution. "Many who were acquainted with the climatic conditions of the region were of the opinion that we ought to winter in Florence," remembered John Ahmanson, one of the few Danes in the company who had a command of English. But Heber Kimball, a senior member of the church leadership, "rode into camp and delivered a speech in which he sternly rebuked those of little faith, and he promised that he would 'stuff into his mouth all the snow they would ever get to see on their journey to the valleys!'"

Staying behind in Florence for the winter was an option, but not a good one. It would have meant that the foreigners, many who didn't speak the language and had few if any skills for making it on the frontier, would have to scrounge for work in the dead of winter among locals who tended not to be friendly to Mormons. Stacked against that, walking a thousand miles to Utah didn't seem quite so daunting.

Savage was voted down, but he took the defeat in stride. "What I have said I know to be true," he told the assembled saints. "But seeing you are to go forward, I will go with you, will help you all I can, will work with you, will rest with you, will suffer with you, and, if necessary, I will die with you."

And the potential for winter weather was not the only concern. Cholera was also a threat. It had dogged General William Harney's army in Nebraska and posed an even greater risk for European emigrants who had already been through an arduous sea voyage that left many weakened from disease or seasickness or both. A company of Texas saints had suffered devastating losses from cholera on the trail the previous year, with twenty-nine people dying in one camp over the course of a few days.

While they outfitted, another six irreplaceable days melted away before the Willie company headed west again on August 19. Just two days later, the train had to stop because the scorching sun was exhausting the travelers and the animals. The irony that the excessive heat had cost them almost a full day would not be lost on the emigrants in months to come.

They lost two more days the first week of September searching for thirty cows that had gone missing. None were found, increasing the burden on those remaining and eliminating a vital source of food should the need arise.

On August 29 the Willie company reached Fort Kearney, where they learned of a Cheyenne attack that had killed several members of a party accompanying Almon Babbitt, Utah's delegate to Congress, on his return to the territory from Washington. The next day Willie's company traveled past the scene of burned-out wagons and charred corpses left to lie in the sun. On August 31, Babbitt caught up with the group and reassured them that he was "perfectly certain of getting through successfully despite the misfortune that had overtaken the men who were carrying his baggage." A week later he was dead at the hands of the Cheyenne.

But the handcart companies encountered few Native Americans, and were untroubled by those they did come across. Willie attempted to soothe any frayed nerves by assuring the travelers that "as their women and children were with them they would do us no harm." A little trading was done with the Omaha, some gifts were presented, a guard was stood at night, and in the morning the Native Americans had gone about their business.

Despite their troubles and the worries about their late start, the company was in good spirits. The Nebraska prairie over which the Mormon handcart companies were crossing was "as fair and fertile as sun ever shone upon," and "the rapidity with which it is being settled is really amazing. . . . To stand on one of the ridges of these prairies, and gaze over their wide expanse, is to enjoy one of the most magnificent spectacles imaginable." European mission coordinator Franklin Richards caught up with them on September 12 and "gave us a stirring address with a view to build up and encourage the people, and his sentiments were seconded by a hearty 'amen' from time to time." Evenings usually involved a good deal of singing. "Several of the songs of zion were sung with firstrate spirit and good effect," Willie recorded in the company journal.

In the happy days of late summer on the Nebraska plains, "Brother Savage's warning was forgotten in the mirthful ease of the hour."

They were moving steadily now across central and western Nebraska, making about fifteen miles a day. They were eating well. Many of the migrants had lived extremely lean lives in their native lands, and "the fare they had on the plains was a feast to them." Later, those feasts would be fondly if wistfully remembered. They reached Fort Laramie on September 30. Pausing there only a day, they were quickly back on the trail, although at a lower food ration. Originally the provisions "were calculated according to a daily ration for each man at one pound of wheat flour, two and a half ounces of meat, two ounces of sugar, two ounces of dried apples, one quarter ounce of coffee, along with a little tea, soda, and soap," remembered John Ahmanson. Now, "In consequence of our limited supply of provisions," Willie "considered it necessary to slightly reduce the supply of the daily ration of flour, which was unanimously and willingly acceded to by the Saints," Willie reported. Twelve days later, rations were cut again, to "10½ oz. for men, 9 oz for women, 6 oz for children, and 3 oz for infants."

A corps of missionaries heading east down the trail and bound for England met up with the Willie company on October 2 and urged them on. But, traveling on the south side of the river, the missionaries missed the Martin company further back.

Martin's company started out with 576 people, 146 handcarts, 7 wagons, 30 oxen, and 50 beef and milk cows. Although an effort was made to divide the healthy young males among the various companies, because they moved out last Martin ended up with a disproportionate share of infants, children, women traveling alone, the elderly, and the sick.

More than a thousand people were heading into the Wyoming winter, with everything they owned bundled up in rickety handcarts, their food already running low. And they still had more than four hundred miles between them and Zion.

"To Drive Hence the Gambler and the Harlot"

If the saintly confines of Winter Quarters and Salt Lake City had an opposite number, it was San Francisco.

The Wild West of Gold Rush San Francisco had seen the rise of a "vigilance committee" in 1851 in response to severe violence growing out of the surge in population (new Kansas governor John Geary had been the city's mayor). Two hundred citizens banded together to do the job they believed the civil authority could not or would not. Before the committee disbanded, four people had been hanged without benefit of trial.

Things got better after that. But by 1856, the settled citizens and business owners of the city were again up in arms about a rise in crime, the corrupt domination of Democratic boss David C. Broderick (a former lieutenant governor and soon-to-be senator), and municipal government's turning of a blind eye to vice. Meanwhile, highwaymen like the notorious Tom Bell gang still wreaked havoc not too many miles from the City by the Bay, robbing stagecoaches and raiding mining claims. A shootout during an attempted robbery on the road from Marysville left several passengers wounded.

In May a new vigilance committee would form, hoping to change the image of San Francisco from the roaring camp of the gold fields to a growing and sophisticated city. In part, it was the reaction of established forces to the growing power of new arrivals, the same force that gave rise to the Know Nothing Party. "Pious laymen, clergymen, lawyers, doctors, merchants, bankers, mechanics, and artizans, in fact and in truth nineteen twentieths of our best and most honored citizens, compose the army who shoulder the musket and rifle, and draw the sword to avenge the wrong deeds of blood and violence that have so long ran rampant in our streets," noted the correspondent for the *Journal of Commerce*.

"The committee claims to represent all the respectability, property, and honesty of San Francisco, and if so, I hope its experiment may succeed," noted George Templeton Strong. "One like it will have to be tried in New York within ten years."

In reality, things in the city were still improving even before the committee formed. Taxes had been cut, a new Consolidation Act had provided the framework for more honest elections, and the forces of reform—in the persons of the Know Nothings—had claimed victory in the city's elections in 1854. The *Alta California* newspaper called that Election Day the "proudest day" the city had ever seen. But as frequently happens, with improved circumstances came increased expectations. Vice, while still present, was on the run. But it had not been running fast enough to satisfy the growing middle class.

It had also not been running fast enough to suit newspaper editor James King, who called himself James King of William, to separate himself from all the other run-of-the-mill James Kings in the city, an affectation that provides a clear picture of his personality. King was editor of the *Evening Bulletin*, a scandal sheet that specialized in publishing innuendo and unproven allegations. A preening, self-righteous anti-Catholic bigot, King fancied himself a crusader, and to a certain extent he was. But he was not a very careful crusader, often getting the facts wrong and not caring very much. Among his allies were local reform society women, the kind of women who supported "Our Jessie" and preached temperance and other Christian values, as one wrote, "to drive hence the gambler and the harlot."

In November 1855, King was given a cause to latch onto when a US marshal named William H. Richardson was murdered in the street and his killer, an otherwise genteel gambler named Charles Cora, walked away free after a hung jury refused to convict him. Cora didn't walk far, for he was rearrested and held for a second trial. Neither King nor Cora would live to see it.

On May 14, less than a week after California's Philemon Herbert murdered the waiter at Willard's in Washington, things came to a head in San Francisco. That day, King published a piece delineating the sordid background of one of Boss Broderick's customs house flunkies, James P. Casey, a member of the city's board of supervisors and editor of a small newspaper who had done a stint in Sing Sing before hightailing it for California. That evening, Casey confronted King at the corner of Montgomery and Washington Streets. Pulling a pistol from his coat, he fired a single shot at the newspaperman, who staggered and fell, mortally wounded. A crowd quickly formed around Casey, who was arrested as the mob called for his immediate hanging.

That mob became the core of the new San Francisco Vigilance Committee. The leadership was claimed by many of the same men who had led the 1851 committee, prominent businessmen and other civic leaders. Recruiting foot soldiers was a simple task, and almost five thousand men signed on. The first order of business for the committee: "What is to be done with that villain, Casey? If the men don't hang him," wrote one female contributor to the house organ, the *Bulletin*, "the ladies will." The ladies need not have worried.

Others less enamored with the idea of self-appointed vigilantes taking the law into their own hands formed a counter-organization, the Law and Order Association, which included many members of the anti-Broderick, pro-southern wing of the Democratic Party. Among the main movers and shakers was the manager of the San Francisco branch of the Saint Louis bankers Lucas, Turner & Company, William Tecumseh Sherman. (The future Civil War hero's brother was Ohio Republican representative John Sherman, author of the Howard Report and of the amendment to bar funding for use of the military to support the Kansas territorial government.) William Sherman was a reluctant participant in the association. He knew Casey, whose *Sunday Times* had been printed on the third floor of the building that housed Sherman's bank—until Sherman decided he "could not tolerate his attempt to print and circulate slanders in our building" and threatened to toss him out the window if he didn't stop. Casey promptly relocated. But "politics had become a regular and profitable business," and Sherman felt like he had to do something.

On Sunday, May 18, more than one hundred of the Law and Order Association's rank-and-file troops, armed with muskets, posted themselves inside the county jail. They were anticipating an attempt by the Vigilance Committee to snatch Casey. They got more than they bargained for. Several thousand armed Vigilance Committee troopers arrived at the jail on Broadway around midday. They also brought artillery and appeared ready to stay for a while. "The vigilance have cannon faced in every direction and bags of sand piled around to defend those that fire the cannon," wrote a witness.

The commander of the Vigilance Committee force demanded that Casey be turned over to them. They also demanded that Charles Cora, still awaiting his retrial for the murder of the US marshal, be handed over as well. Backed by the small Law and Order Association force, county law enforcement officials at first refused. But after a short parley, the sheriff bowed to reality. He had one-twentieth the men and no cannon. The jail guards and Law and Order Association men withdrew, and Vigilance Committee men moved into the jail, seized the two prisoners, and hauled them away under a bright blue sky. "The day was exceedingly beautiful," Sherman remembered.

Four days later, as James King was being buried, Casey and Cora were hanged at the Vigilance Committee headquarters on Clay Street near Front Street, by this point a fortress protected by armed guards and lookouts. The Vigilance Committee was in charge of the city.

One resident who supported the committee reported that while she was not frightened, "many can neither eat, nor sleep, they say the law and order people will plunder the city."

Outsiders, who got their news second- or thirdhand and after long delays, had trouble sorting out the good guys from the bad guys. The Vigilance Committee was "dangerous and bad," observed George Templeton Strong, who had suggested New York might need a dose of such medicine, "but it might be worse." Parents used reports of vigilante justice to scare children into behaving, telling them "it is best to be good and not tease his sister," lest the Vigilance Committee come and take you away, one San Franciscan wrote to a niece.

For many residents, life went on as usual, although not without a hint of concern. One family, planning a post-wedding party for late June, decided to proceed with their celebration—"if we do not all get killed."

Most people simply put their heads down and hoped the trouble would soon pass. This was harder for politicians, but some managed. William M. Gwin, the man named to a full six years in the US Senate when Frémont was appointed to an abbreviated term, opposed Broderick's domination of the Democratic Party and secretly supported the efforts of the committee, but he couldn't risk being seen to do so in public. After a few tentative communications with the leaders, he retreated from view.

But the Law and Order Association did not. California's governor, a Know Nothing named J. Neely Johnson, was indecisive, and the Law and Order men knew they could expect no help from Washington. It was too distant, and too reluctant to create a precedent for using federal power in the states. They appealed to William Sherman—a West Point graduate, veteran of the Mexican War, and major in the state militia—to all but convert his militia troops into the group's military wing. Eventually, the governor recognized that duly constituted authority was under assault by the Vigilance Committee, declared a state of insurrection, and empowered the militia to step in if necessary.

But through the summer, the Vigilance Committee reigned. Guns promised to the state militia by the US Army never arrived. Neither did expected volunteers. Sherman, who "became involved in spite of myself," quickly got fed up. Outright violence was held to a minimum but the threat of violence was ever present, and served its purpose well. The committee issued orders banning a number of people from the state, among them Philemon Herbert, killer of the Willard's waiter, and Edward D. Baker, the attorney who had defended Charles Cora and who was one of Abraham Lincoln's best friends. Baker fled the city and became a prominent statewide speaker on behalf of Frémont's campaign. Sherman would leave later on his own terms, and he had little sympathy for most of those chased out, whom he considered "of that class we could well spare," although his wife referred to the Vigilance Committee as a mob of "traitors and Pharisees." But, excoriated by the city's irresponsible press as a "Mighty Man of War taken from the desk of a counting house," he resigned his commission and resolved to "mind my own business, and leave public affairs severely alone." He also developed a lifelong antipathy toward journalists.

By the end of August, the Vigilance Committee was ready to declare victory and depart the field, its *Bulletin* hailing a "peaceable, joyous termination of the moral revolution."

Sherman was not among the joyous. "Their success has given great stimulus to a dangerous principle, that would at any time justify the mob in seizing all the power of government," he wrote.

"THERE NEVER WAS SEEN . . . A MORE AWFUL CALAMITY"

The planter class of Louisiana was not as yet contemplating any such usurpation of authority as that which worried Sherman (who would soon be a resident of the Pelican State himself). Instead, as a respite from the oppressive humidity and petulant electoral politics, many of the wealthy bundled up their slaves and trundled down to the Gulf Coast.

"We doubt not that the approaching summer will be one of unusual gaiety with us," one local newspaper predicted, "and that Last Island, will become as famous as Nahant"—the Massachusetts summer resort north of Boston peopled by Cabots, Lodges, and Frémont supporter Henry Wadsworth Longfellow that was swankier even than the Frémonts' own Siasconset retreat on Nantucket. "Last Island is environed by one of the most beautiful beaches anywhere to be found in the whole Southern Coast."

Another local promoter trumpeted that "our own coast presents as fine natural attractions for a summer resort as any place in North America—and above all, Last Island. . . . Go to Last Island by all manner of means."

Last Island—Isle Dernière in the French—faced the Gulf of Mexico with Caillou Bay behind it, and the maize of bayous further to the north. An explorer in 1819 called it "a sandy barren marsh scarce fit for anything." But tourism boomed, aided by the transportation revolution, which allowed the well-off to ride trains to embarkation points and then take steamboats to restful islands.

Dozens of large homes and a grand hotel were built on the island, peopled in the summer by the sons of the men who settled Louisiana, their wives, children, and slaves. It was an idyllic spot. A hurricane had hit the island eleven months before, on September 15, 1855, but damage from that storm was minimal, and the 1856 season promised to be the busiest ever.

To accommodate the growing trade, a new steamer, the *Blue Hammock*, captained by Michael Schlatre and serving residents of Lafourche and Iberville Parishes, began ferrying passengers to the island from Dardenne's Landing and Plaquemine on June 16, making the trip every Monday and leaving the dock at 9 AM sharp.

Among the four hundred or so visitors on the island for the weekend of August 9–10 were W. W. Pugh, Speaker of the Louisiana House since 1853, whose family owned eighteen plantations and two thousand slaves. Former governor Paul Octave Hébert also owned an island home, considered to be the sturdiest of the lot. He was not in residence, but had made the house available to some friends.

The highlight of the weekend was to be a Saturday-night ball at the luxurious Last Island Hotel. Guests began arriving on Friday, August 8, to give themselves plenty of time to rest up and prepare. In addition to a fine dance floor, the two-story hotel provided "a well-stocked bar, billiard and boarding saloon, and a livery stable where horses and carriages can be procured to enable visitors to ride or drive on the extensive beach that bounds the island towards the Gulf." Spreading out from the hotel to the west were homes of every shape and size, four miles down the beach.

While the islanders partied, a storm that had been brewing for two days grew steadily worse. "The sea was white with foam and roared like a water fall," boat captain Schlatre reported. When the party, which had begun about nine, ended at midnight, it was clear this was no ordinary summer thunder bumper.

Sunday morning broke cloudy, windy, and wet. "About ten o'clock AM, the wind commenced blowing a regular gale, and some of the cabins in front began to lose their roofs and gradually toppled over," a witness later reported. By 1 PM, "the rain began to come through the roof on the upper floor. Things now began to look squally." An hour later "the rain [was] descending in torrents and . . . the wind at this time increased rapidly." Smaller structures, including some servants' houses, were being blown down. Storm surge was filling Caillou Bay, between the island and the mainland, as the spinning hurricane threw its worst winds from the northeast. By early afternoon, "the waters from Caillou Bay began their slow, relentless march up the back of the island," and the peak winds of 140 miles an hour—today a category 4 storm—were wrecking everything above ground.

As the flimsy beach houses blew apart, people rushed out into the storm, looking for cover anywhere they could find it. There was not much to find. Many made for the hotel, one of the few structures still standing. But by five o'clock, as the winds shifted and began blowing a storm surge from the gulf rather than the shallower Caillou Bay, the hotel began to come apart. Those still inside rushed into the torrent once again. Some found cover in large cisterns used for holding fresh water. One group fleeing the hotel was the family of state house Speaker W. W. Pugh. Exposed to the elements, they quickly became separated, losing two of the older children. These two soon found their way back to the family. But just when Pugh thought he had everyone together, a fresh gale blew up and separated sixteen-month-old Loula and three-year-old Thomas. Pugh searched frantically, but the little ones were nowhere to be seen.

Like Michael Schlatre's *Blue Hammock*, the steamer *Star* carried passengers arriving from New Orleans by train to the embarkation point at Bayou Boeuf on an eight-hour trip to the island. The 147-ton passenger steamer was about to become a lifeboat. Caught in the storm for hours, the pilot was finally able to beach her just before dark. For many Last Island residents huddled in cisterns or in the hotel's turtle pen—a sort-of low-lying pond—the *Star* looked like a refuge. Dozens dashed for her through the fading light. Planter John Beatty was not among them. He stubbornly took his family and slaves in another direction. But his coachman, seeing the *Star* in the distance, left the group and made for the boat. Before he got there, he saw a small body floating on the water, the waves lifting and dropping it like a doll. Barely slowing down, he swept the child into his arms and continued on toward the boat.

Former governor Hébert had asked Iberville Parish planter William Hart to host guests at Hébert's island home for the weekend. Among these was Anna Maria Turner Dickinson, the widow of Charles Henry Dickinson II, son of the man Andrew Jackson killed in a famous duel in 1806. Also in residence for the weekend was ten-year-old Charles Henry Dickinson III, who never knew either of the men whose name he shared (his father had died shortly after Charles Henry III was born). One man he did know, however, was Tom Shallowhorne, a slave long owned by Hébert and a familiar face to the Dickinson family. Luckily for Charles Henry Dickinson III, Shallowhorne was also staying at the house that weekend.

In the middle of the afternoon, as the storm began to reach its peak violence, the dozen or so people gathered in Hébert's home huddled together and prayed the maelstrom would pass. But the temptation to spy on the violence outside grew too great for young Charles. As the rising waters of the Gulf of Mexico rushed across the front yard and toward the house, he stood mesmerized at the front door, watching. In a flash, he was blown outside into the roiling waters, which quickly trapped him against a wooden fence as wave after wave broke over him. His mother, witnessing this, ran to the open door and out into the storm, with her sister close behind. Their attempt at rescue ended quickly, turning potential rescuers into victims. They too were swept into the flooded yard and pulled to the fence by the storm surge. The three clung desperately to the fence—which had pinned Charles down—as the wind howled around them and water raged over their heads again and again. Somehow, the sisters managed to turn toward each other so they could hold Charles's head in their hands and keep it, barely, above water. But the position was untenable. They could not let go of the fence for fear of being swept out to sea. And they knew if they stayed put, they would surely drown.

Things were almost as bad inside the house. As it began coming apart, Hart ordered everyone outside. The group fled together toward a large cistern on the side of the house that might provide some cover.

Except for one: Tom Shallowhorne spied young Charles and his mother and aunt, tied a rope around his waist, and made for the fence. Struggling mightily against wind and wave, he reached them, pulled the women to their feet, and freed Charles from the clutches of the fence. The three grabbed hold of the rope and followed along behind as Shallowhorne led them toward the cistern, and safety.

The Pughs spent the night in another cistern, bloodied and battered, racked by worry about their missing children. As the sun rose on August 11, they began making their way toward the *Star*, where they hoped the children might be. More than a hundred people were crowded onto the ship. Almost as soon as they came aboard, the Pughs found the two older children. They continued wandering across the deck, through the crowd, searching. Then W. W. Pugh heard the voice of an elderly black man, and turned toward it. It was John Beatty's coachman. "Colonel Pugh, I am sure this is your little son," he said, holding out a bedraggled but happy Thomas Pugh for his father to take into his arms.

Newspapers across the country reported the tragedy of the "great summer resort" that was "entirely inundated."

"There never was seen in the world a more awful calamity," a survivor wrote a few months later in a letter published widely. Of the roughly four hundred people on the island, nearly half died, including sixteen-month old Loula Pugh. As for Michael Schlatre, who ferried passengers to and from the island aboard his boat, only three of the seventeen people in his household survived. John Beatty and his family perished. Another 130 or so died aboard nearby ships caught in the storm. The number of fatalities far outstripped the casualties from the violence in Kansas—though it would garner considerably less attention.

"The Mere Thought That
Such a Thing Might Occur"

Louisiana had suffered a hurricane. Maine was about to cause an earthquake.

Somewhere in the United States, some state was holding an election every month save for January, February, June, and July. By August 1856, elections in Iowa and Maine were approaching. Both states had been singled out by Georgia Democrat Alexander Stephens, who identified "Illinois, Iowa, California, Connecticut, and perhaps New Hampshire and Maine" as the fulcrums of the 1856 election. "The contest in all these states," he predicted, "will be the hottest ever waged in politicks."

Iowa was more Republican than Stephens had anticipated, and the party swept to victory in the August state elections. The win provided a morale boost for the Frémont campaign, energizing volunteers and giving stump speakers something to crow about. But it was not altogether unexpected.

Next up was Maine, on September 8. Circumstances were favorable for Republicans, though not as favorable as in Iowa. Everybody thought it was going to be close. A Republican defeat would likely spell doom for the Frémont campaign. "We must not lose Maine," a local Republican, imploring the national party to get involved, wrote to Nathaniel Banks. "If we do the contest is ended."

The Republicans had recruited a strong statewide ticket, headed by Senator Hannibal Hamlin, an anti-Nebraska Democrat who had switched parties only after the Cincinnati convention nominated Buchanan. Hamlin was strong on the nonextension of slavery, but not so scary that he would frighten away winnable Democrats. And as a senator, he had one other advantage: he'd been in Washington during most of the decade when the temperance issue was roiling state politics. Temperance had been a staple of Maine's reform politics for at least as long as antislavery. In 1851, led by Portland mayor Neal Dow, the state legislature had enacted the nation's first statewide prohibition statute, banning the manufacture and sale of liquor. The "Maine Law," as it quickly became known, was an inspiration to temperance advocates in other states and was widely copied. Trying to get organized, Republicans danced around the issue, alert to local sentiment. Prohibition laws had the whiff of nativism, and that was reflected in the partisan news coverage, which tended to focus on the evils of Irish (read: Democratic) whiskey while downplaying the downside of German (read: Republican) beer. But in 1855, violence broke out in Portland. Three thousand Irishmen, none too fond of the Maine Law, rioted, and militias were called in to restore order. On June 2, 1855, one man died and seven were injured by the troops. Order was restored, but Maine's politics had become a minefield. Democrats did well in that year's state elections.

Hamlin, though, had remained focused on national policy and was viewed as above the prohibition fray. He wanted to keep it that way and remain in the Senate. So desperate state Republicans struck a deal, promising to send him back to Washington the following year if he would run for governor and carry a legislative majority into power. (Maine governors served one-year terms.) Similarly, Neal Dow was persuaded to keep his trap shut for a few months about the evils of liquor—as an indication of his inherited zeal, Dow's great-grandfather's name was Hate-Evil Hall—in return for a promise that come 1857, Republicans would assist him in his crusade.

ANTI-DEMOCRATIC CARTOON. *Courtesy of Library of Congress*

With everyone bought off to their satisfaction, the contest commenced. Democrats stuck with incumbent governor Samuel Wells, who had toppled a two-term Whig the previous year. For their part, the moribund Whigs nominated a candidate mostly just to spite the Republicans. Hamlin's campaign ignored prohibition and most other state issues, concentrating on Kansas. Democrats hammered the booze question. "The fight is monstrously hard," Hamlin's Senate colleague William Pitt Fessenden wrote days before the election, "the worst I ever saw."

The most-optimistic Republicans were forecasting a victory margin of 8,000 votes for Hamlin. Most others were expecting half that.

On Election Day, it seemed like the entire state showed up to vote. Turnout was 80 percent, the highest in sixteen years. Those voters gave Hamlin a landslide victory: he won 57 percent of the vote and bested Democrat Wells by an astonishing 25,000 votes. Republicans also won all six House seats and, most importantly for Hamlin, a majority in the state legislature that would elect him to the Senate the following year.

The huge win thrilled Republicans, who saw it as a vindication of their candidate and platform. Party faithful in Philadelphia fired a hundred-gun salute in celebration of the victory in Maine. A smaller but similar salute took place in Cincinnati. George Templeton Strong thought the result would move waverers "down from the fence" and into Frémont's ranks.

While Republicans were overjoyed, the result sent a chill down the spine of Democrats, who for the first time began to take seriously the possibility that Frémont would sweep the North and win the election—and all that might entail. "The 'Kansas outrages' had penetrated the popular heart," a disillusioned Maine Democrat wrote, "and made a deeper impression than any one anticipated. The people were enraged and ready to believe any representation no matter how absurd."

It was as if someone had suggested that men could fly. "The mere thought that such a thing *might* occur is enough to startle one," wrote Buchanan adviser Jeremiah Black.

The realization that the Republicans were not just a temporary aberration but might actually win left Democrats "alarmed for the success of Buchanan and Breckinridge in Pennsylvania" and inspired a turn in Democratic rhetoric. In September in Tippecanoe, Indiana, Breckinridge effectively argued that the majority should not rule, and that if Democrats did not get their way, rebellion was justified. "If the Eastern States were to unite in solid phalanx against the West, or the Southern against the Northern, they happening to have a majority, would you submit to it? I am sure you would not, for I know you to be men," he exhorted. "And, should they further, accompany every act of their triumph with every expression of contumely and contempt, would you not believe revolution a solemn duty?" It was with much justification that Republicans responded, "What does this mean, but 'elect ME as Vice President, or OUR party will dissolve the Union.' Nevertheless this Kentucky slaveholder is howling through the land that the Republicans are disunionists."

Virginia governor Henry Wise threatened "to declare any one who permits his name to go on a Frémont electoral ticket guilty of contemplated treason to the State." Somewhat more practically, Wise issued a call on

September 15 to the other slave state governors to meet in Raleigh, North Carolina, "to admonish ourselves by joint counsel, of the extraordinary duties which may devolve upon us from the dangers which so palpably threaten our common peace and safety." Some of those governors were already beginning to beef up their militia lists, and Wise ordered the Virginia militia to prepare to mobilize.

In the event, only Wise, James Hopkins Adams of South Carolina, and the host, Thomas Bragg of North Carolina, showed up, and Bragg was none too happy about the appearance of the other two. While Wise was attempting without much success to prepare for secession, other Democrats were trying to figure out how to prevent it by winning. The answer, they knew, lay in Pennsylvania.

Samuel L. M. Barlow, the millionaire who had hosted Buchanan's Senate allies in Cincinnati, got together with other moneymen at the New York Hotel on September 25 and pledged to raise $50,000 to save Pennsylvania and Indiana for the party.

Another substantive outcome of the Maine defeat was that Buchanan was roused to publish a letter strengthening the platform's endorsement of the Pacific railroad. Some Democrats questioned whether the federal government had the power to build such a thing. Buchanan anticipated Dwight Eisenhower's "National System of Interstate and Defense Highways" by a century when he cited "the Constitutional power 'to declare war' and the Congressional duty 'to repel invasion'" as the legal foundation for spending federal money on the railroad. The alarm provided by the results in Maine persuaded Democrats that California's 4 electoral votes might be needed, and they weren't taking any chances.

These were all signs that the Democrats were running scared. Republicans were invigorated. Henry Wadsworth Longfellow had long marveled at the exploits of the explorer John C. Frémont, relishing in the comfort of his home, warmed by a blazing fire, his wife reading to him the report of Frémont's 1843 expedition. "What a wild life," Longfellow mused. Now, more than a decade later, the apolitical Longfellow once again was taken with Frémont and found it "difficult to sit still with such excitement in the air."

Following the thrilling victory in Maine, Longfellow was not alone. The intellectual community joined in as never before. Along with Longfellow,

John Greenleaf Whittier, and William Cullen Bryant, joining the Frémont crusade were Ralph Waldo Emerson, Robert Lowell, Washington Irving, and a host of lesser lights.

"A very large class of persons who never before took any interest in elections are zealous Frémonters now," wrote Bryant. "Among these are clergymen and Quakers and indifferents of all sorts."

So not only did the Maine victory provide a sense of enthusiasm and possibility, it also served as a blueprint that could be applied to other states. "Much has been done here by canvassing the rural districts—the back towns; documents and papers of the right stamp have been circulated; numerous lectures have been held in school houses remote from our villages and cities," wrote one Maine resident. "The hard working, honest yeomanry gathered at these meetings were willing listeners, while the real issues in the pending canvass were simply and truthfully portrayed before them. Doubtless much more good has been done, more converts made in this way than by all the great mass meetings that were held in our cities and large villages."

{ 11 }

"A Roseate and Propitious Morn Now Breaking"

As the campaign roared toward the finish line, politicians of all stripes agreed on one thing: there had never been a presidential election like this one. One Hoosier noted, "Men, Women & Children all seemed to be out, with a kind of fervor, I have never witnessed before in six Pres. Elections in which I have taken an active part." George W. Julian stated simply that "the canvass had no parallel in the history of American politics."

As that kind of enthusiasm for Frémont became more and more apparent, slavery men had to begin seriously considering the possibility that a party founded on the idea of freedom might win. The Republican victory in Maine was a jarring moment for many, not all of them from the South. "I will not deny that there is a possibility of Frémont's election," wrote Jeremiah Black, Buchanan's future attorney general. "What is to be done in that event?" A Frémont victory "would place the country in a condition so totally new that we could be guided in our course by no precedents which have been set since the days of the revolution." Buchanan himself was quick to note that in event of a civil war, Maryland and Pennsylvania would be on the front line, and their voters should bear that possibility in mind.

Garrison's *Liberator* reprinted a scathing endorsement of secession from the *Petersburg Intelligencer* in Virginia:

> He who doubts that the election of John C. Frémont to the Presidency would bring about an immediate dissolution of the Union, would deny the existence of the sun in heaven, or any thing else equally palpable to the senses. Frémont could not, for the want of agents, carry on the internal administration of the country. No man in the South can take a commission from him, and no man sent from the North to the South, for the purpose of filling any office under his administration, will be allowed to stay here. He will be notified to leave, and if he disregards the notice, he will be carried off on a rail, and his office shut up. Take our own town as an example. Will any citizen of it accept a commission of Postmaster from Frémont! If one so base could be found, he would not be allowed to remain in his office one day or hour, but would be driven from our midst with the unanimous execrations of the community upon his infamous head. Here, then, would be a stoppage of the mails, and what will follow! Should the President attempt, by any armed force, to open, and keep open, the post office, that force will be resisted by force, and thus we should have revolution or disruption of the government, or in other words, a dissolution of the Union. Of the office of Collector of the Custom, Marshal of the District, and in fact every other federal office in Virginia, and the whole South, the same thing may be said; and then where, we should like to know, would be the administration of the Federal Government! With the mails stopped, the collection of the revenue stopped, and the process of the federal courts struck dead by the want of an officer to execute them, we repeat, what would become of the federal administration! And yet this state of affairs will as surely ensue as Frémont is elected.

Far from objecting, Garrison wholeheartedly endorsed such sentiments, and had for quite a while. "When shall we have a Convention of the Free States with reference to a peaceful dissolution of the Union?" he had written in

1854, in the wake of the Kansas-Nebraska Act. However kindly he felt about Frémont, he hadn't changed his mind about that.

George Templeton Strong had it thirdhand that Virginia governor Henry Wise claimed "if Frémont were elected, he would never be permitted to reach Washington." These were no idle boasts. John Curtiss Underwood, a native New Yorker who lived and practiced law in Wise's state, was "compelled to flee" the Old Dominion after serving as a Frémont delegate at the Republican convention. When John Minor Botts, a former House member from Virginia, defended the Union—not Frémont, just the Union—the *Richmond Enquirer* accused him of treason and suggested he be lynched. University of North Carolina chemistry professor Benjamin S. Hedrick was fired for supporting Frémont.

Thus, in Virginia and elsewhere in the South, there was no real Frémont campaign. Other Frémont supporters gave it a try, planning a rally for August in Wheeling, Virginia, that never really got under way because a mob showed up to assault the attendees. A month later the small but hardy band tried again, with more success. These were "germs of insurrection," but the fever was not spreading.

Governor Wise also recognized the economic element of the contest, telling a Democratic rally in Richmond that "the election of Buchanan would enhance the price of niggers from $1,000 to $5,000!"

Such considerations had real-world implications for people far removed from politics. "There is much opposition to Northern teachers, in the leading papers of the South," noted Tryphena Blanche Holder Fox, a Massachusetts-born woman who had moved to Mississippi to teach a planter's children and stayed to marry a Louisiana doctor, "particularly since Frémont attempted to run."

Certainly, what men like Frederick Douglass and women like Jessie Benton Frémont had in mind was "to administer the bitter dose of subjection to the South." Abolitionist minister Theodore Parker considered Frémont's election "the last chance for a peaceable solution of the quarrel." Should he lose, "then I see nothing but to fight."

Buchanan fully grasped the stakes, but he worried that others might not. "We have so often cried 'wolf,' that now when the wolf is at the door, it is difficult to make the people believe it," he wrote a supporter.

"But yet the sense of danger is slowly & surely making its way in this region."

He told another that he was "in daily receipt of letters from the South which are truly alarming. . . . They say explicitly that the election of Frémont involves the dissolution of the Union & this immediately." A southern merchant writing in the New York–based *Journal of Commerce* flatly predicted "if Frémont is elected, the South will secede." These were not South Carolina hotheads, Buchanan assured his friend, but "prudent, tranquil, and able" Virginians who were "looking on calmly for the North to decide their fate."

Their number also included the somewhat less "tranquil" Howell Cobb of Georgia, who promised to decamp for his home state and preach secession if Frémont was victorious. He was seconded by colleague Robert Toombs, and even by a former president, John Tyler.

Two weeks before Election Day, the *New York Herald* accused Secretary of War Jefferson Davis of shifting army units out of Virginia to clear a path for Wise's militia to mount an insurrection in the event of a Frémont victory—or at least scare northern fence-sitters into voting for Buchanan. The charge was bogus. Not only was Davis not denuding the US Army in the Old Dominion, he had refused Wise's request to upgrade the militia's arsenal with army surplus weaponry. When a visitor to the secretary's Washington office urged him to build up arms at southern military posts, Davis laughed him off. At the same time, though, Davis was warning others to "hasten slowly" to "make all the preparation proper for sovereign States." He would not commit treason, yet. But he would urge others to make ready, just in case.

Many conservative northerners looked at such talk as akin to insanity. "We are told that in case of the election of Colonel Frémont, the South will not, and ought not to submit—that the Union will be dissolved," wrote New York Whig Hamilton Fish, who was supporting Frémont. "Doubtless there are men, both at the North and at the South, who contemplate, and some even who desire a dissolution of the Union. Our Jails and Lunatic Asylums are of sufficient capacity to accommodate them."

Michigan Democrats adopted a resolution promising not to support secession in the event of a Frémont victory. Other northerners, particularly those allied to the business community, were quicker to blame their neighbors for any potential problems. "There is no disguising the fact . . . that the great question of union or disunion has been precipitated upon us by the mad fanatics of the North," opined the *Daily Pennsylvanian*.

Robert Winthrop of Massachusetts, that old-line Whig and Know Nothing supporter of Fillmore, feared the worst, or at least what he considered to be the worst. "When a party composed of only half the States in the Union shall assert its title to the name of a national party, and shall be claimed and recognized as such, it will not be long I fear—it will not be long—before half the States will claim to be recognized as a nation by themselves." Winthrop didn't support Buchanan, but he couldn't have stated Buchanan's case more eloquently.

Even Garrison had to acknowledge that the possibility of a Frémont victory was "exciting an unparalleled anxiety in the breasts of the people." The Republican Party "embodies the whole *political* anti-slavery strength of the country." But that was not enough. The Constitution was a "covenant with death," he insisted, and "as a matter of moral consistency," no true abolitionist could support Frémont or his party. The moral antislavery strength of the country, as opposed to the merely political, must stand outside the process.

It was "an absurdity"—one of Garrison's favorite words—for men like Seward, Sumner, and Banks (he did not mention Frémont) to "stand by the Union to the last" when they could not "hold a public meeting at the South in favor of freedom" and "would be lynched if they should make the attempt."

Fear of disunion played into Democratic hands as surely as outrage over Kansas served Republican purposes. Now it was simply a matter of whether voters were more outraged or more afraid.

"MEET ANY CONTINGENCY THAT MAY ARISE"

Nobody knew what was going to happen.

Fillmore served the purpose, Thurlow Weed noted, of forcing the Democrats to play a little defense on southern soil. The proslavery Know Nothings tried to pin Democrats down on their two-faced interpretation of popular sovereignty, to little avail. They also drew no distinction between Frémont and Buchanan, who were in their eyes both "deadly foes to the Union," a reflection of the Democrats' own overheated rhetoric on the likelihood of disunion if Frémont were victorious. Simultaneously and contradictorily, they complained that the Democratic Party had "abolitionized itself" in trying to counter the Republicans.

Buchanan surmised that the Republicans hoped Fillmore would be strong enough to win a couple of states, thus sending the election "into the House and then they would consider Frémont's election as certain."

Weed, all year long confident of Frémont's defeat, had nevertheless bet a friend $1,250 that his candidate would win Indiana. He apparently ignored advice from the locals. Congressman George W. Julian was not nearly so optimistic. "We have a very mean scurvy pack of politicians in our so-called Republican party—doughfaces at heart—whose knavery for the past two years has been greatly facilitated by Know-Nothingism," the Hoosier wrote to Salmon Chase. Jesse Bright was "confident as to Buchanan's success in Indiana."

Cobb warned Buchanan to be more solicitous of Franklin Pierce, who still had the power to disrupt the campaign if he chose. "In a word," Cobb cautioned the candidate, "I fear that the President and his cabinet are *sore* and unless something is done to conciliate their feelings we shall receive less aid from that quarter than we ought to have." He had no suggestions on what might be done to placate Pierce, but wanted Buchanan to know what was going on so he could "meet any contingency that may arise." Buchanan was in no mood to appease Pierce or his disappointed supporters. "I have too good an opinion of the President to suppose for a moment that he would require a request from me to induce him to employ all proper exertions to render the Democratic cause triumphant," Buchanan whined. And no inducements were forthcoming. Buchanan treated Stephen Douglas in the same disdainful manner. When Douglas sold some property to raise money for the Democratic cause, Buchanan condescended to send a thank you note, and addressed it to "The Hon. Samuel A. Douglas."

In such a state of uncertainty, politicians deployed around the country to make their cases. In a September 25 speech at the Merchants' Exchange on Wall Street, Nathaniel Banks argued that national prosperity would grow out of the increased political power of an industrial North, which would become large enough to crush southern political power. This was just the sort of notion that had frightened southerners for decades. John C. Calhoun had built a career on playing to that fear. Banks repeated for his audience the Republican mantra that the party would do nothing to disturb slavery where it existed, but foresaw that the model of a prosperous, industrial, and free North would inspire southerners to give up slavery on their own. Southerners weren't biting, and although the speech was well received, neither were many of the Yankee business interests Banks hoped to sway. At the exact moment Banks spoke, a few blocks away at the New York Hotel, Democratic moneymen were raising $50,000 to spend in Pennsylvania. The potential profits Banks envisioned were not enough to allay their fears of the chaos brought about by disunion, and their response to Banks's presentation showed they were likely to stick with Buchanan. Just in case, Democrats brought former Virginia governor John Floyd to the same spot a few days later to remind the traders that their business and New York's economic survival depended on the survival of the Union and the preservation of the southern cotton trade.

Charles Sumner had sworn off campaigning to recover from his injuries, "this long divorce from my duties," he called it. He also had to feel, if he could not admit it out loud, that he was more valuable as a symbol of southern and Democratic perfidy than as a rally speaker. His brother reported that "Charles is fretting himself to death, or to death's door, by his anxiety to be in the field." Francis Preston Blair reassured Sumner that he had "done more to gain the victory than any other." Sumner did finally make an appearance on election eve, November 3, still pale and weak, to deliver a few brief remarks in Boston. He got through only a few sentences before handing his prepared remarks to reporters, who would have to print the rest of the speech in their papers the next day. His appearance helped fuel the rumors that Sumner was faking his injuries for political benefit. "The Senatorial sophomore has no doubt done more by playing possum than if he had stumped the entire North with re-hashes and plagiarism from Demosthenes," the *Philadelphia News* reported.

Thomas Hart Benton may have been routed in his final campaign, but that did not keep him off the hustings as the campaign season wore on. In an election-eve speech in Saint Louis, he took one last poke at his daughter's husband in a speech at a new lecture hall downtown. More in sorrow than in anger, he recounted, "at his own hearth and talking as a parent to a child," he had all but begged Frémont not to make the race. But his wise counsel had been ignored, and now voters were faced with a simple choice. Yes, he was against the extension of slavery. But there was a greater principle at stake, he insisted, the "danger of disunion," which was "more imminent than was generally believed." It was Buchanan who could preserve the Union, not John C. Frémont. Nothing, Benton said, mattered more than that.

As he had been all his life, Benton was a metaphor for the country. Born in the east, he moved west, with the nation, to Tennessee, feuded with Jackson, then embraced him. He moved on to Missouri as the country raced further westward. He was a slaveholder but hated slavery. He looked longingly to the West, always, and envisioned, like fellow slaveholder Jefferson, an empire of liberty spreading across the continent. Frémont had been a hero created of that vision, and as Benton's creation, had encapsulated the moment of Manifest Destiny. Now, once again Benton encapsulated the American moment. He longed to be rid of slavery and to stop its spread into the territories. But not at the cost of the Union. Not even if it meant choosing union over family.

As happened in all political campaigns, some partisans went around the bend. One Rochester, New York, skeptic complained of "gatherings of the faithful which are held nightly in various parts of the city [where] 'the spirits' of the illustrious dead are conjured to mingle in concerns of the living, and take part in the present contest for 'bleeding Kansas,' free love, and woman's rights. Those who call up spirits do not invoke any small fry—nothing short of Washington, Jefferson, Franklin, or Milton, will answer their turn."

And, indeed, Republicans focused on Bleeding Kansas nearly to the exclusion of all else. According to one estimate, 80 percent of all the campaign literature produced by the party in 1856 was related to Kansas. Rev. Henry Ward Beecher used the occasion of a New York speech to display leg irons he said had rubbed raw the skin of a free-state official forced by Kansas slavers to wear them.

William Seward, who had offered scant help to Frémont early on, spoke to a crowd in Detroit on October 2 and, as he had done consistently, made a plea for inclusion. After denigrating the southern "apologist" Pierce and the other slave-power leaders whom Seward accused of dominating Congress and the administration, he turned his attention to his own side. Getting rid of northern men with southern loyalties, as well as southerners, the New Yorker insisted, "concerns all persons equally whether they are Protestants or Catholics, native-born or exotic citizens." This election season, he pleaded, "is no time for trials of strength between the native-born and adopted freemen, or between any two branches of one common Christian brotherhood." Two days later in Jackson, he added, "if the great mass of men are ever to exercise control in the affairs of government, they must be willing to take the votes of Irishmen, Scotchmen, Frenchmen, Germans, Catholics, Protestants—Negroes." The day was coming, Seward warned, when people who considered themselves Christians would have to "learn to love freedom more than peace."

Others joined in, eager to be a part of what looked like a certain Frémont victory in Ohio. Kentucky abolitionist Cassius M. Clay toured the state. A crowd of twenty-five thousand gathered in Sandusky to witness a reenactment of a "border ruffian" attack on innocent Kansans.

And as the campaign wore on, women continued to play an unprecedented role. In some of her engagements in Pennsylvania and New York, "lady lecturer" Clarina Howard Nichols was advertised as a speaker to draw a crowd, then gave way to male speakers to avoid stirring up controversy among some still reluctant clergy who opposed women speaking to all-male or even mixed audiences. But more often than not, Nichols spoke for herself. Others did the same all across the contested states of the Old Northwest, speaking, riding in campaign parades, and exhorting the faithful to give money and vote.

Win or lose, women's rights activists—even those not closely associated with the Frémont campaign—saw promise for the future when "women were urged to attend political meetings, and a woman's name was made one of the rallying cries of the party of progress," noted Lucy Stone. "The enthusiasm which everywhere greeted the name of Jessie was so far a recognition of woman's right to participate in politics."

Republicans made much of Buchanan's bachelorhood, and used Jessie to do it. "There is a great hurrahing over J at this moment," a Frémont backer wrote in the *Liberator*. "The Democrats have no feminine element in their two-legged, walking platform; no Jessie to hurrah for; no Jessie to vitalize their manhood and kindle their enthusiasm! Theirs is a *bachelor* party, and it will be a *bachelor* Administration if they get it. No wife, no child, no home, to humanize and save them."

Know Nothings had women working in their campaign, too. Anna Ella Carroll, daughter of a onetime governor of Maryland and descendant of Charles Carroll, a signer of the Declaration of Independence, had been a paid political adviser in the 1840s, while in her twenties, and a prolific pamphleteer for the emerging nativist movement in the early 1850s. In 1856 she campaigned for Fillmore and wrote *The Great American Battle; or, The Contest Between Christianity and Political Romanism*, aimed at preventing the impending Jesuit seizure of power. It sold more than ten thousand copies.

Unlike many of the Republican women, Carroll was explicitly not a women's rights activist, and she made no pitch for either the vote or for equal participation in the political process. "No selfish aspiration, no sordid interest, no political distinction has actuated me," she told Fillmore. It was simply her duty to put her talents to work in the cause.

"No More Chickens to Harry"

Catholicism was a double-edged sword for the Republicans. While Irish and German immigrants were reluctant to support the party because of its ties to the nativists, Democrats were getting some traction with their whispering campaign—at times much louder than a whisper—that Frémont was a closet Catholic, a bastard, and the offspring of bigamy. One particularly bizarre line of argument accosted Frémont for once having eaten "a frozen dead dog!" The latter at least had the virtue of being true, as Frémont himself had recounted in the report of his expedition across the Sierra Nevada in the winter of 1844.

Some of it was true, some wasn't. Republican journals attempted to turn Frémont's illegitimate birth to their advantage, hyping the "man who

has overcome the most formidable obstacles in the path of his advancement
. . . who has hewn out his own path unaided and alone." The *New-York Tribune* ran old quotes from Buchanan praising Frémont, and rounded up old comrades from his western explorations to sing his praises.

A Democratic pamphlet belittled Frémont's "brilliant senatorial career" and concluded that with such a thin resume, he would have to be judged by the company he kept—a motley collection of disunionists and abolitionists, in the pamphleteer's judgment. The screeching Democratic press went full bore on the "Frémont as abolitionist" theme, going so far as to outline—presumably tongue-in-cheek—a prospective Frémont cabinet that included Joshua Giddings as secretary of state, William Lloyd Garrison as secretary of the treasury, David Wilmot as secretary of the interior (not entirely out of the question), Wendell Phillips as secretary of the navy, Frederick Douglass as attorney general, and Henry Ward Beecher as chaplain. The "Female Department" would be manned by Beecher's sister, Harriet Beecher Stowe, and women's rights activists Abby Folsom and Lucy Stone. Somehow, the writer forgot to include a position for Jessie Benton Frémont.

Democrats and Fillmoreites also engaged in character assassination. Democratic papers wildly exaggerated the financial problems at Las Mariposas, accusing Frémont of fraud and land stealing and dubbing him a "landshark" and "monopolist." He was mostly trying to secure claims to the land by getting squatters off parcels they had no right to be on. Pierce, in fact, after the Supreme Court finally confirmed Frémont's claim, had personally handed him a federal patent for the property back in February in the White House, three days before the Republican meeting in Pittsburgh. And old canards of cannibalism during the fourth exploring expedition were rehashed—accusations that Fremont himself had leveled against one of his compatriots during a disastrous winter in the San Juan Mountains—as were untrue allegations of overcharging the government on beef contracts and joining the powerful Palmer, Cook & Company, which handled state finances, in land swindles in California. The *Los Angeles Star*, a particular irritant, rehashed discredited stories about Frémont's supposed execution of prisoners during the Bear Flag Revolt. Frémont was not accused of doing any killing himself, but he was in command of those who did. Former governor Pio Pico rose to Frémont's defense, and former consul Thomas

Larkin offered a detailed testimonial refuting all the charges about bad behavior—personal, military, and otherwise—during Frémont's time in California. Rather, Larkin wrote, Frémont was "a just, correct, and moral man, abstemious, bold, and persevering."

Allegations of extramarital affairs dogged Frémont, dating back to his earliest expedition among the Cherokee in 1837, to his California days, impossible to prove or disprove. The *Los Angeles Star* claimed Frémont had kept "a public harem" while serving in California during the Mexican War. But it was an accusation of more recent vintage that hit closer to home, when Frémont was alleged by one tormenter to have impregnated one of the chambermaids Jessie had brought to the United States from France a few years earlier. The maid was whisked away from the home and nothing was conclusively proven. Jessie's postelection behavior, and John Bigelow's later break with Frémont, indicate this particular unsavory story might have been more than scurrilous campaign gossip.

But it was the charge that Frémont was a closet Catholic that posed the direst threat. It was a false charge that had just enough pieces of supposed

ANTI-FRÉMONT CARTOON. *Courtesy of Library of Congress*

evidence to make it sound credible. Frémont's father was a French Catholic. Frémont had attended Catholic school as a child. He was married—in a rush, to be sure, after two Protestant ministers fearful of Benton had refused to perform the ceremony—by a Catholic priest. And Frémont had sent his niece and ward, Nina, daughter of his late brother, to a Catholic school.

These accusations were heaped with irony, a fact no one missed. "Frémont, who was preferred over me because I was not a bigoted Protestant, is nearly convicted of being a Catholic," laughed Seward. Adding to the irony was the fact that the campaign had made deals in some states with Know Nothing candidates—Nathaniel Banks and Henry Wilson had engineered a fusion ticket in Massachusetts with nativist candidate Henry Gardner, throwing over a credible Republican alternative in the process.

Frémont, who was sufficiently nativist to have been considered by the Know Nothings as a presidential candidate, refused to take the bait, arguing that the question of a man's religion should play no part in whether voters supported him for office. As Lily Frémont put it, "he was used to life in the open and wanted a square fight, not one filled with petty innuendoes and unfounded recriminations." It was a noble sentiment, but men less ethereal than the candidate knew something had to be done to answer. "These Catholic reports must be extinguished," worried Schuyler Colfax. If left unanswered, they threatened Frémont in the must-win states of Pennsylvania, Indiana, and New Jersey.

But the charges were left unanswered for the most part, largely because the campaign feared offending potential Catholic voters by making a point of Frémont's Protestantism. It was a dubious argument—Catholics were going to vote overwhelmingly for Buchanan in any case. Meanwhile, the steady drip of the Frémont-is-a-Catholic campaign daily stripped away those who might actually have considered voting for the candidate.

Meeting little resistance, Frémont's enemies continued the smear campaign. Thousands of pamphlets appeared bearing titles such as "Frémont's Romanism Established," "Papist or Protestant. Which?" and "The Romish Intrigue." Some American Party and Democratic newspapers began referring to the Republican candidate as "John Catholic Frémont" or "John Cross Frémont" and delighted in reprinting the spurious stories of supposed witnesses of Frémont's attendance at Mass. "I have myself seen him a dozen times go to mass, and to the confession, and be sprinkled with holy water," one such "witness" related.

Such allegations were not leveled at Frémont alone. The *New York Herald*'s James Gordon Bennett, until lately a Democrat, was accused of "following the orders of his Jesuit master" and Republicans at large were labeled "the miserable faction which has nominated an instrument of Bishop Hughes."

Finally, Thurlow Weed gathered forty Republican leaders at the Astor House in New York City to come up with a plan. Frémont came to meet with them, and they begged him to make a public statement refuting the allegation that he was Catholic. Frémont stood fast. After the disappointed sachems left, Frémont asked Bennett what he thought. "What are your convictions?" the blustery Bennett asked. Frémont explained again how he believed that he should not appeal for votes based on a person's religion or on another person's religious prejudice. "Follow those convictions, Colonel," Bennett told him, "and I will sustain you to the end."

Gamaliel Bailey sided with Frémont. "Pray Heaven this may be the last election in which a man's religious faith or connection may be brought into the question of his fitness for office. For one, whenever this subject is brought up, we must enter our stern protest against the anti-Christian, anti-American dogma of a miserable bigotry, that none but a Protestant is qualified for civil office." So did Radical Abolition Party candidate Gerrit Smith. "Is it thought necessary that the President should be a Protestant?" Smith wrote. "I see not why it should be. With me it is all one whether the candidate is a Roman Catholic or a Protestant, a foreigner or a native. But Col. Frémont *is* a Protestant—and the lie to the contrary is as base and naked a lie as was ever manufactured by lying politicians."

Without help from the candidate or a definitive statement from the party, state and local organizers did what they could. Rallies were held in cities with large German populations, including New York and Cincinnati. Efforts were made to buy German-language newspapers (a tactic later used successfully by Abraham Lincoln). And always, speakers reminded German audiences that a Republican victory meant more free soil and the spread of free labor.

John Bigelow, writing under a pseudonym (Jim Brown, Staten Island Ferryman), tried to use humor to defuse the charges. "It has just been discovered by the Fillmore men that the *masses* nowadays are all for Fré-mont," he wrote, which must mean that Frémont is a Catholic; that made about as much sense, he concluded, as suggesting that Frémont was a Catholic because he was once seen *"crossing* the streets."

Rev. Henry Ward Beecher used mild public flirtation with the candidate's wife to make his point. Addressing charges that the couple had been married by a Catholic priest, Beecher wrote that "Frémont said that he did not care *who* did it, so that it was done quick and strong. Had we been in Col. Frémont's place, we would have been married if it had required us to walk through a row of priests and bishops as long as from Washington to Rome, winding up with the Pope himself." But by far Beecher's most popular and oft-repeated story was of his dog Noble, who once chased a squirrel into the crevice of a wall. The squirrel never reappeared after that first visit, but Noble persistently revisited the hole again and again. "When there were no more chickens to harry, no pigs to bite, no cattle to chase, no children to romp with, he would walk out of the yard, yawn and stretch himself, and then look wistfully at the hole, as if thinking to himself: 'Well, as there is nothing else to do, I may as well try that hole again.'" The Democrats, Beecher said, were like old Noble. "Col. Frémont is, and always has been as sound a Protestant as John Knox ever was," insisted America's best-known Protestant minister. But, like old Noble and that hole, the Democrats "can never be done barking at it." Gangs of schoolchildren marched to Frémont rallies toting banners depicting old Noble barking at an empty hole.

Even Jessie Frémont herself had to offer reassurances, when an old acquaintance raised the question of her husband's religion. John Robertson, a Scottish scholar with whom Frémont had studied Greek and Latin as a young man in South Carolina, inquired on behalf of a "friend" about his old student's religious proclivities. Responding to his "friendly letter," Jessie hoped to "assure your enquiring friend that Mr. Frémont was born and educated in the Protestant Episcopal Church—for more exactness, at St. Phillips Church in Charleston, that he is now in the same church—that I am too an Episcopalian and our children were all baptized in that church." For good measure, she also reassured Robertson that "neither of us ever owned any slaves, which is the other bugbear."

Hamilton Fish laid bare the obvious contradictions in the Democratic (and radical abolitionist) critiques. "A Southern man by birth and by education," he wrote of Frémont, "he is the candidate of the party which is said to be Northern; he is supported by a party said to be opposed to the Romish religion, and his opponents say that he is a Roman Catholic; his election is opposed as dangerous to the rights of the slaveholders, and the Anti-Slavery Standard (the organ of the Abolitionists), deprecates his success. . . . He is charged at the South with opinions and tendencies dangerous to the rights of the South, and at the North, his votes in the Senate are quoted as evidence of pro-Slavery proclivities."

"Our People Here Don't Give Up the Ship"

As sure a thing as Ohio seemed to be for Frémont, next-door Pennsylvania was the height of uncertainty, and the hinge on which the entire election seemed to hang. State elections scheduled for mid-October would forecast the November outcome, and Democrats panicked by the Maine results were pouring every possible resource into the state.

"The whole canvass depends on Indiana and Pa.," concluded Schuyler Colfax. But Indiana got very little attention; every available resource was hurried to Pennsylvania.

In the days before the state elections, Charles Dana reported "about two hundred orators, great and small" were crisscrossing Pennsylvania on Frémont's behalf. Many of them were women. Indiana had barely any, of either gender. Democrats too understood the importance and shifted their best men to the fight. Howell Cobb made ten speeches in ten days, some in blizzards across the snowy northern tier of Pennsylvania. In a sign of how the political world had been turned upside down, the sons of Whig icons Henry Clay—urged on by vice presidential candidate John Breckinridge—and Daniel Webster came to Pennsylvania to campaign for Buchanan.

Pennsylvania was an organizational mess for the Republicans. The factions that hadn't been able to agree on a vice presidential candidate were still feuding. Know Nothings were strong in the state, and Dayton's presence on the ticket had done nothing to peel any of them away. While the Know Nothings and Republicans were presenting a unified state ticket, it leaned heavily toward the Know Nothing side and offered no guarantee that such unity would be repeated for presidential electors. The state party was so inept that it couldn't coordinate local speakers or get pamphlets printed or distributed. There was virtually no press operation, and Republican newspapers outside Philadelphia were of little use. Thomas Ford, the nativist lieutenant governor of Ohio, was given a stash of cash to buy German-language newspapers, and made a mess of it. "If we hope to carry Pa.," wrote Henry Stanton, "we must literally lift it & carry it." To top it all off, the party was short of money, although most of what little it had ended up in Pennsylvania. "In the old Whig times, we could go out into Market St. and easily get a few thousand dollars," wrote one Philadelphian, "but now of all our Merchants trading with the West and South, we can't get a cent, with two or three exceptions."

"Penna. Is always slow to work in any progressive or new movement," Lucretia Mott had written two years earlier, and now it appeared she was proving a prophet.

Horace Greeley published campaign literature in German and Welsh to distribute to Pennsylvania coal miners. Francis Preston Blair did what he could. Having staunchly opposed Simon Cameron, Frémont's choice for vice president, he now stepped in to mend long-broken fences; the feud went back to 1845, when Cameron played a role in ousting Blair from his editorship of the Democratic newspaper in Washington following James K. Polk's election as president. Cameron eventually stepped up to offer valuable local knowledge and campaign assistance, but many Republicans feared it was a case of too little, too late.

On October 15, the day of the state elections, the weather was cold and drizzly across much of the state but turnout was high. In a year soaked in the blood of political martyrs, this ferociously contested political fight was conducted in peace. Jessie was with the Blairs at the Ninth Street house in New York City. Frémont was in Vermont, meeting with allies.

Early returns from the state on election night looked promising for the Republicans, and despite the weather the streets of Philadelphia were jammed with people pressing in at newspaper offices looking for results. But as the night wore on into the early morning, the fusionist lead dwindled from 10,000 to 4,000 to 3,000 and finally disappeared altogether. It took a couple days for final returns to drift in. When they did, the tally showed Democrats winning by less than 3,000 votes. It was close, but it was a win. Indiana, voting the same day in better weather, yielded an even higher turnout, with the same result: a narrow victory for Democrats across the board at the state level, and gains in the congressional delegation. Ohio, as expected, went heavily Republican, but Frémont had Ohio in the bank. He now had to find some way to turn Pennsylvania and Indiana around, and he had three weeks to do it.

"I heartily regret the defeat we have met and do not look for things to change for the better," wrote a pessimistic Jessie Benton Frémont in the wake of the losses in Pennsylvania and Indiana. But within days she had recovered somewhat and noted that others, including the candidate, were faring better than she. "Our people here don't give up the ship by any means," and Frémont "thinks we shall win."

Republicans cried fraud, and with some justification. It was a staple of nineteenth-century politics, and one at which Democrats were especially adept, particularly at registering recent Irish immigrants who might or might not have been eligible to vote. "We have naturalized a vast mass of men," Buchanan fixer John Forney crowed. Six thousand voters were naturalized in Philadelphia ahead of Election Day, and a city court clerk would eventually go to trial for handing out twenty-seven hundred blank naturalization forms. Some of those around Frémont urged him to challenge the results. Based on the numbers in Philadelphia alone, they probably had a good case. But Frémont and his closest advisers saw no way forward except to redouble efforts in the three weeks remaining to them to unify with the Fillmore campaign in Indiana and Pennsylvania. Neither would be successful.

Weed took out his frustration in a bad-tempered but typical way, by blaming the ignorant voters of places like Cambria County, where "every eighth man does not know the difference between B[ullshit] and an ox-yoke." Local Democratic newspapers took up this observation with a combination of glee and disdain, and it can't have helped in rural parts of the state in November.

Democrats were exultant. Former congressman William Preston of Kentucky quipped, "Now is the winter of our discontent made glorious summer by this son of Lancaster."

Former Kansas governor Andrew Reeder had seen the writing on the wall but also read between the lines. "Buchanan will be elected as I always supposed but the Republican party is bound to sweep the North within the next four years," he wrote a week after Pennsylvania.

"THE MOST EXCITING CONTEST EVER KNOWN IN THIS STATE"

From there, the campaign entered the home stretch. In keeping with the spirit of the year, violence and inspiration were found in almost equal measure.

William Herndon, Lincoln's Springfield law partner, had written abolitionist Wendell Phillips in late September that all they needed was more time to get organized and to foment fusion and Illinois could be won. "Had we a few months longer to go on I think we would carry this State for Frémont. Were the Republicans and the Americans to join, we could easily, now."

But the party was still loosely organized in the state. Illinois was a microcosm of the nation: southern and Democratic in the south, Yankee and Republican in the north, and divided in the middle. Old-line Whigs like Lincoln and former Democrats like Lyman Trumbull had been slow to abandon their parties. While anti-Nebraska fusionists in Illinois were haggling about what to call their party, Democrats dubbed them "anti-Neb-rascals."

Emigrants who had returned from Kansas regaled audiences with lurid tales of slave-state depredations. Democrats found it all quite amusing. "Men and women flocked to political demonstrations as they would to a camp meeting or to a circus," remembered John A. Logan, author of a law to bar free blacks from settling in the state. Democrat Francis Grund told German voters in southern Illinois that Republicans were like the dishonest Yankees peddling defective lightning rods.

Republican appeals to German immigrants included a reminder that "those Germans who wish to see a vast portion of the great West given over to slavery, thus shutting it out from themselves and their children . . . can do much toward it by helping to elect Buchanan." A Frémont victory meant no more slave states and more cheap land for settlement, "open to the sons and daughters of freedom."

Illinois lieutenant governor Gustave Koerner was employed to make the Republican pitch for German Catholic votes in neighboring Wisconsin, an exercise he found "quite uncomfortable." "It was quite dark. I wondered how a meeting could be held at such a time in such a place. But when I arrived at the stand, I found that immense fires had been built around the platform throwing their lurid light over a large space. I was told that all night meetings were held in that style. . . . There was a rough blast from the lake that nearly took one's breath away, and the smoke from the piles of fire was almost stifling. It required a good deal of resolution to attempt a speech under such untoward circumstances. But I had been told that Milwaukee was a Democratic stronghold on account of its very large Catholic population, and so I had to do my best."

Lincoln traveled his own state on behalf of Frémont, focusing his more than fifty campaign speeches in central and southern Illinois, where Republicans were scarce and the crowds were often quite small. He avoided talking about Bleeding Kansas or Bleeding Sumner—quite a departure from most Republican stump speakers and from Lincoln's own history; in the immediate aftermath of the sack of Lawrence, he had told a crowd in Bloomington that Kansas had become a place where men "couldn't think, dream or breathe of a free state there, but what he was kicked, cuffed, shot down, and hung." Now he was aiming a more moderate appeal at Fillmore voters, and pointing out the negative effect of their votes on their own interests. "Suppose Buchanan gets *all* the slave states, and Pennsylvania, and *any other* one state besides; *then he is elected*, no matter who gets all the rest," Lincoln explained. "But suppose Fillmore gets the two slave states of Maryland and Kentucky; *then* Buchanan *is not* elected; Fillmore goes into the House of Representatives, and may be made president by a compromise. But suppose again Fillmore's friends throw away a few thousand votes on him, in *Indiana* and *Illinois*, it will inevitably give these states to Buchanan, which will more than compensate him for the loss of Maryland and Kentucky; will elect him, and leave Fillmore no chance in the H.R. or out of it. This is as plain as the adding up of the weights of three small hogs."

Joining Lincoln in traversing Illinois were Nathaniel Banks, Frank Blair Jr., and Charles Robinson. For the Democrats, Henry Wise and Howell Cobb were among those supplementing home-state icons like Stephen Douglas, who was confident. "We are in the midst of the most exciting contest ever known in this state," Douglas wrote to Buchanan. "The opposition are making desperate efforts, but I think you may rely upon this State with entire certainty."

California may have been the most disappointing state for Republicans. The lone crumb claimed by the North in the Compromise of 1850, its politics were a mishmash of freewheeling entrepreneurialism and southern sympathizing. Leading lights such as Collis P. Huntington, Mark Hopkins, Leland Stanford, and Charles Crocker were in Frémont's corner, but the party was poorly organized and underfunded, and the campaign in what should have been Frémont's home base never really got off the ground. One of the foremost campaigners was Edward D. Baker, Lincoln's friend from his early days in Illinois who had been run out of San Francisco by the Vigilance Committee. Buchanan's cynical endorsement of a Pacific railroad also dampened enthusiasm for the Republicans.

Frémont had other problems in California. His mining interests tended to conflict with those of recent (and numerous) Anglo immigrants, who believed that their mere presence on a piece of land entitled them to mine it. That Frémont had run off a number of squatters at Las Mariposas did not exactly endear him to the miners. His one significant piece of legislation from his Senate tenure, known derisively as "Frémont's Gold Bill," among other provisions barred foreigners from staking a claim, which hurt the economy of the mining region. Frémont was attempting to rationalize a haphazard situation. But Californians wanted the federal government to keep its nose out of their business.

What's more, his allies at Palmer, Cook & Company had recently defaulted on $100,000 worth of San Francisco bonds, and they were also resented as land agents and anti–claim jumpers. Extensive southern immigration into the state also worked to Frémont's disadvantage, although there were pockets of support among antislavery, pro-Jessie women, who boasted that they would "go in for Frémont and freedom."

In the South, unlike the North, the outcome was never in doubt, but that didn't keep the contending sides—Democrats and Know Nothings—from occasionally lunging at one another. An all-day rally in Lexington, Kentucky, on October 23 ended in violence when nativists attacked a torchlight parade and immigrants' homes were stoned. Democrats recruited armed men to guard the polls to prevent a repetition of the violence on Election Day.

Texans seemed to have more fun. On election eve "there is a great deal of drinking going on tonight at least one would think so from the hollering screaming cursing and swearing that is constantly saluting the ear. I have seen more intoxicated men today than I ever did see at one time."

On Election Day, November 4, at least officially the drinking stopped. It snowed in Illinois the night before, leaving snow on the ground mixed with mud and sloppy conditions across much of the state, with bitterly cold temperatures. Farther east it was somewhat warmer but wet. Many New York City voters stood in line for more than two hours to vote. Lydia Maria Child's ninety-year-old father, Convers Francis, was "too feeble to walk" but was so determined to vote for Frémont that his son-in-law carried him from their carriage to his Upstate New York polling place, where he "deposited his vote with trembling hands." In 1788, Francis had voted in the young nation's first presidential election. "My first vote was given for Washington," he said, "and my last shall be given for Frémont."

Just days before Election Day, little Frank Frémont had been felled with a severe fever, and Jesse retired from the campaign to tend to him. "Sleeping in the nursery & starting out of bed a dozen times in the night," she informed Elizabeth Blair Lee. "I don't care for the election. Let it go." Within a few days, though, the baby was feeling better and Jessie was back at the table, tending to business, as she had predicted of herself. "Although I dare say when Frank is well I shall be less careless about it."

On the Sunday before Election Day, she had tried not to jinx things. "I don't dare say anything more than to tell you we may be successful," she wrote to Elizabeth Blair Lee.

Francis Blair was optimistic, and his "intelligent confidence in the results for our side" buoyed the Frémonts. By 11 PM on election night, sizable crowds had gathered in front of the New York offices of the *Tribune*, *Herald*, *Times*, and *Sun* but "learned little that's new and less that's good."

After a depressing night at New York headquarters, a small group retired to the Frémont home for a solemn breakfast that included Lily Frémont, Francis Blair, and John Bigelow. Frémont "took the defeat calmly, cheerfully bowing to the will of the majority." But Lily and Blair did not bear up so well. Trying to lighten the atmosphere, Jessie joked that "Colonel Benton, I perceive, has the best of this family argument." Frémont smiled, but Blair teared up angrily and said, "Tom Benton's stubborn stand cost us many a vote outside Missouri." Blair had been through the wars before, and was "crushed with the bitterness of the defeat." But it was all new to Lily, who had grown up on her mother's tales of life at Jackson's knee and mourned the loss of "a season or two at the White House." Seeing the old family friend so distraught was too much for her, and she was unable to stem her tears. Jessie told her to put on her coat and go for a long walk. After Lily left, Blair rose with a great clamor. "That will do for me too, Jessie Anne. Come, Colonel, let's go to headquarters." While her mother waited, Lily wondered around Washington Square, "retracing my footsteps again and again, weeping copiously the while." When at last she returned home, Jessie took her aside and gently lectured her daughter, ten days shy of her fourteenth birthday, on the necessity of learning to deal with disappointment.

For her part, Jessie bore the defeat well (outwardly at least), telling Bigelow's wife, "I'm very glad that all my little Jessie Annes are too young to weep over the discovery that they are *not* the namesake of a President's wife."

"UP AND AT THEM AGAIN"

Turnout in the North was 83 percent, up 7 percentage points from 1852. Overall turnout was 78.3 percent, the highest since 1840. The voters had understood the stakes and responded.

Buchanan was elected with the lowest percentage of the popular vote— 45.3 percent—than anyone since John Quincy Adams in 1824, whose election had to be settled by the House of Representatives. Frémont won 33.1 percent, all but a smidge of it in the North. Fillmore won 21.5 percent—43.9 percent of the vote in the South and only 13.4 percent in the

North. Buchanan won nineteen states with 174 electoral votes to Frémont's eleven and 114. Fillmore won only Maryland, with 8.

If the results had shifted from the Democrats to the Know Nothings by 8,000 votes across just three states—Kentucky, Tennessee, and Louisiana, where the spread between Buchanan and Fillmore was a mere 1,455 votes total—the race would have been thrown into the House of Representatives. Considering the confused conditions that led to a two-month contest to elect a speaker earlier in the year, what that outcome might have yielded is impossible to determine.

The change over the previous four years had been dramatic. In 1852 Franklin Pierce carried fourteen of sixteen free states, with 49.8 percent of the vote. In 1856, Buchanan won five—California, Illinois, Indiana, Pennsylvania, and New Jersey—three of those by plurality, with bare majorities in Indiana (1,909 votes over the combined totals of Frémont and Fillmore) and Pennsylvania (1,025 votes over the combined totals of Frémont and Fillmore). And it was the southernmost counties in those states that provided his margins of victory, as was also true in Illinois, which was not as close statewide. Even in the North, voters closest to the South elected Buchanan.

Frémont ballots—candidates were listed on separate ballots and you had to ask for the appropriate one before you voted in those days—were available in only four slave states, Delaware, Kentucky, Maryland, and Virginia, where he got a total of 1,194 votes. Kentucky, birthplace of Abraham Lincoln, was Frémont's best slave state, with 314 votes.

Democrats fared better in northern congressional elections than they had in the post-Nebraska election of 1854, and they notched solid majorities in both chambers in the thirty-fifth Congress. But much of that success came in those areas where Republicans and North Americans failed to unite and split the anti-Democratic vote.

Though Buchanan won in Illinois, the state went Republican otherwise, perhaps the most ominous sign of the election for Democrats looking ahead to 1860. "The power of Douglas & slavery is forever broken in Illinois," celebrated one Frémont voter. That wasn't entirely correct, and the agile Douglas had one more trick up his sleeve to win reelection to the Senate in 1858. But the man he would defeat for that seat would eventually prove the celebratory voter right.

It's possible that given the organizational challenges faced by the fledgling party, Frémont could not have won under any circumstances. But that didn't keep the losers from pointing fingers. And there was plenty of blame to go around. "Everybody can tell why," concluded Salmon Chase, "but hardly any dozen men agree in their whys."

Some blamed the Pathfinder himself. Looking back on the contest many years later, Frémont biographer John Bigelow wrote that the candidate "owed such success as he had at this election—and it was very flattering—largely to his wife, a remarkably capable and accomplished woman."

The politicians who couldn't figure out Frémont feared that he would be dominated by the Blairs, or Seward, or Weed. Four years later, they would make the same mistake about Lincoln. Josiah Quincy III, who had served in the House, as mayor of Boston, and as president of Harvard, put it this way: Frémont was "nursed in difficulties, practiced in surmounting them; wise in counsel; full of resource; self-possessed in danger." Historian and women's rights advocate Emma Willard, in her stirring campaign biography, attempted to explain to the political class a crucial point that most of them missed. "No politician can truly understand the claims of Col. Frémont to the public confidence, unless, in connection with his biography, he examines the history of the country during the period of his public service." This is what the politicians, nursed in opportunism and always wary of danger, never understood about Frémont—that there were other types of courage, better types. He possessed those and they often did not. And so they talked past each other.

Simon Cameron blamed narrow-minded Whigs for Frémont's loss in Pennsylvania. Weed blamed Dayton's lack of appeal to the Know Nothings, and the fact that they were outspent by $50,000 in the state. "The first, and I still think fatal error, was in not taking a Vice-President in whose nomination the North Americans would have concurred cordially," Weed wrote to Cameron. On a broader scale, Weed concluded that the inability to create fusion tickets and a cohesive feeling between Republicans and North Americans, of which the vice presidency was only a part, doomed the campaign. For that, his boss Seward's refusal to do business with nativists was at least partly to blame. Frémont's refusal to deal fully with the allegation that he was a Catholic also cost uncounted nativist votes.

Even had all the issues been handled deftly, organization at the state and local levels would have remained a problem for the new party in Pennsylvania and elsewhere. Old arguments between former Democrats and Whigs played a part, with neither side fully trusting the other. "The gentlemen who engineered the Republican party in Indiana are clever, estimable men, every one of them," state fusion leader Michael Garber wrote, "but as political leaders they are imbeciles."

A few contended that Justice John McLean would have been a better presidential candidate, especially in Pennsylvania and New Jersey. It's possible, although the enthusiasm sparked by Frémont was unique to him (and to Jessie) and in no way transferrable to the old fogy McLean. And while he might have gained in the mid-Atlantic, he might well have lost ground in New England.

But there was one overriding reason why John C. Frémont lost and James Buchanan won: because northern voters still feared disunion more than they hated slavery. Voters had seen a country racked by violence in Kansas, San Francisco, and the halls of Congress. Natural disasters like the Louisiana hurricane and the human tragedy of the Margaret Garner case had contributed to the widespread feeling that things were falling apart, that the center could not hold. In that atmosphere, voters craving stability chose what they believed to be the safer path. But not by much, and not for much longer.

Commiserating with John Bigelow, New Yorker Preston King, who had been present at the Blair home the previous Christmas season when talk of Frémont first came to the fore, confidently predicted Buchanan would be "the last pro-slavery President this Country will ever see." How fully the Republican revolution had swept the North was demonstrated most clearly in New York. Of the thirty-nine counties won by Democrat Silas Wright in his 1844 election as governor, Frémont won twenty-nine. The largest state in the Union was now solidly Republican.

Jessie believed that if her husband had become president, her and Frémont's "large family connections through the Southern States" would have allowed them to prevent secession and war and work out a system of gradual abolition with compensation. It's a nice thought, but it seems highly doubtful. For starters, Frémont would have faced a hostile Democratic Congress.

But even outside Washington, the value of those connections was dubious. They had hindered, rather than helped, during the 1856 campaign. And Lincoln, with similar marital ties to Kentucky slaveholders, was not able to halt secession four years later.

The *National Anti-Slavery Standard* concluded that "moderate, non-extension pro-slavery has been beaten by ultra, unlimited pro-slavery. The Union has once more been saved and the slaveholders are triumphant." And the paper predicted desolation on this account. "This nation will be dashed in pieces by force of its own cherished iniquities. It has chosen darkness rather than light. It has made brutal injustice, wrong, and outrage the bond of its Union. At this moment it is impudently dancing with cloven hoofs on millions of down crushed fellow-beings. Let it dance on. It is a death dance. The cup of its wickedness is almost filled. It will not repent. It will not be saved. It is plunging rampantly downwards into the dark and yawning chasm of destruction."

The usually sunny Gerrit Smith had reached the same conclusion. "I have come to despair of the peaceful termination of slavery," he had written in August, well before the outcome of the election could be known. "It must go out in blood. The time for abolishing it at the ballot-box has gone by—never to return."

When his victory was secure, Buchanan spoke to a gathering of neighbors at Wheatland, his "beautifully and tastefully arranged" Lancaster estate, where the house was "plain and unpretending in the extreme," where "everything has the air of unostentatious democracy," as one visitor described it. In that bucolic setting, Buchanan assured them that although the "storm of abolition" had left the nation "tottering on its base," now that his victory was certain "a roseate and propitious morn now breaking upon us promises a long day of peace and prosperity for our country."

James Buchanan, who throughout his long and undistinguished career had been wrong about a great many things, had topped himself. Emerging from the most violent peacetime election year in American history, Buchanan stood staring into the abyss and saw not disunion but a "roseate and propitious morn." His promised "long day of peace and prosperity" would have to wait for a better man. He had defeated such a man in John C. Frémont. But another was waiting, just off stage, who would bring on the "storm of abolition" that Buchanan feared, and in so doing begin to deliver on the long-deferred promise of America.

"The Republicans here are full of grit," Schuyler Colfax wrote from Indiana. "No give up—fuller of elasticity & zeal than any defeated party I ever saw." Lyman Trumbull found his "Republican friends in great spirits for a defeated party. They are bold, confident, and united, ready for another fight and feel that they will certainly win next time." Henry Ward Beecher was likewise unbowed. "I shall sleep on it one night, and be up and at them again the next morning," he enthused.

Frémont was an imperfect vessel for the hopes of antislavery men, but—much more so than in any of the expeditions that earned him the sobriquet Pathfinder—he had now blazed a trail, one that Abraham Lincoln would follow four years hence. "A wedge may be useful in splitting a log," John Bigelow wrote of Frémont, "but useless in converting either of its parts into a chest of drawers." The Pathfinder had split the log in 1856. The Railsplitter would build the chest of drawers.

Epilogue

"Does Any Man Dream That It Would Settle the Controversy?"

On October 4, the James G. Willie handcart company was four days out from Fort Laramie, about halfway between the Upper Crossing, where emigrants left the Platte River to cross a dry plateau, and the next river, the Sweetwater. The company's leaders knew they didn't have a prayer of extending their rations to last until they reached South Pass, 250 miles to the west, where they hoped relief from Utah would be waiting.

That day, Franklin Richards, who had organized the handcart emigration in England back in the spring, reached Salt Lake City after a quick six-week journey by horse and wagon.

Richards reported to Brigham Young that two handcart companies, and two wagon trains behind them carrying baggage, were still on the trail. Young, who had stayed uncharacteristically hands-off on the handcart project since setting it into motion the previous autumn, sprang into action. He gathered church leaders "to find out what we need to do tomorrow," when the semiannual church conference would be convening. At that meeting, Young declared "Many of our brethren and sisters are on the Plains with handcarts, and probably many are now seven hundred miles from this place. They must be brought here, we must send assistance to them. The text will be—to get them here."

Plans were hastily made to gather eleven tons of flour, coats, blankets, shoes, and whatever else might be needed, organize mule teams, hire wagons, and get started. The saints answered the call.

Richards estimated that the Willie company would be nearing the Green River in southwestern Wyoming. When the wagons that were loaded up in Salt Lake City reached Fort Bridger, two days west of the river, though, they still had not encountered any migrants. "Our hearts began to ache when we reached Green River and yet no word of them," one of the rescuers remembered.

Willie company was nowhere close to the Green River. After their rations had been cut twice in two weeks west of Fort Laramie, the company was still making about fifteen miles per day and the weather was holding. But the long journey, the late start, and the reduced rations were beginning to take their toll.

On October 15 Levi Savage noted that the previous night "Caroline Reeder, aged 17 years, died, and was Buried this morning. The peopple are geting weak, and failing very fast. A greate many Sick. Our teams are als[o] failing fast and it requires great exertion to make any progress."

For the next three days they pressed on, though only at about ten miles per day. The weather was "cool but fair," and another handful of people died. Then, just before noon on October 19, a freezing, blustery snowstorm swept in. Several inches fell, and more came the next day. "The cattle, and people, are so much reduced with Short food and hard work," Savage wrote, "that except we get assistance, we Surely, can not move far in this Snow."

George D. Grant, who had been a missionary in England himself and had raced home from Florence with Richards, was leading one of the teams headed back out on the trail from Utah. On October 17, Grant's rescue party was struck by a ferocious snowstorm—the same one that would strike Willie two days later—at South Pass, the relatively flat crossing of the continental divide, 150 miles northeast of Fort Bridger. Fighting the snow, the wind, and freezing temperatures, they left behind carcasses of the game they killed, secure in the knowledge that it would not spoil before anyone would need it. They left some teams behind, too, to speed their progress eastward. More rescue parties coming from Utah joined these teams over the next several days.

Grant pressed forward as far as he dared, but the weather stalled him again the next day at a hollow on Willow Creek, where he moved off the road to find better shelter. Ahead, just one long day's drive to the east, was the Willie company, eating the last of the food they had with them— a bit of flour, some crackers Willie had purchased at Laramie, and two scrawny cows that were on the verge of death. Divided among hundreds, it wasn't much.

On October 19, Willie mounted a mule and headed west with one other man in a desperate search for help, leaving his starving charges behind. At the same moment, Grant dispatched a wagon eastward. They missed each other, but the wagon driver found the starving company, and Willie stumbled across Grant's party thanks to a sign posted on the main trail by one of Grant's men.

The wagon that reached Willie's company brought scant material relief but buoyed the spirit of the haggard band. They would need it, as most of the Grant rescue team continued on to find Edward Martin's company, and the Willie company was told to press on westward through the snow. Nine more died overnight before the carts moved out the next day.

What followed, a harrowing five-mile climb through knee-deep snow into a blinding blizzard and hurricane-force winds up a steep, uneven series of rises and swales called Rocky Ridge, would be remembered forever by all who survived it. Many did not.

"We beried our dead, got up our teams, and about 9 oclock A. M. commenced ascending the Rocky Ridg," recorded Levi Savage. "This was a Severe day. The wind blew awful hard, and colde. The ascent was some five miles long, and Some places, Steep and covered with deep Snow. We became we[a]ry, Set down to rest, and Some become chilled, and commenced to frieze."

Before moving out again on October 24, the company struggled to bury thirteen people in the snow. The travail was too much even for the stout Savage to keep up his spirits. He survived, but he set his journal aside. "We commenced our march again. From this I have not been able to keep a daily journal, but nothing of much note transpired excepte the people ded daily."

The next day, the Willie company reached South Pass, where food and fresh wagon teams greeted them. Famished and exhausted, members would continue to die across the final 250 miles to Salt Lake, which they reached on November 9. But the company, or what was left of it, had been delivered.

Behind them, the Martin company was still awaiting deliverance. After leaving six teams at Willow Creek to aid Willie, George D. Grant continued eastward up the trail in search of Martin. He had eight wagons loaded with supplies and about fifteen men. Again he sent a small party ahead—Abel Garr, Cyrus Wheelock, and Joseph A. Young (Brigham's eldest son)—to reconnoiter, with orders to proceed no further than Devil's Gate, a landmark on the trail formed by the Sweetwater carving out a gash in a granite ridge. There, an abandoned French trading post called Fort Seminoe provided a chance of shelter from the elements, as did a cove across the Sweetwater that had a natural sand dune fronting it that protected it from the winds. Proximity to the river meant better availability of firewood.

The advance team expected to find Martin there, based on Richards's estimate of where the companies would be. But when the team arrived, the handcart emigrants were nowhere to be found. And when Grant brought the rest of his team up, Young, Wheelock, and Garr were still alone.

The Martin company was still sixty-five miles to the east. They had reached Fort Laramie on October 8 and found that Franklin Richards had bought and left a hundred buffalo robes for them. The migrants desperately traded watches, jewelry, and other valuables for whatever provisions they could lay their hands on. Beyond the fort, as Willie had done, Martin was forced to slash rations, and then slash them again. At Deer Creek, near present-day Glenrock, clothes and bedding were cast aside to lighten the load.

Two days later, at Red Buttes near the last crossing of the North Platte, winter howled in. The Martin company hunkered down, and it would be stranded for nine days by a blizzard, along with one of the two wagon trains that had been trailing behind the handcarts. More than fifty members of Martin's corps had already died from exposure, starvation, and exhaustion. Many more were about to follow.

Caught in the same storm, Grant wasted little time, although he was beginning to run low on supplies for his own group. He sent Young, Garr, and Daniel Jones ahead again with a pack mule but no food. It took them three days to reach Red Buttes, where they found a scene of horror. Emaciated and exhausted, the survivors crowded around the three men, who could offer no sustenance but hope. Young told Martin to increase the flour ration to a pound per person per day and to press on westward. Help was three days away. It was their only chance. Then the three men rode on down the trail to find the second wagon train, which was another fifteen miles to the east. Two days later, with both wagon companies united with Martin, the combined troupe wearily picked themselves up and headed west. Several more migrants died on the way.

When they approached the encampment at Devil's Gate on October 26, one of Grant's men observed that "a condition of distress here met my eyes that I never saw before or since. The train was strung out for three or four miles. There were old men pulling and tugging their carts, sometimes loaded with a sick wife or children—women pulling along sick husbands—little children six to eight years old struggling through the mud and snow." One of the handcart emigrants recalled that "the Company gave up and decided they could go no further." The goods that had been sent from Salt Lake were disbursed to a grateful though muted cry of hallelujah, but there was not enough to go around. Some got coats, scarves, blankets, shoes, boots, gloves, hoods. Others had to settle for one of the fourteen neckties some Utah saint had bizarrely included in the donation box.

On November 3, election eve back in the states, a different sort of political meeting was held in the log stockade at Devil's Gate. Should the bedraggled party winter here or press on through to Zion? The old fort offered the stockade, a handful of small cabins, and the sheltered cove beneath the three-hundred-feet-high stone bluffs. They could stay out of the weather and use the riverine wood for fire. If relief trains could get through from Utah, they would have enough to eat.

It seemed a forlorn hope. There was no guarantee that supplies would be able to get through, and if they could, wouldn't travel westward be nearly as practical? And what about the sick? Their only hope was to reach civilization. No matter how comfortable existence in the wilderness might be made, it was still just that. Anyone in need of medical attention was almost certain to die here. They decided to go on.

But that night, another storm blew in, dumping a foot and a half of snow on the camp, with temperatures plummeting to eleven degrees below zero. Those who had been resting in the wagons ran for the stockade and the cabins, but there was barely room for a third of them. Securing tents was nearly impossible with the howling wind and frozen ground. Once up, all too often they blew down. One youngster got caught in a tumbled tent, and the warmth it provided through the night saved his life as others around him froze to death. As the wretched travelers hunkered down as best they could, Joseph Young and Abel Garr once again got astride their horses, this time heading west, in search of help from the rescue companies Grant believed were coming down the trail behind him.

They weren't. Many had turned back when confronted with harsh conditions. Others sincerely believed that the emigrants were either ensconced in camp for the winter or dead. But when a courier from Fort Bridger arrived in Salt Lake with news that some of the teams had turned around, Young dispatched church leaders to intercept them and turn them eastbound again.

Eventually that would make a difference. But at Devil's Gate, the party was in dire straits. With not enough room in the stockade and cabins, Grant moved the Martin company to the cove, about two miles away, necessitating an icy crossing of the Sweetwater River. This has come down through oral tradition as almost a Mormon Golgotha, with exaggerated tales of mythic heroism and redemptive suffering. The truth is, there is no need to exaggerate either the heroism of the rescuers, who helped most across, or the suffering of the emigrants, which was all too real. Wading into the bone-chilling water, two feet deep and more than a hundred feet across and clogged with ice, many seemed certain they were going to their deaths. "I could not keep my tears back," remembered English emigrant Patience Loader. Frozen clothes clung to emaciated bodies. Men faltered, begging not to be made to go on. One broke down weeping as he tried and failed to get his rickety cart through the water. "Don't cry, Jimmy," said his wife, standing beside him. "I'll pull the cart for you."

For five days, as storms swirled around them, the survivors camped at what would come to be known as Martin's Cove. Saints continued to die. Finally, the weather broke, and the wagons were loaded. The last of the handcarts, some of which had already been turned into firewood, were discarded. On November 9, under a clear and warming sky, the company moved out. Nearly every day, at least a few more emigrants died. After another three weeks of trial, the remainder of the Martin company reached Salt Lake City on the last day of November, a Sunday.

All told, more than 200 emigrants died—about 70 in the Willie company, somewhere between 150 and 170 in the Martin company—the worst loss of life of the westward migration. But unlike the Donner Party's Sierra Nevada disaster of 1846–47 and John C. Frémont's 1848–49 expedition to the San Juan Mountains, the saints never resorted to cannibalism to survive. Thousands of immigrants arrived safely. Handcart companies would continue coming to the valley until 1860. And although the population influx was not enough to persuade Washington to overlook polygamy and make Utah a state, the 1856 pioneers would become honored members of the community that was at long last admitted to the Union in 1896, the fortieth anniversary of the first handcart trek.

"The Development of Sectional Feelings"

A wet and weary November in Washington—it rained almost without ceasing for the final ten days of the month—finally gave way to December, with a northeaster blowing in on the evening of December 1, giving the capital one last drenching before winter arrived.

Other than the dreary weather, the *Dred Scott* case, held over in May and scheduled for reargument postelection, now dominated the news. Gone was the anonymity of February. Now the politicians were weighing in, even before the Supreme Court got around to doing its work.

Franklin Pierce's final annual message preempted the court, asserting that the Missouri Compromise was already "a dead letter in the law" and "that Congress does not possess constitutional power to impose restrictions of this character upon any present or future State of the Union." Congress was also getting into the act and began debating the issue as soon as members returned to Washington in the first week of December.

Tennessee Whig James Chamberlain Jones suggested that the legislative branch had failed to resolve the questions at hand, and it was now the purview of the courts to settle it once and for all. He, for one, would be willing to abide by whatever decision was handed down, even if it ran contrary to the interest of his state and section. "Would the Republican Party exhibit equal loyalty, should the decision contravene their wishes and principles?" he asked.

The *National Era* opined that while this position might make "a show of liberality," the reality was that "the Judges of the Supreme Court are men of like passions and infirmities with the rest of us. We may admit that they are upright, honorable, and able, but they are not infallible, or exempt from prejudice." A majority of the justices were from the South. The court had already issued a number of rulings with sectionally split decisions. "Is it too much to assume that Mr. Jones and his friends must feel much less hesitation in submitting their case to such a Tribunal than the Republican Party? . . . But suppose a decision on the main question should be rendered by a majority, the *members from the free States dissenting*, does any man dream that it would settle the controversy? It would only add another element to the agitation."

That politicians were now speaking openly about the case didn't make the stakes any greater, but it did heighten the atmosphere in which the case was being heard, which was one of relief among Democrats that Buchanan would be in the White House, coupled with paranoia among area slave holders. One correspondent who had been following the twists and turns of the case all year noted that "last Spring, when this controversy was in progress in the Court, I made the suggestion that the facts warranted the suspicion that the case had been made up by Washington politicians, in order to enlist the Supreme Court in the electioneering struggles of the day, and to procure from it a decision adverse to the Republican party and the free States. Those grounds of suspicion have not been removed; they are in fact much strengthened by what has since occurred." Secessionist Edmund Ruffin noted in his diary on Christmas Day that "reports of negro plots of designed insurrection have in this neighborhood [near

Richmond, Virginia,] also induced proper measures of vigilance." And while "there are few persons who feel any alarm," nevertheless "patrols, composed of respectable men, have been out every night." If there were to be any trouble, Ruffin was certain, it was "northern incendiaries" who were to blame, and any suffering would fall most heavily on "the deluded victims of these abolition agents."

The fears that had started in Texas had rolled across the South to Virginia. Authorities in Alexandria, just outside Washington, arrested thirty-two slaves in early December, whipped them, and released them back to their masters. Governor Henry Wise rushed a cache of arms to the city. Another group in Clarke County, sixty miles west of the national capital, were arrested "for attempted insurrection." This group said they had heard whites and blacks saying that "if Frémont was elected they would be free, but as he was not they were determined to fight for it." The *New York Herald* sarcastically commented that the state that had only a few months earlier promised secession in the event of a Frémont victory had lost its "military ardor" and couldn't even raise sufficient force "to put down an insurrection feared from some negroes."

When the Supreme Court met on December 15 to hear the second round of oral arguments in *Dred Scott v. Sandford*, the legal lineup had changed slightly. Joining Montgomery Blair in Scott's corner was George Curtis, a noted Boston attorney and the brother of Justice Benjamin Curtis. Just as John McLean's use of the bench to promote his presidential candidacy was not seen as an ethical violation, no one objected to the brother of a sitting justice arguing a case before the court. The defendant was again relying on Missouri senator Henry S. Geyer and former Attorney General Reverdy Johnson, "among the first men of the profession, of the East and the West" as Blair himself described them. And now, unlike in February, everyone was paying attention to the "Missouri Compromise Case," as the papers often referred to it, which "daily attracts large crowds of earnest auditors."

"Mr. Blair opened the case in a luminous argument on the 15th," the *National Era* reported. Blair devoted an hour to the question of whether blacks could be citizens, arguing that mere discrimination by the state or individuals did not deprive a free man of citizenship. Geyer countered that citizenship came from being born a citizen or naturalized; Scott, born a slave, could not enjoy either privilege. But the spotlight shone on Johnson and Curtis, because they were the main combatants on the high-profile question of slavery in the territories.

It was the constitutionality of the Missouri Compromise—not considered by any lower court and barely alluded to during the original Supreme Court hearing in February—that dominated the proceedings and the political class's discussion of it. Curtis argued that Congress of a necessity had to institute governments in territories, which demanded that rules be established. Johnson said such an interpretation stretched the fabric of the Constitution too far. The Missouri Compromise, necessary to the preservation of the Union at the time, was a mere political exercise, not a determining judicial authority. Further, it denied to residents of the southern states the equal protection of the laws guaranteed by the Constitution, by barring their ability to carry their property into any state or territory, a right afforded to all in the North.

Through twelve hours of argument over four days, the lawyers and the justices sparred, parried, and pontificated. The man at the center of the case, an enslaved American named Dred Scott, was all but forgotten.

"We have heard high commendation bestowed upon the ability and courage with which Mr. Blair, from the beginning, has conducted this difficult case," the *National Era* reported, then, in a rare display of even-handedness, noted that "Indeed, the arguments on both sides appear to have been made with signal ability." The *Richmond Dispatch* reported that "[Reverdy] Johnson made a strong argument against the constitutionality of the Missouri Compromise."

Curtis's closing remarks earned some of the highest plaudits. He "commanded marked attention from the Court and attracted the largest audience from Congress which has yet assembled."

In untypically understated fashion, the *National Era* concluded that the case "was reported to have occasioned the development of sectional feelings upon the Bench. . . . Its deliberations have been protracted, but so far as newspaper rumors are to be credited, by no means harmonious."

Antislavery advocates were preparing for the worst and, if not hoping for the best, hopeful enough based on the performance of John C. Frémont and the Republican Party and its first national contest that things might change, perhaps more quickly than anyone had thought imaginable just a few short years before. "If the Supreme Court were today to decide that Congress had no power over slavery in the Territories, the decision would be simply a majority decision, carrying no moral power with it in the North," the *National Anti-Slavery Standard* declared. "And if a speedy change were possible in one or two of the individuals composing the Court, such a decision would be unceremoniously reversed at its very next session."

By Christmas, peace had come to Kansas. Governor John Geary had effectively disarmed both sides' militias, federal control was restored, and a land boom was ensuing.

Having created his imaginary peace in Nebraska, by December General William S. Harney was contemplating an expedition to pacify the Seminole in Florida.

Following their attack on a sitting senator in the halls of Congress, Preston Brooks and Lawrence Keitt had been reelected, but so had Charles Sumner, by the overwhelming total of 333–12 in the Massachusetts legislature, an unheard-of level of agreement for that disjointed body.

On December 29—a year to the day since Francis Preston Blair had organized a meeting at his home that aided greatly in the organizing of a new sectional party—Buchanan told minister to France John Y. Mason that the "great object of my administration will be to arrest, if possible, the agitation of the Slavery question at the North & to destroy sectional parties."

Preston Brooks died on January 27, 1857, at age thirty-seven, of the croup. As he lay dying in his room at Brown's Hotel in Washington, his attending physician was Dr. Cornelius Boyle, who had dressed Charles Sumner's wounds off the floor of the Senate. In its obituary, the *New York Times* called Brooks "a man of generous nature, of kindly feelings, and of manly impulses, warmly attached to his friends, and by no means relentless or vindictive towards his foes."

"A SMALL LIGHT"

Violence and threats of violence chased the country into 1857.

"If Buchanan should secretly favor the free-state men of Kansas, as I see it charged he will, and succeed in bringing it in as a free State, he will richly deserve death, and I hope some patriotic hand will inflict it," Georgia lawyer and newspaper editor Thomas W. Thomas wrote. Thomas need not have worried.

With the *Dred Scott* decision still pending, Supreme Court justice Peter V. Daniel's wife died January 3 in a terrible accident: her clothing caught on fire. Daniel would not return to the court until mid-February. Buchanan wrote to Justice John Catron on February 3, asking if he expected a decision before Inauguration Day. The Tennessean told the president-elect that he wasn't sure, that no action had been taken on the case because of Daniel's absence, but he would keep him informed. Catron wrote again on February 10, telling Buchanan that Daniel was returning that week and a conference was scheduled for the fourteenth. But he also implied that the legality of the Missouri Compromise would not be part of the decision.

The justices finally gathered to consider the case a year and a week after Montgomery Blair filed his original brief. In this meeting, McLean and Curtis both argued that the territorial question should be considered by the court. Following the conference, the opinion was assigned to Justice Samuel Nelson, a New Yorker and appointee of President John Tyler. This signaled bad news for Scott, but also bad news for Buchanan. Nelson would certainly be writing that Scott would remain a slave, but he was unlikely to be entrusted with an opinion as momentous as one that would overturn the Missouri Compromise.

Somewhere between February 14 and February 19, the situation changed. After the conference and the assignment of the opinion to Nelson, Justice James M. Wayne, a Georgian and an appointee of Andrew Jackson, suggested it would be better if Chief Justice Roger Taney took over the opinion and covered all of the contested issues. Over the next several days, Taney was persuaded, perhaps by Wayne's argument that the political situation required a comprehensive response, perhaps by the need to respond to scathing and comprehensive dissents planned by Justices Curtis and McLean (who had leaked some of his own opinion back in the spring as part of his unsuccessful run at the Republican presidential nomination). Whatever the reasons, on February 19, Catron reversed himself, reporting back to Buchanan that he would be safe in saying in his inaugural address that the court was considering the constitutionality of the Missouri

Compromise, and that the court would "decide and settle a controversy" that had "long and seriously agitated the country."

Taney did not want the decision to be viewed as a purely sectional one and put intense pressure on Justice Robert C. Grier, a Pennsylvanian like Buchanan, to join the majority. Grier had hoped to avoid the larger issue. But Buchanan asked for his help, and Grier caved. "I am anxious that it should not appear that the line of latitude should mark the line of division in the court," he wrote to Buchanan, while also tipping off the president-elect that the decision on "this troublesome question" would not be handed down before the inauguration.

Buchanan could now put the finishing touches on his inaugural address.

The president-elect made an "unostentatious entrance" into Washington at 5 PM on March 2, "witnessed by a larger and more enthusiastic assemblage than was ever known to greet under the same circumstances" the incoming chief executive.

Inauguration Day arrived with a beautiful spring morning, the bright blue sky a welcome sight after two days of "blustering disagreeable weather." Buchanan was staying at the National Hotel, and took a carriage with vice president-elect John C. Breckinridge to the Willard Hotel to pick up outgoing president Franklin Pierce. Thousands of people who had poured into the capital lined the streets, many of whom had spent a sleepless inauguration eve on a cold floor or a hard bench because the hotels were filled past capacity. Flags and bunting hung from nearly every window along Pennsylvania Avenue, and a parade of fire engines, militias, bands, and floats led the new president toward the Capitol. Directly in front of the Buchanan carriage was a float drawn by six white horses adorned with a woman dressed as the Goddess of Liberty perched atop a high platform.

On the east portico of the Capitol, Buchanan stopped for a few seconds to chat with Chief Justice Taney before taking his seat. Later, some would suppose this was related to *Dred Scott*, but Buchanan had been fully informed about the decision a month earlier by Catron and Grier.

Taney administered the oath of office "amid the sky-rending shouts of the multitude." Then Buchanan stepped to the lectern.

"A difference of opinion has arisen in regard to the point of time when the people of a territory shall decide this question for themselves,"

NOW READY:
THE
Dred Scott Decision.

OPINION OF CHIEF-JUSTICE ROGER B. TANEY,

WITH AN INTRODUCTION,

BY DR. J. H. VAN EVRIE.

ALSO,

AN APPENDIX,

BY SAM. A. CARTWRIGHT, M.D., of New Orleans,

ENTITLED,

"Natural History of the Prognathous Race of Mankind."

ORIGINALLY WRITTEN FOR THE NEW YORK DAY-BOOK.

THE GREAT WANT OF A BRIEF PAMPHLET, containing the famous decision of Chief-Justice Taney, in the celebrated Dred Scott Case, has induced the Publishers of the DAY-BOOK to present this edition to the public. It contains a Historical Introduction by Dr. Van Evrie, author of "Negroes and Negro Slavery," and an Appendix by Dr. Cartwright, of New Orleans, in which the physical differences between the negro and the white races are forcibly presented. As a whole, this pamphlet gives the *historical*, *legal*, and *physical* aspects of the "Slavery" Question in a concise compass, and should be circulated by thousands before the next presidential election. All who desire to answer the arguments of the abolitionists should read it. In order to place it before the masses, and induce Democratic Clubs, Democratic Town Committees, and all interested in the cause, to order it for distribution, it has been put down at the following low rates, for which it will be sent, free of postage, to any part of the United States. Dealers supplied at the same rate.

Single Copies	$0 25
Five Copies	1 00
Twelve Copies	2 00
Fifty Copies	7 00
One Hundred Copies	12 00
Every additional Hundred	10 00

Address

VAN EVRIE, HORTON, & CO.,

Publishers of DAY-BOOK,

No. 40 Ann Street, New York.

DRED SCOTT DECISION NEWSPAPER ADVERTISEMENT. *Library of Congress*

he said of slavery. "This is, happily, a matter of but little practical importance. Besides, it is a judicial question, which legitimately belongs to the
Supreme Court of the United States, before whom it is now pending,
and will, it is understood, be speedily and finally settled." For good measure, in full knowledge of the outcome, he promised "to their decision,
in common with all good citizens, I shall cheerfully submit, whatever
this may be."

Buchanan misspoke. The court was ruling on whether Congress had
the power to prohibit slavery in a territory, not whether a territorial legislature did. But he would get around to that soon enough, with ever more
disastrous consequences for the people of Kansas and the nation as a whole.

Democrats were ecstatic. Gamaliel Bailey's *National Era* saw only a continuation "of the Pierce dynasty of weakness, vacillation, and unconditional
acquiescence in the demands of the Oligarchy," and deduced it "impossible
to augur a favorable result from a commencement so ominous." Two days
later, when the Supreme Court's decision was announced declaring that
Congress had no authority to ban slavery anywhere, and that blacks had
"no rights which the white man was bound to respect," Republicans reacted
"with mingled derision and contempt. If epithets and denunciation could
sink a judicial body," wrote the *New-York Tribune*, "the Supreme Court of
the United States would never be heard of again."

The slave-power candidate was in the White House. Dred Scott would
remain in bondage. And the entire country, the Supreme Court said, was
now open to slavery. The soaring hopes of summer and fall had descended
into the darkest despair for those who had spied the possibility of freedom
on the horizon.

But a flicker remained. After the election, William Webb, the slave
who at the risk of death had rallied pro-Frémont meetings in Mississippi
during the campaign and talked of inciting the enslaved against their masters, gathered a group of friends from adjoining plantations in Kentucky,
where he had been sent by his master.

Webb believed that God had sent Frémont as a messenger who "gave
the idea of freedom to the colored people" and "made them think that
better times were coming." He asked the group if they thought any more
about being free, and if any of them had heard of Frémont. Some had,

but noted that since he had not been elected, it didn't seem to matter now what Frémont thought about emancipation or anything else.

Webb assured them that it did.

"Frémont was a small light," Webb told them, "and it would keep burning till it was spread over the whole world."

ACKNOWLEDGMENTS

Firt and foremost, I'd like to thank the writers who got here before I did.

Frémont has had many biographers and I am indebted to them all, but Tom Chaffin's *Pathfinder: John Charles Frémont and the Course of American Empire* stands as the definitive work.

Mrs. Frémont has inspired as many writers as her husband—perhaps more—but Pamela Herr's *Jessie Benton Frémont: A Biography* and Sally Denton's *Passion and Principle: John and Jessie Frémont, the Couple Whose Power, Politics, and Love Shaped Nineteenth Century America*, deserve special mention.

I want to warmly thank Stacey Robertson, dean of the College of Arts and Humanities at Central Washington University, for sharing her unpublished paper on Jessie Benton Frémont and women in the 1856 campaign, presented at the Society for Historians of the Early American Republic conference in Philadelphia in July 2014.

I'm indebted to Le Moyne College history professor Douglas Egerton, whose scholarly work on William Webb provided a key element in the narrative for *Lincoln's Pathfinder*.

I am grateful to Natalya Dixon for permission to quote from her late husband Bill Dixon's book, *Last Days of Last Island: The Hurricane of 1856, Louisiana's First Great Storm*.

The editing team at Chicago Review Press have worked with me twice, and both experiences were nothing but positive, particularly the firm and fair hand of Devon Freeny.

Thanks to my agent, Jessica Papin, who took a chance on a cranky old journalist.

And to my wife, Arwen, and son, Thomas, who cannot be surpassed in at least pretending to be interested when I start yapping about the Kansas-Nebraska Act or the courage of Mormon pioneers, no thanks are enough.

NOTES

INTRODUCTION: THE PATHFINDER

Seventeen towns and counties . . . Rolle, *JCF*, 164.
"what is striking about Republican rhetoric . . ." Gienapp, *Origins*, 355.

PROLOGUE: "WE CAN'T CONCEIVE OF
A GREATER PIECE OF MISCHIEF"

Lincoln had traveled extensively . . . Schwartz, "'Egregious Political Blunder,'" 9.
"This is about the only crumb . . ." Abraham Lincoln to Duff Green, May 18, 1849,
   in Lincoln, *CW* 2:49.
"will be an egregious political blunder" . . . Abraham Lincoln to Elisha Embree, May
   25, 1849, in Lincoln, *CW* 2:51 (Lincoln sent essentially the same letter to several
   people).
"fought for Mr. Clay . . ." Abraham Lincoln to Josiah M. Lucas, April 25, 1849, in
   Lincoln, *CW* 2:43.
After failing to secure the land office . . . Abraham Lincoln to John M. Clayton, August
   21, 1849, and to Thomas Ewing, September 23, 1849, in Lincoln, *CW* 2:61, 65;
   Fehrenbacher, *Prelude*, 8, 20–21.
"It is utterly impossible . . ." Johannsen, *Douglas*, 39; Gara, *Presidency*, 90.
"Douglas had his eye fixed . . ." McCormack, *Memoirs of Gustave Koerner*, 1:616.
The bill Douglas reported . . . Johannsen, *Douglas*, 405, 417.
"We can't conceive of a greater piece . . ." *Illinois State Journal*, January 15, 1854, in
   Lehrman, *Lincoln at Peoria*, 76.
"wholly gratuitous and entirely political" . . . Van Deusen, *Weed*, 196.
Douglas was playing a double game . . . Davis, *Jefferson Davis*, 247.

"There cannot be a doubt . . ." Robert Toombs to W. W. Burwell, February 3, 1854, in Toombs et al., *Correspondence*, 342.

"The citizens of the several States . . ." *Congressional Globe*, 33rd Congress, 1st session, 175; Johannsen, *Douglas*, 411.

"inconsistent with the principles of the legislation . . ." Lehrman, *Lincoln at Peoria*, 78.

"It will triumph and impart peace . . ." Stephen A. Douglas to Howell Cobb, April 2, 1854, in Toombs et al., *Correspondence*, 343.

Franklin Pierce, elected in 1852 . . . Davis, *Breckinridge*, 18.

"that lawless ruffian . . ." William Lloyd Garrison to Samuel Gridley Howe, November 12, 1855, in Garrison, *Letters*, 359.

"Gentlemen, you are entering . . ." Holt, *Pierce*, 77; Johannsen, *Douglas*, 414; Lehrman, *Lincoln at Peoria*, 80; Wallner, *Pierce*, 96–97; Davis, *Jefferson Davis*, 249.

Pierce had declared in his first annual message . . . *Congressional Globe*, 32nd Congress, 1st session, 22.

"What a sermon!" . . . Salmon P. Chase journal, January 9, 1853, in Chase, *Papers*, 1:233.

Neither could thousands of others . . . Gara, *Presidency*, 93.

"make stillborn the infant liberty" . . . Theodore Parker to William Herndon, January 2, 1855, in Renehan, *Secret Six*, 80; Lehrman, *Lincoln at Peoria*, 86; Donald, *Sumner*, 259.

"a profanation of the American pulpit" . . . Myers, *Republican Party*, 38.

Anti-Nebraska rallies were called for . . . Woodwell, *Whittier*, 247.

On January 24, Chase asked . . . Blue, *Salmon P. Chase*, 93; Johannsen, *Douglas*, 417.

"a gross violation of a sacred pledge . . ." *National Era*, February 2, 1854.

"lost his temper before he began" . . . Johannsen, *Douglas*, 419–420.

"crowded into and took possession . . ." *New York Times*, February 6, 1854; *Congressional Globe*, 33rd Congress, 1st session, appendix, 134, 140.

"They celebrate a present victory" . . . Donald, *Sumner*, 254–255.

"He says nothing" . . . Ibid., 255–256.

"If we let this opportunity . . ." Robert Toombs to W. W. Burwell, February 3, 1854, in Toombs et al., *Correspondence*, 342 (Burwell was editor of the *Baltimore Patriot*).

"The moral effect of the victory . . ." Alexander Stephens to W. W. Burwell, May 7, 1854, in Toombs et al., *Correspondence*, 344.

They didn't let the opportunity escape . . . *Congressional Globe*, 33rd Congress, 1st session, 532.

The House debate was slightly shorter . . . Gara, *Presidency*, 94–95; Johannsen, *Douglas*, 428, 433–434.

"Nobody says anything now . . ." Alexander Stephens to J. W. Duncan, May 26, 1854, in Toombs et al., *Correspondence*, 345.

"I could travel from Boston to Chicago . . ." Johannsen, *Douglas*, 451.

"the time has come to dissolve . . ." Henry Wilson to WHS, May 28, 1854, in Stahr, *Seward*, 144.

"passage of this Nebraska bill . . ." *New-York Tribune*, May 29, 1854.

"That man must not be sent . . ." John Greenleaf Whittier to Henry I. Bowditch, May 26, 1856, in Woodwell, *Whittier*, 248–249.

"triumphantly carried back . . ." Karcher, *First Woman*, 388.

"we went to bed one night . . ." O'Connor, *Lords of the Loom*, 98.

"simply absurd" . . . William Lloyd Garrison to Samuel J. May, September 24, 1856, in Garrison, *Letters*, 318–319.

The hastily organized meetings . . . Formisano, *Birth*, 242.

"a clear, forcible, and convincing" . . . Illinois State Journal, September 2, 1854 in Lincoln, *CW* 2:227.

"Some men, mostly Whigs . . ." Lincoln, *CW* 2:273, 275.

"antipathy to the Pope . . ." Strong, *Diary*, 182–183, 241.

"I have hoped their organization would die . . ." Abraham Lincoln to Owen Lovejoy, August 11, 1855, in Lincoln, *CW* 2:316.

New York Democrats fell . . . Wallner, *Pierce*, 165–166; Freehling, *Road to Disunion*, 62; Donald, *Sumner*, 268; Holt, *Rise and Fall*, 906–908.

The legislature gathered on February 8 . . . Johannsen, *Douglas*, 463–464; McCormack, *Memoirs of Gustave Koerner*, 1:624–625.

"If we win" . . . David Atchison to R. M. T. Hunter, March 4, 1855, in Landis, *Northern Men*, 138; Etcheson, *Bleeding Kansas*, 55; Freehling, *Road to Disunion*, 74.

"in such a condition that the white man . . ." Wallner, *Pierce*, 92.

"catch the spirit of the people . . ." Salmon P. Chase to James W. Grimes, June 27, 1855, in Chase, *Papers*, 2:421.

1. "A New Man"

"to meet some friends . . ." WHS to Thurlow Weed, December 31, 1856, in Seward, *Seward at Washington*, 264.

"approving of his activity" . . . Ibid.; W. E. Smith, *Blair Family*, 324; Stahr, *Seward*, 158; Bartlett, *Frémont*, 13.

He had named his 250-acre estate . . . Silver Spring Historical Society, accessed June 23, 2014, http://silverspringhistory.homestead.com/; Goodwin, *Team of Rivals*, 24.

Chase was the last to arrive . . . Niven, *Chase*, 179.

But he was more than a member . . . Goodwin, *Team of Rivals*, 24; Remini, *Jackson*, 297.

"The extension of Slavery . . ." E. B. Smith, *Francis Preston Blair*, 219–220; Blair, *Letter*, 2, 6.

"made up . . . for the most part . . ." Washington Star, February 23, 1856.

"in the main" . . . Blair, *Letter*, 2.

The diverging elements . . . Brenzel, *Daughters of the State*, 5, 11, 16.

They agreed on the easy things . . . Niven, *Chase*, 179.

Blair, who was just getting over . . . JBF to EBL, December 14, 1855, in J. B. Frémont, *Letters*, 81; Harrold, *Bailey*, 174; James M. Ashley to Salmon P. Chase, June 16, 1855, in Chase, *Papers*, 2:416.

"I cannot proscribe . . ." McPherson, *Battle Cry*, 142.

"It seems to me . . ." Salmon P. Chase to Kingsley Bingham, October 19, 1855, in Chase, *Papers*, 2:428.

To drive home the point . . . Niven, *Chase*, 179.

Finally the Blair group got around . . . Harrold, *Bailey*, 174.

"hailed with unmeasured satisfaction" . . . F. P. Weisenburger, *McLean*, 144.

"that lonely old man" . . . JBF to EBL, November 21, 1855, in J. B. Frémont, *Letters*, 77; within days of the death of Eliza Benton, John C. Frémont's old trail mate, mapmaker Charles Preuss, committed suicide just a few miles away.

John C. Frémont had been courted . . . Herr, *Jessie Benton Frémont*, 239.

"it became more pleasant . . ." E. B. Frémont, *Recollections*, 74.

"as to nearly terminate the meeting" . . . Denton, *Passion and Principle*, 226–227; Nevins, *Frémont*, 424–425.

"We Democrats are sure to win . . ." Phillips, *Jessie Benton Frémont*, 198–199.

"all that had made my deep rooted . . ." Herr, *Jessie Benton Frémont*, 239.

"It is the choice between . . ." Nevins, *Frémont*, 425.

"There was only one decision possible" . . . Herr, *Jessie Benton Frémont*, 240.

"Isn't it charming . . ." JBF to EBL, December 7 and 14, 1855, in J. B. Frémont, *Letters*, 80, 82.

"She is a noble spirited woman" . . . Seward, *Seward at Washington*, 216–217.

"Mr. Frémont has under consideration . . ." JBF to FPB, August 27, 1855, in J. B. Frémont, *Letters*, 71.

Throughout the late summer and early fall . . . Nevins, *Frémont*, 425–426; Chaffin, *Pathfinder*, 436.

"all that could be wished . . ." JBF to FPB, October 21, 1855, and note, in J. B. Frémont, *Letters*, 72–73.

"impressed me more favorably . . ." Bigelow, *Retrospections*, 141–142.

"until we produced someone . . ." Gienapp, *Origins*, 321–322.

"brave and attractive" qualities . . . E. B. Smith, *Francis Preston Blair*, 218.

"I know both my people . . ." JBF to EBL, April 18 and 25, 1856, in J. B. Frémont, *Letters*, 97, 100; Herr, *Jessie Benton Frémont*, 244.

Blair hoped for better results . . . Gienapp, *Origins*, 321; Harrold, *Bailey*, 174; Niven, *Chase*, 179.

"a new man . . ." Herr, *Jessie Benton Frémont*, 243.

"is a man of great natural sagacity . . ." Read, *Speech*, 35, 37.

On April 4, 1841 . . . Denton, *Passion and Principle*, 67.

He remained enough of a hero . . . Herr, *Jessie Benton Frémont*, 218; Thomas, *Between Two Empires*, 90; Bartlett, *Frémont*, 3.

"I would dissolve the Union . . ." JBF to EBL, November 14, 1851, in Herr, *Jessie Benton Frémont*, 219–220.

Frémont turned his attention . . . Nevins, *Frémont*, 394.

The returns grew spotty . . . Herr, *Jessie Benton Frémont*, 224–225.

"distinctly protest against . . ." WHS to Thurlow Weed, December 31, 1856, in Seward, *Seward at Washington*, 264; Gienapp, *Origins*, 251.

2. "A Fugitive from Freedom"

The boy wonder of New Hampshire . . . Holt, *Pierce*, 1, 10–11.

At the insistence of David Atchison . . . Etcheson, *Bleeding Kansas*, 59, 67.

"no one believed at the time . . ." National Era, January 31, 1856.

"the miserablest doughface . . ." Liberator, January 25, 1856.

"When farmers turn soldiers . . ." Amos Abbot Lawrence to ——, July 20, 1855, in W. Lawrence, *Life of Amos A. Lawrence*, 96; Etcheson, *Bleeding Kansas*, 77.

"my non-resistance has at length . . ." Karcher, *First Woman*, 393.

After Shannon certified the proslavery . . . Etcheson, *Bleeding Kansas*, 74–75.

"the time has come when this armed band. . ." Wilson Shannon to Franklin Pierce, November 28, 1855, in Etcheson, *Bleeding Kansas*, 81–82; Wallner, *Pierce*, 244.

Free staters held their elections . . . Oates, *To Purge This Land with Blood*, 113.

"most determined supporters . . ." New-York Tribune, April 10, 1856; Wallner, *Pierce*, 247.

"inflammatory agitation" and "propagandist immigration" . . . Gara, *Presidency*, 117–118; *Washington Daily Union*, January 25, 1856.

"Whatever irregularities may have occurred . . ." Holt, *Pierce*, 98–99.

"screeches and screams . . ." Washington Daily Union, January 25, 1856.

"disperse and retire peaceably" . . . Wallner, *Pierce*, 249; Blackmar, *Robinson*, 194

"to stab freedom in the heart" . . . Read, *Speech*, 3.

"a fugitive from freedom" . . . Gara, *Presidency*, 118.

"we are on the brink of a crisis . . ." M. W. Delahay to Charles Robinson, James Lane and others, February 16, 1856, via Territorial Kansas Online, www.territorialkansas online.org/~imlskto/cgi-bin/index.php?SCREEN=show_document&SCREEN _FROM=kansas_question&document_id=100646.

"low contemptible trickstering . . ." Andrew Reeder to Charles Robinson, February 16, 1856, via Territorial Kansas Online, www.territorialkansasonline.org/~imlskto /cgi-bin/index.php?SCREEN=show_document&SCREEN_FROM=kansas _question&document_id=101092.

"that ninney Frank Pierce" . . . Etcheson, *Bleeding Kansas*, 93.

"Patience, friends! The eye of God . . ." National Era, March 20, 1856.

"that there will be nothing done . . ." M. W. Delahay to Charles Robinson, James Lane, and others, February 16, 1856, via Territorial Kansas Online, www.territorialkansas online.org/~imlskto/cgi-bin/index.php?SCREEN=show_document&SCREEN _FROM=kansas_question&document_id=100646.

"a deadly tho smiling quiet" . . . Amos Lawrence to Charles Robinson, January 31, 1856, via Territorial Kansas Online, www.territorialkansasonline.org/~imlskto /cgi-bin/index.php?SCREEN=show_document&document_id=101083.

"We seek communion . . ." John Brown Jr. to "Friend Louisa," March 29, 1856, in Renehan, *Secret Six*, 92.

"own conviction remains unshaken . . ." William Lloyd Garrison to Samuel J. May, March 21, 1856, in Garrison, *Letters*, 390.

Stephen A. Douglas prepared . . . Gara, *Presidency*, 118–119; Nichols, *Pierce*, 445; Johannsen, *Douglas*, 471; Etcheson, *Bleeding Kansas*, 29.

"a bomb which hits nothing . . ." Johannsen, *Douglas*, 496, 499.

"a place where the great question . . ." Harry B. Blackwell to Lucy Stone, February 7, 1856, in Wheeler, *Loving Warriors*, 156.

home to about 140,000 people . . . "Population of 100 Largest Urban Places: 1850," US Census Bureau, www.census.gov/population/www/documentation/twps0027/tab08.txt; "Ohio Governor Election Material," Ohio Historical Election Results, http://ohioelectionresults.com/Governor.html.

Maplewood, the plantation of Archibald Gaines . . . S. Weisenburger, *Modern Medea*, 19.

Archibald Gaines's brother . . . Ibid., 20, 28, 34.

In January 1856 . . . Ibid., 49–50.

Sunday dawned warmer . . . Ibid., 50–52.

Sometime before midnight . . . Ibid., 54

"two good horses" . . . Coffin, *Reminiscences*, 558.

From there, crowded together . . . S. Weisenburger, *Modern Medea*, 13, 55.

They passed through the small town . . . Cincinnati Enquirer, January 29, 1856; Coffin, *Reminiscences*, 558–559.

he bore no ill will . . . S. Weisenburger, *Modern Medea*, 57–59.

A crease of dawn appeared . . . Coffin, *Reminiscences*, 558–559; S. Weisenburger, *Modern Medea*, 61.

Safely ashore on the Ohio side . . . Cincinnati Commercial, January 29, 1856; Coffin, *Reminiscences*, 558–559; S. Weisenburger, *Modern Medea*, 62.

By now it was almost 7 AM . . . S. Weisenburger, *Modern Medea*, 64.

"make arrangements to forward them . . ." Coffin, *Reminiscences*, 559.

Kite returned about 8 AM . . . Cincinnati Commercial, January 29, 1856; S. Weisenburger, *Modern Medea*, 72, 74.

The men outside called out . . . Coffin, *Reminiscences*, 559; S. Weisenburger, *Modern Medea*, 72.

The restive crowd made the posse nervous . . . Coffin, *Reminiscences*, 559; S. Weisenburger, *Modern Medea*, 72–73.

As the men in the cabin had begun . . . Coffin, *Reminiscences*, 560, 563; Louisville Daily Courier, January 30, 1856; S. Weisenburger, *Modern Medea*, 74.

Knowing she was on her own . . . Coffin, *Reminiscences*, 560, 563.

"dripping with gore . . ." Louisville Daily Courier, January 30, 1856.

"trickled down their backs . . ." Cincinnati Commercial, January 30, 1856.

John Pendery opened his courtroom . . . S. Weisenburger, *Modern Medea*, 66, 79.

Pendery decided there was not sufficient evidence . . . Reinhardt, *Who Speaks*, 50; S. Weisenburger, *Modern Medea*, 79 (Chase would still be defending himself and his actions eight years later, when he tried and failed to challenge Abraham Lincoln for the Republican presidential nomination in 1864).

"a wild and excited scene . . ." Cincinnati Commercial, January 29, 1856; S. Weisenburger, *Modern Medea*, 79; Reinhardt, *Who Speaks*, 276.

"My brain burned . . ." Lucy Stone to Harry B. Blackwell, February 3, 1856, in Wheeler, *Loving Warriors*, 155.

Before the day was over . . . Reinhardt, *Who Speaks*, 276.

John Jolliffe, the son of a slaveholder . . . S. Weisenburger, *Modern Medea*, 90–94, 103–104.

"It might seem strange . . ." *Cincinnati Daily Gazette*, February 1, 1856.

The courtroom was filled . . . Ibid.; S. Weisenburger, *Modern Medea*, 109–110, 132; Reinhardt, *Who Speaks*, 277.

Jolliffe called witnesses . . . S. Weisenburger, *Modern Medea*, 115.

Chambers, the attorney for the slaveholders . . . S. Weisenburger, *Modern Medea*, 124; *Cincinnati Daily Gazette*, February 1, 1856.

For most in the sizable audience . . . *Cincinnati Daily Gazette*, February 1, 1856.

"I shall not pull off my hat . . ." Coffin, *Reminiscences*, 570.

"clear, cold beautiful Sunday . . ." Harry B. Blackwell to Lucy Stone, February 7, 1856, in Wheeler, *Loving Warriors*, 156.

"to take preliminary steps . . ." *Anti-Slavery Bugle*, February 16, 1856; S. Weisenburger, *Modern Medea*, 139.

On February 6, Jolliffe delivered . . . *Cincinnati Daily Gazette*, February 7, 1856.

"The Constitution expressly declared . . ." Coffin, *Reminiscences*, 561–562.

a Hamilton County grand jury indicted . . . Reinhardt, *Who Speaks*, 277.

"The law of 1850 . . ." *Cincinnati Daily Gazette*, February 1, 1856.

The next day, February 7 . . . S. Weisenburger, *Modern Medea*, 152.

They didn't start out that way . . . S. Weisenburger, *Modern Medea*, 155; Reinhardt, *Who Speaks*, 277.

That day and the next . . . S. Weisenburger, *Modern Medea*, 40, 160.

The light-skinned Margaret Garner . . . Coffin, *Reminiscences*, 562.

"dark calico, with a white handkerchief . . ." *Anti-Slavery Bugle*, February 16, 1856.

After recounting some of her travels . . . *Cincinnati Daily Gazette*, February 12, 1856.

"Our Southern friends who extol . . ." *New-York Tribune*, February 8, 1856.

Jolliffe was not feeling well . . . *Cincinnati Daily Gazette*, February 14, 1856.

"Mrs. [Stone] was not present . . ." S. Weisenburger, *Modern Medea*, 170.

Lucy Stone had indeed visited . . . Lucy Stone to Harry B. Blackwell, February 3, 1856, in Wheeler, *Loving Warriors*, 155.

"I am only sorry . . ." Coffin, *Reminiscences*, 564–566; *Cincinnati Daily Gazette*, February 14, 1856.

Democratic papers in the North . . . *Boston Evening Traveller*, quoted in *Liberator*, February 29, 1856.

"comes into this Court with hands dripping . . ." *Cincinnati Enquirer*, February 8, 1856.

The arguments were over . . . S. Weisenburger, *Modern Medea*, 186.

He was back in court on February 26 . . . *Cincinnati Daily Gazette*, February 27, 1856.

"Had the slaves asserted their freedom . . ." Coffin, *Reminiscences*, 566.

All seven of the "unsuccessful heroes" . . . *Frederick Douglass' Paper*, March 7, 1856; *New-York Tribune*, February 28, 1856.

"and there was great rejoicing . . ." Coffin, *Reminiscences*, 567.

"shell game" . . . Barker, *Fugitive Slaves*, 176.

"I cannot allow myself to doubt . . ." Charles Morehouse to Salmon Chase, March 7, 1856, in Reinhardt, *Who Speaks*, 130.

But it was too late . . . Barker, *Fugitive Slaves*, 176.

In the wee small hours . . . S. Weisenburger, *Modern Medea*, 224–225.

"displayed frantic joy" . . . Reinhardt, *Who Speaks*, 281.

Two days later the surviving Garners . . . Reinhardt, *Who Speaks*, 281–282.

"I wonder if the news of the triumph . . ." *National Era*, October 23, 1857.

3. The First Northern Victory

Even sorting out who was aligned . . . *Washington Star*, January 31, 1856.

the anti-Kansas-Nebraska forces . . . W. E. Smith, *Blair Family*, 319; Gienapp, *Origins*, 240–241.

"exerts more influence upon the destinies . . ." Nevins, *Ordeal of the Union*, 1:170.

"tall, firmly built, coarse featured man . . ." Jenkins and Stewart, *Fighting for the Speakership*, 180; Hesseltine and Fisher, *Trimmers*, 45.

American Party leaders favored . . . Anbinder, *Nativism and Slavery*, 197–198.

On the first ballot . . . Harrington, "First Northern Victory," 191–192; Jenkins and Stewart, *Fighting for the Speakership*, 180.

The anti-Nebraska forces caucused . . . Harrington, "First Northern Victory," 192.

"The present determination . . ." *New York Times*, December 6, 1855.

On December 5, Campbell got . . . Harrington, "First Northern Victory," 192; Jenkins and Stewart, *Fighting for the Speakership*, 181.

"It is a difficult matter to harmonize . . ." *New York Times*, December 10, 1855.

There were shades of gray . . . Harrington, "First Northern Victory," 189; Hollandsworth, *Pretense of Glory*, 26.

But just as Campbell began to fade . . . Harrington, "First Northern Victory," 193.

"this will decide the question" . . . *New York Herald*, December 8, 1855.

If so, it wasn't immediately apparent . . . Harrington, "First Northern Victory," 193.

The North Americans, realizing . . . Jenkins and Stewart, *Fighting for the Speakership*, 182.

"self made man . . ." *Boston Bee*, quoted in *Daily American Organ*, February 6, 1856.

"a genius for being looked at" . . . Hollandsworth, *Pretense of Glory*, 16; Gienapp, *Origins*, 243.

Something similar happened . . . Hollandsworth, *Pretense of Glory*, 23.

" for the Union as it is . . ." Ibid., 26–27.

"It is a point of honor . . ." John Dix to John Bigelow, December, 30, 1856, in Landis, *Northern Men*, 137.

"The third week of the session . . ." Howell Cobb to Mary Ann Cobb, December 23, 1856, in Toombs et al., *Correspondence*, 356.

"The House of Representatives is like . . ." Seward, *Seward at Washington*, 270.

"The House of Representatives is trying . . ." Strong, *Diary*, 247.

"threatened to clog the wheels . . ." *Daily American Organ*, February 4, 1856.

"hundred and forty odd ballots" . . . John C. Frémont to Charles Robinson, March 17, 1856, via Territorial Kansas Online, www.territorialkansasonline.org/~imlskto /cgi-bin/index.php?SCREEN=show_document&SCREEN_FROM=kansas _question&document_id=101103.

"Bostonian, as remarkable as any other . . ." *National Anti-Slavery Standard*, June 28, 1856.

"be allowed to indulge in . . ." Harrington, "First Northern Victory," 197 (also see *Congressional Globe*, 33rd Congress, 1st session, 34, 72, 239, 235, 241).

The House held an all-night session . . . Harrington, "First Northern Victory," 198.

The American Party, meanwhile . . . Anbinder, *Nativism and Slavery*, 200; Harrington, "First Northern Victory," 198–199.

"Is your name Greeley?" . . . *New-York Tribune*, January 31, 1856.

"a stunning blow" . . . Ibid.; Harrington, "First Northern Victory," 200; Hollandsworth, *Pretense of Glory*, 26.

"huddle of strangers" . . . *New-York Tribune*, January 31, 1856

"one of the most powerful men . . ." Ibid.

"I presume this is not . . ." Ibid.

All the while, the Banks forces . . . Harrington, "First Northern Victory," 195; Gienapp, *Origins*, 245.

As February approached . . . Jenkins and Stewart, *Fighting for the Speakership*, 185; Harrington, "First Northern Victory," 200.

The idea came from Georgia's Alexander Stephens . . . Harrington, "First Northern Victory," 200; Anbinder, *Nativism and Slavery*, 200; *Congressional Globe*, 34th Congress, 1st session, 335–336.

The next day, February 2, 1856 . . . Harrington, "First Northern Victory," 201; Jenkins and Stewart, *Fighting for the Speakership*, 187; *Congressional Globe*, 34th Congress, 1st session, 335–336.

The surprise having been spoiled . . . Harrington, "First Northern Victory," 201; Jenkins and Stewart, *Fighting for the Speakership*, 188; *Congressional Globe*, 34th Congress, 1st session, 335–337.

After two months, it had come . . . Harrington, "First Northern Victory," 202; *Washington Daily Union*, February 16, 1856; *Congressional Globe*, 34th Congress, 1st session, 339.

Nathaniel Banks was Speaker of the House . . . Harrington, "First Northern Victory," 186; Seward, *Seward at Washington*, 266.

"brief and neat speech" . . . *Washington Star*, February 4, 1856; *Daily American Organ*, February 4, 1856.

his election as Speaker was "indispensable" . . . Preston King to Francis P. Blair, January 3, 1856, in Gienapp, *Origins*, 247.

"The election of Banks has given . . ." Robert Toombs to Thomas W. Thomas, February 9, 1856, in Toombs et al., *Correspondence*, 359.

"We cannot admit Kansas . . ." Horace Greeley to Charles Dana, February 16, 1856, in Gienapp, *Origins*, 296.

"listen for an instant to the prompting . . ." Daily American Organ, February 4, 1856.

"This was the first victory . . ." Bigelow, *Retrospections*, 141.

"Hell is uncapped" . . . Thomas Harris to Charles Lanphier, February 6, 1856, in Landis, *Northern Men*, 137.

"Amidst the political excitement . . ." National Era, February 21, 1856.

"The public of Washington do not . . ." Washington Star, February 12, 1856.

Chase had been following the case . . . Anti-Slavery Bugle, March 8, 1856; Niven, *Chase*, 178.

Blair was not an abolitionist . . . "Missouri's Dred Scott Case," Missouri Digital Archives, accessed December 22, 2016, www.sos.mo.gov/archives/resources/african american/scott/scott.asp.

Dred Scott was born a slave . . . Dred Scott's biographical sketch and the background of the case are from US Supreme Court, *Dred Scott v. Sandford*, 60 U.S. 393; Missouri Digital Archives, https://www.sos.mo.gov/archives/; and Fehrenbacher, *Dred Scott*, 239–283.

Representing Sanford were . . . Fehrenbacher, *Dred Scott*, 288.

"We had not the pleasure . . ." National Era, February 21, 1856.

"able counsel would have volunteered . . ." Isely, *Greeley*, 226.

"it is expected the judgment . . ." New-York Tribune, February 20, 1856.

"the Court will not decide . . ." Benjamin R. Curtis to George Ticknor, April 8, 1856, in F. P. Weisenburger, *McLean*, 196.

4. "Not a Mere Aggregation of Whigs, Know-Nothings, and Dissatisfied Democrats"

"into any association with Republicans . . ." Gienapp, *Origins*, 251; Harrold, *Bailey*, 172.

"forget, forgive, and unite" . . . Woodwell, *Whittier*, 260.

The meeting went forward . . . Myers, *Republican Party*, 62.

"enlighten the mind . . ." New-York Tribune, February 23, 1856; Julian, *Recollections*, 148.

"to act with us . . ." Isely, *Greeley*, 153; Gienapp, *Origins*, 256.

After the introductory speeches . . . E. B. Smith, *Francis Preston Blair*, 220–221; Gienapp, *Origins*, 255.

"That Blair should, at his time . . ." Washington Star, February 26, 1856; E. B. Smith, *Francis Preston Blair*, 222.

The essence of Blair's message . . . Gienapp, *Origins*, 256–257; Julian, *Recollections*, 148; *Athens (TN) Post*, March 7, 1856.

"for the last twenty years . . ." New-York Tribune, February 23, 1856.

"it is all harmony and enthusiasm" . . . Ibid.

Such Whig-like avoidance . . . Gienapp, "Crime Against Sumner," 218.

When the convention reconvened . . . Myers, *Republican Party*, 63; Gienapp, *Origins*, 257–258; Riddleberger, *Julian*, 111; Clapp, *Forgotten First Citizen*, 100.

The presentation of the resolutions committee . . . Gienapp, *Origins*, 258.

"It was quite manifest . . ." Julian, *Recollections*, 149.

"never be found crouching . . ." Harry B. Blackwell to Lucy Stone, April 3, 1856, in Wheeler, *Loving Warriors*, 157.

"conceding and conceding . . ." Gamaliel Bailey to Salmon P. Chase, April 18, 1856, in Gienapp, *Origins*, 268.

"Can anything more ludicrous . . ." William Lloyd Garrison to Samuel J. May, March 21, 1856, in Garrison, *Letters*, 391; Gienapp, *Origins*, 255–256.

"strong and yet moderate . . ." Charles Sumner to Henry J. Raymond, March 2, 1856, in Donald, *Sumner*, 276

"if anything like the same discretion . . ." John Bigelow to Salmon P. Chase, February 26, 1856, in Clapp, *Forgotten First Citizen*, 100.

"the proper spirit of concession . . ." *National Era*, March 27, 1856.

"little said about Presidents . . ." *Cincinnati Commercial*, February 26, 1856.

"Had the Pittsburgh convention been . . ." F. D. Kimball to Salmon P. Chase, February 28, 1856, in Gienapp, *Origins*, 259.

The attendees had, however, rejected . . . Formisano, *Birth*, 268.

"Judge McLean is more popular . . ." *Washington Star*, February 27, 1856.

"put out of joint the nose . . ." Ibid.

Seward continued to publicly demur . . . JBF to EBL, February 1856 (undated), in J. B. Frémont, *Letters*, 88.

"Jessie Benton seemed to be . . ." McCormack, *Memoirs of Gustave Koerner*, 2:14.

"I'll go, my chief" . . . JBF to EBL, March 8, 1856, in J. B. Frémont, *Letters*, 93, 95n.

In 1852, Pope Pius IX . . . Billington, *Protestant Crusade*, 313–314; Nichols and Klein, "Election of 1856," 1013; "The Mystery of the Pope's Stone," *Boundary Stones* (blog), July 16, 2013, http://blogs.weta.org/boundarystones/2013/07/16/mystery-popes-stone.

A pair of riots . . . Bicknell, *America 1844*, 226; Anbinder, *Nativism and Slavery*, 13.

A larger, more effective organization . . . Anbinder, *Nativism and Slavery*, 14, 23.

"Secrecy is the natural covering . . ." Robert Toombs to T. Lomax, June 6, 1855, in Toombs et al., *Correspondence*, 350.

"a screen—a dark wall . . ." Anbinder, *Nativism and Slavery*, 50; Formisano, *Birth*, 262.

"The moment the new party . . ." *New-York Tribune*, June 2, 1855.

Southern Know Nothings would have . . . Gienapp, *Origins*, 184.

That was too much for the antislavery . . . Rayback, *Fillmore*, 403; Stahr, *Seward*, 155.

When the convention proper opened . . . Nichols and Klein, "Election of 1856," 1020.

"a silly old fellow with a long purse . . ." Hesseltine and Fisher, *Trimmers*, 71.

When Millard Fillmore left the White House . . . Rayback, *Fillmore*, 394–396.

"It is better to wear out . . ." Millard Fillmore to Hugh Maxwell, March 10, 1855, in Rayback, *Fillmore*, 396.

When he got to Rome . . . Finkelman, *Fillmore*, 132.

the "radiant pictures . . ." Le Vert, *Souvenirs*, 164; *Washington Star*, February 8, 1856.

"the cause of unfeigned admiration . . ." *Daily American Organ*, February 27, 1856; Gienapp, *Origins*, 261.

"boldly proclaimed" threats . . . Hesseltine and Fisher, *Trimmers*, 2.

The Monday session opened . . . Hesseltine and Fisher, *Trimmers*, 2, 5; Gienapp, *Origins*, 261–262; *New-York Tribune*, February 27, 1856.

"He labors under the worse hallucination . . ." Cheathem, *Old Hickory's Nephew*, 294–295.

"professing the union doctrine . . ." Hesseltine and Fisher, *Trimmers*, 6–7.

"the perpetuation of the Federal Union . . ." Nichols and Klein, "Election of 1856," 1041.

Southerners, for their part . . . Freehling, *Road to Disunion*, 88.

"To Divide the South . . ." Carey, "Too Southern," 37.

"The American Party are the first . . ." *Daily American Organ*, February 28, 1856.

"The best feature in this Fillmore nomination . . ." Thurlow Weed to WHS, March 5, 1856, in Gienapp, *Origins*, 263.

Technically, Fillmore was not the first . . . Dunn, *Practical Dreamer*, 327, 332.

Fillmore's friends understood the danger . . . Holt, *Rise and Fall*, 965.

"We do not say Millard Fillmore . . ." *Daily American Organ*, February 28, 1856.

"an insurrection of the honest masses . . ." Carey, "Too Southern," 33; Formisano, *Birth*, 249.

"an utter betrayal . . ." Hesseltine and Fisher, *Trimmers*, 11.

"Our real trouble is the K.N. convention . . ." Horace Greeley to Schuyler Colfax, May 6, 1856, in Gienapp, *Origins*, 270.

5. Bleeding Nebraska

The vast wasteland . . . Wishart, *Unspeakable Sadness*, 101–102.

On August 18, 1854, fifteen hundred . . . The accounts of the Grattan fight and Blue Water Creek are from Beck, *First Sioux War*, 39–70; Paul, *Blue Water Creek*, 18–110; G. R. Adams, *Harney*, 120–132; Mattison, "Harney Expedition," 89–130; Warren, *Explorations*, 9–43; and contemporary newspaper accounts, as cited.

"Lieutenant, do you see . . ." Beck, *First Sioux War*, 50.

"to drink your blood . . ." Ibid., 51.

"It is getting late . . ." Ibid., 55.

"After the cannon was fired . . ." Paul, *Blue Water Creek*, 23.

"twenty-four arrows . . ." *Richmond Dispatch*, September 19, 1854.

"it appears to have been a pre-concerted plot . . ." Beck, *First Sioux War*, 74–75.

"the want of adequate military force . . ." *Kansas Weekly Herald*, September 15, 1854.

"school-house officers . . ." *National Era*, September 21, 1854.

On October 26, 1854, Secretary of War . . . G. R. Adams, *Harney*, 122; Beck, *First Sioux War*, 79; Paul, *Blue Water Creek*, 27.

In the wake of the Grattan fight . . . Wishart, *Unspeakable Sadness*, 109.

"flourishing . . . alive with business . . ." Erastus Snow to John Taylor, September 15, 1856, via LDS official website, https://history.lds.org/overlandtravels/sources/8724/snow -erastus-correspondence-of-president-erastus-snow-the-mormon-27-sep-1856-2-3.

When Colonel Harney arrived back . . . G. R. Adams, *Harney*, 125.

While Harney was moving . . . Warren, *Explorations*, 38.

"a single hostile Indian" . . . *Washington Daily Union*, October 2, 1855.

News reports made no distinction . . . *Kansas Herald of Freedom*, July 21, 1855.

"a great stronghold . . ." *Washington Daily Union*, June 1, 1855.

"The probability is there will be nothing . . ." Mattison, "Harney Expedition," 92, 100, 103.

"must be crushed . . ." Beck, *First Sioux War*, 79–80; Paul, *Blue Water Creek*, 47.

"tomorrow the 'Sioux expedition' . . ." Mattison, "Harney Expedition," 108.

For days at a time . . . Warren, *Explorations*, 9, 13, 20.

"gave us no trouble . . ." Ibid., 27–28.

"one of the heaviest thunder storms . . ." Mattison, "Harney Expedition," 110, 111.

"We arrived near their camp . . ." Paul, *Blue Water Creek*, 88; *News of the Day* (Vincennes, IN), November 21, 1855.

"very nearly, if not quite . . ." *Washington Daily Union*, October 2, 1855; Beck, *First Sioux War*, 105.

"The Indian Slaughter . . ." *New-York Tribune*, October 3, 1855.

"The result was what I anticipated . . ." G. R. Adams, *Harney*, 132–133.

"the Indians have become convinced . . ." *Washington Sentinel*, April 26, 1856.

"The scenery is exceedingly solitary . . ." Warren, *Explorations*, 9, 19.

"every nation must have laws . . ." Beck, *First Sioux War*, 127; G. R. Adams, *Harney*, 142.

"appointed one principal Chief . . ." *Nebraska Advertiser*, June 21, 1856; G. R. Adams, *Harney*, 144.

"will insure a general pacification . . ." *Washington Sentinel*, April 26, 1856.

"Military occupation is essential . . ." Warren, *Explorations*, 17–18.

Fort Randall was built . . . Greene, *Fort Randall*, 1, 12–13; Mattison, "Harney Expedition," 130.

The 1849 constitution would have named . . . Arrington, *Brigham Young*, 223–225.

"Our constitution is silent . . ." Brigham Young to Thomas L. Kane, April 14, 1856, in Grow and Walker, *Prophet and Reformer*, 195.

"It should be a national work . . ." Brigham Young to Thomas L. Kane, January 31, 1854, in Grow and Walker, *Prophet and Reformer*, 160.

"The miserable Nebraska-Kansas Measure . . ." Thomas L. Kane to Brigham Young, April 28, 1854, in Grow and Walker, *Prophet and Reformer*, 165.

"We strongly desire . . ." Brigham Young to Thomas L. Kane, April 14, 1856, in Grow and Walker, *Prophet and Reformer*, 194.

"What think you" . . . Brigham Young to Thomas L. Kane, April 14, 1856, in Grow and Walker, *Prophet and Reformer*, 194.

"that there is a poor prospect . . ." Grow and Walker, *Prophet and Reformer*, 191.

"to suppress polygamy . . ." John M. Bernhisel to Brigham Young, July 12, 1856, and January 17, 1857, in Grow and Walker, *Prophet and Reformer*, 192–193.

Franklin D. Richards had been appointed . . . West, *Franklin Richards*, 124–128.

"save this enormous expense . . ." Stegner, *Gathering of Zion*, 224.

"the device of inspiration" . . . Hafen and Hafen, *Handcarts to Zion*, 30, 35.

150 wagon train companies . . . Roberts, *Devil's Gate*, 88.

Franklin Richards's immigration roster . . . West, *Franklin Richards*, 128–129.

From its inception in 1849 . . . Roberts, *Devil's Gate*, 89.

Sea journeys via steamship . . . Strong, *Diary*, 257, 259–261; *New-York Tribune*, April 16, 1856.

For the 1856 migration . . . Stegner, *Gathering of Zion*, 227; Hafen and Hafen, *Handcarts to Zion*, 46.

"This first part of the journey . . ." Hafen and Hafen, *Handcarts to Zion*, 41.

But even this relatively short . . . Edmund Ellsworth handcart company journal, 1856, via LDS official website, https://history.lds.org/overlandtravels/sources/2888 /edmund-ellsworth-emigrating-company-journal-1856-june-sept.

Traveling through Iowa . . . Hafen and Hafen, *Handcarts to Zion*, 82.

"engaged in making yokes, handcarts &c. . . ." James G. Willie handcart company journal, 1856, via LDS official website, https://history.lds.org/overlandtravels/sources/70069 /willie-james-g-synopsis-of-the-fourth-hand-cart-company-s-trip-from-england-to -g-s-l-city-in-1856-in-history-of-brigham-young-9-nov-1856-966-83.

"many strangers seemed to take . . ." Ibid.

"Only one drunken man . . ." Levi Savage journal, 1855–58, via LDS official website, https:// history.lds.org/overlandtravels/sources/7460/savage-levi-journal-1855-mar-1858-oct.

6. A MONTH OF VIOLENCE

At about 11 AM on May 8 . . . The account of the shooting at the Willard is from the *Washington Star*, May 8 and 9, 1856.

"it is quite clear to my mind . . ." *Washington Star*, May 12, 1856.

"high words and stormy scenes" . . . Washington Hunt to Samuel B. Ruggles, November 22, 1855, in Gienapp, "Crime Against Sumner," 218.

"We have before us . . ." Charles Sumner to Gerrit Smith, March 18, 1856, in Gienapp, "Crime Against Sumner," 219.

"a brutal vulgar man . . ." Donald, *Sumner*, 278.

"you appear in the eyes . . ." Samuel Lawrence to Charles Sumner, November 7, 1848, in Donald, *Sumner*, 170.

"Sumner is so much occupied . . ." George S. Hillard to Francis Lieber, November 25, 1846, in Donald, *Sumner*, 171–172.

"His solitude was glacial . . ." H. Adams, *Education*, 31.

He was also utterly humorless . . . Donald, *Sumner*, 218.

"My soul is wrung . . ." Charles Sumner to Salmon P. Chase, May 15, 1856, in Gara, *Presidency*, 120.

Sumner was sincere in his outrage . . . Donald, *Sumner*, 277.

Sumner had been hearing directly . . . Ibid., 278–281.

Sumner wrote the entire speech . . . Ibid., 282, 288.

"I would on no account . . ." Stahr, *Seward*, 160.

Sumner's speaking style . . . Donald, *Sumner*, 214.

And on May 19, there was a horde . . . Ibid., 283; Johannsen, *Douglas*, 503.

"Mr. President," he began . . . Congressional Globe, 34th Congress, 1st session, appendix, 529.

"who, though unlike as Don Quixote . . ." Ibid., 530.

"The Senator from South Carolina . . ." Ibid.

"that damn fool will get . . ." Johannsen, *Douglas*, 503.

"squire of slavery . . ." Congressional Globe, 34th Congress, 1st session, appendix, 531.

"represents that other Virginia . . ." Donald, *Sumner*, 286.

"un-American and unpatriotic" . . . Gara, *Presidency*, 121.

"constrained to hear . . ." Donald, *Sumner*, 287–288.

"the senator is certainly . . ." New-York Tribune, May 28, 1856.

"Is it his object to provoke . . ." Congressional Globe, 34th Congress, 1st session, appendix, 547.

Abolitionists praised Sumner . . . Donald, *Sumner*, 288.

"never seen anything . . ." Ibid.

"rather sophomorical" . . . Strong, *Diary*, 273.

Sumner's enemies were, predictably . . . Donald, *Sumner*, 289.

"unmanly and pernicious . . ." Ibid., 290.

"cordial and agreeable" . . . Hoffer, *Caning*, 69; Congressional Globe, 33rd Congress, 1st session, 1466.

Somewhat hotheaded as a young man . . . Mathis, "Preston Smith Brooks," 298–301.

"a frank, pleasant man" . . . Ibid., 302.

"always a Southern gentleman . . ." National Era, March 19, 1854.

Brooks was not much more . . . Donald, *Sumner*, 214, 289.

He was not interested . . . Ibid., 290–291; Hoffer, *Caning*, 13.

On May 21, Brooks sat outside . . . Gugliotta, *Freedom's Cap*, 239.

"It was time for southern men . . ." US House, *Assault*, 59.

But Sumner did not pass by . . . Donald, *Sumner*, 292; US House, *Assault*, 8; Hoffer, *Caning*, 7.

But again he was foiled . . . Donald, *Sumner*, 292; US House, *Assault*, 59.

Brooks saw that Edmundson . . . Donald, *Sumner*, 92.

"No, I cannot leave . . ." US House, *Assault*, 63.

The Senate adjourned at 12:45 . . . Hoffer, *Caning*, 7; Donald, *Sumner*, 293.

Brooks was getting impatient . . . Hoffer, *Caning*, 7–8.

"he would stand this thing . . ." US House, *Assault*, 60.

"Mr. Sumner, I have read . . ." Ibid., 2, 4.

"immediately left my seat . . ." Ibid., 47; Mathis, "Preston Smith Brooks," 298.

"What is the Union good for . . ." Harrold, *Bailey*, 180.

"If we continue to laugh . . ." New York Post, May 23, 1856.

"will strengthen the Free-soilers . . ." Strong, *Diary*, 274; Donald, *Sumner*, 301–302.

"Those who aid in the extension . . ." Fremont (OH) Journal, May 30, 1856.

"Had it not been . . ." Gienapp, *Origins*, 301–302.

"perhaps did more . . ." Julian, *Recollections*, 153.

"indulge in such attacks . . ." Gienapp, "Crime Against Sumner," 228.

"a chivalric citizen . . ." Benjamin Butler to F. P. Rice, February 15, 1886, in Donald, *Sumner*, 304.

"Every lick went . . ." Preston Brooks to J. H. Brooks, May 23, 1856, in Gienapp, "Crime Against Sumner," 220.

"a heavy gold head . . ." Thomas Shelton Fox to W. H. Fox, June 1, 1856, in Donald, *Sumner*, 304–305.

"Four canes have already . . ." *National Anti-Slavery Standard*, June 28, 1856.

"did not get a lick amiss" . . . James Mason to George M. Dallas, June 10, 1856, in Gienapp, "Crime Against Sumner," 221.

"some sport in the Senate" . . . Junius Hillyer to Howell Cobb, May 28, 1856, in Toombs et al., *Correspondence*, 365.

"the Yankees are greatly excited . . ." Robert Toombs to George W. Crawford, May 30, 1856, in Toombs et al., *Correspondence*, 365.

"not as a reward . . ." *Edgefield Advertiser*, September 3, 1856; *Winchester (TN) Weekly Appeal*, August 30, 1856.

"freedom shriekers" . . . *Spirit of Democracy* (Woodsfield, OH), August 27, 1856.

"have been suffered to run . . ." *Richmond Enquirer*, June 12, 1856.

"atrocious that we believe . . ." C. Adams, *Slavery, Secession and Civil War*, 1–2.

Meetings were held in the North . . . Woodwell, *Whittier*, 259–260.

"Brooks has knocked the scales . . ." Gienapp, "Crime Against Sumner," 231.

"caused many scores of thousands . . ." McClure, *Recollections*, 394.

"to mount the rostrum myself . . ." Karcher, *First Woman*, 391.

When the Senate met to consider . . . Seward, *Seward at Washington*, 272.

The committee named to investigate . . . Hoffer, *Caning*, 71–72.

The committee released its report . . . Ibid.; US House, *Assault*, 3–5.

"The Minority Report . . ." *New-York Tribune*, June 6, 1856.

"The symbol of the North . . ." Hoffer, *Caning*, 91.

the march of violence had slowed . . . Oates, *To Purge This Land with Blood*, 112.

On April 19, Sheriff Samuel Jones rode . . . Etcheson, *Bleeding Kansas*, 100–104; Oates, *To Purge This Land with Blood*, 123.

"I expect before you get this . . ." Etcheson, Bleeding Kansas, 104.

"spring like your bloodhounds . . ." Ibid., 105–106.

In December 1855 . . . Renehan, *Secret Six*, 90–91; Etcheson, *Bleeding Kansas*, 43.

"would rather be ground . . ." Oates, *To Purge This Land with Blood*, 128–129.

At 11 PM on May 24 . . . Details of the Pottawatomie raid are from US Congress, *Howard Report*, 1193–1199; and Oates, *To Purge This Land with Blood*, 119–137.

"I almost hoped to hear . . ." Renehan, *Secret Six*, 102.

"sprinkled from head to foot . . ." *New-York Tribune*, May 26, 1856.

"The lonely cabin . . ." Blackmar, *Robinson*, 252.

"*The doubtful hesitating men . . .*" Edwin D. Morgan to John Bigelow, June 2, 1856, in Gienapp, *Origins*, 303.

7. "THE UNION IS IN DANGER"

"*Frémont bids fair . . .*" *Washington Star*, May 10, 1856.

"*may bring forth Pierce . . .*" Strong, *Diary*, 277.

"*lion of the town*" . . . Chambers, *Old Bullion*, 420.

"*don't know his own mind . . .*" Hesseltine and Fisher, *Trimmers*, 22.

"*by virtue not of his own strength . . .*" *New-York Tribune*, May 24, 1856.

"*If the Democrats don't unite . . .*" Phillips, *Jessie Benton Frémont*, 197.

"*It has been a sore thing . . .*" JBF to EBL, April 29, 1856, in J. B. Frémont, *Letters*, 101, 103n.

"*the strongest northern man . . .*" J. Glancy Jones to James Buchanan, March 7, 1856, in Landis, *Northern Men*, 149.

Franklin Pierce remained in Washington . . . Nichols, *Pierce*, 467.

Patronage, however, was not . . . Holt, *Pierce*, 96–97, 102; Wallner, *Pierce*, 267.

"*The Kansas outrages are all . . .*" Benjamin B. French to Henry French, May 29, 1856, in Gienapp, *Origins*, 305.

"*a foul-mouthed bully . . .*" Hesseltine and Fisher, *Trimmers*, 19.

The success of the Pierce-Douglas combination . . . Nichols, *Pierce*, 466; Wallner, *Pierce*, 266–267.

In addition to the ever-loyal . . . Johannsen, *Douglas*, 506–507, 515.

"*I expect to choose . . .*" Ibid., 515; Holt, *Pierce*, 39.

"*splendid ovations or national gratitude*" . . . Hesseltine and Fisher, *Trimmers*, 17–18.

"*administration blundering*" . . . Strong, *Diary*, 274.

"*arbitrary power*" . . . Buchanan, *Works*, 77–78; Klein, *Buchanan*, 252.

"*acting in good faith toward you*" . . . Johannsen, *Douglas*, 510.

"*I saw Buck in London last summer . . .*" Robert Toombs to Thomas W. Thomas, February 9, 1856, in Toombs et al., *Correspondence*, 359.

"*are very warm for Pierce*" . . . Thomas R. R. Cobb to Howell Cobb, March 4, 1856, in Toombs et al., *Correspondence*, 363.

"*Buck and Douglas are the most prominent . . .*" Robert Toombs to George W. Crawford, May 17 and May 30, 1856, in Toombs et al., *Correspondence*, 364–365.

"*The indications are so strong . . .*" John E. Ward to Howell Cobb, June 3, 1856, in Toombs et al., *Correspondence*, 367.

Buchanan forces set up shop . . . Nichols, *Pierce*, 466–467; Nichols, *Disruption*, 28–29.

"*great political exchange*" . . . Hesseltine and Fisher, *Trimmers*, 23, 25.

"*finest in the United States*" . . . Nichols, *Disruption*, 28.

"*black-hole of Calcutta*" . . . *New-York Tribune*, June 27, 1856; Chambers, *Old Bullion*, 422; Hesseltine and Fisher, *Trimmers*, 26.

"*wild cursing and shouts*" . . . Wallner, *Pierce*, 269; Klein, *Buchanan*, 255; Hesseltine and Fisher, *Trimmers*, 27.

"This is the old story" . . . Hesseltine and Fisher, *Trimmers*, 35.

"non-interference by Congress . . ." For platform, see Nichols and Klein, "Election of 1856," 1035–1039.

"given double rounds . . ." Hesseltine and Fisher, *Trimmers*, 37–39.

"perfectly free to form . . ." Nichols, *Disruption*, 62; J. Glancy Jones to James Buchanan, May 30, 1856, in Gienapp, *Origins*, 307.

"Douglas is a great man . . ." Lincoln, *CW* 2:362.

"Some enterprising individual" . . . Hesseltine and Fisher, *Trimmers*, 40.

"flutter of a thousand fans" . . . Holt, *Pierce*, 103.

"burst of applause . . ." Ibid., 47–49.

And on it went, pretty much unchanged . . . Ibid., 49.

Through fourteen ballots . . . Nichols, *Pierce*, 468.

"The time has come . . ." Hesseltine and Fisher, *Trimmers*, 50–51.

"He was taken up . . ." Holt, *Pierce*, 105.

Most of Pierce's support . . . Nichols, *Pierce*, 468.

"very embodiment of pluck" . . . McCormack, *Memoirs of Gustave Koerner*, 2:1; Hesseltine and Fisher, 46–53.

"This I am decidedly opposed to" . . . Alexander Stephens to W. W. Burwell, June 26, 1854, in Toombs et al., *Correspondence*, 346.

"forty candidates for Vice . . ." Johannsen, *Douglas*, 516.

"the first to plant . . ." Hesseltine and Fisher, *Trimmers*, 59.

"I hold that unless . . ." Ibid.; Davis, *Breckinridge*, 140–144.

Nearly a dozen others . . . Hesseltine and Fisher, *Trimmers*, 60.

"no Democrat has a right to refuse . . ." Hesseltine and Fisher, *Trimmers*, 61.

"Nature seemed to have favored him . . ." Davis, *Breckinridge*, 63.

"on the whole . . ." Hesseltine and Fisher, *Trimmers*, 43.

"proud, defiant, and full of passion . . ." Hesseltine and Fisher, *Trimmers*, 43, 62.

"the studied equivocation . . ." *New-York Tribune*, June 20, 1856.

"No greater service . . ." Jeremiah Black to J. Reynolds, June 9, 1856, in Isely, *Greeley*, 158.

"I look forward to the day . . ." Klein, *Buchanan*, 257.

"no party founded on religious . . ." Buchanan, *Works*, 82–83.

"The Black Republicans must be . . ." James Buchanan to J. Glancy Jones, June 27, 1856, in Klein, *Buchanan*, 257.

"Father, we have them surrounded . . ." Oates, *To Purge This Land with Blood*, 152–153.

"Had I known who I was fighting . . ." *New-York Tribune*, June 17, 1856.

"articles of agreement . . ." Articles of agreement, June 2, 1856, via Territorial Kansas Online, www2.ku.edu/~imlskto/cgi-bin/index.php?SCREEN=show_document &document_id=102530.

"accidentally wounded after the fight . . ." Battle of Black Jack participant and casualty list, June 2, 1856, via Territorial Kansas Online, www.territorialkansasonline.org /~imlskto/cgi-bin/index.php?SCREEN=show_document&document_id=102532.

"civil war is just upon us" . . . *Wellsboro (PA) Gazette*, June 5, 1856.

"*Northern papers have been filled . . .*" *Richmond Dispatch*, July 23, 1856.
THE CIVIL WAR IN KANSAS . . . *Western Democrat* (Charlotte, NC), June 17, 1856.

8. "FREE SOIL, FREE SPEECH, FREE MEN, AND FRÉMONT"

After their preliminary national meeting . . . Gienapp, *Origins*, 278, 282.
"*has laid me prostrate . . .*" Riddleberger, *Julian*, 109.
"*quest for as small a modicum . . .*" Israel Washburn to James G. Blaine, February 26, 1856, in Gienapp, *Origins*, 307.
"*just here & now I am quite . . .*" JBF to EBL, April 18, 1856, in J. B. Frémont, *Letters*, 98; Rolle, *JCF*, 163.
"*Frémont is not the first choice . . .*" Hesseltine and Fisher, *Trimmers*, 82.
"*as you stood by me firmly . . .*" Bartlett, *Frémont*, 16–17; Isely, *Greeley*, 163.
"*apprehensive that the Republican movement . . .*" Gamaliel Bailey to Salmon P. Chase, April 18, 1856, in Chase, *Papers*, 2:434.
"*a regular plot*" . . . Ibid., 2:434–435.
"*martyr to the cause of freedom*" . . . Bartlett, *Frémont*, 6; Gienapp, *Origins*, 327.
Bailey had practical objections . . . Gamaliel Bailey to Salmon P. Chase, April 18, 1856, in Chase, *Papers*, 2:435.
"*We do not want [Seward] nominated . . .*" Stahr, *Seward*, 160.
"*nicely pickled away . . .*" Hesseltine and Fisher, *Trimmers*, 89.
"*own feelings would have inclined . . .*" Seward, *Seward at Washington*, 276.
"*with our principles themselves . . .*" Gamaliel Bailey to Salmon P. Chase, April 18, 1856, in Chase, *Papers*, 2:435.
"*an amiable, honorable Gentleman . . .*" Ibid., 2:436.
"*I am afraid several volumes . . .*" Gienapp, *Origins*, 328.
"*the true metal*" . . . Gienapp, *Origins*, 328.
"*aloofness [that] also helped . . .*" Chaffin, *Pathfinder*, 444
"*bear the responsibility . . .*" Van Deusen, *Weed*, 209.
"*Thurlow Weed says he is . . .*" Stahr, *Seward*, 155; Isely, *Greeley*, 168.
"*Seward is by all odds . . .*" Gamaliel Bailey to George W. Julian, March 9, 1856, in Gienapp, *Origins*, 310.
"*The excited sensibilities . . .*" WHS to Frances Seward, June 13, 1856, in Seward, *Seward at Washington*, 277.
"*There is no name which can find . . .*" Isely, *Greeley*, 165.
"*he has done the very best thing . . .*" WHS to Frances Seward, June 27, 1856, in Seward, *Seward at Washington*, 279; J. B. Frémont, *Letters*, 107n.
Weed worried that defeat . . . Gienapp, *Origins*, 311.
"*to reorganize the defunct Whig Party . . .*" Hesseltine and Fisher, 89.
"*The news of Buchanan's nomination . . .*" Abraham Lincoln to Lyman Trumbull, June 7, 1856, in Lincoln, *CW* 2:342–343.
"*many, very many, tenderfooted Whigs . . .*" Orville H. Browning to Lyman Trumbull, May 19, 1856, in F. P. Weisenburger, *McLean*, 147.

"if McLean is with us at all . . ." Benjamin F. Wade to Salmon P. Chase, May 5, 1856, in Niven, *Chase*, 182; F. P. Weisenburger, *McLean*, 150; Bartlett, *Frémont*, 12.

"I think our U.S. judges . . ." William C. Howells to Joshua R. Giddings, April 29, 1856, in F. P. Weisenburger, *McLean*, 146.

Thurlow Weed was also not a fan . . . Gienapp, *Origins*, 316.

"I never doubted that Congress . . ." John McLean to A. C. M. Pennington, June 6, 1856, in F. P. Weisenburger, *McLean*, 148; Gienapp, *Origins*, 314–315; in an ironic twist, McLean had in January ruled that a federal land claim case in California involving Frémont should go to trial; *Washington Star*, January 16, 1856.

The oddest coupling was McLean . . . Gienapp, *Origins*, 312.

"Bailey worked among anti-slavery men . . ." Hiram Barney to Salmon P. Chase, June 21, 1856, in Chase, *Papers*, 2:443; Harrold, *Bailey*, 181; Gienapp, *Origins*, 314.

But Bailey was not the only . . . F. P. Weisenburger, *McLean*, 151; Myers, *Republican Party*, 69.

"young man of energy and action . . ." *New-York Tribune*, June 21, 1856.

"if McLean is the man . . ." Horace Greeley to Schuyler Colfax, May 6, 1856, in Gienapp, *Origins*, 311.

McLean's backers were not quite . . . Abraham Lincoln to Trumbull, June 7, 1856, in Lincoln, *CW* 2:342–343; Bartlett, *Frémont*, 18.

a "marrowless old lawyer" . . . Charles A. Dana to James S. Pike, May 21, 1856, in F. P. Weisenburger, *McLean*, 147.

"Our only danger . . ." Salmon P. Chase to Edward L. Pierce, April 15, 1856, in Chase, *Papers*, 2:433.

"While he is the ablest and truest . . ." Hesseltine and Fisher, *Trimmers*, 82.

"It seems to me that if . . ." Salmon P. Chase to Edward S. Hamlin, June 12, 1856, in Chase, *Papers*, 2:440.

"the triumph of their schemes . . ." *Washington Star*, June 16, 1856.

Republicans were divided . . . Gienapp, *Origins*, 329–330.

a "joint stock arrangement . . ." Hesseltine and Fisher, *Trimmers*, 67.

"the man who had grit . . ." *New-York Tribune*, June 16, 1856; Hesseltine and Fisher, *Trimmers*, 70.

"Thurlow Weed and his set . . ." *New York Herald*, June 13, 1856.

"melt the whole mass down . . ." Hesseltine and Fisher, *Trimmers*, 71.

What Weed and the others needed . . . Hollandsworth, *Pretense of Glory*, 30; Gienapp, *Origins*, 331–332.

The details were left to a group . . . Gienapp, *Origins*, 333; Bicknell, *America 1844*, 122–123.

"another old fogy . . ." Hesseltine and Fisher, *Trimmers*, 71; Gienapp, *Origins*, 333.

Delegates began making their way . . . Sarah Carroll, "Musical Fund Hall," Phila Place, accessed December 22, 2016, www.philaplace.org/story/1099/.

"nearly every hour in the last . . ." Hesseltine and Fisher, *Trimmers*, 84, 87.

"It is proposed . . ." Hesseltine and Fisher, *Trimmers*, 86–87.

"small eyes glistening . . ." Ibid., 88; Gienapp, *Origins*, 335.

"I am a plain old German . . ." McCormack, *Memoirs of Gustave Koerner*, 2:16.

"attained a fair prospect . . ." Hesseltine and Fisher, *Trimmers*, 100.

"We deny the authority of Congress . . ." Nichols and Klein, "Election of 1856," 1040–1041.

"rapturous enthusiasm" . . . Grow and Walker, *Prophet and Reformer*, 199.

"It includes denationalization . . ." Salmon P. Chase to George W. Julian, July 17, 1856, in Gienapp, *Origins*, 337.

"It is go for the principles . . ." Joshua R. Giddings to George W. Julian, June 24, 1856, in Harrold, *Bailey*, 182.

"The conservative Democrats . . ." McCormack, *Memoirs of Gustave Koerner*, 2:14–15.

To that end . . . Gienapp, *Origins*, 336.

Seward had earlier argued . . . Congressional Globe, 33rd congress, 1st session, appendix, 154.

"state of things at which . . ." Grow and Walker, *Prophet and Reformer*, 200.

"murders, robberies, and arson" . . . Nichols and Klein, "Election of 1856," 1023.

"the foremost statesman of America" . . . Stahr, *Seward*, 163.

"one word from you will give . . ." Ibid.

"would unquestionably have been . . ." Gienapp, *Origins*, 339.

"a hearty and vigorous . . ." Hesseltine and Fisher, *Trimmers*, 93–94.

"caused a fierce sensation . . ." Ibid.; Gienapp, *Origins*, 340.

"It was enough to knock a man down . . ." Hesseltine and Fisher, *Trimmers*, 95–96; Gienapp, *Origins*, 340.

After the final vote was cast . . . Clapp, *Forgotten First Citizen*, 102.

It was an act of faith . . . Strong, *Diary*, 283–284.

"borrowing the self-forgetting devotion . . ." Julian, *Recollections*, 153.

The obvious choice . . . Gienapp, *Origins*, 343–344.

"of decided Whig antecedents" . . . Donald, *Lincoln*, 193; Burlingame, *Life*, 422.

Illinoisans worked through the evening . . . Donald, *Lincoln*, 193; Burlingame, *Life*, 422.

Joshua Giddings had tried . . . Bartlett, *Frémont*, 19; Gienapp, *Origins*, 287, 344; Fehrenbacher, *Prelude*, 43.

"grey-haired old gent . . ." Hesseltine and Fisher, *Trimmers*, 98–99; *New-York Tribune*, June 20, 1856.

"we can lick Buchanan anyway . . ." Myers, *Republican Party*, 70.

After the speeches . . . Hesseltine and Fisher, *Trimmers*, 98; *New-York Tribune*, June 20, 1856.

"a poultice on the sore . . ." Hesseltine and Fisher, *Trimmers*, 98.

Back in New York . . . Bartlett, *Frémont*, 22–23.

"an act of positive injustice" . . . Gienapp, *Origins*, 342.

"desponding for the future" . . . Browning, *Diary*, 244–245.

"not fit to discharge . . ." John McLean to J. Teesdale, September 3, 1859, in F. P. Weisenburger, *McLean*, 151.

"a vast deal of enthusiasm" . . . J. B. Frémont, *Letters*, 109n.

"if we can get rid of . . ." Abraham Lincoln to Lyman Trumbull, June 27, 1856, in Lincoln, *CW* 2:346.

Seward sensed an "alarm" . . . WHS to Frances Seward, June 27 and 28, 1856, in Seward, *Seward at Washington*, 279.

"the fusion ranks of Black Republicanism . . ." Alexander Stephens to Thomas W. Thomas, June 16, 1856, in Toombs et al., *Correspondence*, 368; James Guthrie to John C. Breckinridge, July 18, 1856, in Gienapp, *Origins*, 348.

"the greatest farce upon earth" . . . Sally McDowell to John Miller, June 25, 1856, in McDowell and Miller, *"If You Love That Lady,"* 622.

"ten years hence" . . . Strong, *Diary*, 282.

"Nothing is clearer in the history . . ." Nevins, *Frémont*, 437.

"If this writer could flatter himself . . ." Burleigh, *Signal Fires*, viii.

"There was no 'dash' in our marriage . . ." JBF to Charles Upham, May 31, 1856, in J. B. Frémont, *Letters*, 102; see also letters of June 4, 12, 25, and 30.

Newspaperman John Bigelow . . . JBF to John Bigelow, July 7, 1856, in J. B. Frémont, *Letters*, 114; Bigelow, *Retrospections*, 143; Clapp, *Forgotten First Citizen*, 101, 103–105.

Jessie used her opening chapters . . . Herr, *Jessie Benton Frémont*, 264; Pierson, *Free Hearts*, 119–120.

"the only biography which contains . . ." *National Era*, August 14, 1856.

The books contained illustrations . . . Herr, *Jessie Benton Frémont*, 259.

"imagine her place to be hers" . . . Jeffrey, "Permeable Boundaries," 91.

"All Ladies have politics . . ." Robertson, "Women, Morality, and Politics," 2–3.

"attended all the Republican meetings" . . . Elizabeth Cady Stanton to Susan B. Anthony, November 4, 1855, in DuBois, *Stanton-Anthony*, 59.

Whigs had brought women into the arena . . . Pierson, *Free Hearts*, 140–141; JBF to Lydia Maria Child, late July/August 1856, in J. B. Frémont, *Letters*, 121.

"dar[ing] to run away with a senator's daughter . . ." *New York Post*, July 12, 1856.

"noble young Jessie the flower . . ." *True American* (Steubenville, OH), August 6, 1856.

"Give us Jessie" . . . Herr, *Jessie Benton Frémont*, 254–255.

"sun-burnt and frost-blistered . . ." Hesseltine and Fisher, *Trimmers*, 84; Nevins, *Frémont*, 437; Pierson, *Free Hearts*, 130–131.

"Is Jessie a candidate for the presidency?" . . . *Richmond Dispatch*, September 22, 1856.

"FOR PRESIDENT, john c. Frémont, husband . . ." Pierson, *Free Hearts*, 146.

Newspapers readily promoted the idea . . . Robertson, "Women, Morality, and Politics," 6.

"Sound, sound the trumpet fearlessly . . ." John Greenleaf Whittier, *The Poetical Works in Four Volumes* (1892), via Bartleby.com, www.bartleby.com/372/526.html.

"unparalleled in bitterness . . ." McCormack, *Memoirs of Gustave Koerner*, 2:18.

"a civil war rages . . ." C. Adams, *Slavery, Secession and Civil War*, 1.

The commission that the House sent . . . Gienapp, *Origins*, 351–352; US Congress, *Howard Report*, 67–68.

"they were sent by their abolition friends . . ." *Western Democrat* (Charlotte, NC), June 17, 1856.

"we hear that Franklin Pierce means . . ." John Brown to Mary Ann Brown, February 20, 1856, in Oates, *To Purge This Land with Blood*, 115.

Shannon was an empty suit . . . Etcheson, *Bleeding Kansas*, 113–116; Tate, *Sumner*, 52–53.

"the most painful duty of my whole life" . . . *New-York Tribune*, July 10, 1856; Etcheson, *Bleeding Kansas*, 116.

"to shoot the citizens . . ." Oates, *To Purge This Land with Blood*, 115.

"the 'border ruffian' legislation . . ." William Lloyd Garrison to Samuel J. May, March 21, 1856, in Garrison, *Letters*, 390.

"Freedom," he now said . . . William Lloyd Garrison to Ann R. Bramhall, August 8, 1856, in Garrison, *Letters*, 401.

Alexander Stephens worked with Robert Toombs . . . Johannsen, *Douglas*, 524–528; Nichols, *Pierce*, 475–477.

"Douglas and others are scared . . ." Strong, *Diary*, 283.

"Do you want some nasty fix-up . . ." Horace Greeley to Schuyler Colfax, July 10, 1856, in Isely, *Greeley*, 184.

Greeley need not have worried . . . Fehrenbacher, *Dred Scott*, 205–207.

"Our difficulties are numerous . . ." Nathaniel Banks to Charles Robinson, March 19, 1856, via Territorial Kansas Online, www.territorialkansasonline.org/~imlskto /cgi-bin/index.php?SCREEN=show_document&document_id=101104.

"No man who has the least regard . . ." *Congressional Globe*, 34th Congress, 1st session, appendix, 754; Nichols and Klein, "Election of 1856," 1092; Gara, *Presidency*, 119.

"All these gentlemen want . . ." *Congressional Globe*, 34th Congress, 1st session, appendix, 844.

"Suppose we abandon the Republican party . . ." Republican Association, *Republican Campaign Documents*, 236.

After the failed back-and-forth . . . Etcheson, *Bleeding Kansas*, 118.

Congress had washed its hands . . . Ibid., 119–122.

"carrying a Presidential candidate" . . . Gienapp, *Origins*, 350.

"Jefferson Davis especially thirsts . . ." *New-York Tribune*, September 8, 1856.

"carrying a presidential candidate" . . . John W. Geary to William Bigler, November 28, 1856, in Gienapp, *Origins*, 351.

"accessory after the fact" . . . Etcheson, *Bleeding Kansas*, 130, 135.

"He must be met . . ." John W. Forney to James Buchanan, October 5, 1856, in Gienapp, *Origins*, 352.

9. "THE SEVEREST DEADLIEST BLOW UPON SLAVERY"

"for good or evil" . . . William Dayton to Edwin Morgan, June 30, 1856, in Gienapp, *Origins*, 384.

Following the conventions . . . Gienapp, *Origins*, 382–385.

"A party is not national . . ." Hamilton Fish to James A. Hamilton, September 12, 1856, in Fish and Hamilton, *Correspondence*, 3.

"I admit that Col. Frémont . . ." National Anti-Slavery Standard, September 6, 1856.

Republicans could not match . . . Nichols, *Disruption*, 56; Fischer, "Republican Presidential Campaigns," 127, 129.

"was so extremely cautious . . ." Gienapp, *Origins*, 376.

So the men of the national committee . . . Gienapp, *Origins*, 376–377; J. B. Frémont, *Letters*, 99n.

"blue penciled by my mother" . . . E. B. Frémont, *Recollections*, 77; Phillips, *Jessie Benton Frémont*, 212.

"Quite at the beginning . . ." Herr, *Jessie Benton Frémont*, 263.

"personal and friendly . . ." Denton, *Passion and Principle*, 258.

"second mind" . . . Ibid., 249; Rolle, *JCF*, 165.

"This house has people . . ." Herr, *Jessie Benton Frémont*, 253; Phillips, *Jessie Benton Frémont*, 205–206.

One of the first visitors . . . Phillips, *Jessie Benton Frémont*, 205, 211.

"Nearly all the girl babies . . ." Indiana American (Brookville), July 25, 1856.

"There will be neither bustling . . ." Rolle, *JCF*, 172.

An estimated sixty thousand . . . Herr, *Jessie Benton Frémont*, 260; Denton, *Passion and Principle*, 247; Rolle, *JCF*, 172.

A rally in Beloit, Wisconsin . . . Pierson, "'Prairies on Fire,'" 104–118.

"to receive their political christening" . . . Fehrenbacher, *Prelude*, 15–16.

"The question of slavery . . ." Lincoln, *CW* 2:361, 366.

"I have always had a pretty firm . . ." James Buchanan to Howell Cobb, July 22, in Toombs et al., *Correspondence*, 377.

"Success, if it comes . . ." JBF to EBL, April 18, 1856, in J. B. Frémont, *Letters*, 97–98.

"I am above family . . ." New York Times, June 27, 1856.

the "fractional parties" . . . Chambers, *Old Bullion*, 421–422.

"We are treading upon a volcano . . ." New-York Tribune, August 18, 1856.

"there was nothing which a father . . ." Chaffin, *Pathfinder*, 441–442.

In a similar vein . . . Denton, *Passion and Principle*, 65–66; Nichols and Klein, "Election of 1856," 1026.

"all must admit . . ." Eaton (OH) Democrat, July 17, 1856.

"has come out from the corruption . . ." National Anti-Slavery Standard, September 6, 1856.

Jessie Benton Frémont was not the only . . . Cheathem, *Old Hickory's Nephew*, 300.

In August Frank Blair was elected . . . E. B. Smith, *Francis Preston Blair*, 235; Chambers, *Old Bullion*, 424.

"very much thinner and so still" . . . JBF to EBL, September 16, 1856, in J. B. Frémont, *Letters*, 137.

On a campaign swing . . . Frank Leslie's Weekly, September 6, 1856.

Frémont's campaign was gathering steam . . . Gienapp, *Origins*, 378.

"I want to fight . . ." JBF to EBL, August 20, 1856, in J. B. Frémont, *Letters*, 131.

"an excellent Stump Speaker". . . Charles Robinson to John C. Frémont, July 28, 1856, via Territorial Kansas Online, www.territorialkansasonline.org/~imlskto/cgi-bin /index.php?SCREEN=show_document&document_id=100504.

Also coming from Kansas . . . Jonathan Watson et al. to Cyrus Holliday, July 29, 1856, via Territorial Kansas Online, www.territorialkansasonline.org/~imlskto/cgi-bin /index.php?SCREEN=show_document&document_id=101590.

"speech in favor of Frémont . . ." Read, *Speech*, 35, 37.

"To think that all in me . . ." Elizabeth Cady Stanton to Susan B. Anthony, September 10, 1855, in DuBois, *Stanton-Anthony*, 58–59.

"these gadders abroad" . . . Blackwell and Oertel, *Frontier Feminist*, 164.

"in view of the absorbing interest . . ." Lucretia Mott to Lucy Stone, October 31, 1856, in Mott, *Letters*, 254.

Stone was on the stump that summer . . . Blackwell, *Lucy Stone*, 189; a plaque now marks the spot where Stone delivered her speech; Pierson, *Free Hearts*, 134.

Stone herself was suspicious . . . Gustafson, *Women*, 16–17.

"impeachment of the tyrant" . . . Pierson, *Free Hearts*, 149.

"If old Penn. is to be carried . . ." Blackwell and Oertel, *Frontier Feminist*, 165.

"Everywhere the Republicans had said . . ." *Liberator*, December 5, 1856.

"Frémont Barbecue is to be held . . ." *National Anti-Slavery Standard*, August 23, 1856.

"held great meetings and had speeches . . ." Webb, *History*, 13; Egerton, "Slaves' Election," 36.

Across the South in 1856 . . . Egerton, "Slaves' Election," 36.

"Frémont was at the head . . ." *National Era*, December 18, 1856.

Estimates vary and records are scarce . . . Egerton, "Slaves' Election," 37.

Democrats were largely to blame . . . Ibid., 39.

"had got hold of some indistinct . . ." Ibid., 39–41.

"led on by white men" . . . Ibid., 44–45.

"distributing fire-arms . . ." Ibid., 44, 56.

"The negroes manifested . . ." Ibid., 59.

"an unwelcome surprise" . . . *Frederick Douglass' Paper*, August 15, 1856; Stahr, *Seward*, 154.

"While the Republican Party has not . . ." *Frederick Douglass' Paper*, August 15, 1856; see also Oakes, *Scorpion's Sting*, for a full discussion of the idea of constricting slavery.

"The greatest triumphs of Slavery . . ." *Frederick Douglass' Paper*, August 15, 1856.

"As between the contending political parties . . ." William Lloyd Garrison to Ann R. Bramhall, August 8, 1856, in Garrison, *Letters*, 401; Mayer, *All on Fire*, 456.

"I know he has battled . . ." *Liberator*, August 8, 1856.

"a mere squirm and wriggle . . ." Strong, *Diary*, 282.

"if the Slave-Power is checked . . ." Karcher, *First Woman*, 391, 398.

"the rich fruitage of seed" . . . Mayer, *All on Fire*, 454.

"Mrs. Frémont told me . . ." *National Era*, August 21, 1856.

"abounded in side-splitting fun . . ." Applegate, *Most Famous Man*, 286–287.

"If Jessie is an abolitionist . . ." *Liberator*, August 8, 1856.

"Isn't it pleasant . . ." Lydia Maria Child to Sarah Shaw, August 3, 1856, in Karcher, *First Woman*, 398.

"There are cases in which . . ." Thomas Hart Benton to Thomas L. Price, August 10, 1856, in *New-York Tribune*, August 18, 1856.

"Father's silence . . ." JBF to FPB, August 25, 1856, in J. B. Frémont, *Letters*, 132–133.

"the feminine partner . . ." *Saint Louis Mirror*, quoted in *Eaton (OH) Democrat*, July 17, 1856.

"I've climbed the Rocky Mountains . . ." *Morning Comet* (Baton Rouge, LA), September 9, 1856.

"Ah Jessie! Sweet Jessie! . . ." *Lewisburg (PA) Chronicle*, October 3, 1856.

"these demented females . . ." *Dallas Herald*, September 6, 1856.

"luckily, they have no votes . . ." *Richmond Dispatch*, September 22, 1856.

Frémont events invariably included . . . Gustafson, *Women*, 19.

"At an impromptu gathering . . ." *Frank Leslie's Weekly*, July 5, 1856; "Give 'em Jesse" was a common New England idiom for years before the 1856 campaign, meaning to harshly rebuke someone.

"would have been the better candidate" . . . Gienapp, *Origins*, 377.

"I would as soon place my children . . ." JBF to Lydia Maria Child, late July/August 1856, in J. B. Frémont, *Letters*, 122–123.

"Rather California should be a slave state . . ." Pierson, *Free Hearts*, 132.

"no newspapers, no ideas . . ." Herr, *Jessie Benton Frémont*, 270.

"Head of his 'kitchen cabinet'" . . . Pierson, *Free Hearts*, 131.

"some 400 ladies" . . . Herr, *Jessie Benton Frémont*, 261; *Dallas Herald*, September 6, 1856; Robertson, "Women, Morality, and Politics," 6.

"Ladies attending court . . ." Diary of Henrietta Baker Embree, December 30, 1856, in Wink, *Tandem Lives*, 45.

"will not hinder me . . ." Diary of Henrietta Baker Embree, April 22, 1856, in Wink, *Tandem Lives*, 25.

Buchanan's allies in Congress . . . *New-York Tribune*, August 11, 1856.

"could by one line set right . . ." JBF to EBL, August 12 and 20, 1856, in J. B. Frémont, *Letters*, 124, 130; Herr, *Jessie Benton Frémont*, 271.

"Should Frémont be elected . . ." Buchanan, *Works*, 88.

Buchanan assigned John Breckinridge . . . Davis, *Breckinridge*, 150–151.

"If we cannot get the head . . ." Ibid., 158–159

"He must be blind indeed" . . . Ibid., 155; Johannsen, *Douglas*, 536.

Like Buchanan, Fillmore had been . . . Rayback, *Fillmore*, 405–406.

But there would be much more . . . Ibid., 407.

"We see a political party presenting . . ." Cheathem, *Old Hickory's Nephew*, 303.

"canker worm that has been gnawing . . ." *National Intelligencer*, June 27, 1856.

"my idea throughout the canvass . . ." Andrew Jackson Donelson to Millard Fillmore, October 2, 1856, in Cheathem, *Old Hickory's Nephew*, 303–304.

Vitriolic criticism of Frémont himself . . . Gienapp, *Origins*, 369.

Back on the firmer ground . . . Anbinder, *Nativism and Slavery*, 222.

"One-third part Missouri Compromise . . ." Bartlett, *Frémont*, 31.
"The best safety of the Union . . ." O'Connor, *Lords of the Loom*, 122–123.
"Americans should govern America" . . . Anbinder, *Nativism and Slavery*, 223.
It was an appeal that worked better . . . Carey, "Too Southern," 26.
"that slavery is an evil . . ." Marten, *Texas Divided*, 27–28.
Such broad-based response . . . Cheathem, *Old Hickory's Nephew*, 304.
"rally multitudes of the solid & conservative men . . ." James Hamilton to Hamilton
   Fish, March 7, 1856, in Holt, *Rise and Fall*, 968.
The goal for these Silver Grays . . . Holt, *Rise and Fall*, 968–969.
"ephemeral factions of the day" . . . Ibid., 968.
How to go about calling a convention . . . Ibid., 972.
Leading southern Whigs . . . Ibid., 970.
"The truth is . . ." Carey, "Too Southern," 24.
"men who cannot see . . ." Millard Fillmore to William C. Rives, July 23, 1856, in
   Holt, *Rise and Fall*, 974.
"Civil War and anarchy . . ." Millard Fillmore to Edward Everett, July 7, 1856, in
   Holt, *Rise and Fall*, 981; Millard Fillmore to William C. Rives, July 23, 1856,
   in ibid., 974; Katula, *Eloquence*, 94–95.
"the fossil remains . . ." Holt, *Rise and Fall*, 975.
"a Historical Society or Congress . . ." Strong, *Diary*, 293; Holt, *Rise and Fall*, 977.
"Without adopting or referring . . ." Whig Party platform, September 17, 1856, via
   American Presidency Project, www.presidency.ucsb.edu/ws/?pid=25857.
"your pretended friends . . ." Lewis Levin to Millard Fillmore, September 26, 1856,
   in Holt, *Rise and Fall*, 978.
"These gentlemen are evidently incapable . . ." Nichols and Klein, "Election of 1856,"
   1031.
"The question now to be decided . . ." Seward, *Seward at Washington*, 292.
"We must defeat the Republicans . . ." Hiram Ketcham to Daniel Dewey Barnard,
   September 21, 1856, in Rayback, *Fillmore*, 411–412.
"Every day makes it . . ." Howell Cobb to James Buchanan, July 27, 1856, in Toombs
   et al., *Correspondence*, 378.
"Convince the people that Frémont . . ." Simon Cameron to Edward Morgan, August
   18, 1856, in Anbinder, *Nativism and Slavery*, 239.
"The Republican leaders . . ." Stephen Sammons to Millard Fillmore, November 7,
   1856, in Anbinder, *Nativism and Slavery*, 244.
"material for mischief" . . . Daily American Organ, June 26, 1856.
"is disposed to defend himself . . ." Washington Star, July 23, 1856.
"looked upon the act . . ." Preston, *Argument*, 4–5.
The jury began deliberations . . . Ibid., 5.
Brooks was arrested . . . Hoffer, *Caning*, 80–82.
In the meantime, the House voted . . . Ibid., 78.
"several interruptions from the gallery" . . . Congressional Globe, 34th Congress, 1st
   session, appendix, 831–832.

"He was welcomed, as he left the House . . ." Strong, *Diary*, 284–285.

"If we are pushed too long . . ." *Congressional Globe*, 34th Congress, 1st session, appendix, 656; Gienapp, "Crime Against Sumner," 237.

"express to you my sympathy . . ." *Anti-Slavery Bugle*, October 25, 1856.

"I felt it to be my duty . . ." Preston Brooks to J. H. Brooks, May 23, 1856, in Donald, *Sumner*, 290.

"his whole constituency sympathise . . ." *Edgefield Advertiser*, July 30, 1856.

"one of the most magnetic . . ." Shelden, *Washington Brotherhood*, 143.

"the only hope of the South . . ." Nevins, *Frémont*, 448.

"You can have little idea of the depth . . ." Gienapp, "Crime Against Sumner," 223.

10. "THE HARDSHIPS THAT WE SHOULD HAVE TO ENDURE"

"We remained in camp today . . ." Edmund Ellsworth handcart company journal, 1856, via LDS official website, https://history.lds.org/overlandtravels/sources/2888/edmund-ellsworth-emigrating-company-journal-1856-june-sept.

"To day we commenced preparing . . ." Levi Savage journal, 1855–58, via LDS official website, https://history.lds.org/overlandtravels/sources/7460/savage-levi-journal-1855-mar-1858-oct.

"Brother Willey Exorted the Saints . . ." Ibid.

"Many who were acquainted . . ." John Ahmanson, *Secret History* (trans. 1984), via LDS official website, https://history.lds.org/overlandtravels/sources/7422/ahmanson-john-secret-history-translation-of-vor-tids-muhamed-trans-gleason-l-archer-1984-28-35.

"What I have said I know . . ." Hafen and Hafen, *Handcarts to Zion*, 96–97.

And the potential for winter weather . . . Olch, "Plenty of Doctoring," 98, 108–109.

"perfectly certain of getting through . . ." John Ahmanson, *Secret History* (trans. 1984), via LDS official website, https://history.lds.org/overlandtravels/sources/7422/ahmanson-john-secret-history-translation-of-vor-tids-muhamed-trans-gleason-l-archer-1984-28-35.

"as their women and children were with them . . ." Euphemia Mitchell Bain, "Pioneer Sketch," via LDS official website, https://history.lds.org/overlandtravels/sources/12764/bain-euphemia-mitchell-pioneer-sketch-in-daughters-of-utah-pioneers-salt-lake-city-utah-scrapbooks; Margaret Ann McFall Caldwell Bennett, *Reminiscences*, via LDS official website, https://history.lds.org/overlandtravel/sources/91273965056491581650-eng/bennett-margaret-ann-mc-fall-caldwell-reminiscences-4-5-trail-excerpt-transcribed-from-pioneer-history-collection-available-at-pioneer-memorial-museum-daughters-of-utah-pioneers-museum-salt-lake-city-utah-some-restrictions-apply.

"as fair and fertile . . ." *Washington Sentinel*, August 7, 1856.

"gave us a stirring address . . ." James G. Willie handcart company journal, 1856, via LDS official website, https://history.lds.org/overlandtravels/sources/70069

/willie-james-g-synopsis-of-the-fourth-hand-cart-company-s-trip-from-england-to
-g-s-l-city-in-1856-in-history-of-brigham-young-9-nov-1856-966-83.

"Brother Savage's warning was forgotten . . ." Hafen and Hafen, *Handcarts to Zion*, 99.

"the fare they had . . ." John Ahmanson, *Secret History* (trans. 1984), via LDS official website, https://history.lds.org/overlandtravels/sources/7422/ahmanson-john
-secret-history-translation-of-vor-tids-muhamed-trans-gleason-l-archer-1984-28-35.

"In consequence of our limited supply . . ." James G. Willie handcart company journal, 1856, via LDS official website, https://history.lds.org/overlandtravels/sources/70069
/willie-james-g-synopsis-of-the-fourth-hand-cart-company-s-trip-from-england-to
-g-s-l-city-in-1856-in-history-of-brigham-young-9-nov-1856-966-83.

Martin's company started out . . . Hafen and Hafen, *Handcarts to Zion*, 93–94; Bartholomew and Arrington, *Rescue*, 2.

The Wild West of Gold Rush San Francisco . . . Thomas, *Between Two Empires*, 89.

In May a new vigilance committee formed . . . Secrest, *Perilous Trails*, 29–30.

"Pious laymen, clergymen . . ." Washington Star, September 3, 1856.

"The committee claims to represent . . ." Strong, *Diary*, 282.

In reality, things in the city . . . Lotchin, *San Francisco*, 247.

the "proudest day" the city . . . Ibid.

King was editor of the Evening Bulletin . . . Ibid., 252–258.

"to drive hence the gambler . . ." Ibid., 258.

In November 1855 . . . O'Meara, *Vigilance Committee*, 11.

On May 14, less than a week . . . Ibid.; Lotchin, *San Francisco*, 258–259.

That mob became the core . . . O'Meara, *Vigilance Committee*, 3–4.

"What is to be done . . ." Lotchin, *San Francisco*, 259.

Others less enamored with the idea . . . O'Meara, *Vigilance Committee*, 12; O'Connell, *Fierce Patriot*, 47.

"could not tolerate his attempt . . ." Sherman, *Memoirs*, 138.

On Sunday, May 18 . . . O'Meara, *Vigilance Committee*, 14–15.

"The vigilance have cannon . . ." Mary Jane Megquier to Angeline Megquier Gilson, June 19, 1856, in Megquier, *Apron*, 165.

The commander of the Vigilance Committee . . . O'Meara, *Vigilance Committee*, 15.

"The day was exceedingly beautiful" . . . Sherman, *Memoirs*, 143.

"many can neither eat . . ." Mary Jane Megquier to Angeline Megquier Gilson, June 19, 1856, in Megquier, *Apron*, 165.

"dangerous and bad" . . . Strong, *Diary*, 280.

"it is best to be good . . ." Mary Jane Megquier to Jennie Gilson, May 1856, in Megquier, *Apron*, 163.

"if we do not all get killed" . . . Mary Jane Megquier to Angeline Megquier Gilson, June 19, 1856, in Megquier, *Apron*, 165.

Most people simply put their heads down . . . Thomas, *Between Two Empires*, 119.

But the Law and Order Association did not . . . O'Meara, *Vigilance Committee*, 23–24.

But through the summer . . . O'Meara, *Vigilance Committee*, 28, 34.

"became involved in spite of myself" . . . Sherman, *Memoirs*, 137, 144, 149.

"Mighty Man of War . . ." Marszalek, *Sherman*, 166.

"peaceable, joyous termination . . ." Lotchin, San Francisco, 270.

"Their success has given . . ." Sherman, *Memoirs*, 150.

"We doubt not that . . ." Thibadoux Minerva, March 15, 1856.

"our own coast presents . . ." Houma Ceres, June 12, 1856.

"a sandy barren marsh . . ." Dixon, *Last Days*, 10.

To accommodate the growing trade . . . Southern Sentinel, June 14, 1856.

Among the four hundred or so . . . Dixon, *Last Days*, 2, 28.

The highlight of the weekend . . . Ibid., 7, 22.

"The sea was white with foam . . ." Schlatre, "Disaster," 705.

"About ten o'clock AM *. . ."* Dixon, *Last Days*, 3, 59, 65.

As the flimsy beach houses blew apart . . . Ibid., 75–76.

Like Michael Schlatre's Blue Hammock . . . Ibid., 29–30, 38–39, 75, 101.

Former Governor Hébert . . . Ibid., 60; David E. Cann, personal genealogy homepage, Ancestry.com, accessed December 22, 2016, http://homepages.rootsweb.ancestry .com/~decann/genealogy/master/b357.htm.

In the middle of the afternoon . . . Dixon, *Last Days*, 60–61.

The Pughs spent the night . . . Ibid., 110–111.

"great summer resort" . . . Daily American Organ, August 18, 1856.

"There never was seen in the world . . ." Spirit of Democracy (Woodsfield, OH), November 12, 1856.

Of the roughly four hundred people . . . Dixon, *Last Days*, 233; Schlatre, "Disaster," 704.

Somewhere in the United States . . . Nichols, *Disruption*, 21.

"Illinois, Iowa, California, Connecticut . . ." Alexander Stephens to Thomas W. Thomas, June 16, 1856, in Toombs et al., *Correspondence*, 368.

"We must not lose Maine" . . . Stephen Hoyt to Nathaniel Banks, August 22, 1856, in Gienapp, *Origins*, 389.

The Republicans had recruited . . . Okrent, *Last Call*, 11–12; Fehrenbacher, *Prelude*, 13.

Hamlin, though, had remained . . . Gienapp, *Origins*, 391; Okrent, *Last Call*, 11.

"The fight is monstrously hard" . . . William Pitt Fessenden to Edwin Morgan, September 5, 1856, in Gienapp, *Origins*, 392.

The huge win thrilled Republicans . . . New-York Tribune, September 12, 1856.

"down from the fence" . . . Strong, *Diary*, 292.

"The 'Kansas outrages' had penetrated . . ." Etcheson, *Bleeding Kansas*, 128.

"The mere thought that such a thing . . ." Jeremiah S. Black to Howell Cobb, September 22, 1856, in Toombs et al., *Correspondence*, 382.

"alarmed for the success . . ." New-York Tribune, September 12, 1856.

"If the Eastern States . . ." Western Reserve Chronicle (Warren, OH), October 1, 1856.

"to declare any one . . ." Frank Leslie's Weekly, September 6, 1856.

"to admonish ourselves . . ." Nichols, *Disruption*, 57; Landis, *Northern Men*, 154.

Samuel L. M. Barlow, the millionaire . . . Nichols, *Disruption*, 58.

"the Constitutional power 'to declare war' . . ." Ibid., 56–57.

"What a wild life" . . . Bicknell, *America 1844*, 110.

"difficult to sit still . . ." Gienapp, *Origins*, 375.
The intellectual community joined in . . . Denton, *Passion and Principle*, 251.
"A very large class of persons . . ." Chaffin, *Pathfinder*, 448.
"Much has been done here . . ." New-York Tribune, September 18, 1856.

11. "A Roseate and Propitious Morn Now Breaking"

As the campaign roared toward . . . Gienapp, *Origins*, 375–376.
"I will not deny that there is a possibility . . ." Jeremiah S. Black to Howell Cobb, September 22, 1856, in Toombs et al., *Correspondence*, 382; Bartlett, *Frémont*, 28.
"He who doubts . . ." Liberator, October 3, 1856.
"When shall we have a Convention . . ." William Lloyd Garrison to Samuel J. May, September 24, 1854, in Garrison, *Letters*, 319.
"if Frémont were elected . . ." Strong, *Diary*, 286–287.
"compelled to flee" . . . William Lloyd Garrison to Helen E. Garrison, May 13, 1857, and footnote, in Garrison, *Letters*, 438–439. Underwood was later a federal district court judge in Virginia.
When John Minor Botts . . . Nevins, *Frémont*, 449; Rolle, *JCF*, 168.
Other Frémont supporters gave it a try . . . Bartlett, *Frémont*, 50.
"germs of insurrection" . . . Strong, *Diary*, 287.
"the election of Buchanan would enhance . . ." National Anti-Slavery Standard, June 28, 1856.
"There is much opposition . . ." Tryphena Blanche Holder Fox to Anna Rose Holder, November 18, 1856, in King, *Northern Woman*, 45.
"to administer the bitter dose . . ." JBF to EBL, October 20, 1856, in J. B. Frémont, *Letters*, 140.
"the last chance for a peaceable solution . . ." Theodore Parker to Mr. Bramhall, June 25, 1856, in Bigelow, *Retrospections*, 162.
"We have so often cried 'wolf' . . ." James Buchanan to Nahum Capen, August 27, 1856, in Buchanan, *Works*, 87.
"in daily receipt of letters . . ." James Buchanan to William B. Reed, September 14, 1856, in Buchanan, *Works*, 92.
"if Frémont is elected . . ." Journal of Commerce, September 25, 1856.
Their number also included . . . Bartlett, *Frémont*, 27.
"hasten slowly" . . . Davis, *Jefferson Davis*, 253–254.
"We are told that in case . . ." Hamilton Fish to James. A. Hamilton, September 12, 1856, in Fish and Hamilton, *Correspondence*, 11.
"There is no disguising the fact . . ." Bartlett, *Frémont*, 27, 49.
"When a party composed of only half . . ." O'Connor, *Lords of the Loom*, 123.
"exciting an unparalleled anxiety . . ." William Lloyd Garrison to James Miller McKim, October 14, 1856, in Garrison, *Letters*, 405–408.
It was "an absurdity" . . . William Lloyd Garrison to James Miller McKim, October 14, 1856, in Garrison, *Letters*, 410.

Fillmore served the purpose . . . Carey, "Too Southern," 38–39.

sending the election "into the House . . ." James Buchanan to Howell Cobb, July 10, 1856, in Toombs et al., *Correspondence*, 374.

Weed, all year long confident . . . Van Deusen, *Weed*, 211.

"We have a very mean scurvy pack . . ." George W. Julian to Salmon P. Chase, July 22, 1856, in Bartlett, *Frémont*, 46.

"confident as to Buchanan's success . . ." Jesse Bright to William Corcoran, October 12, 1856, in Landis, *Northern Men*, 154.

"In a word" . . . Howell Cobb to James Buchanan, July 14, 1856, and Buchanan to Cobb, July 22, 1856, in Toombs et al., *Correspondence*, 375–376.

"The Hon. Samuel A. Douglas" . . . Klein, *Buchanan*, 259.

In a September 25 speech . . . Hollandsworth, *Pretense of Glory*, 31–32; Nichols, *Disruption*, 58–59; see also *New York Herald*, September 26, 1856.

"this long divorce . . ." Donald, *Sumner*, 323.

"Charles is fretting . . ." Ibid.; Charles Sumner to John Bigelow, October 9, 1856, and George Sumner to John Bigelow, October 3, 1856, in Bigelow, *Retrospections*, 173, 172.

"done more to gain the victory . . ." Francis P. Blair to Charles Sumner, September 12, 1856, in Gienapp, "Crime Against Sumner," 245.

"The Senatorial sophomore . . ." Donald, *Sumner*, 319.

"at his own hearth and talking . . ." Chambers, *Old Bullion*, 426.

"gatherings of the faithful . . ." *Grand River (MI) Times*, October 22, 1856.

And, indeed, Republicans focused . . . Bartlett, *Frémont*, 31, 36.

"concerns all persons . . ." Formisano, *Birth*, 269–270.

"if the great mass of men . . ." *Weekly Indiana State Sentinel*, October 16, 1856.

Others joined in . . . Bartlett, *Frémont*, 48.

And as the campaign wore on . . . Blackwell and Oertel, *Frontier Feminist*, 165–166.

"women were urged to attend . . ." Pierson, *Free Hearts*, 134.

"There is a great hurrahing . . ." *Liberator*, October 3, 1856.

Know Nothings had women working . . . Coryell, "Superseding Gender," 87–88.

"No selfish aspiration . . ." Ibid., 88–89.

"a frozen dead dog!" . . . *Green-Mountain Freeman* (Montpelier, VT), August 14, 1856; J. C. Frémont, *Exploring Expedition*, 234.

the "man who has overcome . . ." Pierson, *Free Homes*, 121; Isely, *Greeley*, 191.

"brilliant senatorial career" . . . Nichols and Klein, "Election of 1856," 1067.

"Fremont as abolitionist" theme . . . *Washington Sentinel*, July 26, 1856.

"landshark" and "monopolist" . . . Denton, *Passion and Principle*, 256.

"a just, correct, and moral man . . ." Rolle, *JCF*, 167; Johnson, *Roaring Camp*, 265; Chaffin, *Pathfinder*, 446.

"a public harem" . . . Herr, *Jessie Benton Frémont*, 266; Denton, *Passion and Principle*, 257; Rolle, *JCF*, 167; Chaffin, *Pathfinder*, 448.

"Frémont, who was preferred over me . . ." WHS to Frances Seward, August 17, 1856, in Stahr, *Seward*, 164; Gienapp, *Origins*, 388.

"he was used to life . . ." E. B. Frémont, *Recollections*, 77.

"These Catholic reports . . ." Schuyler Colfax to Francis P. Blair, August 15, 1856, in Gienapp, *Origins*, 370.

Thousands of pamphlets appeared . . . Billington, *Protestant Crusade*, 429.

Some American Party and Democratic newspapers . . . *Weekly Portage Sentinel* (Ravenna, OH), July 24, 1856; *Ashland (OH) Union*, August 27, 1856.

"I have myself seen him . . ." *Cadiz (OH) Democratic Sentinel*, October 8, 1856.

"following the orders . . ." *Daily American Organ*, July 7, 1856.

Thurlow Weed gathered forty . . . Nevins, *Frémont*, 445.

"Pray Heaven this may be . . ." *National Era*, October 23, 1856.

"Is it thought necessary . . ." *National Anti-Slavery Standard*, September 6, 1856.

Without help from the candidate . . . Bartlett, *Frémont*, 29.

"It has just been discovered . . ." Clapp, *Forgotten First Citizen*, 106.

"Frémont said that he did not care . . ." Applegate, *Most Famous Man*, 287.

when an old acquaintance . . . JBF to Dr. John Robertson, June 30, 1856, in J. B. Frémont, *Letters*, 110.

"A Southern man by birth . . ." Hamilton Fish to James. A. Hamilton, September 12, 1856, in Fish and Hamilton, *Correspondence*, 10.

"The whole canvass depends . . ." Schuyler Colfax to Charles M. Heaton Sr., August 15, 1856, in Gienapp, *Origins*, 395.

"about two hundred orators . . ." Nevins, *Frémont*, 453; Bartlett, *Frémont*, 63; Klein, *Buchanan*, 260.

Pennsylvania was an organizational mess . . . Nevins, *Frémont*, 454.

"If we hope to carry Pa." . . . Henry Stanton to Horace Greeley, August 5, 1856, and M. L. Hallowell to Simeon Draper, August 18, 1856, in Gienapp, *Origins*, 397, 399.

"Penna. Is always slow to work . . ." Lucretia Coffin Mott to Thomas Wentworth Higginson, April 6, 1854, in Mott, *Letters*, 230.

Greeley published campaign literature . . . Denton, *Passion and Principle*, 251; Gienapp, *Origins*, 410.

"I heartily regret the defeat . . ." JBF to EBL, October 20 and undated late October, 1856, in J. B. Frémont, *Letters*, 140, 141.

"We have naturalized a vast mass . . ." Gienapp, *Origins*, 404–406.

"every eighth man . . ." *Ebensburg (PA) Democrat and Sentinel*, October 29, 1856.

"Now is the winter of our discontent . . ." William Preston to John C. Breckinridge, October 18, 1856, in Davis, *Breckinridge*, 161.

"Buchanan will be elected . . ." Andrew Reeder to John A. Halderman, October 22, 1856, via Territorial Kansas Online, www.territorialkansasonline.org/~imlskto /cgi-bin/index.php?SCREEN=show_document&document_id=100278.

"Had we a few months longer . . ." Burlingame, *Life*, 431.

But the party was still loosely organized . . . *Ottawa Free Trader*, June 14, 1856.

"Men and women flocked . . ." Bartlett, *Frémont*, 43.

Democrat Francis Grund . . . Ibid., 42.

"those Germans who wish . . ." *New-York Tribune*, July 26, 1856.

"quite uncomfortable" . . . McCormack, *Memoirs of Gustave Koerner*, 2:22; Frémont would win Wisconsin by more than 10 percentage points.

"couldn't think, dream or breathe . . ." Lincoln, *CW* 2:340–341.

"Suppose Buchanan gets . . ." Ibid., 374; Donald, *Lincoln*, 194; Burlingame, *Life*, 425; coverage of Lincoln's 1856 campaign speeches can be found in Lincoln, *CW* 2:344–380; three of the towns he spoke in were the homes of future presidents: Galena (Ulysses Grant), Dixon (Ronald Reagan), and Springfield (himself).

"We are in the midst . . ." Stephen A. Douglas to James Buchanan, September 28, 1856, in Johannsen, *Douglas*, 536.

California may have been . . . Bartlett, *Frémont*, 37–38.

Frémont had other problems . . . Ibid., 39; Johnson, *Roaring Camp*, 261–262.

"go in for Frémont . . ." Johnson, *Roaring Camp*, 267; Rolle, *JCF*, 174.

An all-day rally in Lexington . . . Davis, *Breckinridge*, 162.

"there is a great deal of drinking . . ." Diary of Henrietta Baker Embree, November 2, 1856, in Wink, *Tandem Lives*, 41.

On Election Day, November 4 . . . Browning, *Diary*, 261.

"too feeble to walk" . . . Karcher, *First Woman*, 401.

"Sleeping in the nursery . . ." JBF to EBL, late October, 1856, in J. B. Frémont, *Letters*, 141.

"I don't dare say anything . . ." JBF to EBL, November 2, 1856, in J. B. Frémont, *Letters*, 143.

"intelligent confidence in the results . . ." JBF to EBL, November 2, 1856, in J. B. Frémont, *Letters*, 142.

"learned little that's new . . ." Strong, *Diary*, 308.

"took the defeat calmly . . ." E. B. Frémont, *Recollections*, 79–80.

"Colonel Benton, I perceive . . ." Phillips, *Jessie Benton Frémont*, 214.

"a season or two at the White House" . . . E. B. Frémont, *Recollections*, 79–80.

"This will do for me . . ." Phillips, *Jessie Benton Frémont*, 214

"retracing my footsteps . . ." E. B. Frémont, *Recollections*, 79–80; Clapp, *Forgotten First Citizen*, 106.

"I'm very glad . . ." Phillips, *Jessie Benton Frémont*, 215.

Turnout in the North . . . Election totals are from Nichols and Klein, "Election of 1856."

The change over the previous four years . . . Freehling, *Road to Disunion*, 105.

"The power of Douglas & slavery . . ." Landis, *Northern Men*, 157.

"Everybody can tell why" . . . Salmon P. Chase to E. L. Pierce, December 7, 1856, in Gienapp, *Origins*, 415.

"owed such success as he had . . ." Bigelow, *Retrospections*, 144.

"nursed in difficulties . . ." Rolle, *JCF*, 172.

"No politician can truly understand . . ." Willard, *Late American History*, 3.

Simon Cameron blamed . . . Van Deusen, *Weed*, 211.

"The first, and I still think fatal error . . ." Thurlow Weed to Simon Cameron, November 12, 1856, in Denton, *Passion and Principle*, 244.

"The gentlemen who engineered . . ." Gienapp, *Origins*, 415.

"the last pro-slavery President . . ." Preston King to John Bigelow, November 10, 1856, in Gienapp, *Origins*, 442.

How fully the Republican revolution . . . Holmes County (OH) Republican, December 18, 1856.

"large family connections . . ." Chaffin, *Pathfinder*, 448.

"moderate, non-extension pro-slavery . . ." National Anti-Slavery Standard, November 22, 1856.

"I have come to despair . . ." National Anti-Slavery Standard, September 6, 1856.

"beautifully and tastefully arranged" . . . New-York Tribune, September 18, 1856; Buchanan, *Works*, 96–97.

"The Republicans here are full of grit" . . . Schuyler Colfax to Alfred Wheeler, November 13, 1856, in Isely, *Greeley*, 194.

"Republican friends in great spirits . . ." Landis, *Northern Men*, 158.

"I shall sleep on it one night . . ." Applegate, *Most Famous Man*, 288.

"A wedge may be useful . . ." Bigelow, *Retrospections*, 145.

EPILOGUE: "DOES ANY MAN DREAM THAT IT WOULD SETTLE THE CONTROVERSY?"

"to find out what we need to do . . ." Bartholomew and Arrington, *Rescue*, 6.

"Many of our brethren . . ." Arrington, *Brigham Young*, 404.

"Our hearts began to ache . . ." Bartholomew and Arrington, *Rescue*, 11.

"Caroline Reeder, aged 17 . . ." Levi Savage journal, 1855–58, via LDS official website, https://history.lds.org/overlandtravels/sources/7460/savage-levi-journal-1855-mar-1858-oct.

"cool but fair" . . . Ibid.

On October 19, Willie mounted a mule . . . Bartholomew and Arrington, *Rescue*, 16.

"We beried our dead . . ." Levi Savage journal, 1855–58, via LDS official website, https://history.lds.org/overlandtravels/sources/7460/savage-levi-journal-1855-mar-1858-oct.

"We commenced our march again . . ." Ibid.

"a condition of distress . . ." Bartholomew and Arrington, *Rescue*, 24–25.

"the Company gave up . . ." Roberts, *Devil's Gate*, 228.

Eventually that would make a difference . . . Bartholomew and Arrington, *Rescue*, 27.

A wet and weary November . . . Robert Toombs to Alexander Stephens, December 1, 1856, in Toombs et al., *Correspondence*, 383.

"a dead letter in the law" . . . Richardson, *Messages*, www.gutenberg.org/files/11125/11125-h/11125-h.htm.

"Would the Republican Party exhibit . . ." National Era, December 25, 1856.

"a show of liberality" . . . Ibid.

"last Spring, when this controversy . . ." National Anti-Slavery Standard, December 27, 1856.

"reports of negro plots . . ." Ruffin, *Diary*, 18–19.

The fears that had started in Texas . . . Egerton, "Slaves' Election," 47–48.

"among the first men . . ." *National Era*, January 1, 1857.

"daily attracts large crowds . . ." *Washington Star*, December 17, 1856.

"Mr. Blair opened the case . . ." *National Era*, December 25, 1856; Fehrenbacher, *Dred Scott*, 294.

Blair devoted an hour . . . Fehrenbacher, *Dred Scott*, 295–296.

It was the constitutionality . . . Fehrenbacher, *Dred Scott*, 300–301; *National Anti-Slavery Standard*, December 27, 1856.

"We have heard high commendation . . ." *National Era*, December 25, 1856.

"[Reverdy] Johnson made a strong argument . . ." *Richmond Dispatch*, December 18, 1856.

"commanded marked attention . . ." *National Anti-Slavery Standard*, December 27, 1856.

"was reported to have occasioned . . ." *National Era*, December 25, 1856.

"If the Supreme Court were today . . ." *National Anti-Slavery Standard*, December 27, 1856.

By Christmas, peace had come . . . Renehan, *Secret Six*, 106.

Preston Brooks and Lawrence Keitt had been reelected . . . Donald, *Sumner*, 322.

the "great object of my administration . . ." James Buchanan to John Y. Mason, December 29, 1856, in Buchanan, *Works*, 100.

Preston Brooks died . . . Hoffer, *Caning*, 103.

"a man of generous nature . . ." *New York Times*, January 29, 1856.

"If Buchanan should secretly favor . . ." Thomas W. Thomas to Alexander Stephens, January 12, 1857, in Toombs et al., *Correspondence*, 392.

justice Peter V. Daniel's wife died . . . Fehrenbacher, *Dred Scott*, 305, 307.

After the conference and the assignment . . . Ibid., 308–309.

"decide and settle a controversy" . . . John Catron to James Buchanan, February 19, 1857, in Buchanan, *Works*, 106.

"I am anxious . . ." Robert C. Grier to James Buchanan, February 23, 1856, in Buchanan, *Works*, 106–107.

"unostentatious entrance" . . . *Washington Star*, March 3, 1857

"witnessed by a larger . . ." *Frank Leslie's Weekly*, March 14, 1857.

Inauguration Day arrived . . . Klein, *Buchanan*, 271–272.

"blustering disagreeable weather" . . . *Washington Star*, March 4, 1857.

"amid the sky-rending shouts . . ." Ibid.

"A difference of opinion has arisen . . ." Richardson, *Messages*, www.gutenberg.org /files/11021/11021.txt.

Buchanan misspoke . . . Fehrenbacher, *Dred Scott*, 313–314.

a continuation "of the Pierce dynasty . . ." *National Era*, April 2, 1857.

"with mingled derision and contempt . . ." *New-York Tribune*, March 7, 1857.

"gave the idea of freedom . . ." Webb, *History*, 26, 69–70.

BIBLIOGRAPHY

BOOKS, ARTICLES, AND GOVERNMENT DOCUMENTS

Adams, Charles. *Slavery, Secession and Civil War: Views from the United Kingdom, 1856–1865.* Lanham, MD: Scarecrow, 2007.

Adams, George Rollie. *General William S. Harney: Prince of Dragoons.* Lincoln: University of Nebraska Press, 2001.

Adams, Henry. *The Education of Henry Adams.* New York: Oxford University Press, 1999.

Anbinder, Tyler. *Nativism and Slavery: The Know Nothings and the Politics of the 1850s.* New York: Oxford University Press, 1992.

Applegate, Debby. *The Most Famous Man in America: The Biography of Henry Ward Beecher.* New York: Doubleday, 2006.

Arrington, Leonard J. *Brigham Young: American Moses.* Urbana: University of Illinois Press, 1986.

Barker, Gordon S. *Fugitive Slaves and the Unfinished American Revolution: Eight Cases, 1848–1856.* Jefferson, NC: McFarland, 2013.

Bartholomew, Rebecca, and Leonard J. Arrington. *Rescue of the 1856 Handcart Companies.* Provo, UT: Brigham Young University Charles Redd Center for Western Studies, 1992.

Bartlett, Ruhl J. *John C. Frémont and the Republican Party.* New York: Da Capo, 1970.

Beck, Paul N. *The First Sioux War: The Grattan Fight and Blue Water Creek, 1854–1856.* Lanham, MD: University Press of America, 2004.

Bicknell, John. *America 1844: Religious Fervor, Westward Expansion and the Presidential Election That Transformed the Nation.* Chicago: Chicago Review Press, 2014.

Bigelow, John. *Memoir of the Life and Public Services of John Charles Frémont.* New York: Derby & Jackson, 1856.

———. *Retrospections of an Active Life.* Vol. 1, *1817–1863.* New York: Baker & Taylor, 1909.

Billington, Ray Allen. *The Protestant Crusade 1800–1860: A Study of the Origins of American Nativism*. New York: Macmillan, 1938.

Blackmar, Frank W. *The Life of Charles Robinson, the First State Governor of Kansas*. Topeka, KS: Crane, 1902.

Blackwell, Alice Stone. *Lucy Stone: Pioneer of Woman's Rights*. Boston: Little, Brown, 1930.

Blackwell, Marilyn S., and Kristen T. Oertel. *Frontier Feminist: Clarina Howard Nichols and the Politics of Motherhood*. Lawrence: University Press of Kansas, 2010.

Blair, Francis Preston. *Letter of Francis P. Blair, Esq. to the Republican Association of Washington, D.C.* Washington, DC: Buell & Blanchard, 1856.

Blue, Frederick J. *Salmon P. Chase: A Life in Politics*. Kent, OH: Kent State University Press, 1987.

Brenzel, Barbara M. *Daughters of the State: A Social Portrait of the First Reform School for Girls in North America, 1856–1905*. Cambridge, MA: MIT Press, 1983.

Browning, Orville Hickman. *Diary of Orville Hickman Browning*. Vol. 1. Edited by Theodore Calvin Pease and James G. Randall. Springfield: Trustees of the Illinois State Historical Library, 1925.

Buchanan, James. *The Works of James Buchanan, Comprising his Speeches, State Papers and Private Correspondence*. Vol. 10, *1856–1860*. Edited by John Bassett Moore. New York: Antiquarian Press, 1960.

Burleigh, George S. *Signal Fires on the Trail of the Pathfinder*. New York: Dayton and Burdick, 1856.

Burlingame, Michael. *Abraham Lincoln: A Life*. Vol. 1. Baltimore: Johns Hopkins University Press, 2008.

Carey, Anthony Gene. "Too Southern to Be Americans: Proslavery Politics and the Failure of the Know-Nothing Party in Georgia, 1854–1856." *Civil War History* 41, no. 1 (March 1995): 22–40.

Chaffin, Tom. *Pathfinder: John Charles Frémont and the Course of American Empire*. New York: Hill and Wang, 2002.

Chambers, William Nisbet. *Old Bullion Benton: Senator from the New West*. Boston: Atlantic Monthly Press, 1956.

Chase, Salmon P. *The Salmon P. Chase Papers*. Vol. 1, *Journals, 1829–1872*. Kent, OH: Kent State University Press, 1993.

———. *The Salmon P. Chase Papers*. Vol. 2, *Correspondence, 1823–1857*. Kent, OH: Kent State University Press, 1994.

Cheathem, Mark R. *Old Hickory's Nephew: The Political and Private Struggles of Andrew Jackson Donelson*. Baton Rouge: Louisiana State University Press, 2007.

Clapp, Margaret. *Forgotten First Citizen: John Bigelow*. Boston: Little, Brown, 1947.

Coffin, Levi. *Reminiscences of Levi Coffin*. New York: Arno Press, 1968.

Congressional Globe. 32nd Congress, 1st session.

———. 33rd Congress, 1st session.

———. 34th Congress, 1st session.

Coryell, Janet L. "Superseding Gender: The Role of the Woman Politico in Antebellum Partisan Politics." In *Women and the Unstable State in Nineteenth-Century*

America, edited by Alison M. Parker and Stephanie Cole. Arlington: Texas A&M University Press, 2000.

Davis, William C. *Breckinridge: Statesman, Soldier, Symbol.* Baton Rouge: Louisiana State University Press, 1992.

———. *Jefferson Davis: The Man and His Hour.* Baton Rouge: Louisiana State University Press, 1991.

Day, Robert O. *The Enoch Train Pioneers: Trek of the First Two Handcart Companies—1856.* Oviedo, FL: Day to Day Enterprises, 2003.

Denton, Sally. *Passion and Principle: John and Jessie Frémont, the Couple Whose Power, Politics, and Love Shaped Nineteenth Century America.* New York: Bloomsbury, 2007.

Dixon, Bill. *Last Days of Last Island: The Hurricane of 1856, Louisiana's First Great Storm.* Lafayette: University of Louisiana, 2009.

Donald, David Herbert. *Charles Sumner and the Coming of the Civil War.* New York: Alfred A. Knopf, 1960.

———. *Lincoln.* London: Jonathan Cape, 1995.

DuBois, Ellen Carol, ed. *The Elizabeth Cady Stanton–Susan B. Anthony Reader: Correspondence, Writings, Speeches.* Boston: Northeastern University Press, 1992.

Dunn, Norman. *Practical Dreamer: Gerrit Smith and the Crusade for Social Reform.* Hamilton, NY: Log Cabin Books, 2009.

Egerton, Douglas R. "The Slaves' Election: Frémont, Freedom, and the Slave Conspiracies of 1856." *Civil War History* 61, no. 1 (March 2015): 35–63.

Etcheson, Nicole. *Bleeding Kansas: Contested Liberty in the Civil War Era.* Lawrence: University Press of Kansas, 2004.

Fehrenbacher, Don E. *The Dred Scott Case: Its Significance in American Law and Politics.* New York: Oxford University Press, 1978.

———. *Prelude to Greatness: Lincoln in the 1850s.* Stanford, CA: Stanford University Press, 1961.

Finkelman, Paul. *Millard Fillmore.* New York: Henry Holt, 2011.

Fischer, Roger A. "The Republican Presidential Campaigns of 1856 and 1860: Analysis Through Artifacts." *Civil War History* 27, no. 2 (June 1981): 123–137.

Fish, Hamilton, and James A. Hamilton. *Frémont, the Conservative Candidate: Correspondence Between Hon. Hamilton Fish, U.S. Senator from New York and James A. Hamilton, son of Alexander Hamilton.* N.p., 1856.

Formisano, Ronald P. *The Birth of Mass Political Parties: Michigan, 1827–1861.* Princeton, NJ: Princeton University Press, 1971.

Freehling, William W. *The Road to Disunion.* Vol. 2, *Secessionists Triumphant.* New York: Oxford University Press, 2007.

Frémont, Elizabeth Benton. *Recollections of Elizabeth Benton Frémont.* New York: F. H. Hitchcock, 1912.

Frémont, Jessie Benton. *Letters of Jessie Benton Fremont.* Edited by Pamela Herr and Mary Lee Spence. Champaign: University of Illinois Press, 1992.

Frémont, John C. *The Exploring Expedition to the Rocky Mountains, Oregon and California*. Washington, DC: Gales and Seaton, 1845.

Gara, Larry. *The Presidency of Franklin Pierce*. Lawrence: University Press of Kansas, 1991.

Garrison, William Lloyd. *The Letters of William Lloyd Garrison*. Vol. 4, *From Disunionism to the Brink of War, 1850–1860*. Edited by Louis Ruchames. Cambridge, MA: Belknap Press, 1975.

Gienapp, William E. "Crime Against Sumner: The Caning of Charles Sumner and the Rise of the Republican Party." *Civil War History* 25, no. 3 (September 1979): 218–245.

———. *The Origins of the Republican Party, 1852–1856*. New York: Oxford University Press, 1987.

Goodwin, Doris Kearns. *Team of Rivals: The Political Genius of Abraham Lincoln*. New York: Simon & Schuster, 2005.

Greene, Jerome A. *Fort Randall on the Missouri, 1856–1892*. Pierre: South Dakota State Historical Society, 2005.

Grow, Matthew J., and Ronald W. Walker. *The Prophet and the Reformer: The Letters of Brigham Young & Thomas L. Kane*. New York: Oxford University Press, 2015.

Gugliotta, Guy. *Freedom's Cap: The United States Capitol and the Coming of the Civil War*. New York, Hill and Wang, 2012.

Gustafson, Melanie S. *Women and the Republican Party, 1854–1924*. Champaign: University of Illinois Press, 2001.

Hafen, LeRoy R., and Ann W. Hafen. *Handcarts to Zion: The Story of a Unique Western Migration, 1856–1860*. Glendale, CA: Arthur H. Clark, 1976.

Hamand, Wendy F. "The Woman's National Loyal League: Feminist Abolitionists and the Civil War." *Civil War History* 35, no. 1 (March 1989): 39–58.

Harrington, Fred Harvey. "The First Northern Victory." *The Journal of Southern History* 5, no. 2 (May 1939): 186–205.

Harrold, Stanley. *Gamaliel Bailey and Antislavery Union*. Kent, OH: Kent State University Press, 1986.

Herr, Pamela. *Jessie Benton Frémont: A Biography*. Norman: University of Oklahoma Press, 1988.

Hesseltine, William B., and Rex G. Fisher. *Trimmers, Trucklers & Temporizers: Notes of Murat Halstead from the Political Conventions of 1856*. Madison: State Historical Society of Wisconsin, 1961.

Hoffer, Williamjames Hull. *The Caning of Charles Sumner: Honor, Idealism and the Origins of the Civil War*. Baltimore: Johns Hopkins University Press, 2010.

Hollandsworth, James G., Jr. *Pretense of Glory: The Life of General Nathaniel P. Banks*. Baton Rouge: Louisiana State University Press, 1998.

Holt, Michael F. *Franklin Pierce*. New York: Henry Holt, 2010.

———. *The Political Crisis of the 1850s*. New York: John Wiley & Sons, 1978.

———. *The Rise and Fall of the American Whig Party: Jacksonian Politics and the Onset of the Civil War*. New York: Oxford University Press, 1999.

Isely, Jeter Allen. *Horace Greeley and the Republican Party, 1853–1861: A Study of the New York Tribune.* Princeton, NJ: Princeton University Press, 1947.

Jeffrey, Julie Roy. "Permeable Boundaries: Abolitionist Women and Separate Spheres." *Journal of the Early Republic* 21, no. 1 (June 2002): 101–122.

Jenkins, Jeffrey A., and Charles Stewart III. *Fighting for the Speakership: The House and the Rise of Party Government.* Princeton, NJ: Princeton University Press, 2013.

Johannsen, Robert W. *Stephen A. Douglas.* New York: Oxford University Press, 1973.

Johnson, Susan Lee. *Roaring Camp: The Social World of the California Gold Rush.* New York: W. W. Norton, 2000.

Julian, George W. *Political Recollections 1840–1872.* Chicago: Jansen, McClurg, 1884.

Karcher, Carolyn L. *The First Woman in the Republic: A Cultural Biography of Lydia Maria Child.* Durham, NC: Duke University Press, 1994.

Katula, Richard. A. *The Eloquence of Edward Everett: America's Greatest Orator.* New York: Peter Lang, 2010.

King, Wilma. *A Northern Woman in the Plantation South: Letters of Tryphena Blanche Holder Fox, 1856–1876.* Columbia: University of South Carolina Press, 1993.

Klein, Philip S. *President James Buchanan.* Newtown, CT: American Political Biography Press, 1995.

Landis, Michael Todd. *Northern Men with Southern Loyalties: The Democratic Party and the Sectional Crisis.* Ithaca, NY: Cornell University Press, 2014.

Lawrence, Mary Chipman. *The Captain's Best Mate: The Journal of Mary Chipman Lawrence on the Whaler Addison 1856–1860.* Edited by Stanton Garner. Providence, RI: Brown University Press, 1966.

Lawrence, William. *Life of Amos A. Lawrence, with Extracts from His Diary and Correspondence.* Boston: Houghton Mifflin, 1888.

Le Vert, Madame Octavia Walton. *Souvenirs of Travel.* Vol. 1. New York: S. H. Goetzel, 1857.

Lehrman, Lewis E. *Lincoln at Peoria: The Turning Point.* Mechanicsburg, PA: Stackpole Books, 2008.

Lincoln, Abraham. *Collected Works.* Vol. 2. Ann Arbor: University of Michigan Digital Library Production Services, 2001. http://quod.lib.umich.edu/l/lincoln/.

Lotchin, Roger W. *San Francisco, 1846–1856: From Hamlet to City.* Urbana: University of Illinois Press, 1997.

Marszalek, John F. *Sherman: A Soldier's Passion for Order.* New York: Free Press, 1993.

Marten, James. *Texas Divided: Loyalty and Dissent in the Lone Star State 1856–1874.* Lexington: University Press of Kentucky, 1990.

Mathis, Robert Neil. "Preston Smith Brooks: The Man and His Image." *South Carolina Historical Magazine* 79 (October 1978): 296–310.

Mattison, Ray H., ed. "The Harney Expedition Against the Sioux: The Journal of Capt. John B. S. Todd." *Nebraska History* 43 (1962): 89–130.

Mayer, Henry. *All on Fire: William Lloyd Garrison and the Abolition of Slavery.* New York: St. Martin's, 1998.

McClure, Alexander: *Recollections of Half a Century.* Salem, MA: Salem Press, 1902.

McCormack, Thomas, ed. *Memoirs of Gustave Koerner, 1809–1896, Life-Sketches Written at the Suggestion of His Children.* Vols. 1 and 2. Cedar Rapids, IA: Torch Press, 1909.

McDowell, Sally, and John Miller. *"If You Love That Lady Don't Marry Her:" The Courtship Letters of Sally McDowell and John Miller, 1854–1856.* Edited by Thomas E. Buckley. Columbia: University of Missouri Press, 2000.

McPherson, James M. *Battle Cry of Freedom: The Civil War Era.* New York: Oxford University Press, 1988.

Megquier, Mary Jane. *Apron Full of Gold: The Letters of Mary Jane Megquier from San Francisco, 1849–1856.* Albuquerque: University of New Mexico Press, 1994.

Mott, Lucretia Coffin. *Selected Letters of Lucretia Coffin Mott.* Edited by Beverly Wilson Palmer. Urbana: University of Illinois Press, 2002.

Mueller, Ken S. *Senator Benton and the People: Master Race Democracy on the Early American Frontier.* DeKalb: Northern Illinois University Press, 2014.

Myers, William Starr. *The Republican Party: A History.* New York: Century, 1928.

Nevins, Allan. *Frémont: Pathmarker of the West.* Lincoln: University of Nebraska Press, 1992.

———. *Ordeal of the Union.* Vol. 1, *Fruits of Manifest Destiny, 1847–1852.* New York: Scribner's, 1992; orig. publ. 1947.

Nichols, Roy F. *The Disruption of American Democracy.* New York: Collier Books, 1962, originally published 1948.

———. *Franklin Pierce: Young Hickory of the Granite Hills.* Newtown, CT: American Political Biography Press, 1993, originally published 1931.

Nichols, Roy F., and Philip S. Klein. "Election of 1856," in *History of American Presidential Elections, 1789–2008,* 3:1007–1094. Edited by Arthur M. Schlesinger Jr. and Fred L. Israel. New York: Chelsea House Publishers, 2002.

Niven, John. *Salmon P. Chase: A Biography.* New York: Oxford University Press, 1995.

Oakes, James. *The Radical and the Republican: Frederick Douglass, Abraham Lincoln and the Triumph of Antislavery Politics.* New York, W. W. Norton, 2007.

———. *The Scorpion's Sting: Antislavery and the Coming of the Civil War.* New York: W. W. Norton, 2014.

Oates, Stephen B. *To Purge This Land with Blood: A Biography of John Brown.* Amherst: University of Massachusetts Press, 1970.

O'Connell, Robert L. *Fierce Patriot: The Tangled Lives of William Tecumseh Sherman.* New York: Random House, 2014.

O'Connor, Thomas H. *Lords of the Loom: The Cotton Whigs and the Coming of the Civil War.* New York: Charles Scribner's Sons, 1968.

Okrent, Daniel. *Last Call: The Rise and Fall of Prohibition.* New York: Scribner, 2010.

Olch, Peter D. "Plenty of Doctoring to Do: Health-Related Problems on the Oregon Trail." With commentary by Roger P. Blair. *Overland Journal* 33, no. 3 (Fall 2015): 96–113.

O'Meara, James. *The Vigilance Committee of 1856.* San Francisco: James H. Barry, 1887.

Paul, R. Eli. *Blue Water Creek and the First Sioux War, 1854–1856.* Norman: University of Oklahoma Press, 2004.

Phillips, Catherine Coffin. *Jessie Benton Frémont: A Woman Who Made History*. Lincoln: University of Nebraska Press, 1995; orig. publ. 1935.

Pierson, Michael D. *Free Hearts, Free Homes: Gender and American Antislavery Politics.* Chapel Hill: University of North Carolina Press, 2003.

———. "'Prairies on Fire': The Organization of the 1856 Mass Republican Rally in Beloit, Wisconsin." *Civil War History* 48, no. 2 (June 2002): 101–122.

Potter, David M. *The Impending Crisis: 1848–1861*. Completed and edited by Don E. Fehrenbacher. New York, Harper & Row, 1976.

Preston, William P. *An Argument in the Case of the United States Versus Philemon T. Herbert*. Washington, DC: C. Alexander, 1856.

Rayback, Robert J. *Millard Fillmore: Biography of a President*. Newtown, CT: American Political Biography Press, 1959.

Read, John M. *Speech of Hon. John M. Read on the Power of Congress over the Territories, and in Favor of Free Kansas, Free White Labor and of Frémont and Dayton*. Philadelphia: C. Sherman & Son, 1856.

Reinhardt, Mark. *Who Speaks for Margaret Garner?* Minneapolis: University of Minnesota Press, 2010.

Remini, Robert V. *Andrew Jackson: The Course of American Freedom, 1822–1832*. Baltimore: Johns Hopkins University Press, 1981.

Renehan, Edward J., Jr. *The Secret Six: The True Tale of the Men Who Conspired with John Brown*. New York: Crown, 1995.

Republican Association of Washington. *Republican Campaign Documents of 1856: A Collection of the Most Important Speeches and Documents Issued by the Republican Association of Washington, During the Presidential Campaign of 1856*. Washington, DC: Lewis Clephane, 1857.

Richardson, James D., ed. *Compilation of the Messages and Papers of the Presidents*. Volume 5, pt. 3, *Franklin Pierce*. www.gutenberg.org/files/11125/11125-h/11125-h.htm.

Riddleberger, Patrick W. *George Washington Julian, Radical Republican: A Study in Nineteenth-Century Politics and Reform*. Indiana Historical Bureau, 1966.

Roberts, David. *Devil's Gate: Brigham Young and the Great Mormon Handcart Tragedy*. New York: Simon & Schuster, 2008.

Robertson, Stacey. "Women, Morality, and Politics: Jessie Frémont and the Election of 1856." Paper presented at SHEAR, Philadelphia, PA, July 2014.

Rolle, Andrew F. *John C. Frémont: Character as Destiny*. Norman: University of Oklahoma Press, 1999.

Ruffin, Edmund. *The Diary of Edmund Ruffin*. Vol. 1, *Toward Independence, October 1856–April 1861*. Baton Rouge: Louisiana State University Press, 1972.

Schlatre, Michael. "The Last Island Disaster of August 10, 1856: Personal Narrative of His Experiences by One of the Survivors; Introduction by Walter Prichard." *Louisiana Historical Quarterly* 20, no. 3 (1937): 690–737.

Schwartz, Thomas F. "'An Egregious Political Blunder': Justin Butterfield, Lincoln, and Illinois Whiggery." *Journal of the Abraham Lincoln Association* 8, no. 1 (1986): 9–19.

Secrest, William B. *Perilous Trails, Dangerous Men: Early California Stagecoach Robbers and Their Desperate Careers, 1856–1900*. Clovis, CA: Quill Driver, 2002.

Seward, Frederick. *Seward at Washington as Senator and Secretary of State: A Memoir of His Life, with Selections from His Letters, 1846–1861*. New York: Derby and Miller, 1891.

Shelden, Rachel A. *Washington Brotherhood: Politics, Social Life, and the Coming of the Civil War*. Chapel Hill: University of North Carolina Press, 2013.

Sherman, William Tecumseh. *Memoirs of General W. T. Sherman*. New York: Library of America, 1990.

Silbey, Joel H. "After 'The First Northern Victory': The Republican Party Comes to Congress, 1855–1856." *Journal of Interdisciplinary History* 20 (Summer 1989): 1–24.

———. *Party Over Section: The Rough and Ready Presidential Election of 1848*. Lawrence: University Press of Kansas, 2009.

Smith, Elbert B. *Francis Preston Blair*. New York: Free Press, 1980.

Smith, William Ernest. *The Francis Preston Blair Family in Politics*. Vol. 1. New York, Macmillan, 1933.

Stahr, Walter. *Seward: Lincoln's Indispensable Man*. New York: Simon & Schuster, 2012.

Stegner, Wallace. *The Gathering of Zion: The Story of the Mormon Trail*. Lincoln: University of Nebraska Press, 1992.

Strong, George Templeton. *The Diary of George Templeton Strong: The Turbulent Fifties, 1850–1859*. Edited by Allan Nevins and Milton Halsey Thomas. New York: Macmillan, 1952.

Tate, Thomas K. *General Edwin Vose Sumner, USA: A Civil War Biography*. Jefferson, NC: McFarland, 2013.

Thomas, Lately. *Between Two Empires: The Life Story of California's First Senator, William McKendree Gwin*. Boston: Houghton Mifflin, 1969.

Toombs, Robert, Alexander H. Stephens, and Howell Cobb. *The Correspondence of Robert Toombs, Alexander H. Stephens and Howell Cobb*. Edited by Ulrich Bonnell Phillips. New York: Da Capo, 1970.

Upham, Charles Wentworth. *Life, Explorations and Public Services of John Charles Frémont*. Boston: Ticknor and Fields, 1856.

US Congress. *Report of the Special Committee Appointed to Investigate the Troubles in Kansas* (Howard Report). Report no. 200. 34th Congress, 1st session. Washington, DC: Wendell, Printer, 1856.

US House of Representatives. *Alleged Assault Upon Senator Sumner*. House report no. 182. *Congressional Globe*, 34th Congress, 1st session.

US Supreme Court. *Dred Scott v. Sandford*, 60 U.S. 393.

Van Deusen, Glyndon G. *Thurlow Weed: Wizard of the Lobby*. Boston: Little, Brown, 1947.

Wallner, Peter A. *Franklin Pierce: Martyr for the Union*. Concord, NH: Plaidswede Publishing, 2007.

Warren, Gouverneur Kemble. *Explorations in the Dacota Country, in the Year 1855*. Washington, DC: A. O. P. Nicholson, Senate Printer, 1856.

Webb, William. *The History of William Webb, Composed by Himself.* Detroit: Egbert Hoekstra, 1873.

Weisenburger, Francis P. *The Life of John McLean: A Politician on the United States Supreme Court.* New York, Da Capo, 1971.

Weisenburger, Steven. *Modern Medea: A Family Story of Slavery and Child-Murder from the Old South.* New York: Hill and Wang, 1998.

West, Franklin L. *Life of Franklin D. Richards: President of the Council of the Twelve Apostles Church of Jesus Christ of Latter-Day Saints.* Salt Lake City, UT: Deseret News Press, 1924.

Wheeler, Leslie. *Loving Warriors: Selected Letters of Lucy Stone and Henry B. Blackwell, 1853 to 1893.* New York: Dial Press, 1981.

Willard, Emma. *Late American History: Containing a Full Account of the Courage, Conduct, and Success of John C. Frémont.* New York: Barnes, 1856.

Wilson, Dick. *Sawdust Trails in the Truckee Basin: A History of Lumbering Operations, 1856–1936.* Nevada City: Nevada County Historical Society, 1992.

Wink, Amy L., ed. *Tandem Lives: The Frontier Texas Diaries of Henrietta Baker Embree and Tennessee Keys Embree, 1856–1884.* Knoxville: University of Tennessee Press, 2008.

Wishart, David J. *An Unspeakable Sadness: The Dispossession of the Nebraska Indians.* Lincoln: University of Nebraska Press, 1994.

Woodwell, Roland H. *John Greenleaf Whittier: A Biography.* Haverhill, MA: Trustees of the John Greenleaf Whittier Homestead, 1985.

WEBSITES

Accessible Archives, www.accessible-archives.com

American Presidency Project, www.presidency.ucsb.edu

Ancestry.com

Bartleby.com

Collected Works of Abraham Lincoln, http://quod.lib.umich.edu/l/lincoln/

Missouri Digital Archives, www.sos.mo.gov/archives/

"Mormon Pioneer Overland Travel," LDS official website, https://history.lds.org /overlandtravel/

Ohio Historical Election Results, http://ohioelectionresults.com/

Silver Spring Historical Society, http://silverspringhistory.homestead.com/

Territorial Kansas Online, www.territorialkansasonline.org

US Census Bureau, www.census.gov/

NEWSPAPERS

Anti-Slavery Bugle (New Lisbon, OH)
Ashland (OH) Union
Athens (TN) Post
Cadiz (OH) Democratic Sentinel
Cincinnati Commercial
Cincinnati Daily Gazette
Cincinnati Enquirer
Daily American Organ (Washington, DC)
Dallas Herald
Eaton (OH) Democrat
Ebensburg (PA) Democrat and Sentinel
Edgefield Advertiser
Frank Leslie's Weekly
Frederick Douglass' Paper
Fremont (OH) Journal
Grand River (MI) Times
Green-Mountain Freeman (Montpelier, VT)
Holmes County (OH) Republican
Houma Ceres
Indiana American (Brookville)
Journal of Commerce
Kansas Herald of Freedom
Kansas Weekly Herald
Lewisburg (PA) Chronicle
Liberator
Louisville Daily Courier
Morning Comet (Baton Rouge, LA)

National Anti-Slavery Standard
National Era
National Intelligencer
Nebraska Advertiser
New York Herald
New York Post
New York Times
New-York Tribune
News of the Day (Vincennes, IN)
Ottawa Free Trader
Provincial Freeman
Revolution
Richmond Dispatch
Richmond Enquirer
Southern Sentinel
Spirit of Democracy (Woodsfield, OH)
Thibadoux Minerva
True American (Steubenville, OH)
Washington Daily Union
Washington Sentinel
Washington Star
Weekly Indiana State Sentinel
Weekly Portage Sentinel (Ravenna, OH)
Wellsboro (PA) Gazette
Western Democrat (Charlotte, NC)
Western Reserve Chronicle (Warren, OH)
Winchester (TN) Weekly Appeal

INDEX